Fault-Tolerant Distributed Transactions on Blockchain

Synthesis Lectures on Data Management

Editor
H.V. Jagadish, *University of Michigan*

Founding Editor
M. Tamer Özsu, *University of Waterloo*

Synthesis Lectures on Data Management is edited by H.V. Jagadish of the University of Michigan. The series publishes 80–150 page publications on topics pertaining to data management. Topics include query languages, database system architectures, transaction management, data warehousing, XML and databases, data stream systems, wide scale data distribution, multimedia data management, data mining, and related subjects.

Fault-Tolerant Distributed Transactions on Blockchain
Suyash Gupta, Jelle Hellings, and Mohammad Sadoghi
2021

Skylines and Other Dominance-Based Queries
Apostolos N. Papadopoulos, Eleftherios Tiakas, Theodoros Tzouramanis, Nikolaoes Georgiadis, and Yannis Manalopoulos
2020

Cloud-Based RDF Data Management
Zoi Kaoudi, Ioana Manolescu, and Stamatis Zampetakis
2020

Community Search over Big Graphs
Xin Huang, Laks V.S. Lakshmanan, and Jianliang Xu
2019

On Transactional Concurrency Control
Goetz Graefe
2019

Data-Intensive Workflow Management: For Clouds and Data-Intensive and Scalable Computing Environments
Daniel C.M. de Oliveira, Ji Liu, and Esther Pacitti
2019

Answering Queries Using Views, Second Edition
Foto Afrati and Rada Chirkova
2019

Transaction Processing on Modern Hardware
Mohammad Sadoghi and Spyros Blanas
2019

Data Management in Machine Learning Systems
Matthias Boehm, Arun Kumar, and Jun Yang
2019

Non-Volatile Memory Database Management Systems
Joy Arulraj and Andrew Pavlo
2019

Scalable Processing of Spatial-Keyword Queries
Ahmed R. Mahmood and Walid G. Aref
2019

Data Exploration Using Example-Based Methods
Matteo Lissandrini, Davide Mottin, Themis Palpanas, and Yannis Velegrakis
2018

Data Profiling
Ziawasch Abedjan, Lukasz Golab, Felix Naumann, and Thorsten Papenbrock
2018

Querying Graphs
Angela Bonifati, George Fletcher, Hannes Voigt, and Nikolay Yakovets
2018

Query Processing over Incomplete Databases
Yunjun Gao and Xiaoye Miao
2018

Natural Language Data Management and Interfaces
Yunyao Li and Davood Rafiei
2018

Human Interaction with Graphs: A Visual Querying Perspective
Sourav S. Bhowmick, Byron Choi, and Chengkai Li
2018

On Uncertain Graphs
Arijit Khan, Yuan Ye, and Lei Chen
2018

Answering Queries Using Views
Foto Afrati and Rada Chirkova
2017

Databases on Modern Hardware: How to Stop Underutilization and Love Multicores
Anatasia Ailamaki, Erieta Liarou, Pınar Tözün, Danica Porobic, and Iraklis Psaroudakis
2017

Instant Recovery with Write-Ahead Logging: Page Repair, System Restart, Media
Restore, and System Failover, Second Edition
Goetz Graefe, Wey Guy, and Caetano Sauer
2016

Generating Plans from Proofs: The Interpolation-based Approach to Query
Reformulation
Michael Benedikt, Julien Leblay, Balder ten Cate, and Efthymia Tsamoura
2016

Veracity of Data: From Truth Discovery Computation Algorithms to Models of
Misinformation Dynamics
Laure Berti-Équille and Javier Borge-Holthoefer
2015

Datalog and Logic Databases
Sergio Greco and Cristina Molinaro
2015

Big Data Integration
Xin Luna Dong and Divesh Srivastava
2015

Instant Recovery with Write-Ahead Logging: Page Repair, System Restart, and Media
Restore
Goetz Graefe, Wey Guy, and Caetano Sauer
2014

Similarity Joins in Relational Database Systems
Nikolaus Augsten and Michael H. Böhlen
2013

Information and Influence Propagation in Social Networks
Wei Chen, Laks V.S. Lakshmanan, and Carlos Castillo
2013

Data Cleaning: A Practical Perspective
Venkatesh Ganti and Anish Das Sarma
2013

Data Processing on FPGAs
Jens Teubner and Louis Woods
2013

Perspectives on Business Intelligence
Raymond T. Ng, Patricia C. Arocena, Denilson Barbosa, Giuseppe Carenini, Luiz Gomes, Jr.,
Stephan Jou, Rock Anthony Leung, Evangelos Milios, Renée J. Miller, John Mylopoulos, Rachel
A. Pottinger, Frank Tompa, and Eric Yu
2013

Semantics Empowered Web 3.0: Managing Enterprise, Social, Sensor, and Cloud-based
Data and Services for Advanced Applications
Amit Sheth and Krishnaprasad Thirunarayan
2012

Data Management in the Cloud: Challenges and Opportunities
Divyakant Agrawal, Sudipto Das, and Amr El Abbadi
2012

Query Processing over Uncertain Databases
Lei Chen and Xiang Lian
2012

Foundations of Data Quality Management
Wenfei Fan and Floris Geerts
2012

Incomplete Data and Data Dependencies in Relational Databases
Sergio Greco, Cristian Molinaro, and Francesca Spezzano
2012

Business Processes: A Database Perspective
Daniel Deutch and Tova Milo
2012

Data Protection from Insider Threats
Elisa Bertino
2012

Deep Web Query Interface Understanding and Integration
Eduard C. Dragut, Weiyi Meng, and Clement T. Yu
2012

P2P Techniques for Decentralized Applications
Esther Pacitti, Reza Akbarinia, and Manal El-Dick
2012

Query Answer Authentication
HweeHwa Pang and Kian-Lee Tan
2012

Declarative Networking
Boon Thau Loo and Wenchao Zhou
2012

Full-Text (Substring) Indexes in External Memory
Marina Barsky, Ulrike Stege, and Alex Thomo
2011

Spatial Data Management
Nikos Mamoulis
2011

Database Repairing and Consistent Query Answering
Leopoldo Bertossi
2011

Managing Event Information: Modeling, Retrieval, and Applications
Amarnath Gupta and Ramesh Jain
2011

Fundamentals of Physical Design and Query Compilation
David Toman and Grant Weddell
2011

Methods for Mining and Summarizing Text Conversations
Giuseppe Carenini, Gabriel Murray, and Raymond Ng
2011

Probabilistic Databases
Dan Suciu, Dan Olteanu, Christopher Ré, and Christoph Koch
2011

Peer-to-Peer Data Management
Karl Aberer
2011

Probabilistic Ranking Techniques in Relational Databases
Ihab F. Ilyas and Mohamed A. Soliman
2011

Uncertain Schema Matching
Avigdor Gal
2011

Fundamentals of Object Databases: Object-Oriented and Object-Relational Design
Suzanne W. Dietrich and Susan D. Urban
2010

Advanced Metasearch Engine Technology
Weiyi Meng and Clement T. Yu
2010

Web Page Recommendation Models: Theory and Algorithms
Sule Gündüz-Ögüdücü
2010

Multidimensional Databases and Data Warehousing
Christian S. Jensen, Torben Bach Pedersen, and Christian Thomsen
2010

Database Replication
Bettina Kemme, Ricardo Jimenez-Peris, and Marta Patino-Martinez
2010

Relational and XML Data Exchange
Marcelo Arenas, Pablo Barcelo, Leonid Libkin, and Filip Murlak
2010

User-Centered Data Management
Tiziana Catarci, Alan Dix, Stephen Kimani, and Giuseppe Santucci
2010

Data Stream Management
Lukasz Golab and M. Tamer Özsu
2010

Access Control in Data Management Systems
Elena Ferrari
2010

An Introduction to Duplicate Detection
Felix Naumann and Melanie Herschel
2010

Privacy-Preserving Data Publishing: An Overview
Raymond Chi-Wing Wong and Ada Wai-Chee Fu
2010

Keyword Search in Databases
Jeffrey Xu Yu, Lu Qin, and Lijun Chang
2009

Fault-Tolerant Distributed Transactions on Blockchain

Suyash Gupta, Jelle Hellings, and Mohammad Sadoghi

ISBN: 978-3-031-00749-1   paperback
ISBN: 978-3-031-01877-0   ebook
ISBN: 978-3-031-00104-8   hardcover

DOI 10.1007/978-3-031-01877-0

A Publication in the Springer series
SYNTHESIS LECTURES ON DATA MANAGEMENT

Lecture #64
Series Editor: H.V. Jagadish, *University of Michigan*
Founding Editor: M. Tamer Özsu, *University of Waterloo*
Series ISSN
Print 2153-5418   Electronic 2153-5426

Fault-Tolerant Distributed Transactions on Blockchain

Suyash Gupta, Jelle Hellings, and Mohammad Sadoghi
University of California, Davis

SYNTHESIS LECTURES ON DATA MANAGEMENT #64

ABSTRACT

Since the introduction of *Bitcoin*—the first widespread application driven by blockchain—the interest of the public and private sectors in blockchain has skyrocketed. In recent years, blockchain-based fabrics have been used to address challenges in diverse fields such as trade, food production, property rights, identity-management, aid delivery, health care, and fraud prevention. This widespread interest follows from fundamental concepts on which blockchains are built that together embed the notion of trust, upon which blockchains are built.

1. Blockchains provide data transparancy. Data in a blockchain is stored in the form of a *ledger*, which contains an ordered history of all the transactions. This facilitates oversight and auditing.

2. Blockchains ensure data integrity by using strong cryptographic primitives. This guarantees that transactions accepted by the blockchain are authenticated by its issuer, are immutable, and cannot be repudiated by the issuer. This ensures accountability.

3. Blockchains are decentralized, democratic, and resilient. They use consensus-based replication to decentralize the ledger among many independent participants. Thus, it can operate completely decentralized and does not require trust in a single authority. Additions to the chain are performed by consensus, in which all participants have a democratic voice in maintaining the integrity of the blockchain. Due to the usage of replication and consensus, blockchains are also highly resilient to malicious attacks even when a significant portion of the participants are malicious. It further increases the opportunity for fairness and equity through democratization.

These fundamental concepts and the technologies behind them—a generic ledger-based data model, cryptographically ensured data integrity, and consensus-based replication—prove to be a powerful and inspiring combination, a catalyst to promote computational trust. In this book, we present an in-depth study of blockchain, unraveling its revolutionary promise to instill computational trust in society, all carefully tailored to a broad audience including students, researchers, and practitioners. We offer a comprehensive overview of theoretical limitations and practical usability of consensus protocols while examining the diverse landscape of how blockchains are manifested in their permissioned and permissionless forms.

KEYWORDS

blockchains, bitcoin, transactions, fault-tolerance, replication, consensus, consistency, concurrency, cryptocurrency, proof-of-work

To my wife, my mother
Nasim Sadoghi, Lili Taghavi

– Mohammad Sadoghi

Contents

Preface xix

1 Introduction 1
    1.1   Blockchains and Their Usage in Bitcoin 1
        1.1.1   The Tamper-Proof Design of Bitcoin 2
        1.1.2   A Formalization of Blockchains 3
        1.1.3   The Components of a Blockchain 3
        1.1.4   Permissionless and Permissioned Blockchains 4
    1.2   On Distributed Systems 5
        1.2.1   The CAP Theorem 5
        1.2.2   CAP and Permissionless Blockchains 6
        1.2.3   CAP and Permissioned Blockchains 6
    1.3   On Resilient Distributed Systems 7
        1.3.1   Notations for Resilient Distributed Systems 8
        1.3.2   Coordination in Resilient Distributed Systems 8
        1.3.3   Failure Models 12
        1.3.4   Communication Models 13
        1.3.5   Authenticated vs. Signed Messages 14
        1.3.6   The Complexity and Cost of Consensus 16
    1.4   Outline of This Book 17
    1.5   Bibliographic Notes 18

2 Practical Byzantine Fault-Tolerant Consensus 21
    2.1   An Overview of PBFT 25
    2.2   The Byzantine Commit Algorithm of PBFT 27
    2.3   Primary Replacement and Recovery 35
        2.3.1   Failure Detection 36
        2.3.2   Requesting a View Change 38
        2.3.3   Proposing the New View 39
        2.3.4   Validate the New View 39
        2.3.5   Move into the New View 41

2.3.6   Guaranteeing Successful View-Changes 45

2.4   Termination via Checkpoints 50

      2.4.1   The Checkpoint Algorithm 51

      2.4.2   Integrating Checkpoints into View-Changes 53

2.5   PBFT and Client Behavior 55

2.6   PBFT is a Consensus Protocol 57

2.7   Optimizing and Fine-Tuning PBFT 59

      2.7.1   Eliminating Redundant Messages 59

      2.7.2   Limiting Message Size Using Message Digests 60

      2.7.3   Dealing with Unreliable Communication 62

2.8   PBFT Without Using Digital Signatures 63

      2.8.1   Dropping Signatures on Client Requests 63

      2.8.2   Dropping Signatures on All Other Messages 65

2.9   Concluding Remarks 69

2.10   Bibliographic Notes 71

3   Beyond the Design of PBFT **73**

3.1   Modeling the Performance of PBFT 73

      3.1.1   Determining the Performance Variables 74

      3.1.2   The Single-Round Cost of PBFT 74

      3.1.3   The Throughput of PBFT 75

3.2   Implementation Techniques for PBFT 76

      3.2.1   Batching of Client Requests 76

      3.2.2   Out-of-Order Processing 78

      3.2.3   Overlapping Communication Phases 80

3.3   Primary-Backup Consensus Beyond PBFT 81

      3.3.1   Threshold Signatures 81

      3.3.2   Speculative Execution 84

      3.3.3   Optimistic Execution 87

3.4   Trusted Components 88

      3.4.1   Systems With Trusted Components 89

      3.4.2   Proactive Recovery 90

      3.4.3   High Failure Resilience 90

3.5   Limitations of Primary-Backup Consensus 93

      3.5.1   Gossip Protocols 95

      3.5.2   Consensus via a Subset of Replicas 96

	3.5.3	Sharding	96
	3.5.4	Concurrent Consensus	97
3.6	Improving Resilience		105
	3.6.1	Throttling Attacks	105
	3.6.2	Ordering Attacks	107
3.7	Concluding Remarks		109
3.8	Bibliographic Notes		111

4   Toward Scalable Blockchains **115**

4.1	Toward Scalable Ledger Storage		116
	4.1.1	Information Dispersal	116
	4.1.2	Encoding the Ledger	117
	4.1.3	Reconstructing the Ledger (Simple Checksums)	118
	4.1.4	Reconstructing the Ledger (Tree Checksums)	120
	4.1.5	Scalable Storage Using Information Dispersal	122
4.2	Scalability for Read-Only Workloads		123
	4.2.1	Optimistic Read-Only Transaction Processing	123
	4.2.2	Role-Specialization via Learners	124
4.3	Coordination Between Blockchains		128
	4.3.1	Formalizing Cluster-Sending	130
	4.3.2	Lower Bounds for Cluster-Sending	134
	4.3.3	Cluster-Sending via Bijective Sending	138
	4.3.4	Optimal Cluster-Sending via Partitioning	140
4.4	Geo-Scale Aware Consensus		146
	4.4.1	Optimistic Inter-Cluster Sending	147
	4.4.2	Ordering and Execution	150
	4.4.3	On the Geo-Scale Performance of GeoBFT	150
4.5	General-Purpose Sharded Blockchains		152
	4.5.1	Traditional Permissioned Blockchains	152
	4.5.2	Processing Multi-Shard Transactions	154
	4.5.3	Practical Sharding in a Byzantine Environment	157
4.6	Concluding Remarks		165
4.7	Bibliographic Notes		167

5   Permissioned Blockchains **169**

| 5.1 | Hyperledger Fabric .... | | 169 |
| | 5.1.1 | Motivation .... | 170 |

      5.1.2   Architecture 170

  5.2 ResilientDB 172

      5.2.1   Architecture 174

      5.2.2   Experimental Analysis 179

  5.3 Concluding Remarks 182

  5.4 Bibliographic Notes 183

6 **Permissionless Blockchains** **185**

  6.1 Proof-of-Work Consensus 186

      6.1.1   Core Algorithm 186

      6.1.2   Merkle Tree Hashing 188

  6.2 Bitcoin 189

      6.2.1   General Working 189

      6.2.2   Challenge String 191

      6.2.3   Consensus and Miner Incentives 192

      6.2.4   Bitcoin Transactions 194

      6.2.5   Pooled Mining 198

      6.2.6   Special Hardware 200

      6.2.7   Bitcoin Wallets 201

      6.2.8   Attacks on Bitcoin 202

  6.3 Energy-Aware Proof-of-X Protocols 204

      6.3.1   Proof-of-Stake 204

      6.3.2   Peercoin 205

      6.3.3   Proof-of-Activity 207

      6.3.4   Other Proof-of-Stake Variants 210

      6.3.5   Proof-of-Space 211

  6.4 Ethereum 214

      6.4.1   Accounts in Ethereum 214

      6.4.2   Ethereum Virtual Machine 215

      6.4.3   Storage and Querying 215

      6.4.4   Ethash Proof-of-Work Protocol 219

      6.4.5   Attacks on Ethereum 220

  6.5 Concluding Remarks 221

  6.6 Bibliographic Notes 222

Bibliography **225**

Authors' Biographies **247**

Preface

In this book, we introduce blockchains as fully-replicated resilient distributed systems. We examine the problem of *consensus*—the core technique to operate resilient distributed systems. In the first part of the book, we focus on *permissioned blockchains*, as these systems are best-suited for high-throughput transaction processing in managed environments. We study in-depth the techniques behind *permissioned blockchains*.

- In Chapter 2, we describe the working of the *Practical Byzantine Fault Tolerance protocol* (PBFT) [54–56], a consensus protocol that inspired almost all protocols used in modern permissioned systems.

- In Chapter 3, we describe implementation techniques to maximize throughput of PBFT and to improve beyond PBFT. Furthermore, we examine the techniques that are at the core of modern PBFT-like consensus protocols such as FastBFT [174], HotStuff [249], MinBFT [239], PoE [120], RCC [121, 122], SBFT [109], and ANameZyzzyva [2, 3, 161–163].

- In Chapter 4, we consider ways to make permissioned blockchains *scalable*. We study several cutting-edge techniques such as enabling scalable storage, read-only optimizations [137], reliable cluster communication [135, 136], geo-aware designs (e.g., GeoBFT [123]), and sharding (e.g., Cerberus [134] and ByShard [138]).

In the second part of the book, we offer a comprehensive study of modern blockchain systems while expanding our scope to *permissionless setting*.

- In Chapter 5, we observe the key components of a blockchain system and analyze the design of two state-of-the-art permissioned blockchain frameworks, Hyperledger Fabric [14, 231] and ResilientDB [120–124, 138, 214].

- In Chapter 6, we move beyond the traditional way of designing consensus and illustrate the design of Byzantine fault-tolerant consensus protocols that support *open membership*. We start by investigating the *Proof-of-Work* protocol, which is at the core of the first blockchain application. Next, we discuss the design of two of the well-known *Proof-of-X* protocols: PoS and PoC [26, 88, 155]. Further, we illustrate the architecture of two famous permissionless blockchains: *Bitcoin* [193], and *Ethereum* [244].

Suyash Gupta, Jelle Hellings, and Mohammad Sadoghi
February 2021

C H A P T E R   1

Introduction

Fueled by the emergence of Bitcoin and other blockchain-based cryptocurrencies, we see a corresponding surge in interest of the public and private sector in blockchain technology. This interest has already led to the development of specific blockchain-based systems that address challenges in the financial sector, the trade of valuable commodities, food production, managing land property rights, managing identities, supporting transparent aid delivery, managing health care data, insurance fraud prevention, energy production and energy trading, advertisements, and managing compliance with privacy regulations. At the same time, we also see the development of blockchain-based frameworks, transaction processing engines, and data management systems that aim to combine the promises of blockchain technology with the power of general-purpose data management.

In this book, we will unravel blockchains and their promises of computational trust (i.e., fault tolerance). We do so by exploring blockchain technology to offer *resilient transaction processing* through its democratic (i.e., consensus) and decentralized (i.e., replicated) design. In this chapter, as the first step toward understanding blockchain transaction processing, we provide an introduction as to what blockchains are.

1.1   BLOCKCHAINS AND THEIR USAGE IN BITCOIN

As a first step toward describing what a blockchain is, we look at their usage in the *Bitcoin network*, the first widespread application that employed them. A main purpose of the Bitcoin network is to provide a *monetary token*, the Bitcoin, together with a fully open and decentralized way to transfer these tokens from one owner to the next. In Figure 1.1, we provide a high-level visualization of a blockchain.

All participants in the Bitcoin network hold a full copy of the blockchain, which allows them to validate incoming transactions that transfer Bitcoins. The blockchain held by each of the participants consists of a chain of blocks that starts with a pre-defined initial *genesis block*. Each block contains a list of transactions, that each transfer Bitcoins, and a hash pointing to the previous block in the chain. Typically, the ordered list of transactions represented by a blockchain is referred to as the *ledger*. Furthermore, each block contains a solution to a *computational complex puzzle* (that has the hash and transactions of the block as inputs). These puzzle solutions are used to make the blockchain *tamper-proof* by imposing a huge cost on any malicious participant that wants to change blocks that are already part of the blockchain. We illustrate this next.

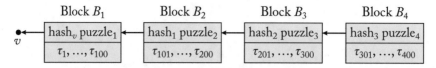

Figure 1.1: A visualization of a Bitcoin-based blockchain holding the ledger of transactions $\tau_1, \ldots, \tau_{500}$ with some *genesis block* with value v. The i-th block holds a *hash value* $hash_{i-1}$ that identifies the preceding block and a *puzzle solution* $puzzle_i$ that is used to make the structure *tamper-proof*.

1.1.1   THE TAMPER-PROOF DESIGN OF BITCOIN

Assume some malicious participant P wants to replace transaction τ_{123} in the second block B_2 of Figure 1.1 by τ', resulting in block B_2'. This replacement will invalidate the puzzle solution $puzzle_2$. Furthermore, as the content of block B_2 changed, its hash also changes. Hence, $hash_3$ of the third block B_3 will not point to B_2'. Consequently, we end up with a *fork* in the blockchain, as illustrated in Figure 1.2. As participants in the Bitcoin network are incentivized to build upon the longest sequence of blocks, no participant will accept the chain ending at B_2' over the original chain ending at B_4. Hence, if P truly wants to replace τ_{123}, it not only needs to reconstruct block B_2, but also needs to produce blocks B_3', B_4', and B_5' to assure that the chain with second block B_2' is the longest. This task is further complicated as by the time P is able to finish B_5', the other participants have likely already extended the original blockchain, e.g., by adding blocks B_5 and B_6.

To assure that the cost for P to create all these blocks is *too high*, Bitcoin uses the Proof-of-Work consensus protocol [193]. Proof-of-Work relies on solving the computational complex puzzles that are part of each block. As solving these puzzles is costly, the cost to construct any single block is high. Hence, P can only reliably replace a chain of blocks in the blockchain if it has access to the majority of all computational resources. Otherwise, P will compete against a majority that is building upon the longest chain, due to which P will fail to replace the longest chain by its own tampered-with chain. Hence, to guarantee proper operation of a Bitcoin network, it is assumed that a majority of all computational resources is owned by participants that play by the rules. Under this majority assumption, a long chain of valid blocks following a block B serves as a *proof* that a majority of all computational resources of the network are dedicated to maintaining B and are protecting B against tampering. Such majority assumptions are at the basis of any *resilient system* that can deal with malicious behavior by some participants and although these majority assumptions cannot be strictly enforced, the design of Bitcoin incentivizes participants that play by the rule.

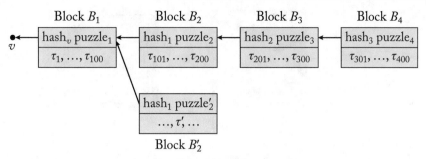

Figure 1.2: A visualization of a fork in the blockchain of Figure 1.1.

1.1.2 A FORMALIZATION OF BLOCKCHAINS

The above high-level overview of Bitcoin and its blockchain is sufficient to illustrate the main properties of a blockchain. In Chapter 6, we will expand on the working of Bitcoin in full detail. Using the above overview, we formalize what a blockchain is.

Definition 1.1   A *blockchain* is a resilient tamper-proof ledger that is maintained collectively by many independent participants, meaning:

1. *Resilient.* Blockchains are distributed fully replicated systems that can deal, without interruption, with failures and malicious behavior of a minority of the participants.

2. *Tamper-proof.* Blockchains are design to support append-only addition of transactions by adding new blocks, whereas the structure of the blockchain makes it practically impossible to replace existing blocks (without support of a majority of the participants).

3. *Ledger.* The blockchain represents an ordered list of transactions.

1.1.3 THE COMPONENTS OF A BLOCKCHAIN

To further answer what blockchains are, we consider the typical operations and design of blockchain systems. A blockchain is a *system* operated by a set of *replicas* (each controlled by one of the participants), some of which are faulty. Depending on the type of behavior a blockchain is designed to deal with, these faulty replicas can crash, omit sending messages, send arbitrary messages, or even coordinate with each other and operate in malicious manners.

In a blockchain, each replica holds a copy of the ledger of *transactions*. These transactions are requested by clients which, over time, will request new transactions to be appended to the ledger. The core component in any blockchain is the mechanisms by which participants coordinate which client transactions are appended to the ledger, and in which order. This coordination is typically provided by a *consensus protocol* such as the Proof-of-Work protocol employed

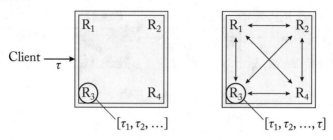

Figure 1.3: A sketch of a blockchain system with four replicas. The ledger in this system holds individual transactions. *Left*, a client requests transaction τ. *Right*, the replicas coordinate (via consensus), resulting in appending τ to their ledgers.

by Bitcoin. In blockchain systems, the consensus protocol is operated in *rounds*. Consider the ρ-th round. In this round, all participants use consensus to reach a decision on a single value (e.g., a transaction or a block of transactions) that is appended as the ρ-th value to the ledger. This design is sketched in Figure 1.3.

1.1.4   PERMISSIONLESS AND PERMISSIONED BLOCKCHAINS

To complete our initial exploration of *what* a blockchain is, we study at the two types of blockchain systems in practical use. Bitcoin, Ethereum, and most other cryptocurrencies are *permissionless blockchains*. In permissionless blockchains, anyone can freely participate when they want and as long as they want. Hence, the defining characteristic of these blockchain is that participants are not known and will constantly change. The rationale for this stems from the objective of operating a *fully decentralized* and *open* currency that is not controlled by any overarching institution (including institutions that vet participants). As there is no way to vet participants, permissionless blockchains need to defend against so-called *Sybil attacks* in which malicious participants try to control the blockchain by controlling a vast amount of participants. A typical way to defend against such Sybil attacks is by binding the control each participant has over the blockchain to a *resource* that cannot be shared between participants, e.g., in Proof-of-Work (as used by Bitcoin), the control of each participant on the creation of new blocks is ultimately tied to the computational power they can contribute. Permissionless designs are *flexible* in the sense that they can typically scale to thousands of participants and can easily deal with changing participants due to network failures. This comes at the price of low transaction processing throughputs, very high transaction latencies, and weak consensus guarantees, e.g., Bitcoin can only process a handful of transactions per second and reaching strong-enough consensus on a transaction can easily take up an hour.

Many data management and transaction processing systems are managed and deployed by a well-defined set of participants. Such systems can be built on top of blockchain technology, but they do not require the fully decentralized design of permissionless blockchains. To illustrate this, we consider two examples. First, consider a data management system that manages internal records of a single company. This system can be deployed on trusted servers owned and controlled by that company, and, in this setting, blockchain technology can be used to *only* harden the system against crashes. Second, consider an patient e-health system that keeps track of patient records and is managed by a consortium of health-care providers. In this setting, the individual participants are known (e.g., hospitals, clinics, labs) and their access to the system is vetted by the consortium. Here, blockchain technology can be used to bridge the different systems operated by each participant and to deal with individual system failures (e.g., software, hardware, and network failures at some participants), while assuring that the remaining participants can all access and update patient records. Most permissioned blockchain systems built upon the technology used in traditional fully replicated resilient distributed systems can operate with dozens of participants, and can easily process thousands of transactions per second with low latencies. The downside of permissioned systems is that there typically is no easy way to change the participants.

1.2 ON DISTRIBUTED SYSTEMS

In the previous section, we introduced blockchains and provided a high-level description of what a blockchain is. From this description, we learned that blockchains are operated by many independent participants. Hence, blockchains are *distributed systems*. Furthermore, in typical blockchains all participants hold and maintain a full copy of the ledger. Hence, blockchains are also *fully replicated distributed systems*. Finally, as blockchains can tolerate malicious behavior by some participants, blockchains are *resilient distributed systems*. Fully replicated and resilient distributed systems have been studied in many forms over the years, resulting in plenty of theory that clearly demarcates what such systems *can* and *cannot* do. Here, we take a brief look at the theory applicable to any fully replicated distributed system. In the next section, we expand to the theory applicable to resilient distributed systems.

1.2.1 THE CAP THEOREM

All blockchain systems are distributed systems in which individual replicas work together to maintain a shared state (the ledger). Hence, as a first step in exploring what blockchains can and cannot do, we look at what such distributed systems can and cannot do. Typically, distributed systems try to provide desirable properties from three categories [46, 47].

Consistency In *strong consistent* systems, all replicas have a single up-to-date copy of the shared data. Such strong consistent systems are typically operated in a *linearizable* manner: all replicas perform exactly the same data updates in the same order on all data. In *weak consistent* systems, individual replicas can hold a different state. Weak consistent systems typically allow replicas to perform updates in different order, while only guaranteeing convergence on the shared data eventually (e.g., after all updates are processed).

Availability A system with *high availability* is able to always process updates such that every valid request received by any good (non-faulty) replica is eventually processed and will result in a response.

Partitioning A system that has *high tolerance to partitioning* of the network can operate in an environment in which arbitrarily large groups of replicas are unable to communicate with each other.

In 2000, Brewer conjectured that any distributed system in which individual replicas work together to maintain a shared state can only provide two out of these three properties. This conjecture was later formalized and proven to hold.

Theorem 1.2   The CAP Theorem [47, 108].   *Consider a distributed system in which individual replicas work together to maintain a shared state. This system can only provide two-out-of-three of consistency, availability, and partitioning.*

As most distributed systems operate on unreliable networks (e.g., the Internet), they require tolerance of partitioning. Hence, due to the CAP Theorem, such systems have to choose between providing strong consistency or high availability. This strict interpretation of the CAP Theorem is misleading; however, the formalization of the CAP Theorem uses rather specific definitions of consistency, availability, and partitioning. In practice, many systems operate on a spectrum and can deal with some network failures, will provide a form of consistency, while being highly available. Next, we shall see which CAP choices are made by blockchains [46].

1.2.2   CAP AND PERMISSIONLESS BLOCKCHAINS

As described in Section 1.1.4, permissionless blockchains are designed to deal with the fact that replicas are not known and will constantly change. This open design requires that these systems have a *high tolerance to partitioning*. Furthermore, permissionless blockchains provide high availability, as any functioning replica can always create new blocks that holds client transactions. This comes at the cost of *consistency*. If the system is partitioned, then the individual partitions will append different blocks to their copies of the ledger. Furthermore, if the partitioning happens for a longer time, then these different blocks will each collect proofs of their validity (by being followed by a long chain of blocks). Hence, permissionless blockchains can end up with an inconsistent state in which some clients consider their transactions to be executed, even though this is not guaranteed. This CAP-trade-off is sketched in Figure 1.4.

1.2.3   CAP AND PERMISSIONED BLOCKCHAINS

Permissioned blockchains typically provide *strong consistency* at all costs. Specifically, permissioned blockchains guarantee that if a client receives confirmation that a requested transaction is appended to the ledger as the ρ-th transaction, then this transaction will always stay in the

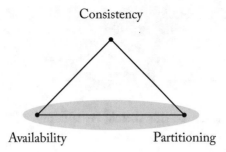

Figure 1.4: The CAP-trade-off for permissionless blockchains, where the focus is on high availability and tolerance to partitioning.

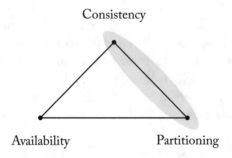

Figure 1.5: The CAP-trade-off for permissioned blockchains, where the focus is on consistency.

ledger as the ρ-th transaction. This strong consistency is maintained independent of the reliability of the network. This comes at the cost of availability: permissioned blockchains provide *limited availability*, as client requests can only be processed if they are received by good replicas in partitions holding a majority of all the good replicas. In practice, permissioned blockchains will provide reliable services whenever communication is sufficiently reliable and do not provide any services whenever communication is not reliable, while always guaranteeing consistency of the already-constructed ledger. This CAP-trade-off is sketched in Figure 1.5.

1.3   ON RESILIENT DISTRIBUTED SYSTEMS

In the previous section, we explored the CAP Theorem, which provides a broad-stroke classification of the properties that can be provided by blockchains. To gain a more fine-grained classification of the properties of blockchains, we will take a closer look at the theory behind fault-tolerant systems.

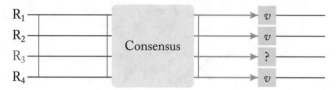

Figure 1.6: A sketch of *consensus*. In this sketch, R_3 is faulty, while all other replicas are good. As R_3 is faulty, the replica can decide anything.

1.3.1   NOTATIONS FOR RESILIENT DISTRIBUTED SYSTEMS

A blockchain is a *system* operated by a set of *replicas* $\mathfrak{R}$. We write $\mathcal{F} \subseteq \mathfrak{R}$ to denote the set of *faulty replicas* that can exhibit Byzantine behavior. Depending on the type of behavior a blockchain is designed to deal with, these faulty replicas can crash, omit sending messages, send arbitrary messages, or even coordinate with each other and operate in malicious manners. We write $\mathcal{G} = \mathfrak{R} \setminus \mathcal{F}$ to denote the *good (non-faulty) replicas* and we write $\mathbf{n} = |\mathfrak{R}|$, $\mathbf{f} = |\mathcal{F}|$, and $\mathbf{g} = |\mathcal{G}|$ to denote the number of replicas, faulty replicas, and good replicas, respectively. We assume that the replicas $\mathfrak{R}$ are ordered uniquely and, based on this ordering, have unique identifiers. Hence, each replica $R \in \mathfrak{R}$ has an identifier $0 \leq id(R) < \mathbf{n}$.

1.3.2   COORDINATION IN RESILIENT DISTRIBUTED SYSTEMS

The problem of coordinating good replicas in a resilient system has been studied formally in several forms, the most prominent of which are *consensus*, *interactive consistency*, and *Byzantine broadcast* (itself sometimes referred to as *Byzantine generals*). First, we define the most abstract of these problems, the consensus problem [102].

Definition 1.3   Let $\mathfrak{R}$ be a system. An protocol solves the *consensus problem* if, upon completion of the protocol, the following holds:

Termination Each good replica $R \in \mathcal{G}$ decides on a value $v(R)$.

Non-divergence All good replicas decide on the same value. Hence, if $R_1, R_2 \in \mathcal{G}$, then $v(R_1) = v(R_2)$.

Non-triviality In different runs of the protocol, replicas can decide on different values.

In Figure 1.6, we have sketched the definition of *consensus*.

We note that the *non-triviality* guarantee of consensus excludes trivial solutions (e.g., an protocol in which all good replicas always decide on a pre-defined constant value). In practice,

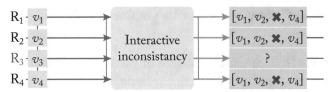

Figure 1.7: A sketch of *interactive consistency*. In this sketch, R_3 is faulty, while all other replicas are good. As R_3 is faulty, the value ✖ can be anything and the replica can decide anything.

most application-oriented definitions of *consensus* expand on non-triviality by putting restrictions on the decided values.

Example 1.4   The obvious example of non-trivial decisions can be found in systems that process client transactions. In such systems, one wants replicas to reach *consensus* and decide on valid client-requested transactions that have not yet been executed. More involved examples can also be found. Consider a system of temperature sensors distributed in a room, some of which can be unreliable. The goal of *consensus* in this system is to determine the average temperature in the room. Hence, in this case, the final decision on the temperature should be based on the average of the temperatures measured by each of the sensors (possibly excluding outliers, as these could indicate sensor failures).

Most blockchain systems utilize consensus to decide on client-requested transactions (as in the first example above). We will consider such a *practical* client-oriented definition of consensus in Chapter 2. Next, we examine interactive consistency [207].

Definition 1.5   Let $\mathfrak{R}$ be a system in which each replica R holds an initial value $v(R)$. An protocol solves the *interactive consistency problem* if, upon completion of the protocol, the following holds:

Termination Each good replica $R \in \mathcal{G}$ decides on a list $L(R)$ of n values, one for each replica.

Non-divergence All good replicas decide on the same list. Hence, if $R_1, R_2 \in \mathcal{G}$, then $L(R_1) = L(R_2)$.

Dependence If replica $R \in \mathfrak{R}$ is a good replica and good replica $Q \in \mathcal{G}$ decided on $L(Q)$, then $L(Q)[\text{id}(R)] = v(R)$.

In Figure 1.7, we have sketched the definition of *interactive consistency*.

The interactive consistency problem is a *concrete* problem that clearly specifies both the input values and the decided-upon values, whereas consensus is *abstract* as it only specifies requirements on the decided-upon values (without specifying where these values come from or are based upon). Still, the interactive consistency problem is a powerful tool that can easily solve consensus problems:

Example 1.6   Consider the consensus problems of Example 1.4. First, we use interactive consistency to reach consensus on client transactions. To do so, each client simply sends their transactions to one or more replicas. Next, each good replica R chooses a valid transaction it received (and has not yet executed) as their initial value $v(R)$. Then, all replicas participate in interactive consistency, after which each good replica decides upon the same list L of **n** transactions. Finally, all good replicas use the same method to choose one of these transactions, e.g., by choosing the first valid transaction in L that has not yet been executed.

Next, we use interactive consistency to reach consensus on the room temperature. In this case, each good replica R chooses their sensor-value as the initial value. Then, all replicas participate in interactive consistency, after which each good replica decides upon the same list L of **n** temperatures, **g** of which are provided by good replicas. Finally, all good replicas use the same method to remove outliers from L and to compute the average of L.

Finally, we consider the Byzantine broadcast problem [167].

Definition 1.7   Let $\mathfrak{R}$ be a system in which some replica $G \in \mathfrak{R}$ holds an initial value w. A protocol solves the *Byzantine broadcast problem* if, upon completion of the protocol, the following holds:

Termination   Each good replica $R \in \mathcal{G}$ decides on a value $v(R)$.

Non-divergence   All good replicas decide on the same value. Hence, if $R_1, R_2 \in \mathcal{G}$, then $v(R_1) = v(R_2)$.

Dependence   If replica G is a good replica and good replica $R \in \mathcal{G}$ decided on $v(R)$, then $v(R) = w$.

In Figure 1.8, we have sketched the definition of *Byzantine broadcast*.

The Byzantine broadcast problem is also a *concrete* problem that can be used to provide consensus, as we illustrate next.

Example 1.8   Consider again the consensus problems of Example 1.4. Next, we use Byzantine broadcasts to reach consensus on client transactions. To do so, we appoint one replica as the *primary* that is responsible for broadcasting transactions. For simplicity, we assume that primaries are assigned based on replica-identifiers. Hence, the i-th primary is the replica $R \in \mathfrak{R}$ with $id(R) = i$.

We assume that clients send valid transactions to all replicas. To start, the first primary uses Byzantine broadcast, after which all replicas decide on the same value w. If this value is a valid transaction that has not been executed yet, then consensus is reached. Otherwise, the next

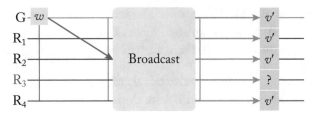

Figure 1.8: A sketch of *Byzantine broadcast*. In this sketch, G holds initial value w. If G is good, then all replicas will decide w ($v' = w$). Otherwise, v' can be anything. Replica R_3 is faulty, and can decide anything.

primary repeats the process. As long as there are good replicas in the system, this process will eventually use a good replica as a good primary, after which consensus will be reached on a valid transaction that has not yet been executed.

As we shall see in Chapters 2 and 3, the client-oriented consensus protocol of Example 1.8 is very close to the basic design of many *practical* consensus protocols. Indeed, the design of the influential *Practical Byzantine Fault Tolerance (*PBFT*) consensus protocol* [54–56] that we present in Chapter 2 matches the basic approach outlined in Example 1.8 (if we ignore all aspects related to dealing with possible-unreliable communication).

The interactive consistency problem and the Byzantine broadcast problem are closely related and solutions to these problems can be used to solve each other, which we show next.

Theorem 1.9   *Let $\mathfrak{R}$ be a system with reliable communication in which the good replicas outnumber the faulty replicas (**g** > **f**).*

1. *If one can solve the* interactive consistency problem *in $\mathfrak{R}$, then one can solve the* Byzantine broadcast problem.

2. *If one can solve the* Byzantine broadcast problem *in $\mathfrak{R}$, then one can solve the* interactive consistency problem.

Proof. First, we solve Byzantine broadcast using interactive consistency. Let $G \in \mathfrak{R}$ be a replica that wants to broadcast initial value w. To do so, G broadcasts w to all other replicas. Let $w'(R)$ be the value R receives from G. Next, R will use $w'(R)$ as its initial value $v(R)$ and then participates in interactive consistency. After interactive consistency, each replica in $\mathfrak{R}$ has decided on an identical list L that contains the values $w'(R)$ received from G by each good replica $R \in \mathcal{G}$. Finally, each good replica deterministically decides on the most-frequent value in L. As the majority of all replicas are good, a good replica G will be able to assure that the majority of the values in L are w. Next, we solve interactive consistency using Byzantine broadcasts. Let $v(R)$

be the initial value held by $R \in \mathfrak{R}$. To perform interactive consistency, each replica R performs Byzantine broadcast of $v(R)$. Finally, each good replica $Q \in \mathfrak{R}$ constructs $L(Q) = [v_0, \dots, v_{n-1}]$, in which v_i, $0 \leq i < \mathbf{n}$, is the value $v(R_i)$ broadcasted by replica R_i with $\mathrm{id}(R_i) = i$ $\qquad\square$

Finally, we remark that consensus is also closely related to both interactive consistency and Byzantine broadcasts. In Examples 1.6 and 1.8, we already showed how specific types of *consensus* can be solved using interactive consistency and Byzantine broadcasts. Likewise, both interactive consistency and Byzantine broadcasts can be seen as variations of the consensus problem in which the *non-triviality* condition is expressed in terms of the initial state of the participating replicas.

In the following sections, we will take a deep dive in the theory behind consensus to determine the environments in which resilient distributed systems can be built and how resilient such systems can be against failures. Specifiically, we will consider the failure model, the communication model, the usage of authenticated communication and digital signatures, and, finally, the complexity and cost of consensus.

1.3.3   FAILURE MODELS

Resilient distributed systems can be designed to deal with a variety of faulty behavior. The total *resilience* of such systems, the ratio of replicas that can turn faulty, is depending on the *failure model*: systems can be designed to deal with replicas that are initially crashed, crash, can omit messages, or exhibit Byzantine behavior.

Definition 1.10   Consider a system $\mathfrak{R}$ operated by some distributed protocol A. An *initially crashed replica* does never perform any steps (it performs no steps related to A, does not send messages, and does not receive messages). A *crashing replica* performs the steps of A correctly up till some point, after which it stops performing any step. An *omitting replica* executes steps of A correctly, but can decide to not send a message when A requires to and to ignore messages it receives. Finally, a *Byzantine replica* can behave in arbitrary manners. Byzantine replicas can be malicious and actively take steps to disrupt A, e.g., by sending wrong messages, corrupting messages, and ignoring messages of other replicas. Furthermore, Byzantine replicas can coordinate together in attempts to disrupt A.

In some practical applications, a fifth type of faulty behavior is considered: replicas that can behave Byzantine, but also have trusted components (that will not behave faulty). Such trusted components are typically used to curtail the most egregious forms of Byzantine behavior, due to which such systems can behave more closely to systems that only have to deal with omitting replicas. We take an in-depth view at the usage of trusted components in Section 3.4.

Finally, we observe that Byzantine replicas can omit messages, that omitting replicas can behave as if they are crashed, and crashed replicas can crash before performing any steps. Hence, dealing with crashing replicas is harder than dealing with initially crashed replicas, dealing with omitting replicas is harder than dealing with crashing replicas and, finally, dealing with Byzantine replicas is harder than dealing with omitting replicas. In the following sections, we shall see how the failure model influences failure resilience.

1.3.4   COMMUNICATION MODELS

Distributed systems rely on a network to enable communication between the replicas. Typically, the communication services of the underlying network are modeled by, on the one hand, *synchronous communication*, and, on the other hand, *asynchronous communication*.

In distributed systems that use *synchronous communication*, messages sent by any good replica will be delivered within some known bounded delay. Without loss of generality, any distributed computations in such systems can be modeled via *pulses*.

Definition 1.11   A distributed systems is *synchronous* if its operations can be modeled via *pulses* in which replicas perform three steps:

1. first, replicas receive all messages sent to them in the previous pulse;

2. then, replicas perform internal computations; and

3. finally, replicas send messages to other replicas (which will be received in the next pulse).

Synchronous communication is reliable and enables individual replicas to detect whether other replicas did sent the necessary messages to them (as part of a protocol). Hence, synchronous communication simplifies the detection of faulty replicas that are crashed or omit sending messages when they are supposed to send them. Practical wide-area deployments of distributed systems operate via *unreliable networks* (e.g., via the Internet). Communication in such networks is typically modeled by *asynchronous communication*.

Definition 1.12   In a distributed systems that uses *asynchronous communication*, messages can get arbitrary delayed, duplicated, or dropped.

As messages can get arbitrarily delayed in asynchronous systems, messages can also arrive in a different order as in which they are sent. Furthermore, asynchronous communication complicates the detection of faulty behavior: it is impossible to distinguish between a faulty replica that is crashed or refuses to send messages, and a good replica whose messages are dropped (or delayed for very long times).

Although one typically wants blockchain systems to operate on networks with asynchronous communication, a well-known result of Fisher, Lynch, and Paterson (FLP) shows that this is impossible.

Theorem 1.13   FLP Impossibility Theorem [102, 189].   *Let $\Re$ be a system using asynchronous communication. The consensus problem cannot be solved for $\Re$ if there are any faulty replicas that can crash.*

A straightforward interpretation of the FLP Impossibility Theorem would rule out the construction of blockchain systems that operate in *practical* network environments. Fortunately, there are several ways to circumvent the FLP Impossibility Theorem.

First, many blockchains weaken the termination requirement of *consensus* toward *weak termination*. Such blockchain systems simply opt to not provide services in all circumstances. Instead, they utilize *consensus* to make new decisions in periods of sufficiently reliable communication, while not making new decisions whenever communication becomes too unreliable. Hence, strictly speaking such systems fail to provide *termination* whenever communication becomes too unreliable and, consequently, such systems do not solve consensus. Another approach is to weaken the termination requirement of *consensus* toward *probabilistic termination*. In systems that operate using probabilistic termination, all replicas coordinate their operations in probabilistic steps and during each step, each replica decides on a value with high probability. Systems using asynchronous communication can solve both the *weak consensus problem* (in which termination is replaced by weak termination) and the *probabilistic consensus problem* (in which termination is replaced by probabilistic termination).

Theoretically speaking, one can also weaken the failure model: the FLP Impossibility Theorem states that consensus cannot be solved in asynchronous systems in which faulty replicas can crash. In asynchronous systems in which faulty replicas cannot crash, but are always *initially crashed* (and never participate in the system), one can solve consensus effectively [102].

Remark 1.14   The FLP Impossibility Theorem is closely related to the CAP Theorem, as we shall argue next. First, solving the consensus problem requires providing *termination*, which is closely related to providing *availability* (in the CAP Theorem). Additionally, solving the consensus problem also requires providing *non-divergence*, which is closely related to providing *consistency* (in the CAP Theorem). Finally, supporting asynchronous communication is closely related to *tolerance to partitioning* (in the CAP Theorem).

1.3.5   AUTHENTICATED vs. SIGNED MESSAGES

In traditional distributed systems and permissioned blockchain systems, the set of participating replicas is predetermined. Furthermore, for their correct operations, these systems require that faulty replicas can only impersonate each other, and not impersonate good replicas. To do so, these systems typically assume *authenticated communication*.

Definition 1.15   Let $\mathfrak{R}$ be a system with replicas $R, Q \in \mathfrak{R}$ and consider a message m sent from R to Q. The system $\mathfrak{R}$ provides *authenticated communication* if Q can, on receipt of m, determine that m was sent by R whenever R is a good replica, and determine that m was sent by a faulty replica whenever R is faulty. Hence, faulty replicas are able to impersonate each other, but are not able to impersonate good replicas.

Authenticated communication can be implemented using inexpensive *symmetric cryptography*, e.g., via *message authentication codes*. Systems that use authenticated synchronous communication can solve consensus if sufficient good replicas are participating [82, 83, 167, 207].

Theorem 1.16   *Let $\Re$ be a system using synchronous communication.*

1. *If $\Re$ deals with crashing or omitting replicas, then the consensus problem can be solved whenever* **n > 2f.**

2. *If $\Re$ deals with Byzantine replicas, then the consensus problem can be solved whenever* **n > 3f.**

The main drawback of authenticated communication is that it does not prevent faulty replicas from corrupting the messages they forward: recipients of messages forwarded by faulty replicas only have a guarantee that they received a message from a faulty replica. To deal with this, many systems employ *digital signatures* to make messages tamper-proof.

Definition 1.17   The system $\Re$ uses digital signatures if every replica R can *sign* arbitrary messages m, resulting in a certificate $\text{cert}(m, R)$. These certificates are non-forgeable and can be constructed only if R cooperates in constructing them. Hence, if Q receives $\text{cert}(m, R)$ from *any* replica, then Q can determine that m was originally signed by R whenever R is good, and can determine that m was originally signed by a faulty replica whenever R is faulty. Hence, when faulty replicas forward messages, they are able to corrupt messages originating from other faulty replicas, but are not able to corrupt messages originating from good replicas.

In practice, *digital signatures* can be implemented using *public-key (asymmetric) cryptography* in which every replica is equipped with a privately held key used for *signing* and a publicly-known key used for *signature verification*. Digital signatures and public-key cryptography can be used to implement authenticated communication, although other methods are preferable due to the high costs associated with public-key cryptography. More importantly, digital signatures can be used to curtail the most egregious forms of Byzantine behavior, due to which such systems can behave more closely to systems that only have to deal with omitting replicas, as we show next [85, 167, 207].

Theorem 1.18   *Let $\Re$ be a system using synchronous communication and digital signatures. If $\Re$ deals with Byzantine replicas, then the consensus problem can be solved whenever* **n > f.**

We directly note that Theorem 1.18 claims a resilience against failures that typical systems *cannot* provide. Typical systems do not operate independent of the outside world, but instead provide services to the outside world. For external users of the service (e.g., clients requesting transactions), it is impossible to distinguish between outcomes produced by good replicas and outcomes falsified by faulty replicas whenever the majority of all replicas can be faulty. Hence, practical consensus-based systems require $n > 2f$, even when using synchronous communication and digital signatures.

The FLP Theorem already showed that the consensus problem cannot be solved in systems using asynchronous communication. We can consider the resilience of weak consensus or probabilistic consensus, however. In this respect, Theorem 1.16 generalizes to systems using asynchronous communication, whereas Theorem 1.18 does not. Specifically, we have the following [44].

Theorem 1.19   *Let $\mathfrak{R}$ be a system using asynchronous communication.*

1. *If $\mathfrak{R}$ deals with crashing or omitting replicas, then both the weak and the probabilistic consensus problem can be solved whenever $n > 2f$.*

2. *If $\mathfrak{R}$ deals with Byzantine replicas, then both the weak and the probabilistic consensus problem can be solved whenever $n > 3f$.*

The above conditions also apply when digital signatures are used.

Remark 1.20   The results of Theorems 1.16, 1.18, and 1.19 assume an environment in which each participating replica has a *unique identity*, has an *equal vote*, and no new identities can be added. Such assumptions are fundamentally at odds with the design goals of permissionless blockchains. Still, these results indicate what kinds of resilience can be obtained in permissionless blockchains, e.g., consider a permissionless blockchain with a stable set of participants that each have equal computational resources. If this blockchain uses the Proof-of-Work protocol of Bitcoin, then this blockchain satisfies the assumptions of Theorems 1.16 and 1.18.

1.3.6   THE COMPLEXITY AND COST OF CONSENSUS

In the previous sections, we provided a fine-grained classification of the types of environments in which one can build consensus-based resilient distributed systems and we provided insight in the resilience to failures such systems can provide. From these results, we can already conclude that resilience to failures is *resource intensive*, as one at-least requires more good replicas than faulty replicas. Next, we shall discuss some results on the *complexity* of consensus in terms of the amount of communication required to reach consensus. First, we inspect the number of communication steps [85, 101].

Theorem 1.21   *Let $\mathfrak{R}$ be a system using synchronous communication. Worst-case protocols that solve the consensus problem in $\mathfrak{R}$ while tolerating up-to-f faulty replicas requires at-least $f + 1$ phases of communication. Optimistic protocols that solve the consensus problem while encountering $t \leq f$ faults require at-least $t + 2$ communication phases, even if faulty replicas only omit messages.*

Next, we determine the amount of messages exchanged [84, 128].

Theorem 1.22   *Let $\Re$ be a system using synchronous communication. Any protocol that solves the consensus problem in $\Re$ requires the exchange of at least* **nf** *signatures and the exchange of at least* $\mathbf{n} + \mathbf{f}^2$ *messages.*

Finally, we analyze the connectivity of the network [82, 83]:

Theorem 1.23   *Let $\Re$ be a system using synchronous communication. Consensus can only be solved in $\Re$ if there are at least* $2\mathbf{f} + 1$ *disjoint communication paths between every pair of replicas (hence, the removal of all* **f** *faulty replicas will leave* $\mathbf{f} + 1$ *communication paths between every pair of replicas).*

In practice, Theorem 1.23 is satisfied whenever all replicas have direct connections to all other replicas. Such a clique network is not feasible for large-scale deployments of blockchains, however, and most practical blockchains are employed on a best-effort network in which consensus can fail whenever the network becomes too unreliable (weak consensus).

Remark 1.24   We notice that Theorem 1.23 puts a hard limit on the reliability of communication within a blockchain system and, hence, indicates that consensus cannot be solved in systems with a high tolerance of partitioning. Hence, this result is in line with the FLP Impossibility Theorem.

1.4   OUTLINE OF THIS BOOK

In the previous three sections, we introduced blockchains as fully replicated resilient distributed systems, we surveyed the limitations of fully replicated systems, we focused at *consensus*—the core technique to operate resilient distributed systems—and we surveyed the limitations of consensus. This introduction provides a sufficient background to start inspecting the design and implementation of *practical* high-performance blockchains that are designed for transaction processing.

The remainder of this book is split into two parts. First, we focus on *permissioned blockchains*, as these blockchains are best-suited for high-throughput transaction processing in managed environments. Specifically, we study in-depth the techniques behind *permissioned blockchains*.

- In Chapter 2, we describe the working of the PBFT [54–56], a practical consensus protocol that inspired almost all consensus protocols used in modern permissioned blockchains.

- In Chapter 3, we describe implementation techniques to maximize throughput of PBFT and to improve beyond PBFT. Furthermore, we examine the techniques that are at the core of modern PBFT-like consensus protocols such as FASTBFT [174], HotStuff [249], MinBFT [239], PoE [120], RCC [121, 122], SBFT [109], and Zyzzyva [2, 3, 161–163].

- In Chapter 4, we consider ways to make permissioned blockchains *scalable*. To do so, we study several cutting-edge techniques to step away from the unscalable fully replicated design of permissioned blockchains, while enabling scalable storage, read-only optimizations [137], reliable cluster communication [135, 136], geo-aware designs (e.g., GEOBFT [123]), and sharding (e.g., CERBERUS [134] and BYSHARD [138]).

In the second part, we offer a detailed view of practical blockchain systems.

- in Chapter 5, we observe the key components of a blockchain system and analyze the design of two state-of-the-art permissioned blockchain frameworks, HYPERLEDGER Fabric [14, 231] and RESILIENTDB [116–124, 138, 214].

- In Chapter 6, we move beyond the traditional way of designing consensus and illustrate the design of Byzantine fault-tolerant consensus protocols that support *open membership*. We start by focusing on the *Proof-of-Work* protocol, which is at the core of the first blockchain application. Next, we discuss the design of two of the well-known *Proof-of-X* protocols: PoS and PoC [26, 88, 155]. Further, we illustrate the architecture of two well-established permissionless blockchains: *Bitcoin* [193] and *Ethereum* [244].

1.5   BIBLIOGRAPHIC NOTES

Blockchains have received considerable attention over the years. As such, many recent surveys cover the current state of permissioned and permissionless blockchain technology, e.g., [30, 51, 72, 247], and their usage in various fields, e.g., [110, 149, 168, 215, 233, 246]. Outside the specific scope of blockchain systems, distributed systems have been built and studied with considerable depth and there are many textbooks on such systems, e.g., earlier work focused on resilient fully-replicated database systems that can deal with partitioning [92, 93], and textbooks that focus on distributed system architecture [235], distributed protocols [229], and distributed databases [199]. Next, we cover specific background for the topics discussed in this chapter.

Bitcoin and permissionless blockchains   Bitcoin [193] started in 2009 and marked the first widespread deployment of a *permissionless blockchain*. It is frequently observed that Bitcoin was built on the shoulders of giants, as Bitcoin draws inspiration from many techniques. Examples include digital currencies, consensus-based replication, gossip-based communication, and the usage of cryptography to construct tamper-proof data structures [142, 194]. Still, the novel way in which Bitcoin combined and extended these techniques turned out to be a major breakthrough for resilient decentralized systems: Bitcoin was the first to show that large-scale problems (namely managing a currency) can be solved by a resilient blockchain that is managed by thousands of participants. The design of Bitcoin comes at a price, however. In practice, Bitcoin can only handle a handful of transactions per second, while consuming vast amounts of energy to do so [76, 241].

Since Bitcoin, many other cryptocurrencies and their supporting permissionless blockchains have been proposed, developed, and deployed. Of these, we mention Ethereum [244], whose blockchain is designed with the express purpose to process transactions that perform general-purpose computations in the form of smart contracts. Due to the flexibility of smart contracts in Ethereum, Ethereum sees a significant amount of development of new and innovative (permissionless) blockchain techniques. Examples include relays that enable observing transactions occurring in other blockchains [141] and atomic swaps that enable strict coordination between independent blockchains [141]. These techniques are at the basis of future designs such as Polkadot and Cosmos whose system architecture consists of many independent blockchains that cooperate together to achieve scalability [164, 245].

Permissioned blockchains   Bitcoin was not the first practical resilient system. Functional resilient systems have been designed and implemented for decades. A well-known example is the Byzantine File System proposed by Castro and Liskov [54–56] in 1999. This distributed file system—a Byzantine fault-tolerant version of the well-known Network File System [131]—utilizes the Practical Byzantine Fault Tolerance consensus protocol, which is a classical (permissioned) consensus protocol and could already handle hundreds of transactions per second back in 1999.

Limitations of blockchain systems   The CAP Theorem was conjectured by Brewer in 2000 [46, 47] and a formalization of the CAP Theorem was proven to hold not long after [108].

The FLP Impossibility Theorem, proving that consensus cannot be solved in an asynchronous environment, was proven by Fisher, Lunch, and Paterson in 1985 [102]. The FLP Impossibility Theorem has been generalized to many other situations, e.g., to other fault-tolerant decision tasks [189] and to shared-memory systems [226]. Bounds on the resilience of systems solving consensus in a synchronous environment, together with accompanying consensus protocols, have been proven in several works, e.g., [82, 83, 167, 207]. Likewise, the refinements of these bounds on resilience in systems that employ digital signatures and accompanying consensus protocols have been shown in several works, e.g., [85, 167, 207]. Finally, there are also several works that show results on the complexity of consensus in terms of the number of phases [85, 101], in terms of the number of signatures and messages [84, 128], and in terms of the network connectivity [82, 83].

A first attempt to circumvent the FLP Impossibility Theorem by solving probabilistic consensus was made in 1983 by Ben-Or [25]. In 1985, Bracha and Toueg showed limits on the resilience of probabilistic consensus that deal with crash failures and Byzantine failures, while also introducing their influential probabilistic Byzantine broadcast protocols [44]. Recently, these broadcast protocols have found a new place in the design of high-performance interactive consistency protocols [79] and in consensus protocols such as HoneyBadgerBFT [186], BEAT [86], and Dumbo [115]. Probabilistic consensus protocols have also been studied in the shared-memory model, e.g. [61, 62]. Most practical asynchronous systems use weak consensus protocols such as PBFT to coordinate their actions, however. This includes protocols such as FastBFT [174], HotStuff [249], MinBFT [239], PoE [120], RCC [121, 122], SBFT [109], Zyzzyva [2, 3, 161–163], GeoBFT [123]), Cerberus [134], and ByShard [138].

CHAPTER 2

Practical Byzantine Fault-Tolerant Consensus

In the previous chapter, we characterized blockchains as fully replicated resilient distributed systems. Furthermore, we introduced the *consensus problem*, the problem of coordinating between possibly faulty replicas, that is at the core of such systems, and studied consensus from a theoretical perspective. From this theoretical perspective, the consensus problem can be stated in terms of only the replicas in a distributed system. This layer of abstraction simplifies the study of impossibility results and complexity results, as this perspective eliminates any reliance on specific details of practical distributed systems (e.g., client behavior). In practice, resilient distributed systems do not operate in a vacuum, however. Instead, systems usually provide useful services to one or more clients. Examples include systems that provide transaction processing services to clients, systems that provide data storage services to clients, and the likes.

In the following, we assume that our system of interest provides general-purpose transaction processing to clients, and the step to more basic services is easily made. We model such a resilient distributed system via *state machine replication* of *client transactions*. Specifically, when a client needs a service, it requests this service by sending a transaction to the system. This transaction contains all the specific instructions to be performed by the system to honor the client request. The system proceeds with replicating this transaction among all good replicas using a *consensus protocol*. After successful replication, the replicas execute the transaction (if necessary) and inform the client of the result. As all replicas execute the same transaction, each replica maintains the same state. Next, we illustrate this client-server model with two examples.

Example 2.1 Consider a resilient distributed system that provides the services of a traditional *relational database management system* as sketched in Figure 2.1. In this setting, the system maintains a database consisting of a set of tables and clients can query and update these tables via standard SQL queries. Hence, a client transaction in this setting is simply a set of SQL queries. If a transaction queries for data (e.g., via SELECT-queries), then the replicas execute these queries on the database and return the query result to the client. Otherwise, if the transaction updates the data (e.g., via INSERT, UPDATE, or DELETE-queries), then the replicas simply acknowledge these updates, e.g., by sending the number of affected rows to the client.

Next, consider a resilient distributed system that provides the services of the *Network File System*. In this setting, the system provides network access to a file system consisting of files and directories. Clients can perform file operations on this file system, e.g., creating, reading

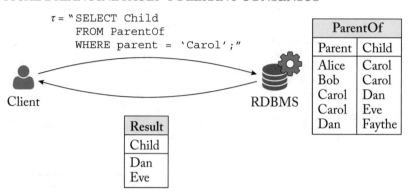

Figure 2.1: Interactions between a client and relational database management system (RDBMS) that maintains a ParentOf table. The client transaction τ requests the children of Carol.

from, writing to, moving, and deleting files and creating, moving, and deleting directories. In this case, a client transaction is simply such a file operation. If the file operation reads data, then the replicas return this data to the client. Otherwise, replicas simply acknowledge whether the file operation was performed successfully.

We are working in a resilient setting in which some replicas in the distributed system can be malicious. This complicates the above client-server service view slightly: both the system and the client need to protect themselves against malicious behavior. Specifically, the following malicious behavior needs to be guarded against in practical resilient distributed systems.

1. Malicious replicas can attempt to insert forged client transactions—that have not been requested by any clients—into the system. To protect against this, all replicas must have means to distinguish between transactions that are requested by clients and transactions that are forged.

2. Malicious replicas can attempt to prevent replication of client transactions from some or all clients. Hence, the system needs to provide means for clients to send their requests to good replicas, even though it is impossible for clients to know which replicas are good.

3. Malicious replicas can send invalid results to the client. To protect against this, the system must provide means for clients to distinguish between invalid results and correct results such that clients can learn the correct results.

4. Also, clients can be malicious and can attempt to interfere with the correct working of a distributed system, e.g., by trying to convince replicas that other good replicas are malicious.

5. Finally, malicious replicas can attempt to prevent replication of client transactions by disrupting the consensus protocol. Fortunately, protecting against such disruptions is the core task of any correct consensus protocol.

Besides dealing with malicious behavior by replicas and clients, the execution of transactions requires the usual application-specific verification and validation steps, e.g., in the resilient database system of Example 2.1, only syntactically correct queries requested by users with sufficient access rights should be executed. As one can see, the practical requirements on a resilient distributed system that processes transactions go further than the properties provided by the consensus problem (as stated in Definition 1.3). Indeed, a solution to the consensus problem only addresses the last of the above practical requirements. Moreover, in practical systems some internal state is maintained at each replica (e.g., database tables or file system data). This state needs to remain consistent among all replicas. To keep the internal state consistent among all replicas, practical systems typically guarantee that all replicas process and execute *the same transactions* in exactly the same order.

Remark 2.2 Executing transactions in exactly the same order among all replicas is not always sufficient to keep the internal state of each replica consistent: if a transaction is non-deterministic, then its execution can modify the internal state of different replicas in different ways. To illustrate this, consider the following high-level transaction τ that modifies the ParentOf table in Figure 2.1:

$$\tau = \text{``Remove a child of Carol from the ParentOf table.''}$$

Upon execution of this transaction, a replica can choose to either remove Dan or Eve. Hence, different replicas can end up removing different rows from the ParentOf table after executing τ, which would make the internal states of these replicas inconsistent with each other.

To provide proper state machine replication, in which all replicas maintain consistent internal states, practical resilient distributed systems typically enforce that all transactions are *deterministic* and that their execution on a given state will always yield the same resultant state and client result. In the above example, determinism can be enforced by requiring that the transaction specifies which child needs to be removed from the table (e.g., the first child in an alphabetic ordering on their names).

As observed, practical resilient distributed systems provide services by processing transactions in sequence. Hence, these systems do not make a single isolated consensus decision, but continuously make consensus decisions. We will formalize these requirements on practical systems in terms of good replicas learning a *ledger*.

Definition 2.3 Let $\mathfrak{R}$ be a system. Each replica $\mathsf{R} \in \mathfrak{R}$ maintains an append-only *ledger* $\mathcal{L}_{\mathsf{R}}$ that represents a sequence of *client transactions*. In practical resilient systems, a *consensus protocol* operates in rounds $\rho = 0, 1, 2, 3, \ldots$ that satisfies the following requirements.

1. *Termination.* In each round ρ, each good replica in $\mathcal{G}$ will append a single client transaction τ to their ledger such that—after round ρ—$\mathcal{L}_R[\rho] = \tau$.

2. *Validity.* If good replica $R \in \mathcal{G}$ appended a transaction to its ledger in round ρ, then $\mathcal{L}_R[\rho]$ is a transaction requested by some client.

3. *Non-divergence.* If good replicas $R_1, R_2 \in \mathcal{G}$ appended transactions to their ledger in round ρ, then $\mathcal{L}_{R_1}[\rho] = \mathcal{L}_{R_2}[\rho]$.

4. *Response.* If good replica $R \in \mathcal{G}$ appended a transaction to its ledger in round ρ, then the client that requested $\mathcal{L}_R[\rho]$ will eventually learn the result of executing $\mathcal{L}_R[\rho]$.

5. *Service.* If a good client requests τ, then eventually a good replica will append τ to its ledger.

The differences between this practical definition of consensus and the theoretical definition of Definition 1.3 are twofold. First, *non-triviality* is replaced by the application-specific client-oriented *validity* requirement. Second, the *response* and *service* requirements have been added to better capture the semantics of client-oriented services.

Due to differences in message delivery times (due to asynchronous communication) and differences in transaction processing times at replicas, we cannot assume that all good replicas append transactions to their ledger at exactly the same time. Consequently, we can only assume that, given a pair of good replicas $R_1, R_2 \in \mathcal{G}$, either $\mathcal{L}_{R_1} \preceq \mathcal{L}_{R_2}$ or $\mathcal{L}_{R_2} \preceq \mathcal{L}_{R_1}$.

Example 2.4   Consider a system $R = \{R_1, R_2, R_3, B\}$ with

$$\mathcal{L}_{R_1} = [\tau_0, \tau_1, \tau_2, \tau_3, \tau_4, \tau_5, \tau_6, \tau_7]; \qquad \mathcal{L}_{R_2} = [\tau_0, \tau_1, \tau_2, \tau_3, \tau_4, \tau_5, \tau_6];$$
$$\mathcal{L}_{R_3} = [\tau_0, \tau_1, \tau_2, \tau_3, \tau_4, \tau_5, \tau_6]; \qquad \mathcal{L}_B = [\tau_0, \tau_1, \tau_2, \tau_3', \tau_4'].$$

The ledger of replica B diverges from the other replicas and, hence, B must be Byzantine. The three good replicas share the ledger $[\tau_0, \tau_1, \tau_2, \tau_3, \tau_4, \tau_5, \tau_6]$. Currently, the system is deciding on the eight transaction, τ_7. This transaction is already appended by R_1, whereas replicas R_2 and R_3 are still processing this transaction.

Notice that we defined the internal state of replicas in terms of the ledger. In practical systems, the ledger is maintained as part of the processes that replicate and execute transactions. Besides this ledger, systems also need to maintain application-specific internal state (e.g., database tables or file system data). While explaining practical consensus protocols, the abstraction of representing the internal state of replicas by a ledger suffices, however.

There are many consensus protocols that provide the guarantees outlined in Definition 2.3 and can be used to construct practical resilient systems. Most practical consensus protocols are based on the influential primary-backup design of the PBFT [54–56] of Castro and Liskov. In this chapter, we will lay out the working of such practical consensus protocols by presenting the design and working of PBFT.

2.1   AN OVERVIEW OF PBFT

In this section, we provide an overview of the design of the PBFT that provides Byzantine fault-tolerant replication of client transactions in an unique order among a set of replicas. In the following sections, we will review in-depth the individual parts of this design.

PBFT, as many other practical consensus protocols, uses a *primary-backup design*, in which a single replica is elected the *primary* and all replicas are *backups*. In this design, the primary is responsible for handling client transactions: it receives client transactions from clients and coordinates replication and execution of these transactions by initiating consensus. At the same time, the backups participate in the consensus process, execute transactions on which consensus is reached, and inform clients on the outcome of execution.

The tasks performed by PBFT can be grouped into two distinct tasks.

1. *Normal-case operations.* In the normal-case, the primary receives client transactions and initiates consecutive rounds of the consensus protocol to add these transactions to the ledgers of all good replicas. During normal-case operations, backups exchange state information among themselves, which allows them to recover from failures and detect any failures that prevent successful completion of consensus rounds. In PBFT, the backups do so by running a simple *two-phase Byzantine fault-tolerant commit algorithm* that guarantees that any committed transaction can be recovered during primary replacement. If failure is detected, backups will blame the current primary and initiate primary replacement and recovery. If no failures are detected, then backups end up committed to the proposed transaction, append the transaction to their ledger, execute the transaction, and inform the client of the result. In Figure 2.2, we have sketched the working of the normal-case operations of PBFT.

2. *Primary replacement and recovery.* When backups detect failure of the normal-case working, they attempt to reach agreement on replacing the primary. During successful primary replacement a new primary is elected and this new primary is responsible for recovering the consensus protocol back to normal-case operations. In PBFT, primary replacement happens via a *view-change* algorithm that, on success, guarantees that any previously committed transaction will be recovered. When a backup considers recovery to be successful, it will switch back to the normal-case operations, this time coordinated by the newly elected primary.

The popularity of the primary-backup design of PBFT is motivated by the relative simplicity of the normal-case, which allows for efficient high-performance implementation of the normal-case that can achieve high transaction throughput. Furthermore, the primary-backup design fits well with client-server services typically provided by resilient distributed systems: the client only has to send its transactions to the primary and it will eventually get responses from the good replicas.

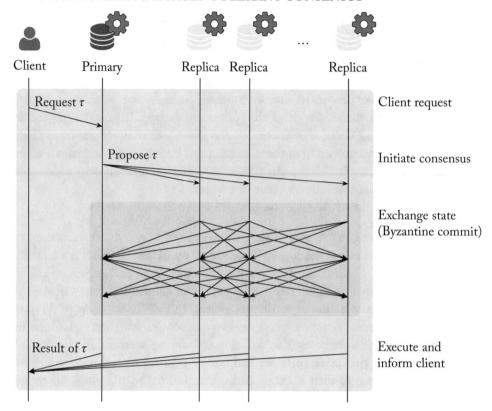

Figure 2.2: High-level working of the normal-case of primary-backup consensus protocols.

To keep the presentation of PBFT as simple as possible, we first present a simplified design of PBFT that uses digital signatures for all messages and that assumes reliable asynchronous communication in which all messages that are sent by good replicas are eventually received. Under these assumptions, Section 2.2 describes the normal-case *Byzantine commit algorithm* of PBFT. Next, in Section 2.3, we describe the *view-change algorithm* of PBFT. In Section 2.4, we detail the usage of *checkpoints* in PBFT, which are used to deal with malicious behavior not covered by view-changes. In Section 2.5, we detail how clients interact with PBFT, how PBFT protects against faulty clients, and how good clients can enforce service. In Section 2.6, we complete our presentation and show that the presented design of PBFT satisfies Definition 2.3. Next, in Section 2.7, we discuss some optimizations that can be applied to the presented design and how PBFT can operate with message loss. Then, in Section 2.8 we sketch how PBFT can operate without using digital signatures. Finally, we close the chapter in Sections 2.9 and 2.10 with some concluding remarks and bibliographic notes.

2.2   THE BYZANTINE COMMIT ALGORITHM OF PBFT

Under normal-case operations, PBFT operates in *views* $v = 0, 1, \ldots$. In each view v a single replica, the replica P with $id(P) = v \bmod \mathbf{n}$, is elected primary and will coordinate consensus rounds. To do so, this primary P will coordinate the replication and execution of client transactions using a *Byzantine commit algorithm*.

To bootstrap this commit algorithm, a client C needs to send a transaction τ to the primary P of the current view v, this by sending a signed request message $\langle \tau \rangle_C$ to the primary. The signature used on the request $\langle \tau \rangle_C$ allows replicas to determine *validity* of the request, as only client C can produce this signature (assuming the client did not hand over its private-keys to others). Moreover, the signature prevents clients from *repudiating their transactions*, limiting malicious behavior by clients.

The primary P can *propose* a ρ-th transaction by choosing such a client request $\langle \tau \rangle_C$ and then proposing this request to all replicas via a PrePrepare message of the form $m :=$ PrePrepare($\langle \tau \rangle_C, v, \rho$). In response, all replicas (the *backups*) participate in a two-phase Byzantine commit algorithm. This commit algorithm can succeed if at least $\mathbf{n} - 2\mathbf{f}$ good replicas received the same PrePrepare message m, in which case success of the commit algorithm guarantees that good replicas can always recover the client request $\langle \tau \rangle_C$ proposed by the PrePrepare message.

After replica R receives a PrePrepare message from P, R will enter the *prepare phase*. In the prepare phase, R will *prepare* the first proposal $m =$ PrePrepare($\langle \tau \rangle_C, v, \rho$) for round ρ it received from P by broadcasting Prepare(m) messages to all replicas. After broadcasting Prepare(m), replica R waits until it receives Prepare messages identical to the message it send from $\mathbf{g}$ distinct replicas. When R receives these $\mathbf{g}$ messages Prepare(m), it reaches the *prepared state* for proposal m. Notice that R can only expect to receive at most $\mathbf{g}$ such Prepare messages: we only have the assurance that the $\mathbf{g}$ good replicas will sent messages to R, whereas the malicious replicas might end up not sending anything. This does not mean that the first $\mathbf{g}$ such Prepare messages R receives all come from good replicas: in the worst case, $\mathbf{f}$ such messages come from malicious replicas. Hence, if R receives these messages, then R has the assurance that at least $\mathbf{g} - \mathbf{f}$ good replicas received m and entered the prepare phase for m. This assurance plays an important role in enforcing *non-divergence*: as we shall prove in Proposition 2.5, this assurance guarantees that replicas can only reach the prepared state for a single PrePrepare message in round ρ of view v. We write $\mathrm{Prepare}_R(m)$ to denote the *prepared certificate* of m, consisting of m and the set of $\mathbf{g}$ Prepare messages used to reach the prepared state for proposal m.

After replica R reaches the prepared state for any proposal $m =$ PrePrepare($\langle \tau \rangle_C, v, \rho$), R will enter the *commit phase*. In the commit phase, R will *commit* to m by broadcasting signed Commit(m) messages to all replicas. After broadcasting Commit(m), R waits until it receives Commit messages identical to the message it send from $\mathbf{g}$ distinct replicas. When R receives these $\mathbf{g}$ messages Commmit(m), it reaches the *committed state* for proposal m. When R reaches the committed state for m, it has the assurance that at least $\mathbf{g} - \mathbf{f}$ good replicas prepared m. As

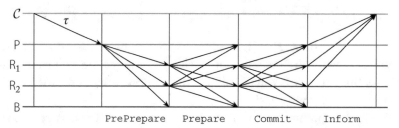

Figure 2.3: A schematic representation of the Byzantine commit algorithm of PBFT: a client C requests transaction τ, the primary P proposes this request to all replicas, all replicas prepare and commit this proposal, and, finally, all replicas will execute τ and inform the client of the result. Replica B is Byzantine, but as it is the only faulty replica it will fail to interfere with the outcome of PBFT.

we shall discuss in Section 2.3, the assurance that $\mathbf{g} - \mathbf{f}$ good replicas prepared m guarantees that in every set of $\mathbf{g}$ replicas, at least a single good replica prepared m, which plays an important role in enabling *recovery of m after failure*. We write $\text{Commit}_R(m)$ to denote the *committed certificate* of m, consisting of m and the set of $\mathbf{g}$ Commit messages used to reach the committed state for proposal m.

After replica R reaches the committed state for any proposal $m = \text{PrePrepare}(\langle \tau \rangle_C, v, \rho)$, R will schedule τ for execution as the ρ-th transaction. To do so, R first waits until all transactions of rounds before ρ are executed and appended to $\mathcal{L}_R$. Then, after all preceding transactions are executed, R appends τ to $\mathcal{L}_R$ and executes τ. After execution, R informs the client of the order of execution and of any execution result r by sending a message $\text{Inform}(\langle \tau \rangle_C, \rho, r)$ to C.

The client C considers the requested transaction τ successfully executed after it receives $\mathbf{f} + 1$ identical messages $\text{Inform}(\langle \tau \rangle_C, \rho, r)$ from distinct replicas. This guarantees that at least one good replica Q appended τ to its ledger in round ρ, executed τ as the ρ-th transaction, and obtained execution result r. Due to the requirements on PBFT stated in Definition 2.3, this guarantees that all good replicas will eventually reach the same conclusions as Q.

If the client does not know the current primary or does not get any timely response on its requests, then it can broadcast its request to all replicas. On receiving such a request, each good replicas will check whether they already executed the request. If a good replica did execute, it will resent the outcome of execution to the client via a fresh Inform message. Otherwise, when a good replica did not yet execute the request, it will forward this request to the current primary and validate that the primary will initiate successful proposal of this request via a PrePrepare message in a timely manner (see Section 2.3 for further details).

In the above, we assume that replicas will discard any messages that are not well formed or have invalid signatures. The communication of the Byzantine commit algorithm of PBFT is sketched in Figure 2.3 and the full pseudo-code of the algorithm can be found in Figures 2.4 and 2.5.

Client-role (used by client C to request transaction τ) :

1: Send $\langle\tau\rangle_C$ to the primary P.
2: Await receipt of messages $\texttt{Inform}(\langle\tau\rangle_C, \rho, r)$ from $\mathbf{f}+1$ replicas.
3: Considers τ executed, with result r, as the ρ-th transaction.

Primary-role (running at the primary P of view v, id(P) $= v \bmod \mathbf{n}$) :

4: Let view v start after execution of the ρ-th transaction.
5: **while** P is the primary **do**
6:     P awaits receipt of message $\langle\tau\rangle_C$ of some client C.
7:     **if** $\langle\tau\rangle_C$ is a well-formed request, signed by client C, for transaction τ **then**
8:         Broadcast $\texttt{PrePrepare}(\langle\tau\rangle_C, v, \rho)$ to all replicas.
9:         $\rho := \rho + 1$.
10:    **end if**
11: **end while**

Figure 2.4: The Byzantine commit algorithm of PBFT (client and primary roles).

The Byzantine commit algorithm of PBFT is designed such that only a single PrePrepare message can reach the commit phase in each round of a view. This implies that only a single prepared certificate can be constructed in each round of a view. This technical property is central to the correctness of PBFT. Next, we will prove this technical property.

Proposition 2.5 *Let* R_i, $i \in \{1, 2\}$, *be two replicas. If* $\mathbf{n} > 3\mathbf{f}$ *and replica* R_i, $i \in \{1, 2\}$, *is able to construct a prepared certificate* $\texttt{Prepare}_{R_i}(m_i)$ *with* $m_i = \texttt{PrePrepare}(\langle\tau_i\rangle_{C_i}, v, \rho)$, *then* $\langle\tau_1\rangle_{C_1} = \langle\tau_2\rangle_{C_2}$.

Proof. To prove the statement of this proposition, we will show that replicas R_1 and R_2 can only construct prepared certificates $\texttt{Prepare}_{R_1}(m_1)$ and $\texttt{Prepare}_{R_2}(m_2)$ after both receiving a Prepare message from a good replica Q. As replica Q is good, it will only send out a single such Prepare message and, hence, $m_1 = m_2$. Next, we formalize this argument.

Replica R_i can only construct $\texttt{Prepare}_{R_i}(m_i)$ after R_i received identical messages $\texttt{Prepare}(m_i)$ from $\mathbf{g}$ distinct replicas (Line 17 of Figure 2.5). Let $\texttt{Prepare}_{R_i}(m_i)$ be this set of messages, let S_i be the set of $\mathbf{g}$ distinct senders of messages in $\texttt{Prepare}_{R_i}(m_i)$, and let $T_i = S_i \setminus \mathcal{F}$ be the good replicas in S_i. By construction, we have $|S_i| = \mathbf{g}$ and $|T_i| \geq \mathbf{g} - \mathbf{f}$. We have sketched these sets in Figure 2.6.

Using the above, we are ready to prove that $\langle\tau_1\rangle_{C_1} = \langle\tau_2\rangle_{C_2}$ by contradiction. Assume that $\langle\tau_1\rangle_{C_1} \neq \langle\tau_2\rangle_{C_2}$. Notice that the good replicas in T_1 and T_2 will only broadcast a single Prepare message for the ρ-th transaction in view v (Line 14 of Figure 2.5). Hence, the sets T_1 and T_2 cannot overlap. Consequently, $|T_1 \cup T_2| = |T_1| + |T_2|$, and we must have $|T_1 \cup T_2| \geq 2(\mathbf{g} - \mathbf{f})$. Remember that all replicas in $T_1 \cup T_2$ are good, hence, $|T_1 \cup T_2| \leq \mathbf{g}$ must also hold. These two

---

Backup-role (running at every replica $R \in \mathfrak{R}$) :

12: **event** R receives message $m = \text{PrePrepare}(\langle \tau \rangle_C, v, \rho)$ such that:

    (i) v is the current view;

    (ii) m is sent by the primary of view v;

    (iii) R did not prepare a ρ-th proposal in view v; and

    (iv) $\langle \tau \rangle_C$ is a well-formed request, signed by client C, for transaction τ

  do

13:      Prepare m as the proposal for round ρ in view v.

14:      Broadcast $\text{Prepare}(m)$ to all replicas.

15: **end event**

16: **event** R receives **g** messages $\text{Prepare}(m)$ such that:

    (i) each message was sent by a distinct replica; and

    (ii) R started the prepare phase for m

  do

17:      Reach the prepared state for m and log the **g** received Prepare messages as $\text{Prepare}_R(m)$.

18:      Broadcast $\text{Commit}(m)$ to all replicas.

19: **end event**

20: **event** R receives **g** messages $\text{Commit}(m)$ such that:

    (i) each message was sent by a distinct replica; and

    (ii) R started the commit phase for m (logged $\text{Prepare}_R(m)$)

  do

21:      Reach the committed state for m and log the **g** received Commit messages as $\text{Commit}_R(m)$.

22: **end event**

23: **event** R committed $m = \text{PrePrepare}(\langle \tau \rangle_C, v, \rho)$ (logged $\text{Commit}_R(m)$) and $|\mathcal{L}_R| = \rho$ **do**

24:      Append τ to $\mathcal{L}_R$, execute τ, and let r be any (optional) result of execution.

25:      Send $\text{Inform}(\langle \tau \rangle_C, \rho, r)$ to C.

26: **end event**

Figure 2.5: The Byzantine commit algorithm of PBFT (backup role).

conditions can only hold if $2(\mathbf{g} - \mathbf{f}) \leq \mathbf{g}$. We have $\mathbf{n} = \mathbf{g} + \mathbf{f}$. Hence,

$$2(\mathbf{g} - \mathbf{f}) \leq \mathbf{g} \quad \text{iff} \quad 2\mathbf{g} - 2\mathbf{f} \leq \mathbf{g} \quad \text{iff} \quad \mathbf{g} \leq 2\mathbf{f} \quad \text{iff} \quad \mathbf{n} \leq 3\mathbf{f},$$

which contradicts the assumption that $\mathbf{n} > 3\mathbf{f}$. By contradiction, we must conclude that $\langle \tau_1 \rangle_{C_1} = \langle \tau_2 \rangle_{C_2}$. $\qquad\square$

    Next, we show that the Byzantine commit algorithm of PBFT provides consensus when the primary is good and communication is reliable.

Theorem 2.6   *Consider a system in view v in which, for all good replicas $R \in \mathcal{G}$, $|\mathcal{L}_R| = \rho$. If the primary is good, communication is reliable, and the primary receives $\langle \tau \rangle_C$, then the primary can use the*

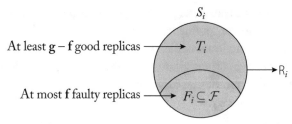

The **g** distinct senders of messages Prepare(m_i) received by R$_i$.)

Figure 2.6: Replica R$_i$ receives **g** messages Prepare(m_i). The set S_i represents the senders of these messages. The set T_i represents the good replicas in S_i. As all messages are sent by distinct replicas, we must have $|T_i| \geq$ **g** $-$ **f**.

Byzantine commit algorithm of PBFT *(Figures 2.4 and 2.5) to ensure that consensus is reached on* τ *in round* ρ *(according to Definition 2.3), this independent of any malicious behavior by faulty replicas.*

Proof. We follow the Byzantine commit algorithm of PBFT (Figures 2.4 and 2.5). After receiving $\langle\tau\rangle_C$, the primary proposes $m = $ PrePrepare($\langle\tau\rangle_C, v, \rho$) by broadcasting m to all replicas (Line 8 of Figure 2.4). As the primary is good, no faulty replica can impersonate the primary. Hence, m is the only well-formed PrePrepare message replicas will receive for round ρ of view v.

In response, all **g** good replicas will broadcast Prepare(m) (Line 14 of Figure 2.5). As there are at most **f** $<$ **g** faulty replicas, the faulty replicas can only forge up-to-**f** invalid Prepare messages. Consequently, each good replica will only receive the message Prepare(m) from at least **g** distinct replicas and every good replica will reach the prepared state for m (Line 17 of Figure 2.5). Likewise, all **g** good replicas will broadcast Commit(m) (Line 18 of Figure 2.5), only receive the message Commit(m) from at least **g** distinct replicas, and reach the committed state for m (Line 21 of Figure 2.5).

As we assumed $|\mathcal{L}_R| = \rho$ for all good replicas R $\in \mathcal{G}$, every good replica R will directly proceed with appending τ to $\mathcal{L}_R$. Hence, the Byzantine commit algorithm provides *termination* and *non-divergence*. Next, each good replica will execute τ and inform the client. As all good replicas behave deterministic, execution will yield the same result r across all good replicas. Hence, when the good replicas inform $\mathcal{C}$, they do so by all sending identical messages Inform($\langle\tau\rangle_C, \rho, r$) to $\mathcal{C}$ (Lines 23–25 of Figure 2.5). Consequently, the client will conclude that τ is executed yielding result r (Line 3 of Figure 2.4). Hence, the Byzantine commit algorithm provides *response*. As a good primary will propose any client request it receives, the Byzantine commit algorithm also provides *service*.

We notice that requested client transactions are digitally signed by the requesting client. Under standard assumptions on the computational complexity of digital signatures, only the client can generate such signed transactions, while any replica can check whether a transaction has a valid signature. Hence, by verifying the signatures of transaction forwarded by the primary, every replica can check whether the transaction originated from a client. Hence, the Byzantine commit algorithm also guarantees *validity*.   □

Remark 2.7   Even though we assumed all messages sent in the Byzantine commit algorithm of PBFT are digitally signed by the sender, digital signatures only play a limited role in the algorithm (and in Proposition 2.5 and Theorem 2.6). As stated in Section 1.3.5, digital signatures serve two purposes: digital signatures can be used to implement *authenticated communication*, as receivers can always identify the sender of a message via the signature (if the sender is good); and signed messages can be *reliably forwarded* without the forwarding replicas being able to corrupt the messages.

As shown in Theorem 2.6, the Byzantine commit algorithm only needs reliable forwarding to provide *validity* (Definition 2.3): replicas depend on client signatures to verify whether *some* client requested the transaction proposed by the primary. All other parts of the algorithm only require authenticated communication, as such channels already enable counting the number of distinct senders of Prepare and Commit messages. In Section 2.3, we will see that the digital signatures on internal messages (PrePrepare, Prepare, and Commit) enables a straightforward way to provide primary replacement and recovery. To eliminate the computational costs associated with digital signatures, signatures on internal messages can be completely eliminated, even though this results in a more complicated approach toward primary replacement and recovery. We discuss the elimination of digital signatures on internal messages in Section 2.8.

Theorem 2.6 only covers the working of PBFT under normal-case operations. We also need to show how PBFT deals with failures. Specifically, we need to consider how PBFT operates when the normal-case operations of PBFT is interrupted. Looking at the conditions under which Theorem 2.6 holds, such interruptions have only two possible causes: faulty primaries or unreliable communication.

Example 2.8   A malicious primary can attempt to compromise PBFT by not conforming to the Byzantine commit algorithm in several ways.

1. *By sending proposals for different transactions to different good replicas.* In this case, Proposition 2.5 already guarantees that at most a single such proposed transaction will get committed by any good replica. We have sketched such a behavior in Figure 2.7.

2. *By keeping some good replicas in the dark by not sending proposals to them.* In this case, the remaining good replicas can still end up committing and executing transactions as long as at least $g - f$ good replicas receive proposals: the faulty replicas in $\mathcal{F}$ can collude with the primary and take over the role of up-to-f good replicas that are left in the dark.

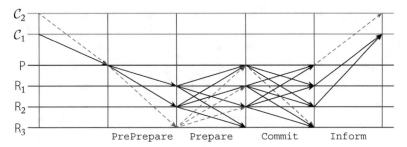

Figure 2.7: A schematic representation of a Byzantine primary that tries to propose two distinct client transactions. All other replicas behave in accordance to the Byzantine commit algorithm of PBFT. In this case, we have $n = 4, f = 1$, and $g = 3$. Due to Proposition 2.5, at most a single such proposal will get committed by good replicas. In this case, the proposal for the request of C_1 will be committed by good replicas, and only C_1 gets sufficient $(f + 1)$ Inform messages to conclude *response*.

3. *By preventing execution of committed transactions.* In this case, the primary skips or sabotages proposing an ρ-th transaction, even though transactions following the ρ-th transaction are being proposed and committed.

We notice that when the network is unreliable and messages do not get delivered (or not on time), the behavior of a good primary can match that of the malicious primary of the second and third case.

Some malicious primary behavior is easily detected: if, for example, the primary sends conflicting PrePrepare messages, then—on receipt of these conflicting messages—any replica can determine that the primary is faulty. This is not true for all malicious behavior, unfortunately. It is especially hard to detect whether a primary is maliciously trying to keep good replicas in the dark:

Example 2.9   Consider a system with four replicas $\{P, R_1, R_2, R_3\}$, of which P is the current primary. We distinguish the following two situations.

1. We have $R_3 \in \mathcal{G}$ and $P \in \mathcal{F}$. The faulty primary behaves normally, except that it keeps R_3 in the dark by never sending messages to R_3. Consequently, R_3 detects that it does not receive messages, and notifies replicas R_1 and R_2 of this misbehavior of the primary.

2. We have $R_3 \in \mathcal{F}$ and $P \in \mathcal{G}$. Independent of the actions of the good primary, the faulty replica R_3 notifies replicas R_1 and R_2 of misbehavior of the primary.

We have sketched these two situations in Figure 2.8. In both situations, replicas R_1 and R_2 receives exactly the same set of messages. Consequently, replicas R_1 and R_2 cannot distinguish

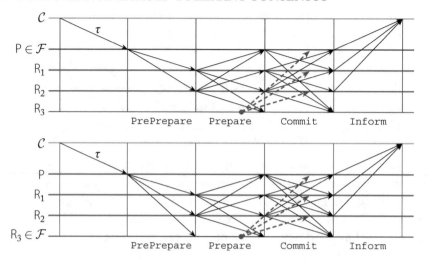

Figure 2.8: A schematic representation of two *different* situations in which good replicas R_1 and R_2 receive exactly the same information. The *dashed* arrows indicate failure messages sent by R_3 to indicate its belief that the primary is malicious. In the situation at the *top*, primary P is faulty, whereas in the situation at the *bottom*, replica R_3 is faulty. As R_1 and R_2 receive exactly the same information, they cannot distinguish between these two situations and, hence, are unable to detect the Byzantine behavior of P in the situation at the top.

between the two situations and cannot determine whether P or R_3 is faulty and which of these replicas is good. We can easily generalize this example to show that malicious behavior by a Byzantine primary that keeps at-most-f good replicas in the dark cannot be detected, as this behavior cannot be distinguished from at-most-f faulty replicas falsely claiming that a good primary keeps them in the dark.

In Section 1.3.4, we already saw that there is no way to guarantee services when communication is unreliable (e.g., when the network is partitioned) and in Example 2.8, we saw that it is not always possible to distinguish between unreliable communication and primary failure. To deal with this, replicas always assume failure of the current primary if the Byzantine commit algorithm of PBFT is interrupted. Next, to deal with such failure, replicas will replace the primary. To assure that this does not lead to issues when communication is unreliable, the design of PBFT assures that unreliable communication only affect termination and that the system will be able to fully recover during periods of reliable communication. The replacement of primaries is done via the *view-change algorithm*, which we discuss in the next section.

Remark 2.10   For clarity, we summarize the terminology introduces in this section and used throughout this and future chapters. The normal-case Byzantine commit algorithm of PBFT has three phases.

1. In the *preprepare phase*, the *primary* proposes a client request via a `PrePrepare` message m to all other replicas. After receiving this proposal m, replicas enter the *prepare phase*.

2. In the *prepare phase*, replicas *prepare* m by sending a `Prepare` message to all other replicas. Then each replica waits until it receives matching `Prepare` messages for m from **g** replicas. After receiving these `Prepare` messages, the replica is *prepared* for m, can construct a *prepared certificate* for m based on the **g** `Prepare` messages, and enters the *commit phase*.

3. In the *commit phase*, replicas *commit* m by sending a `Commit` message to all other replicas. Then each replica waits until it receives matching `Commit` messages for m from **g** replicas. After receiving these `Commit` messages, the replica is *committed* to m and can construct a *committed certificate* for m based on the **g** `Commit` messages.

A replica that is *committed* to m can append m to its ledger and execute it.

2.3   PRIMARY REPLACEMENT AND RECOVERY

If PBFT observes failure of the primary P of view v, then PBFT will elect a new primary and move to the next view, view $v + 1$, via the *view-change algorithm*. The goals of the view-change algorithm are

1. to assure that every request that *could be considered executed* by any client is preserved under all circumstances; and

2. to assure that the replicas are able to agree on a new view whenever communication is reliable.

As described in Section 2.2, a client will consider its request executed if it gets identical `Inform` responses from at-least $f + 1$ distinct replicas. Of these $f + 1$ responses, at-most **f** can come from faulty replicas. Hence, a client can already consider its request executed whenever the requested transaction was executed by *only a single* good replica in the system.

Consequently, to assure that the necessary requests are preserved, the view-change algorithm must assure that every request $\langle \tau \rangle_C$ that *could* have been executed by at least one good replica R is *always* preserved. Hence, any proposal $m := \mathtt{PrePrepare}(\langle \tau \rangle_C, v, \rho)$ committed by R must *always* be preserved. As any R can only reach the committed state for m after receiving `Commit` messages for m from **g** distinct replicas, execution of m by R can only happen if at least $g - f$ good replicas *prepared* m, and the view-change algorithm of PBFT that we will detail next will guarantee that such requests will always be preserved.

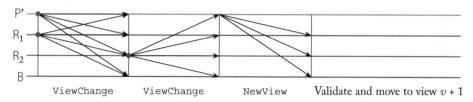

Figure 2.9: The current primary B of view v is faulty and needs to be replaced. The next primary, P′, and the replica R_1 detected this failure first and request a view-change via ViewChange messages. As R′ and R_1 halted the Byzantine commit algorithm of PBFT, the Byzantine commit algorithm cannot make further progress. Eventually, R_2 also detects failure, due to receiving $f + 1$ ViewChange messages, and sends a ViewChange message. Next, the new primary proposes a new view based on the information it received by broadcasting a NewView message. Finally, if the received new-view proposal is valid, then replicas enter the new view with P′ as the new primary.

To do so, the view-change algorithm consists of five steps. First, failure of the current primary needs to be detected by all good replicas. Second, the good replicas elect the replica P′ with $\mathrm{id}(P') = (v + 1) \bmod \mathbf{n}$ as the new primary and provide this replica with the necessary information to establish which transactions could have been committed. Third, the new primary P′ proposes a new view. This new view proposal contains a list of all transactions the new primary considers proposed in previous views (based on the information exchanged in the previous step). Fourth, all replicas validate the new view proposed by P′. Fifth and finally, if the new view proposal is valid, then replicas switch to this view; otherwise, replicas detect failure of P′ and initiate a view-change for the next view, view $v + 2$. The communication of the view-change algorithm of PBFT is sketched in Figure 2.9 and the full pseudo-code of the algorithm can be found in Figure 2.10. Next, we discuss each step of the view-change algorithm in full detail.

2.3.1   FAILURE DETECTION

The only reliable way to detect failure (of the current primary or of the network) is by monitoring the progress of the Byzantine commit algorithm of PBFT: if a replica does not detect any progress for some time, then it will assume a failure happened. To implement this, each replica R relies on *timers* and some internal *time-out value*. Whenever R can expect progress of the Byzantine commit algorithm of PBFT (e.g., when R received a PrePrepare proposal from the primary or when R forwards a client request to the primary), R will set its timer using its internal time-out value. If the timer expires before progress is made (e.g., the PrePrepare message is not committed or the forwarded client request is not proposed by the primary), then R detects failure of the current primary.

View-change request role (used by replica R to request a view-change) :

1: **event** R detects failure of the primary in view v **do**
2:     R halts the Byzantine commit algorithm of PBFT (Figures 2.4 and 2.5) for view v.
3:     Let E be the set of all requests m prepared by R (R logged $\text{Prepare}_R(m)$).
4:     Broadcast $\text{ViewChange}(E, v)$ to all replicas.
5: **end event**
6: **event** R receives $f + 1$ messages $m_i = \text{ViewChange}(E_i, v_i)$, $1 \leq i \leq f + 1$, such that:

(i) all $f + 1$ messages are well-formed (see Section 2.3.3);

(ii) these messages are sent by a set S of $|S| = f + 1$ distinct replicas; and

(iii) v_i is *at least* the current view v ($v_i \geq v$).

do
7:     R detects failure of the primary in view v (if not yet done so).
8: **end event**

New view proposal role (used by replica P$'$ to become the new primary) :

9: **event** P$'$ receives g messages $m_i = \text{ViewChange}(E_i, v_i)$, $1 \leq i \leq g$, such that

(i) all g messages are well-formed (see Section 2.3.3);

(ii) these messages are sent by a set S of $|S| = g$ distinct replicas;

(iii) v_i is the current view v; and

(iv) P$'$ is the next primary ($\text{id}(P') = (v + 1) \bmod n$)

do
10:     $V := \{m_i \mid 1 \leq i \leq g\}$.
11:     $M := \{\text{Prepare}_Q(m) \mid (\text{Prepare}_Q(m) \in E_i) \wedge (1 \leq i \leq g)\}$.
12:     $\{M$ is the set of all prepared certificates contained in $m_1, \ldots, m_g.\}$
13:     $\rho_{\text{all}} := \{\rho \mid (\text{Prepare}_Q(m) \in M) \wedge (m = \text{PrePrepare}(\langle \tau \rangle_C, w, \rho))\}$.
14:     $\{\rho_{\text{all}}$ is the set of all rounds for which M contains prepared certificates.$\}$
15:     $N := \{\text{PrePrepare}(\langle \text{nop} \rangle_{P'}, v + 1, \rho) \mid (\rho \notin \rho_{\text{all}}) \wedge (1 \leq \rho \leq \max(\rho_{\text{all}}))\}$.
16:     $\{N$ contains a $\langle \text{nop} \rangle_{P'}$ proposal for each round missing in $\rho_{\text{all}}.\}$
17:     Broadcast $\text{NewView}(v + 1, V, N)$ to all replicas.
18: **end event**

Figure 2.10: The view-change algorithm of PBFT (message exchange). See Section 2.3.4 for the steps taken by replicas to validate received NewView messages and Section 2.3.5 for steps taken by replicas to move into a validated new view.

2.3.2   REQUESTING A VIEW CHANGE

If a replica R detects failure of the primary of view v, then it will halt the Byzantine commit algorithm of PBFT for view v and inform all replicas, including the new primary P′, id(P′) = $(v + 1)$ mod $\mathbf{n}$, of this failure by requesting a view-change. The replica R does so by broadcasting a message ViewChange(E, v), in which E details all PrePrepare messages R prepared before failure (Line 1 of Figure 2.10).

As detailed in Section 2.3.1, the view-change algorithm relies on time-outs, which are chosen by replicas individually, to detect failure. Ideally, these time-out values are in line with real-world communication latencies. Otherwise, a replica might time-out and detect failure long before the primary had any chance to assure progress. In Section 2.3.6, we show that when communication is reliable, the view-change algorithm of Figure 2.10 assures sufficient *synchronization* between replicas and also that eventually time-outs are sufficiently large to enable successful view-changes. As we shall show in Section 2.3.6, it is for this synchronization that replicas broadcast their ViewChange messages to *all* replicas instead of sending their ViewChange messages to only the new primary P′ (Line 4 of Figure 2.10).

For now, we only provide the intuition behind these broadcasted ViewChange messages. If any good replica R received ViewChange messages from $\mathbf{g}$ distinct replicas, then it received ViewChange messages from at least $\mathbf{g} - \mathbf{f} > \mathbf{f}$ good replicas. These at-least-$\mathbf{f} + 1$ good replicas will have broadcasted their ViewChange message to all replicas. Hence, when R received the $\mathbf{g}$-th message, it has the guarantee that all good replicas have received ViewChange messages from at least $\mathbf{f} + 1$ distinct replicas, will join the view-change algorithm (via Line 6 of Figure 2.10), and that within a message delay all replicas will have received ViewChange messages from at least $\mathbf{g}$ distinct replicas. This assures that within a message delay of R receiving $\mathbf{g}$ distinct replicas, the new primary must be able to construct a valid NewView message, which R can expect to receive in two message delays. Hence, at this point, R can start a timer to detect failure of the new primary to propose a new view.

Remark 2.11   Good replicas halt participation in the Byzantine commit algorithm of PBFT after they detect failure. Hence, after $\mathbf{f} + 1$ good replicas detect failure, at most $\mathbf{n} - (\mathbf{f} + 1) = \mathbf{g} - 1$ replicas still participate in the Byzantine commit algorithm of PBFT (which includes all $\mathbf{f}$ faulty replicas). After this point, it is guaranteed that no good replica will be able to reach the commit phase for any further proposals of the view. Consequently, all good replicas will eventually time-out—causing a *cascade of failure* detections—and request a view-change. The view-change algorithm of Figure 2.10 does not rely on this cascade to assure that all good replicas detect failure, however. Indeed, via Line 6 of Figure 2.10, replicas can detect failure of the primary *indirectly* by using ViewChange messages of other replicas. Example 2.8(2) already showed that replicas cannot directly trust such ViewChange messages to determine that the current primary is faulty. To alleviate this, each replica R only acts when it receives ViewChange messages from $\mathbf{f} + 1$ distinct replicas: in this case, R can safely conclude that a good replica detected failure (as there are at most $\mathbf{f}$ faulty replicas that might lie about failures), and detect failure itself (before any time-out).

2.3.3   PROPOSING THE NEW VIEW

To start view $v + 1$, the new primary P' (with $\mathrm{id}(\mathsf{P}') = (v + 1) \bmod \mathbf{n}$) needs to propose a new view by proposing a valid final state for the views preceding view $v + 1$. To do so, P' first awaits until it receives sufficient information to determine this final state. Specifically, P' waits until there is a set $S \subseteq \mathfrak{R}$ of $|S| = \mathbf{g}$ distinct replicas from which P' received well-formed view-change requests (Line 9 of Figure 2.10). The message $\mathtt{ViewChange}(E_i, v_i)$, $1 \leq i \leq \mathbf{g}$, is well-formed if $v = v_i$ and each value in E_i is a valid $\mathrm{Prepare}_{\mathsf{R}_i}(m)$ entry: a set of $\mathbf{g}$ well-formed $\mathtt{Prepare}$ messages, all for the same well-formed $\mathtt{PrePrepare}$ message m' and each signed by a distinct replica.

To propose a new view $v + 1$, the new primary P' sends a message $\mathtt{NewView}(v + 1, V, N)$. This $\mathtt{NewView}$ message contains a set V of $\mathbf{g}$ $\mathtt{ViewChange}$ messages and a set N of special no-op requests $\langle \mathrm{nop} \rangle_{\mathsf{P}'}$ proposed by P'. These no-op requests are used to fill up any holes in the sequence of requests proposed by previous primaries (e.g., due to Example 2.8(3)). Computation of N proceeds in two steps. First, P' determines the set ρ_{all} of all rounds for which requests have been successfully proposed by previous primaries (Line 13 of Figure 2.10). This set can be constructed using the prepared certificates in the received $\mathtt{ViewChange}$ message (Line 11 of Figure 2.10). Next, P' will construct a set N that contains a message $\mathtt{PrePrepare}(\langle \mathrm{nop} \rangle_{\mathsf{P}'}, v + 1, \rho)$ for each round $\rho \in \{0, \ldots, \max(\rho_{\mathrm{all}})\}$ for which no request has been proposed, hence, with $\rho \notin \rho_{\mathrm{all}}$ (Line 15 of Figure 2.10). As the set N is deterministically determined by the content of V, any malicious attempts by P' to place requests in N other than those described by the view-change algorithm will be detected as malicious behavior by good replicas during validation of the new view (see Section 2.3.4 for details).

The goal of the $\mathtt{NewView}$ message is to provide all replicas with sufficient information to derive a final common state for the views preceding view $v + 1$ (see Section 2.3.5), after which all replicas can resume the Byzantine commit algorithm of PBFT with the new primary P'. In the next sections, we discuss how replicas validate these $\mathtt{NewView}$ messages and incorporate these messages into their own state.

2.3.4   VALIDATE THE NEW VIEW

Let R be a replica in view v. After a replica R receives a new-view proposal $\mathtt{NewView}(v', V, N)$ of a new primary P' (with $v' > v$ and $\mathrm{id}(\mathsf{P}') = v' \bmod \mathbf{n}$), the replica first verifies whether the $\mathtt{NewView}$ message is well-formed: the set V must be a set of $\mathbf{g}$ well-formed $\mathtt{ViewChange}$ messages for view $v' - 1$ signed by distinct replicas and N must be a set of proposals of the form $\mathtt{PrePrepare}(\langle \mathrm{nop} \rangle_{\mathsf{P}'}, v', \rho)$ (see Section 2.3.3). Next, R will verify whether N is correctly constructed. To do so, R executes Lines 11–13 of Figure 2.10, this to construct ρ_{all} out of V. Using

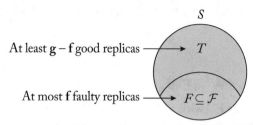

S

At least $\mathbf{g} - \mathbf{f}$ good replicas $\longrightarrow$ T

At most $\mathbf{f}$ faulty replicas $\longrightarrow$ $F \subseteq \mathcal{F}$

(A set of $\mathbf{g}$ distinct senders of `ViewChange` messages.)

Figure 2.11: Construction of a `NewView` message using $\mathbf{g}$ `ViewChange` messages. The set S represents the distinct senders of these messages and the set T represents the good replicas in S. As all messages are sent by distinct replicas, we must have $|T| \geq \mathbf{g} - \mathbf{f}$.

ρ_{all}, R can determine for which round numbers P′ should propose special no-op requests $\langle \mathrm{nop} \rangle_{\mathsf{P}'}$: `PrePrepare`$(\langle \mathrm{nop} \rangle_{\mathsf{P}'}, v', \rho)$ should be in N if and only if $\rho \in \{0, \ldots, \max(\rho_{all})\} \setminus \rho_{all}$. We notice that well-formed `NewView` messages have the following helpful property.

Proposition 2.12   *Let* `NewView`$(v + 1, V, N)$ *be a well-formed* `NewView` *message. If* $\mathbf{n} > 3\mathbf{f}$ *and* $\mathbf{g} - \mathbf{f}$ *good replicas prepared* $m =$ `PrePrepare`$(\langle \tau \rangle_C, v, \rho)$, *then there exists a message* `ViewChange`$(E, v) \in V$ *of good replica* $\mathsf{Q} \in \mathcal{G}$ *with* `Prepare`$_{\mathsf{Q}}(m) \in E$.

Proof. To prove the statement of this proposition, we will show that at least one good replica Q that prepared m must also have participated in the view-change. As replica Q is good, any `ViewChange` message it produces after it prepared m will contain a prepared certificate for m. Next, we formalize this argument.

Let C be the set of good replicas that prepared m. Each of the replicas $\mathsf{R} \in C$ only prepared m if they have logged `Prepare`$_{\mathsf{R}}(m)$ (Line 18 of Figure 2.5). Let S be the set of replicas that constructed the `ViewChange` messages in V and let $T = S \setminus \mathcal{F}$ be the good replicas in S. By construction, we have $|S| = \mathbf{g}$ and $|T| \geq \mathbf{g} - \mathbf{f}$. We have sketched these sets in Figure 2.11.

Notice that if T and C overlap, then there exists a good replica $\mathsf{Q} \in (T \cap C)$. This replica Q will have prepared m, logged `Prepare`$_{\mathsf{Q}}(m)$, have a message `ViewChange`$(E, v) \in V$, and have `Prepare`$_{\mathsf{Q}}(m) \in E$ (Line 4 of Figure 2.10). Hence, it only remains to prove that T and C have overlap. We do so by contradiction. Assume that $(T \cap C) = \emptyset$. Under this assumption, we have $|T \cup C| = |T| + |C|$ and, as $|T| \geq \mathbf{g} - \mathbf{f}$ and $|C| \geq \mathbf{g} - \mathbf{f}$, we also have $|T \cup C| \geq 2(\mathbf{g} - \mathbf{f})$. Remember that all replicas in $T \cup C$ are good, hence, $|T \cup C| \leq \mathbf{g}$ must also hold. Using the same reasoning as used in the proof of Proposition 2.5, we can derive $\mathbf{n} \leq 3\mathbf{f}$, a contradiction. Hence, we conclude that T and C have overlap, completing the proof. $\square$

Proposition 2.12 provides a sufficient condition for requests proposed in the previous view to be included in the next view-change. It does not provide a necessary condition, however, e.g., where only a single faulty replica R was able to construct a prepared certificate $\text{Prepare}_R(m)$, this replica can still provide a valid message $\text{ViewChange}(E, v)$ with $\text{Prepare}_R(m) \in E$ to the new primary. In that case, m will be included in the next view-change, even though no good replica prepared m.

Any request m committed by good replicas must have been prepared by at least $\mathbf{g} - \mathbf{f}$ good replicas. Hence, the sufficient condition provided by Proposition 2.12 has important consequences on *committed (and possibly executed) requests*.

Corollary 2.13 *Let* $R \in \mathcal{G}$ *be a good replica and* $\text{NewView}(v + 1, V, N)$ *be a well-formed* NewView *message. If* $\mathbf{n} > 3\mathbf{f}$ *and* R *committed* $m = \text{PrePrepare}(\langle \tau \rangle_C, v, \rho)$, *then there exists a message* $\text{ViewChange}(E, v) \in V$ *of good replica* $Q \in \mathcal{G}$ *with* $\text{Prepare}_Q(m) \in E$.

Proof. If replica R committed m in view v, then R received Commit messages for m from $\mathbf{g}$ distinct replicas (Line 21 of Figure 2.5). Let S be the set of $\mathbf{g}$ replicas that did send these Commit messages and let $T = S \setminus \mathcal{F}$ be the good replicas in S. By construction, we have $|S| = \mathbf{g}$ and $|T| > \mathbf{g} - \mathbf{f}$. As the replicas in T are good and sent Commit messages to R, each replica in T must have prepared m (Line 18 of Figure 2.5). Hence, Proposition 2.12 can be applied to complete the proof. □

Due to Corollary 2.13, a request committed and executed by any good replica will always be included in the next view-change. In Theorem 2.15, presented in the following section, we further generalize this by showing that such committed requests will always be included in future view-changes. This is crucial to guarantee *response* (Definition 2.3): if a good replica R committed a message $m = \text{PrePrepare}(\langle \tau \rangle_C, v, \rho)$, then it will eventually be picked up by all other good replicas. Hence, even if only a single good replica committed and executed m in a view, client C is still guaranteed to end up considering τ executed (Line 3 of Figure 2.4), as other good replicas will pick up m during view-changes.

2.3.5 MOVE INTO THE NEW VIEW

If R determines that the received new-view proposal $\text{NewView}(v', V, N)$ of a new primary P' is well-formed, then R enters the new view by updating its internal state according to the information received. We notice that the set of ViewChange messages in V can contain conflicting information: different replicas could provide conflicting prepared certificates for the same round number in different views. We illustrate this next.

Example 2.14 We consider views v, $v + 1$, and $v + 2$. View v has faulty primary P, $v + 1$ has faulty primary P_1, and view $v + 2$ has primary P_2. View v ended in round ρ, during which P assured that only good replica R_1 prepared message $m_1 = \text{PrePrepare}(\langle \tau_1 \rangle_{C_1}, v, \rho)$.

When constructing a NewView message, primary P_1 ignored any messages received from R_1. As R_1 is the only replica with a prepared certificate for m_1, the constructed NewView message will not contain m_1. Hence, according to the NewView message constructed by P_1, the last

New view role (used by replica R to move into a new view) :

1: **event** R receives $\texttt{NewView}(v', V, N)$ from P' such that:

    (i) v' follows the current view v ($v' > v$);

    (ii) $v' \bmod n = \text{id}(P')$; and

    (iii) $\texttt{NewView}(v', V, N)$ is well-formed

  do

2:    $M := \{\text{Prepare}_Q(m) \mid (\texttt{ViewChange}(E, v') \in V) \wedge (\text{Prepare}_Q(m) \in E)\}$.

3:    $\rho_{\text{all}} := \{\rho \mid (\text{Prepare}_Q(m) \in M) \wedge (m = \texttt{PrePrepare}(\langle \tau \rangle_C, w, \rho))\}$.

4:    **for** $\rho \in \{0, \ldots, \max(\rho_{\text{all}})\}$ **do**

5:        **if** $\text{Prepare}_Q(m) \in M$ with $m = \texttt{PrePrepare}(\langle \tau \rangle_C, w, \rho)$ **then**

6:            $w_\rho := \max(\{w \mid (\text{Prepare}_Q(m) \in M) \wedge (m = \texttt{PrePrepare}(\langle \tau \rangle_C, w, \rho))\})$.

7:            Choose a $\text{Prepare}_Q(m) \in M$ with $m = \texttt{PrePrepare}(\langle \tau \rangle_C, w_\rho, \rho))$.

8:            Enter the commit phase for m using the $\texttt{Prepare}$ messages in $\text{Prepare}_Q(m)$.

9:            Resume the Byzantine commit algorithm of PBFT for m (Figure 2.5).

10:        **else**

11:            Choose $m = \texttt{PrePrepare}(\langle \text{nop} \rangle_{P'}, v', \rho) \in N$.

12:            Enter the prepare phase for m as the first proposal for round ρ in view v'.

13:            Resume the Byzantine commit algorithm of PBFT for m (Figure 2.5).

14:        **end if**

15:    **end for**

16: **end event**

Figure 2.12: The local state update algorithm of PBFT.

round of v was round $\rho - 1$. Next, primary P_1 proposes $m_2 = \texttt{PrePrepare}(\langle \tau_2 \rangle_{C_2}, v + 1, \rho)$ to all replicas except R_1. Consequently, some replica R_2 prepared m_2, after which P_2 fails.

In view $v + 2$, primary P_2 receives $\texttt{ViewChange}$ messages from both R_1 and R_2. As R_1 was excluded by P_1, the $\texttt{ViewChange}$ message of R_1 will contain a prepared certificate for m_1, while the $\texttt{ViewChange}$ message of R_2 will contain a prepared certificate for m_2.

We can easily deal with Example 2.14: by Corollary 2.13, we can conclude that no replica committed m_1, as otherwise it would have been included in the $\texttt{NewView}$ message constructed by P_1. Hence, it is safe to drop m_1 in favor of m_2. To do so, each replica will use the following rule of thumb to update its own state: *for each round number for which prepared certificates are in V, R picks the prepared certificate constructed in the latest view.* The special no-op requests $\texttt{PrePrepare}(\langle \text{nop} \rangle_{P'}, v', \rho) \in N$ will only be considered by R for round numbers ρ for which no prepared certificates can be found in V. The full pseudo-code to implement these rules can be found in Figure 2.12. Next, we discuss each step in full detail.

During the local state update algorithm, R determines which local state needs updating. Let $\texttt{NewView}(v', V, N)$ be the well-formed $\texttt{NewView}$ message that triggered local state update. To update the local state, R first constructs the set M of all prepared certificates contained in the $\texttt{ViewChange}$ messages in V (Line 2 of Figure 2.12). Based on these prepared certificates,

R computes the set of round numbers ρ_{all} for which proposals are included in the new-view proposal (Line 3 of Figure 2.12). From ρ_{all}, R determines that requests will be kept for rounds $0, \ldots, \max(\rho_{all})$. Next, for each round $\rho \in \{0, \ldots, \max(\rho_{all})\}$, R will determine whether a local state update is necessary (Line 4 of Figure 2.12). For each round ρ, two distinct cases are possible.

1. The set M contains prepared certificates for proposals in round ρ (Lines 5–9 of Figure 2.12). In this case, R applies the rule of thumb and chooses $\text{Prepare}_Q(m) \in M$ with $m = \text{PrePrepare}(\langle \tau \rangle_C, w_\rho, \rho))$ such that w_ρ is the latest view for which a prepared certificate for proposals in round ρ is in M. Next, R commits to this message m (by logging the prepared certificate) and resumes the Byzantine commit algorithm of PBFT for this message.

2. Otherwise, if M contains no prepared certificates for proposals in round ρ, then the set N must contain a $\langle \text{nop} \rangle_{P'}$ proposal for round ρ in N (Lines 10–13 of Figure 2.12). In this case, R selects the PrePrepare message $m \in N$, constructed by P', that proposes a no-op request in round ρ. Next, R prepares m and resumes the Byzantine commit algorithm of PBFT for this message.

After updating the local state, R moves into view v' with new primary P' ($\text{id}(P') = v' \bmod \mathbf{n}$) and will await new PrePrepare proposals for view v'. These new proposals all must have round numbers starting at $\max(\rho_{all}) + 1$. Next, we prove correctness of this new view process. We proceed in two steps. Here, we show that the new view process preserves all committed proposals. Next, in Section 2.3.6, we show that the new view process will eventually restore PBFT to a state in which the Byzantine commit algorithm can operate when communication is reliable, this by assuring that all good replicas will eventually attempt to view-change to the same new view.

Theorem 2.15   *Let* $Q \in \mathcal{G}$ *be a good replica that committed* $m = \text{PrePrepare}(\langle \tau \rangle_C, v, \rho)$, *and let* $\text{NewView}(w, V, N)$ *be a well-formed* NewView *message with* $w > v$. *If* $\mathbf{n} > 3\mathbf{f}$, *then any good replica* $R \in \mathcal{G}$ *will commit to* m *when updating its local state via the algorithm of Figure 2.12.*

Proof. We prove this theorem by induction on $w - v$. The base case is $w - v = 1$. In this case, Corollary 2.13 guarantees that m is included in a ViewChange message in V. By Proposition 2.5, we know that m is the only prepared proposal with round number ρ in view v. As $w = v + 1$, no other proposals with round number ρ will be prepared in a later view. Hence, Q will commit to m when executing the algorithm of Figure 2.12.

Next, consider the case $w - v > 1$. As the induction hypothesis, we assume that any good replica $R' \in \mathcal{G}$ that updated its local state when entering view u, $v < u < w$, will commit to m during this update. Now consider replica $R \in \mathcal{G}$ entering view w and consider any ViewChange message $\text{ViewChange}(E, w) \in V$ with $\text{Prepare}_{R'}(m') \in E$ and $m' = \text{PrePrepare}(\langle \tau' \rangle_{C'}, v', \rho)$. By contradiction, we will prove that $v' \leq v$. Assume that $v < v' < w$. Let S be the set of g replicas whose Prepare messages are included in $\text{Prepare}_{R'}(m')$, let $T = S \setminus \mathcal{F}$ be the good replicas in S, and let P' be the primary of view v'. By construction, we have $|T| \geq \mathbf{g} - \mathbf{f} \geq 1$. Consider any such good replica $R'' \in T$. As R'' is good and participated in view v', $v < v' < w$, it must have updated its local state when entering view v'. Hence, we can apply the induction hypothesis to conclude that R'' committed to m during this update. Consequently, while updating its local state when entering view v', the replica will not prepare any special no-op requests for round ρ (Figure 2.12, Lines 5–13). Moreover, as round ρ was updated, R'' will only prepare new PrePrepare proposals from P' in view v' for rounds ρ'', $\rho'' > \rho$. Hence, R'' could not have produced a Prepare message for m', a contradiction, and we must conclude that $v' \leq v$.

Finally, it only remains to prove that there exists a message $\text{ViewChange}(E, w) \in V$ with $\text{Prepare}_{R'}(m) \in E$. Similar to the proof of Corollary 2.13, we can construct set C' of $\mathbf{g}$ replicas that did send Commit messages for m to R and set $C = C' \setminus \mathcal{F}$. Similar to the proof of Proposition 2.12, we can also construct set S of replicas that constructed the ViewChange messages in V and set $T = S \setminus \mathcal{F}$. We have $|T| \geq \mathbf{g} - \mathbf{f}$ and $|C| \geq \mathbf{g} - \mathbf{f}$. Hence, using the reasoning of Proposition 2.12, we conclude that $T \cap C \neq \emptyset$, completing the proof. □

We notice that Theorem 2.15 only provides guarantees on *committed* PrePrepare messages, it does not provide any guarantees on any other proposals. Indeed, if a message is only prepared by one or more good replicas, then this message can still be replaced in later views. We illustrate this next.

Example 2.16   Consider a system $\mathfrak{R} = \{R_0, \dots, R_6\}$ with $\mathcal{F} = \{R_0, R_6\}$. In view 0, the replica R_0 is the primary and manages to replicate client requests $\langle \tau_0 \rangle_{c_0}$, $\langle \tau_1 \rangle_{c_1}$, and $\langle \tau_2 \rangle_{c_2}$. Hence, at the start of round $\rho = 3$, all replicas have executed the sequence

$$\mathcal{L}_{R_0} = \dots = \mathcal{L}_{R_6} = [\tau_0, \tau_1, \tau_2].$$

At this point, R_0 starts behaving malicious. We consider two distinct situations.

1. In the first situation, R_0 proposes $m_3 = \text{PrePrepare}(\langle \tau_3 \rangle_{c_3}, 0, 3)$ to replicas R_0, R_1, R_2, R_3, and R_6. Next, the faulty replicas R_0 and R_6 only send Prepare messages to R_2. Consequently, only R_2 prepared m_3 and broadcasts $\text{Commit}(m_3)$ to all replicas. Eventually, with the help of the faulty replicas, failure of R_0 is detected and a view change is initiated.

   The new primary—R_1—receives any ViewChange message of R_2 later than other ViewChange messages and, hence, proposes a new view that does not include m_3. As this new view proposal is valid, all replicas decide that view 0 resulted in requests $\langle \tau_0 \rangle_{c_0}$, $\langle \tau_1 \rangle_{c_1}$, and $\langle \tau_2 \rangle_{c_2}$. Hence, the first proposal considered in view 1 has round number 3 and will eventually overwrite m_3 in R_2.

2. In the second situation, R_0 proposes $m_3 = \text{PrePrepare}(\langle \tau_3 \rangle_{c_3}, 0, 3)$ to replicas R_0, R_1, R_2, R_3, and R_6, and $m_4 = \text{PrePrepare}(\langle \tau_4 \rangle_{c_4}, 0, 4)$ to all replicas. Notice that the Byzantine commit algorithm of PBFT (Figure 2.5) does not require that proposals are prepared and

committed in order. Moreover, R_0 can commence proposing m_4 long before replicas start to detect failure of round three. Next, the replicas R_0 and R_6 only send Prepare messages for m_3 to R_2, while behaving normally for m_4. Consequently, R_2 prepared m_3, and all replicas prepared m_4.

Similar to the first situation, the new primary—R_1—receives any ViewChange message of R_2 later than other ViewChange messages and, hence, proposes a new view that does not include m_3 but does include m_4. Consequently, this new view message includes a message PrePrepare($\langle nop \rangle_{R_1}$, 1, 3)—which will eventually overwrite m_3 at R_2—and the first new proposal considered in view 1 has round number 4.

The issues in Example 2.16 cannot easily be resolved: as we are dealing with up-to-f faulty replicas that can decide to not participate in any part of the view-change algorithm, every step of the algorithm must be able to successfully proceed with participation of only g replicas as, with reliable communication, only the $g = n - f$ good replicas are guaranteed to participate. Hence, new views are based on ViewChange messages of only g replicas. As replicas do not know which replicas are faulty, this means that new views can be based on the state of only $g - f$ good replicas, whereas the state of the remaining f good replicas is ignored in favor of the state of an equal amount of faulty replicas.

2.3.6   GUARANTEEING SUCCESSFUL VIEW-CHANGES

In Sections 2.3.1–2.3.5, we presented the view-change algorithm and argued that on success the view-change algorithm always preserves PrePrepare messages committed by good replicas. We have not yet argued that the view-change algorithm will succeed. Unfortunately, success is not guaranteed for all replicas.

Example 2.17   In practice, the view-change algorithm can fail in several ways. Assume all good replicas detect failure of view v and let P' be the replica with $id(P') = (v + 1) \bmod n$.

1. *The new primary is faulty.* If all good replicas detect failure in view v and the replica P' is faulty, then P' can choose to not respond by never broadcasting well-formed NewView proposals. Moreover, as in Example 2.8(2), a malicious primary can choose to keep up-to-f good replicas in the dark by never sending them NewView messages, this while behaving normally to all other replicas.

2. *Communication is unreliable.* If all good replicas detect failure in view v and the replica P' is good, then P' might still be unable to construct a well-formed NewView message: the necessary ViewChange messages can be dropped or severely delayed if communication is unreliable. Moreover, even if P' is able to construct and broadcast a well-formed NewView message, the broadcasted message m can also be dropped or severely delayed.

Notice the similarities with Example 2.8: one once again cannot distinguish between failure of replicas and failure of communication.

As shown in Example 2.17, good replicas cannot reliably detect *why* a view-change did not succeed. Hence, good replicas only have a single choice: assuming that the new primary is faulty, detect this failure, and request another view-change. Again, these failures are detected via some internal *time-out value*. This reliance on time-out values in itself introduces difficulties, however.

Example 2.18   Consider a system $\Re = \{P, R_1, R_2, R_3\}$ in view v with $id(P) = v \bmod \mathbf{n}$. Each replica uses internal time-out value $\delta = 10\,\mu s$. As the replicas do not operate in a fully synchronous environment, each replica starts round ρ of the current view v at a different time, e.g., at

$$t(R_1) = 2\,\mu s, \qquad t(R_2) = 5\,\mu s, \qquad t(R_3) = 1\,\mu s.$$

Next, we explore a simple failure detection scheme: each replica expects to enter a new view at most $\delta\,\mu s$ after detecting failure. A failure is triggered when the current primary—replica P— fails to propose any transaction for round ρ. Notice that each replica $R \in \Re$ detects this failure at $t(R) + \delta$. After detection, ViewChange messages are exchanged and each replica resets its timer and waits for the NewView proposal of the next primary, replica R_1. We consider two scenarios.

1. Assume that the current message delay is $\gamma = 11\,\mu s$. Notice that R_1 will only receive sufficient ViewChange messages at $t(R_2) + \delta + \gamma = 26\,\mu s$. At this point, some replicas have already timed out as $\delta < \gamma$. Hence, independent of what R_1 does, the view-change will be unsuccessful. We have sketched this situation in Figure 2.13, *top*.

2. Assume that the current message delay is $\gamma = 4\,\mu s$. Notice that R_1 will only receive sufficient ViewChange messages at $t(R_2) + \delta + \gamma = 19\,\mu s$. Assuming that R_1 can instantaneously construct a well-formed NewView message, all replicas will receive this message at $t(R_2) + \delta + 2\gamma = 23\,\mu s$. At this point R_3 will already have timed out as it started its timer long before R_1 could start constructing a NewView message. Hence, assuring that the view-change will be unsuccessful. We have sketched this situation in Figure 2.13, *bottom*.

When communication is unreliable, PBFT cannot guarantee success of the view-change algorithm. Next, we will discuss how PBFT guarantees *eventual* success of the view-change algorithm when communication is reliable. To do so, the view-change algorithm of PBFT relies on three principles, two of which deal with view-change failures due to timing issues such as those illustrated in Example 2.18. First, to enable a new primary to construct and broadcast a NewView message before any replica times out, the internal time-out values of individual replicas need to eventually become sufficiently larger than the current message delays. Second, all good

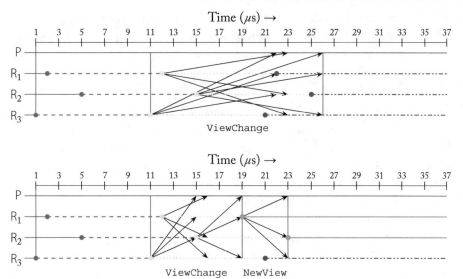

Figure 2.13: Illustration of the failure of a simple timer-based failure detection scheme. First, all replicas start a new round. Then, after 10 µs, this round fails and the view-change algorithm takes place. The line - - - - - indicates the interval during which a replica expects a `PrePrepare` message. The line ⋯⋯⋯ indicates the interval during which a replica expects a `NewView` message. The line -⋯-⋯- indicates the interval during which a replica detects failure of the new primary. The line ——— indicates the interval during which a replica entered the new view successfully. At the *top*, R_1 is able to propose a new view at 26 µs, at which all replicas already timed out. At the *bottom*, R_1 is able to propose a new view at 19 µs, which arrives at R_3 at 23 µs, at which point R3 already timed out.

replicas need to sufficiently *synchronize* their timers at the start of a view-change to assure that there is an overlapping window of time in which all good replicas are waiting for a `NewView` message. Finally, as consecutive views cycle through all **n** replicas, it is assured that eventually a good replica will be the next primary and can construct and broadcast a well-formed `NewView` message. The two timing-related principles are achieved using the following two rules.

1. Each replica will double its internal time-out value after each unsuccessful view-change.

2. Each replica starts the timer for the `NewView` message for view $v + 1$ only after it has received well-formed messages $m_i = \texttt{ViewChange}(E_i, v_i)$ with $v_i \geq v$ from **g** distinct replicas.

During periods of unreliable communication, repeated application of the first rule can increase the internal time-out values of replicas far beyond the message delay when communication is reliable. To not waste time during future view-changes while communication is reliable, replicas can reset their internal time-out values to a sensible default after successful view-changes.

These rules easily resolve the issues illustrated in Example 2.18.

Example 2.19   Consider the situations described in Example 2.18.

1. In the first situation, replicas initially have internal time-out value $\delta = 10\,\mu s$ and message delay $\gamma = 11\,\mu s$. This time, due to the second rule, all replicas will start their timer for a NewView message from R_1 after receiving the ViewChange message of R_2, which they receive at $t(R_2) + \delta + \gamma = 26\,\mu s$. All replicas will receive a NewView message from R_1 at $t(R_2) + \delta + 2\gamma = 37\,\mu s$. Unfortunately, replicas will already detect failure at $t(R_2) + 2\delta + \gamma = 36\,\mu s$, however. Hence, this view-change is unsuccessful. Due to the first rule, all replicas will then update their internal time-out value to $2\delta = 20\,\mu s$, which is larger than γ. Hence, the view-change coordinated by the next primary following R_1—R_2—will succeed. We have sketched this situation in Figure 2.14, *top*.

2. In the second situation, replicas initially have internal time-out value $\delta = 10\,\mu s$ and message delay $\gamma = 4\,\mu s$. This time, due to the second rule, all replicas will start their timer for a NewView message from R_1 after receiving the ViewChange message of R_2, which they receive at $t(R_2) + \delta + \gamma = 19\,\mu s$. All replicas will receive a NewView message from R_1 at $t(R_2) + \delta + 2\gamma = 23\,\mu s$, long before any replica times out. Hence, this view-change will succeed. We have sketched this situation in Figure 2.14, *bottom*.

Next, we show that these rules are sufficient to guarantee successful view-changes when communication is reliable.

Theorem 2.20   *Consider a system in which view v failed to get any transaction committed in round ρ. If communication is reliable, then the view-change algorithm (Figures 2.10 and 2.12) will move the system into a view v', $v' > v$, in which the Byzantine commit algorithm of PBFT (Section 2.2) is able to get a transaction committed in round ρ.*

Proof. Assume that communication is reliable and that the current message delay to construct and send any message is upper-bounded by γ. Now consider a replica R that received g ViewChange messages from a set of S replicas at time t. If communication is reliable and the current message delay is γ, then R can conclude that *all replicas* will receive at least $g - f \geq f + 1$ ViewChange messages from the replicas in $S \setminus \mathcal{F}$ at time $t + \gamma$. Hence, all g good replicas will have detected failure of view v (Line 6 of Figure 2.10) at time $t + \gamma$ and broadcast ViewChange messages themselves. Consequently, at time $t + 2\gamma$, all replicas will have received g ViewChange messages and must have started their timers for the NewView message for view $v + 1$ somewhere during $[t - \gamma, t + 2\gamma]$, assuring that all good replicas are awaiting a NewView message for view $v + 1$ at roughly the same time. Furthermore, if the primary of view $v + 1$, the replica P' with

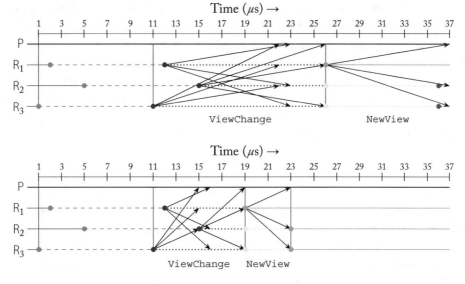

Figure 2.14: Illustration of the improved timer-based failure detection scheme. First, all replicas start a new round. Then, after 10 µs, this round fails and the view-change algorithm takes place. At the *top*, R_1 is able to propose a new view at 26 µs. Unfortunately, this proposal still arrives after all replicas timed out. At the *bottom*, R_1 is able to propose a new view at 19 µs, which arrives at all replicas at 23 µs, long before any replica times out.

$id(P') = (v + 1) \bmod \mathbf{n}$, is good, then all replicas will have received a well-formed `NewView` message at $t + 3\gamma$.

Now let R be a replica with internal time-out value δ in view v. If $\delta < 3\gamma$, then R could time-out before receiving a `NewView` message from the primary of round $v + 1$, in which case the view-change is unsuccessful. Due to R doubling its internal time-out value after every unsuccessful view-change, it will use an internal time-out value of $\delta \cdot 2^{i-1}$ when waiting for a `NewView` message for view $v + i$, $i \geq 1$. We have

$$\delta \cdot 2^{i-1} \geq 3\gamma \quad \text{iff} \quad 2^i \geq 6\frac{\gamma}{\delta} \quad \text{iff} \quad i \geq \log_2\left(6\frac{\gamma}{\delta}\right).$$

Hence, starting at view $v + \max\left(\lceil \log_2\left(6\frac{\gamma}{\delta}\right)\rceil, 1\right)$, replica R is guaranteed to receive `NewView` messages before any time-outs if any such messages are sent. Let $v + j$ be the first view for which all good replicas are guaranteed to receive `NewView` messages for that view before any time-outs if any such messages are sent.

Now assume that all view-changes before the change to view $v + k$ where unsuccessful, $k \geq j$, and consider replica P_k with $id(P_k) = (v + k) \bmod \mathbf{n}$. As all $\mathbf{g}$ good replicas will detect failure of all previous views, replica P_k will receive $\mathbf{g}$ `ViewChange` messages from distinct replicas. Hence, replica P_k can construct a valid `NewView` message m and broadcast this to all replicas.

As $k \geq j$, all good replicas will receive this message m before timing out. Hence, on receipt of this message m, each good replica R will update its internal state to the common state proposed in m, after which all g good replicas are able to participate in the Byzantine commit algorithm of Figures 2.4 and 2.5 and get a transaction committed in round ρ.

Finally, consider the case where also the view-change to view $v + k$ is unsuccessful. Due to the above, the view-change will only fail when P_k is faulty. As there are at most f faulty replicas, at most f consecutive view-changes after view $v + j$ can fail this way. Hence, the system will successfully view-change to a view $v + k$, $j \leq k \leq j + f$, and get a transaction committed in round ρ.   □

Remark 2.21   In the proof of Theorem 2.20, we assumed that there is a constant upper-bound on the cost to construct any message. Such an upper-bound can only exists if there is a strict upper-bound on the size of messages. In the presented design, this is not the case, as ViewChange and NewView messages have an unbounded size that grows linearly with the number of rounds that have passed. In Section 2.4.2, we resolve this issue by assuring that ViewChange and NewView messages only need state information on a fixed number of rounds. Finally, in Section 2.7.2, we show how one can guarantee that the necessary state information for each of these round is of constant size, even if individual transactions have an arbitrary size.

2.4   TERMINATION VIA CHECKPOINTS

At this point, we have introduced the main algorithms of PBFT: the Byzantine commit algorithm presented in Section 2.2 and the view-change algorithm presented in Section 2.3. These parts are primarily focused on guaranteeing *non-divergence*: only at most a single transaction will be committed per round by good replicas and such committed transactions are always preserved (Theorem 2.15). Close inspection shows that the proposed algorithms do not guarantee *termination*, however: even if communication is fully reliable, malicious primaries can always keep some good replicas in the dark, both during the Byzantine commit algorithm, as illustrated in Example 2.8(2), as during view-changes, as illustrated in Example 2.17(1). In the presented design, good replicas that are left in the dark will be unable to ever *terminate*.

Besides not providing termination, the presented algorithms of PBFT also have practical issues: the view-change algorithm presented in Section 2.3 will repeatedly replicate information that is already available to all good replicas (namely, all requests already committed by every good replica).

Both issues are resolved in the design of PBFT by using *checkpoints*, which we describe next. First, in Section 2.4.1 we will introduce the *checkpoint algorithm* of PBFT, which will allow PBFT to guarantee termination. Then, in Section 2.4.2, we show how checkpoints can be used to reduce the amount of work during view-changes, this by reducing the size of ViewChange messages.

Checkpoint-role (running at every replica $R \in \Re$) :
1: **event** R appends τ to $\mathcal{L}_R$ (and committed $m = \mathtt{PrePrepare}(\langle\tau\rangle_C, v, \rho)$) **do**
2:     Broadcast $\mathtt{Checkpoint}(m)$ to all replicas.
3: **end event**
4: **event** R receives $f + 1$ identical messages $\mathtt{Checkpoint}(m)$ from distinct replicas **do**
5:     Reach the committed state for m (if not yet done so).
6: **end event**
7: **event** R receives g messages $\mathtt{Checkpoint}(m)$ such that:

   (i) each message was sent by a distinct replica; and

   (ii) R broadcasted $\mathtt{Checkpoint}(m)$

   do
8:     Checkpoint m and log the g messages as $\mathtt{Checkpoint}_R(m)$.
9: **end event**

Figure 2.15: The checkpoint algorithm of PBFT.

2.4.1 THE CHECKPOINT ALGORITHM

Based on the results presented in Sections 2.2 and 2.3, we already know which kind of issues the checkpoint algorithm needs to resolve: the checkpoint algorithm must be able to propagate each committed transaction to all good replicas, this even when only $g - f \geq f + 1$ good replicas have committed to the transaction (if less than $g - f$ good replicas have committed to a transaction, then the view-change algorithm will take over). At the same time, the checkpoint algorithm must be able to deal with any malicious behavior by at most f faulty replicas. Based on these constraints, the checkpoint algorithm is rather straightforward, and operates in three phases.

1. First, if a replica R *committed* a message $m = \mathtt{PrePrepare}(\langle\tau\rangle_C, v, \rho)$ and appended τ to its ledger $\mathcal{L}_R$ (indicating that R also committed transactions for all rounds before ρ), then R informs all other replicas of this by broadcasting $\mathtt{Checkpoint}(m)$.

2. If a replica R receives messages $\mathtt{Checkpoint}(m)$ for the same message $m = \mathtt{PrePrepare}(\langle\tau\rangle_C, v, \rho)$ from $f + 1$ replicas, then R has the guarantee that at least a single good replica committed m. Hence, R can safely treat m as committed.

3. If a replica R receives messages $\mathtt{Checkpoint}(m)$ for the same message $m = \mathtt{PrePrepare}(\langle\tau\rangle_C, v, \rho)$ from g replicas, then R considers the checkpoint for round ρ established. We write $\mathtt{Checkpoint}_R(m)$ to denote the *checkpoint certificate* of m, consisting of m and the set of g $\mathtt{Checkpoint}$ messages used to reach the checkpointed state for proposal m.

The full pseudo-code of the algorithm can be found in Figure 2.15.

Remark 2.22   We notice that the checkpoint algorithm is fully *decentralized*: individual replicas initiate steps from the algorithm without external coordination. In doing so, the checkpoint algorithm side-steps the shortcomings of the Byzantine commit algorithm and the view-change algorithm: any *centralized* algorithm that is coordinated by a single replica will be susceptible to in-the-dark attacks similar to those illustrated in Examples 2.8(2) and 2.17(1).

At the core of the checkpoint algorithm are the following two technical properties of *committed* and *checkpoint* decisions made by the checkpoint algorithm (Line 5 of Figure 2.15).

Proposition 2.23   *If* $n > 3f$ *and a good replica committed* $m = \texttt{PrePrepare}(\langle \tau \rangle_c, v, \rho)$ *as a consequence of the checkpoint algorithm of Figure 2.15, then a good replica committed* m *via the Byzantine commit algorithm of Figure 2.5.*

Proof. As some good replica committed m as a consequence of the checkpoint algorithm of Figure 2.15, there must be a *first* good replica $R \in \mathcal{G}$ that did so. Due to the conditions at Line 4 of Figure 2.15, replica R committed m only if it has received messages $\texttt{Checkpoint}(m)$ from at least $f + 1$ replicas. Let S be the set of replicas from which R received these messages and let $T = S \setminus \mathcal{F}$. By construction, $|S| = f + 1$ and $|T| \geq (f + 1) - f \geq 1$. Let $Q \in T$. As R is the first replica that committed m as a consequence of the checkpoint algorithm of Figure 2.15, Q must have committed m via the Byzantine commit algorithm of Figure 2.5.   □

If replica R committed m via the checkpoint algorithm, then R will *not* have obtained a prepared certificate for m. Hence, R cannot participate in the preservation of m during view-changes. This is not an issue, however. As a consequence of Proposition 2.23, messages m can only be committed by R if at least a single good replica committed m via the Byzantine commit algorithm. Consequently, Theorem 2.15 assures that m will always be preserved during view-changes. Next, we formalize this important preservation property.

Corollary 2.24   *Let* $Q \in \mathcal{G}$ *be a good replica that committed* $m = \texttt{PrePrepare}(\langle \tau \rangle_c, v, \rho)$ *as a consequence of the checkpoint algorithm of Figure 2.15, and let* $\texttt{NewView}(w, V, N)$ *be a well-formed* $\texttt{NewView}$ *message with* $w > v$. *If* $n > 3f$, *then any good replica* $R \in \mathcal{G}$ *will commit to* m *when updating its local state via the algorithm of Figure 2.12.*

Next, we show that a successful checkpoint guarantees *termination* when communication is reliable.

Proposition 2.25   *If* $n > 3f$, *a replica can construct a checkpoint certificate for* $m = \texttt{PrePrepare}(\langle \tau \rangle_c, v, \rho)$, *and communication is reliable, then all good replicas will reach the committed state for* m.

Proof. Let $R \in \mathfrak{R}$ be the replica that can construct a checkpoint certificate for m. Due to the structure of a checkpoint certificate, R can only do so after receiving messages $\texttt{Checkpoint}(m)$ from g distinct replicas. Hence, at least $g - f$ good replicas must have provided such messages.

These $\mathbf{g} - \mathbf{f}$ good replicas only provide these messages by broadcasting them to all replicas (Line 2 of Figure 2.15). Consequently, all good replicas will receive the message Checkpoint(m) from at least $\mathbf{g} - \mathbf{f} \geq \mathbf{f} + 1$ distinct good replicas and, hence, meet the conditions of Line 4 of Figure 2.15 and reach the committed state for m. □

Finally, we use Proposition 2.25 to finally prove that PBFT guarantees termination.

Theorem 2.26 *Consider a system in which communication is reliable. If a good replica committed* $m = \texttt{PrePrepare}(\langle \tau \rangle_c, v, \rho)$, *then all good replicas will eventually reach the committed state for m and checkpoint m.*

Proof. First, consider a view v in which at least $\mathbf{g} - \mathbf{f}$ good replicas committed m via the Byzantine commit algorithm of Section 2.2. In this case, at least $\mathbf{g} - \mathbf{f} \geq \mathbf{f} + 1$ good replicas will meet the conditions of Line 1 of Figure 2.15 and broadcast Checkpoint(m). Hence, every good replica that has not yet committed m will eventually receive these Checkpoint messages from at least $\mathbf{f} + 1$ distinct replicas, meet the conditions of Line 4 of Figure 2.15, reach the committed state for m, and broadcast Checkpoint(m). Consequently, all $\mathbf{g}$ good replicas will have broadcasted Checkpoint(m), all replicas will meet the conditions of Line 7 of Figure 2.15, and, finally, all good replicas will checkpoint m.

Otherwise, consider a view v in which less than $\mathbf{g} - \mathbf{f}$ good replicas committed m via the Byzantine commit algorithm of Section 2.2. In this case, failure of the primary of view v will be detected. Theorem 2.20 already showed that, in this case, a series of view-changes happen until a new view is established in which the Byzantine commit algorithms of PBFT can be resumed. By Corollary 2.24, any replica that enters the established new view will commit to m. As the Byzantine commit algorithm of PBFT will eventually resume, at least $\mathbf{g} - \mathbf{f}$ good replicas will eventually reach the committed state for m, and we can fall back to the first case. □

Remark 2.27 Most implementations of PBFT are optimistic in that they assume that primaries are usually good. In this case, checkpoints only add additional costs to PBFT. Furthermore, even if the primary is faulty, checkpoints are not necessary to guarantee successful operation of the Byzantine commit algorithm of PBFT: they are used to deal with certain types of attacks that do *not prevent* progress of the normal-case operations. Hence, to reduce the cost of checkpoints, these implementations typically perform checkpoints in bulk, e.g., by making a checkpoint of all previous c rounds via a single Checkpoint message carrying c PrePrepare messages after every c-th round (rounds ρ with $\rho \bmod c = c - 1$).

2.4.2 INTEGRATING CHECKPOINTS INTO VIEW-CHANGES

As noted before, the view-change algorithm presented in Section 2.3 uses ViewChange messages whose size grows linearly with the number of rounds that have passed, as transactions for all previous rounds are included. In this simple design, establishing new views will get progressively more expensive. Furthermore, as already noted in Remark 2.21, this reliance on non-constant-sized `ViewChange` messages conflicts with some of the timing assumptions made in Theorem 2.20. Next, we will incorporate checkpoints in the view-change algorithm as a first partial step to address these issues.

1. Each replica only prepares, commits, and executes some upper-bounded number c of new proposals via the Byzantine commit algorithm of PBFT after the latest successfully checkpointed proposal.

2. Each replica R that sends a `ViewChange` message includes the latest checkpointed certificate $\text{Checkpoint}_R(\text{PrePrepare}(\langle\tau\rangle_C, v, \rho))$ and *only* includes prepared certificates $\text{Prepare}_R(m)$ for proposals of rounds after ρ: proposals $m = \text{PrePrepare}(\langle\tau'\rangle_C, v', \rho')$ with $\rho < \rho' \leq \rho + c$.

3. For the verification of `ViewChange` messages, straightforward checks are added to verify the validity of checkpoint certificates, verify whether all prepared certificates are for proposals of rounds after ρ, and verify whether at most c prepared certificates are included in each `ViewChange` message.

4. A new primary P$'$ will only consider rounds after the last round for which it received a checkpoint certificate via the `ViewChange` messages. Specifically, after receiving **g** messages $m_i = \text{ViewChange}(C_i, E_i, v_i)$, it will compute

$$\rho_{\text{cp}} := \{\rho \mid (C_i = \text{Checkpoint}_Q(m)) \wedge (m = \text{PrePrepare}(\langle\tau\rangle_C, w, \rho)\};$$
$$\rho_{\text{all}} := \{\rho \mid (\text{Prepare}_Q(m) \in M) \wedge (m = \text{PrePrepare}(\langle\tau\rangle_C, w, \rho))\};$$
$$N := \{\text{PrePrepare}(\langle\text{nop}\rangle_{P'}, v + 1, \rho) \mid (\rho \notin \rho_{\text{all}}) \wedge (\max(\rho_{\text{cp}}) < \rho \leq \max(\rho_{\text{all}})\}$$

and broadcast the message $\text{NewView}(v + 1, V, N)$ to all replicas.

5. For the verification of `NewView` messages, individual replicas can verify the content of N based on the selected `ViewChange` messages in V using the above computations.

6. Finally, when a replica R receives a valid message $\text{NewView}(v + 1, V, N)$, it runs the local state update algorithm only for the rounds since the latest checkpoint included in V. Hence, it computes ρ_{cp} and ρ_{all} using the above and executes the loop at Line 4 of Figure 2.12 only for all $\rho \in \{\max(\rho_{\text{cp}}) + 1, \ldots, \max(\rho_{\text{all}})\}$.

In Figure 2.16, we have summarized the impact of applying checkpoints on the size of `ViewChange` and `NewView` messages. As can be seen in this summary, the size of these messages is linear in the size of the ledger without checkpoints, and are constant in the size of the ledger whenever checkpoints are applied.

Notice that not every good replica will necessary have received proposals for all rounds before $\max(\rho_{\text{cp}})$. Let R be such a replica that misses proposals for some rounds before $\max(\rho_{\text{cp}})$.

Message Component	Contains	Size
Prepared certificate	**g** `Prepare` messages	$\mathcal{O}(\mathbf{g})$
Checkpoint certificate	**g** `Checkpoint` messages	$\mathcal{O}(\mathbf{g})$
`ViewChange` message	$\leq \rho$ prepared certificates	$\mathcal{O}(\rho\mathbf{g})$
`NewView` message	**g** `ViewChange` messages	$\mathcal{O}(\rho\mathbf{g}^2)$
`ViewChange` message with checkpoints	$\leq c + 1$ prepare and checkpoint certificates	$\mathcal{O}(c\mathbf{g})$
`NewView` message with checkpoints	**g** `ViewChange` messages	$\mathcal{O}(c\mathbf{g}^2)$

Figure 2.16: Overview of the size of `ViewChange` messages and `NewView` messages for a view-change after round ρ. When using checkpoints, each replica supports, commits, and accepts at-most-c new proposals after the latest successfully checkpointed proposal. We assume all transactions have a constant size.

Due to Proposition 2.25, this can only happen when communication is unreliable, as otherwise R already learned the missing proposals via the checkpoint algorithm. Still, in this case, the information in the `NewView` message provides R with sufficient information to eventually retrieve proposals for all missing rounds: the checkpoint certificate identifies **g** replicas that have checkpointed everything up-till-round $\max(\rho_{\mathrm{cp}})$. At least $\mathbf{g} - \mathbf{f} > \mathbf{f}$ of these replicas are good and can reliably provide the proposals up-till-round $\max(\rho_{\mathrm{cp}})$.

We notice that incorporating checkpoints upper-bounds the number of proposals included in `ViewChange` and `NewView` messages. It does not limit the size of these messages, however, as we have not put an upper bound on the size of individual transactions. In Section 2.7.2, we discuss how to deal with arbitrarily sized transactions.

2.5   PBFT AND CLIENT BEHAVIOR

In the previous sections, we have presented in detail the algorithms of PBFT used by replicas in a service to reliably replicate client transactions among themselves. To simplify the presentation, we have kept the details on the roles of clients to a bare minimum, however. Next, we shall take a close look at how clients interact with PBFT. Specifically, we shall focus on how PBFT enforces *validity*, *response*, and—most importantly—*service*. To do so, we will provide a full description of how a client can use a PBFT-replicated service.

First, we revisit the standard way in which clients can request services from a PBFT-replicated service. Recall, from Section 2.2, that client C can request transaction τ from the service by sending $\langle \tau \rangle_C$ to the current primary. If the current primary is good, then it will eventually select $\langle \tau \rangle_C$ and propose $\langle \tau \rangle_C$ in some round ρ, after which the client will receive response in the form of at least $\mathbf{f} + 1$ identical `Inform` messages. If the client does not know the current primary, then it can send $\langle \tau \rangle_C$ to an arbitrary replica, whom will then forward the request to the current primary. This forwarding-mechanism is also utilized to deal with malicious primaries that *ignore* requests from C, as described in Section 2.3.1: if a replica R forwards $\langle \tau \rangle_C$ to the current primary, then R expects a positive response—execution of τ—before some internal time-out passes. By asking all replicas to forward requests to the primary, a client can either force replication of its request or force failure detection of the primary by all good replicas (after which the primary will be replaced).

Malicious clients can try to abuse the sketched forwarding system, e.g., this in an attempt to replace the primary or to deny service to other client.

Example 2.28   Consider a system with n replicas and a malicious client C. The client C can attempt to compromise PBFT in several ways.

1. *Attempt to force a failure detection.* The client prepares requests $\langle \tau_0 \rangle_C, \ldots, \langle \tau_{n-1} \rangle_C$ and sends request $\langle \tau_i \rangle_C$, $0 \leq i < n$, to replica R with $\mathrm{id}(R) = i$. All good replicas will forward the request they receive to the current primary P. Hence, the current primary has to propose at least g requests before any replica times out, as otherwise it will be considered *faulty*.

2. *Attempt to deny services to other clients.* The client continuously sends requests to all replicas, all replicas forward these requests to the primary, and the primary is always expected to propose requests for C, giving it no time to propose requests of other clients.

To eliminate the impact of malicious clients, replicas can employ two simple strategies. First, if a replica R forwards $\langle \tau \rangle_C$ to the primary, then it only waits until *any* request of C is committed. Second, a replica R can refuse to forward any client requests of C if R recently committed another proposal of C (e.g., in the last c rounds, with c the number of clients, or based on some period of inactivity). Combined, these approaches will limit the resources the primary (and any other replica) is required to spend on requests of any individual client and, hence, will negate the misbehavior of Example 2.28.

Many practical data processing applications utilize a *data model* in which the order of execution of transactions is meaningful. To maintain consistency, these applications usually require that consecutive transactions of a client C will be executed in the order in which C requests these transactions.

Example 2.29   Consider a banking system in which a client C manages accounts for Alice, Bob, and Eve. The client wants to transfer \$500 from Alice to Bob and \$400 from Bob to Eve. Hence, C issues the following two requests:

$$m_1 = \langle \mathtt{transfer}(\$500, \mathrm{Alice}, \mathrm{Bob}) \rangle_C,$$
$$m_2 = \langle \mathtt{transfer}(\$400, \mathrm{Bob}, \mathrm{Eve}) \rangle_C.$$

If m_1 is executed before m_2, then we avoid any situation in which Bob has a negative balance. If m_2 is executed before m_1 and Bob initially has a balance below \$400, then Bob will temporarily have a negative balance.

Good clients can always enforce a desired ordering of the execution of their transactions by *always* waiting for the outcome on a transaction before requesting any following transactions. This will limit per-client throughput of the system, however. Consequently, many high-performance PBFT-replicated systems allow clients to propose several requests in parallel. In such a setting, a specific ordering of execution of requests is hart to guarantee, however, especially when clients can be malicious.

Example 2.30   Consider a client C with requests $\langle \tau_0 \rangle_C, \langle \tau_1 \rangle_C, \langle \tau_2 \rangle_C, \langle \tau_3 \rangle_C$. To make explicit the order of execution desired by the client, each transaction contains some client-specific timestamp, e.g.,

$$\mathrm{ts}(\tau_0) = 2389; \quad \mathrm{ts}(\tau_1) = 5367; \quad \mathrm{ts}(\tau_2) = 7937; \quad \mathrm{ts}(\tau_3) = 9521.$$

The client sends these requests to primary P. Unfortunately, the requests arrive out-of-order, and the primary receives the requests in the order $\langle \tau_0 \rangle_C, \langle \tau_2 \rangle_C, \langle \tau_3 \rangle_C, \langle \tau_1 \rangle_C$. When P receives $\langle \tau_2 \rangle_C$, it has no way of knowing whether any transaction with timestamp $t \in \{2390, \ldots, 7936\}$ was proposed. Hence, P choses to propose $\langle \tau_0 \rangle_C$ in round ρ and $\langle \tau_2 \rangle_C$ in round $\rho + 1$. After P receives request $\langle \tau_1 \rangle_C$, request $\langle \tau_2 \rangle_C$ is already committed and executed. Hence, P cannot propose $\langle \tau_1 \rangle_C$ without violating the order of execution intended by the client.

One way to avoid situations such as those of Example 2.30 is by annotating the t-th transaction $\langle \tau \rangle_C$ client C wants to see executed with identifier t. With this setup, any replica (including the primary) can simply put the t-th transactions requested by C on hold until they have committed all preceding transactions (e.g., the $t - 1$-th transaction). To assure that clients cannot abuse this ability to overload replicas with requests, replicas can put a threshold on the number of transactions they put on hold per client, as clients can always reissue transactions. This scheme does, however, require clients to keep track of the number of requests they requested (or to be able to obtain this number).

2.6   PBFT IS A CONSENSUS PROTOCOL

In the previous sections, we have introduced the main parts of the design of PBFT: the Byzantine commit algorithm that deals with normal-case operations (Section 2.2), the view-change algorithm that deals with detectable failures of primaries (Section 2.3), the checkpoint algorithm that deals with undetectable malicious behavior of primaries (Section 2.4), and the way in which clients interact with PBFT (Section 2.5). Next, we will show that together the presented parts provide a solution to the consensus problem of Definition 2.3.

Theorem 2.31   *If* $\mathbf{n} > 3\mathbf{f}$ *and communication is reliable, then* PBFT *provides consensus.*

Proof. Consider any request $\langle \tau \rangle_C$ accepted by a good replica R. Replica R will only accept $\langle \tau \rangle_C$ if it is well-formed and has a valid digital signature. Hence, a well-formed request $\langle \tau \rangle_C$ can only be constructed with cooperation of C. Consequently, *validity* of $\langle \tau \rangle_C$ is provided under the assumption that digital signatures cannot be forged (and C is good and did not share its private-keys with others). Using the forward-mechanism detailed in Section 2.5, client C can force that either a request $\langle \tau \rangle_C$ will be accepted by a good replica in some round ρ, or that the current primary is replaced. We distinguish between these two cases.

1. *A request $\langle \tau \rangle_C$ is proposed, and this proposal is committed by a good replica.* As the proposal reached the committed state at a good replica in some round ρ, Theorem 2.26 guarantees that all good replicas will eventually also reach the committed state for the proposal in round ρ, providing *service, non-divergence,* and *termination.* When a good replica committed the proposel, it will execute τ and inform C of the outcome of execution via an `Inform` message (Line 25 of Figure 2.5). Consequently, C will eventually receive $\mathbf{g} \geq \mathbf{f} + 1$ identical `Inform` messages. Under the assumption that digital signatures cannot be forged, faulty replicas can only forge up-to-$\mathbf{f}$ such `Inform` messages. Hence, by receiving identical `Inform` messages from at least $\mathbf{f} + 1$ distinct replicas, C can conclude that these messages provide the outcome to execution of the requested transaction, providing *response.*

2. *The current primary is replaced.* Due to Theorem 2.6, a good primary will have proposed $\langle \tau \rangle_C$, in which case this proposal would have been committed by some good replica. Hence, the current primary was faulty. As there are $\mathbf{f}$ faulty replicas, this case can only happen at-most $\mathbf{f}$ times, after which we either end up with a good replica—in which case it is guaranteed that a proposal for $\langle \tau \rangle_C$ will get committed—or with a faulty replica that gets a proposal for $\langle \tau \rangle_C$ committed. In both situations, eventually the conditions of the previous case apply. $\square$

Theorem 2.31 *relies* on reliable communication. Only with reliable communication are good replicas able to successfully utilize the Byzantine commit algorithm to replicate client requests and able to detect and replace faulty primaries via the view-change algorithm. When communication is not reliable, PBFT still keeps the internal state of good replicas consistent. We have the following.

Theorem 2.32   *If* $\mathbf{n} > 3\mathbf{f}$, *then* PBFT *provides* validity *and* non-divergence.

Proof. In the proof of Theorem 2.31, we only relied on the assumption that digital signatures cannot be forged to prove that PBFT provides *validity.* Hence, the same proof can also be used when communication is unreliable.

To prove that PBFT always provides *non-divergence,* we consider two good replicas R_i, $i \in \{1, 2\}$, that committed proposals $m_i = \texttt{PrePrepare}(\langle \tau_i \rangle_{C_i}, v_i, \rho)$ for client requests $\langle \tau_i \rangle_{C_i}$ in round ρ. Notice that R_i could have committed m_i via the Byzantine commit algorithm of Section 2.2 or via the checkpoint algorithm of Section 2.4. Due to Proposition 2.23, we can assume, without loss of generality, that R_i committed m_i via the Byzantine commit algorithm of Section 2.2.

First consider the possibility that these two requests are accepted in distinct views. Without loss of generality, we can assume that $v_1 < v_2$. As m_2 was committed as part of view v_2 by good replica R_2 and $v_1 < v_2$, replica R_2 must have performed state update while entering view v_2. Hence, by Theorem 2.15, replica R_2 committed to m_1 while entering view v_2 and will only prepare and commit proposals in view v_2 for rounds after ρ. Consequently, R_2 could not have committed m_2 as part of view v_2, and we must conclude that R_1 and R_2 accepted the two requests in the same view. In this case, Proposition 2.5 proves that $\tau_1 = \tau_2$ and $C_1 = C_2$.   □

2.7   OPTIMIZING AND FINE-TUNING PBFT

As stated in Section 2.1, we presented a *simplified* design of PBFT in which we focus on its working and its correctness. As shown in Section 2.6, this simplified design is *effective*, as it keeps the state of all good replicas consistent under all circumstances, while it provides consensus whenever communication is reliable. In this presentation, we have omitted some fine-grained optimizations that can be applied to the design of PBFT. Furthermore, we have also omitted details on how to deal with *arbitrary-sized transactions*, and how to deal with *unreliable communication*. Next, we shall briefly discuss each of these topics.

2.7.1   ELIMINATING REDUNDANT MESSAGES

The first and most straightforward fine-tuning is to reduce the number of *redundant messages that* are sent around, this by by implementing the following two rules:

1. a PrePrepare message m sent by primary P is also interpreted as the Prepare message Prepare(m) sent by primary P; and

2. no replica sends messages to itself (as this would not introduce any extra knowledge).

These changes can be applied to *all* parts of PBFT: the Byzantine commit algorithm of Section 2.2, the view-change algorithm of Section 2.3, and the checkpoint algorithm of Section 2.4. These changes do affect the "*receive* g" and "*receive* f + 1" conditions used in these algorithms in straightforward ways: replicas should include their own messages when evaluating these conditions where applicable (even though these messages are not received) and count PrePrepare messages of the primary as a Prepare message.

To illustrate the effect of these minor changes, we revisit the Byzantine commit algorithm detailed in Section 2.2. In that algorithm, the primary sends 3**n** messages per round, as it broadcasts PrePrepare, Prepare, and Commit messages to *all* replicas, whereas all other replicas send 2**n** messages per round, as they broadcast Prepare and Commit messages to *all* replicas. With the above changes in place, *all* replicas—including the primary—only send 2(**n** − 1) messages per round: the primary will send **n** − 1 PrePrepare and Commit messages, whereas all other replicas will send **n** − 1 Prepare and Commit messages.

The elimination of redundant messages is a first step in reducing the communication for the primary drastically. In the next section, we shall see how to further reduce the size of all non-PrePrepare messages drastically, thereby further reducing the communication costs for all replicas involved.

2.7.2 LIMITING MESSAGE SIZE USING MESSAGE DIGESTS

A further effective way to reduce cost of communication of PBFT is by reducing the size of the messages exchanged. In the presented design, the size of all messages is ultimately determined by the size of client requests. Indeed, client requests $\langle \tau \rangle_C$ are directly embedded in the PrePrepare messages m that propose $\langle \tau \rangle_C$. Next, as part of the Byzantine commit algorithm and the checkpoint algorithm, all replicas will broadcast Prepare, Commit, and Checkpoint messages that themselves embed m. To further illustrate this, consider the replication of a single client request $\langle \tau \rangle_C$ of size $s = \|\langle \tau \rangle_C\|$ bytes:

1. the primary broadcasts $\mathbf{n} - 1 = \mathcal{O}(\mathbf{n})$ PrePrepare messages of size $\mathcal{O}(s)$ each and $\mathbf{n} - 1 = \mathcal{O}(\mathbf{n})$ Commit and Checkpoint messages, also of size $\mathcal{O}(s)$ each; and

2. all other replicas broadcast $\mathbf{n} - 1 = \mathcal{O}(\mathbf{n})$ Prepare, Commit, and Checkpoint messages of size $\mathcal{O}(s)$ each.

Hence, in total $3\mathbf{n}(\mathbf{n} - 1)$ messages are sent with a total size of $\mathcal{O}(s(\mathbf{n} + \mathbf{n}^2))$. Furthermore, even ViewChange and NewView messages embed PrePrepare messages. Consequently, all these messages have a size that is determined by the size of client requests.

Unfortunately, the size of the transactions clients can request is application dependent and can range from dozens of bytes (e.g., single read or write operations in a key-value store) to practically unlimited (e.g., complex programs in the form of smart contracts, or file operations). Hence, in *many* applications, the transactions clients request do not have a bounded size, in which case embedding client requests in all messages puts a high burden on communication and, moreover, invalidates the assumption used by the view-change algorithm that messages can be delivered in bounded time when communication is reliable.

A frequently used technique to limit the size of Prepare, Commit, ViewChange, NewView, and Checkpoint messages is by *not* including client requests in PrePrepare messages, but by only including a *digest* of the client request in PrePrepare messages. To create these digests, one relies on a *collision-resistant hash function* that maps arbitrary values v into a small bounded-size *digest*. A hash function digest$(\cdot)$ is collision-resistant if, for any value v, it is practically impossible to find another value v', $v \neq v'$, such that digest$(v) = $ digest(v'). In this, practically impossible implies that finding such a collision v' is only feasible by spending an exorbitant amount of resources (e.g., computational time).

Let digest$(\cdot)$ be a collision-resistant hash function and let $m = $ PrePrepare$(\langle \tau \rangle_C, v, \rho)$ be a PrePrepare message used to propose $\langle \tau \rangle_C$ in round ρ of view v (in the original design of PBFT). In the relevant parts of PBFT, we replace message m by the pair (PrePrepare(digest$(\langle \tau \rangle_C), v, \rho), \langle \tau \rangle_C$). Now, the message $m' = $ PrePrepare(digest$(\langle \tau \rangle_C), v, \rho)$ has an upper-bounded size and it is this message that is

	Message Type	Size per Message	Messages per Replica	Total Communication Cost
Without Digests	PrePrepare	$\mathcal{O}(s)$	$\mathcal{O}(n)$ (only primary)	$\mathcal{O}(sn)$
	Prepare	$\mathcal{O}(s)$	$\mathcal{O}(n)$	$\mathcal{O}(sn^2)$
	Commit	$\mathcal{O}(s)$	$\mathcal{O}(n)$	$\mathcal{O}(sn^2)$
	Checkpoint	$\mathcal{O}(s)$	$\mathcal{O}(n)$	$\mathcal{O}(sn^2)$
	ViewChange	$\mathcal{O}(csg)$	$\mathcal{O}(n)$	$\mathcal{O}(csn^2)$
	NewView	$\mathcal{O}(csg^2)$	$\mathcal{O}(n)$ (only new primary)	$\mathcal{O}(csng^2)$
With Digests	PrePrepare	$\mathcal{O}(s)$	$\mathcal{O}(n)$ (only primary)	$\mathcal{O}(sn)$
	Prepare	$\mathcal{O}(1)$	$\mathcal{O}(n)$	$\mathcal{O}(n^2)$
	Commit	$\mathcal{O}(1)$	$\mathcal{O}(n)$	$\mathcal{O}(n^2)$
	Checkpoint	$\mathcal{O}(1)$	$\mathcal{O}(n)$	$\mathcal{O}(n^2)$
	ViewChange	$\mathcal{O}(cg)$	$\mathcal{O}(n)$	$\mathcal{O}(cn^2)$
	NewView	$\mathcal{O}(cg^2)$	$\mathcal{O}(n)$ (only new primary)	$\mathcal{O}(cng^2)$

Figure 2.17: Overview of the message complexity of PBFT for replicating requests $\langle\tau\rangle_C$ of size $s = \|\langle\tau\rangle_C\|$ bytes. For ViewChange and NewView messages, we assume that checkpoints are made every c rounds.

embedded in all other messages, guaranteeing that these messages all also have an upper-bounded size. To illustrate the impact, consider again the replication of a single client request $\langle\tau\rangle_C$ of size $s = \|\langle\tau\rangle_C\|$ bytes. Without using digests, PBFT would replicate $\langle\tau\rangle_C$ using messages with a total size of $\mathcal{O}(s(n + n^2))$. By using digests, the size of all Prepare, Commit, and Checkpoint messages is reduced from $\mathcal{O}(s)$ to $\mathcal{O}(1)$. Hence, the total size of all messages is reduced from $\mathcal{O}(s(n + n^2))$ to only $\mathcal{O}(sn + n^2)$. In Figure 2.17, we summarized the message complexity of the original design of PBFT without using digests (after eliminating redundant messages, see Section 2.7.1), and with using digests.

We notice that this change does affect the *view-change algorithm* and *checkpoint algorithm*: ViewChange, NewView, and Checkpoint messages no longer embed client requests $\langle\tau\rangle_C$, but embed digest($\langle\tau\rangle_C$) instead. This means that replicas kept in the dark can no longer directly learn client requests from NewView and Checkpoint messages. Next, we briefly describe how such replicas can recover the client request.

Let R be a replica that is left in the dark and is unaware of client request $\langle\tau\rangle_C$. During a view-change, R receives a well-formed NewView message that embedded the message m'. From m', R can reliably learn the digest digest($\langle\tau\rangle_C$). To obtain $\langle\tau\rangle_C$, R can simply query other replicas for the request of round ρ (which should have digest digest($\langle\tau\rangle_C$)). As NewView messages only embed PrePrepare messages with prepared certificates signed by g distinct replicas, R has a list of g replicas it can query for $\langle\tau\rangle_c$, of which $g - f$ are guaranteed to be good and able to provide the client request. In a similar fashion, R only accepts m' via the checkpoint protocol after receiving $f + 1$ identical messages $\mathtt{Checkpoint}(m')$, after which it has a list of $f + 1$ replicas it can query for $\langle\tau\rangle_c$, of which at least one is guaranteed to be good and able to provide the client request.

2.7.3   DEALING WITH UNRELIABLE COMMUNICATION

Up until now, we have assumed that PBFT operates in an environment with *reliable asynchronous communication*: we do not know when messages arrive, but we do know that messages sent by good replicas will eventually arrive. Such a strong form of reliability is hard to achieve in practice, however, as messages can get duplicated, arrive out-of-order, or get lost.

No part of the design of PBFT assumes that messages arrive only once. Indeed, as faulty replicas can purposely resend messages, the design of PBFT has straightforward ways to deal with any duplicates: each replica only processes a single PrePrepare message per round (per view) and only a single NewView message per view, and all other messages are only processed once per sending replica. Hence, dealing with duplicated messages is straightforward, as one can simply drop the later-arriving copies.

Likewise, no part of the design of PBFT makes assumptions about the order in which messages arrive. As with message duplication, the design of PBFT has to be able to deal with faulty replicas that purposely send messages out-of-order. Hence, the design of PBFT ensures that no amount of out-of-order message delivery will influence the order in which client requests are executed, as the execution order is enforced independently by individual replicas. To deal with out-of-order message delivery, messages that arrive too early (e.g., Prepare messages that arrive before their corresponding PrePrepare message, or Commit messages that arrive before their corresponding Prepare messages) can be placed in a temporary holding buffer where these messages are kept until they can be processed by the relevant parts of PBFT. The capacity of such temporary holding buffers is necessary finite, unfortunately. As such PBFT is able to deal with only a finite number of messages arriving out-of-order. Consequently, if communication becomes *too unreliable* and many messages arrive out-of-order at once, then implementations of PBFT are forced to drop messages.

Finally, we inspect lost messages. On the one hand, PBFT can deal with up-to-f replicas that are unable to communicate (as the faulty replicas could not participate at all). On the other hand, message loss *does* affect PBFT, as it needs reliable communication between a sufficient number of replicas to ensure progress. This is a direct consequence of the CAP Theorem (Section 1.2.1) and the FLP Impossibility Theorem (Section 1.3.4): PBFT provides consensus (a strong form of *data consistency*) in an asynchronous environment (which can have *network partitioning*), hence, PBFT can only guarantee *availability* whenever communication is reliable. If communication becomes sufficiently unreliable, then view-changes will fail as good replicas will not receive sufficient ViewChange messages to either construct NewView messages or set time-outs for the next primary. The only way PBFT can deal with this is by waiting until communication becomes sufficiently reliable, after which primary replacement can recommence. To assure that this is the case, replicas will rebroadcast their `ViewChange` messages for view v until they receive a well-formed `NewView` message or time-out for this message (after which they start broadcasting `ViewChange` messages for view $v + 1$).

2.8   PBFT WITHOUT USING DIGITAL SIGNATURES

The version of PBFT presented in the previous sections utilizes digital signatures. As already discussed in Remark 2.7 and explained in Section 1.3.5, the reason for this is that signed messages can be forwarded reliable without the forwarding replicas being able to corrupt the message. Unfortunately, digital signatures are typically computational expensive and, hence, simple *authenticated communication* is often preferable. Next, we shall sketch how PBFT can be tuned toward using authenticated communication.

Inspection of PBFT shows that only a few message types are forwarded. Namely, client requests $\langle \tau \rangle_C$ are forwarded as part of `PrePrepare` messages; `PrePrepare` messages are forwarded as part of `Prepare`, `Commit`, and `Checkpoint` messages; `Prepare` messages are forwarded as part of prepared certificates included in `ViewChange` messages; `Checkpoint` messages are forwarded as part of checkpoint certificates included in `ViewChange` messages; and `ViewChange` messages are forwarded as part of `NewView` messages.

First, we shall consider removing signatures from client requests, then we will sketch how the techniques used to eliminate signatures from client requests can be applied to remove all signatures.

2.8.1   DROPPING SIGNATURES ON CLIENT REQUESTS

Let $\langle \tau \rangle_C$ be a *signed* client request. In PBFT, the signature on $\langle \tau \rangle_C$ provided by C is used to assure *validity* (Definition 2.3): only with the involvement of C can such signatures be constructed. Hence, even if a primary P is malicious and proposes $\langle \tau \rangle_C$ via a `PrePrepare` request, we have the guarantee that P did not forge the proposed request.

If we drop signatures on client requests, then good replicas need another way to determine *validity*. There is an obvious way to do so.

1. Good replica R considers request $\langle \tau \rangle_C$ valid if it receives that request directly from the client.

Indeed, if clients and communication are reliable, then we can simply rely on clients to distribute their requests to all replicas. Unfortunately, we must also take care of the situation in which either clients are faulty or communication is unreliable. In that case, some good replicas Q might never be able to learn some client request $\langle \tau \rangle_C$ directly from the client. In that case, Q would not be able to determine whether any `PrePrepare` message that proposes $\langle \tau \rangle_C$ is well-formed, as Q cannot determine whether $\langle \tau \rangle_C$ is requested by C. Hence, to deal with faulty or malicious clients

---

Client-role (used by client C to request transaction τ) :
1: Broadcast $\langle\tau\rangle_C$ to *all* replicas.
2: Await receipt of messages $\texttt{Inform}(\langle\tau\rangle_C, \rho, r)$ from $\mathbf{f}+1$ replicas.
3: Considers τ executed, with result r, as the ρ-th transaction.

Validity-role (running at every replica $\mathsf{R} \in \mathfrak{R}$) :
4: **event** R receives $\langle\tau\rangle_C$ directly from C **do**
5:     Mark client request $\langle\tau\rangle_C$ as a valid request from C.
6:     Broadcast $\texttt{AckClient}(\langle\tau\rangle_C)$ to all replicas.
7: **end event**
8: **event** R receives $\mathbf{f}+1$ identical messages $\texttt{AckClient}(\langle\tau\rangle_C)$ from distinct replicas **do**
9:     Mark client request $\langle\tau\rangle_C$ as a valid request from C (if not yet done so).
10:     Broadcast $\texttt{AckClient}(\langle\tau\rangle_C)$ to all replicas (if not yet done so).
11: **end event**

Primary-role (running at the primary P of view v, $\text{id}(\mathsf{P}) = v \bmod \mathsf{n}$) :
12: Let view v start after execution of the ρ-th transaction.
13: **while** P is the primary **do**
14:     P awaits receipt of message $\langle\tau\rangle_C$ of some client C together with messages $\texttt{AckClient}(\langle\tau\rangle_C)$ from $\mathbf{g}$ distinct replicas.
15:     **if** $\langle\tau\rangle_C$ is a well-formed request for transaction τ **then**
16:         Broadcast $\texttt{PrePrepare}(\langle\tau\rangle_C, v, \rho)$ to all replicas.
17:         $\rho := \rho + 1$.
18:     **end if**
19: **end while**

Figure 2.18: The first steps of the Byzantine commit algorithm of PBFT (client, validity, and primary roles) when client signatures are dropped. The processing of $\texttt{PrePrepare}$ messages continues as normally. We refer to Figure 2.5 and Section 2.2 for details.

and with unreliable communication, we need a way in which replicas can determine validity of requests without help of the client and in which primaries can determine whether a client request is considered valid by all good replicas. To do so, we can rely on a less-obvious technique.

2. Good replica R considers request $\langle\tau\rangle_C$ valid if another good replica claims it is valid. As R does not know which other replicas are good, replica R considers request $\langle\tau\rangle_C$ valid only after $\mathbf{f}+1$ distinct replicas—of which at least one is good—claim it is valid.

To implement the above rule, we let replicas *broadcast* a message acknowledging that they consider a client request valid. To do so, we make minimal changes to the initial phases of the Byzantine commit protocol of Section 2.2. We refer to Figure 2.18 for the full details on these changes.

We notice that the validity-role of Lines 4–11 of Figure 2.18 is directly based on the two techniques that replicas can use to determine validity of a request. Using a—by now standard—counting argument on the number of `AckClient` messages, we can prove the following.

Proposition 2.33 *If* $n > 3f$, *communication is reliable, and a good primary proposed* $m =$ `PrePrepare`$(\langle \tau \rangle_C, v, \rho)$ *as a consequence of the Byzantine commit algorithm of Figure 2.18, then all good replicas will be able to verify that* $\langle \tau \rangle_C$ *was sent by client* C.

Proposition 2.33 shows that we can use *authenticated communication* to simulate *message signatures*, this at the cost of additional communication. There is one aspect of forwarding client requests that we have not yet discussed. Remember that—as part of the view-change algorithms—replicas forward client requests to the primary. To assure that good replicas only forward client requests that are already considered valid by all good replicas, good replicas only forward client requests for which they already received $n - f$ `AckClient` messages, in which case we can use another counting argument to prove that also the primary will receive $n - f$ such messages, which it needs to propose the client request via the algorithm of Figure 2.18.

2.8.2 DROPPING SIGNATURES ON ALL OTHER MESSAGES

First, we consider `PrePrepare` messages forwarded as part of `Prepare`, `Commit`, and `Checkpoint` messages. Here, we can easily drop digital signatures, as replicas only accept `Prepare` and `Commit` messages that match the `PrePrepare` message they received from the primary themselves. For `Checkpoint` messages, we see that one only trusts such a message after receiving it from at least $f + 1$ replicas, in which case one such copy must be forwarded by a good replica. Hence, digital signatures are also not required in `Checkpoint` messages. Lastly, messages are forwarded in `ViewChange` and `NewView` messages, this as part of the view-change algorithm. Here, the removal of digital signatures has a much bigger impact, which we shall explore next.

In the view-change algorithm presented in Section 2.3, digital signatures serve several distinct and essential purposes. First, it is important to remember a *main* goal of the view-change algorithm of Section 2.3: the view-change algorithm must assure that every request $\langle \tau \rangle_C$ that *could* have been executed by at least one good replica R is *always* preserved. Hence, any proposal $m := $ `PrePrepare`$(\langle \tau \rangle_C, v, \rho)$ that has been committed by at least one good replica R must *always* be preserved. As any R can only reach the committed state for m after receiving `Commit` messages for m from g distinct replicas, R only committed m if at least $g - f$ good replicas *prepared* m, and only for such m does the view-change algorithm guarantee preservation (Theorem 2.15).

The view-change algorithm of Section 2.3 achieves its goals by heavily relying on digital signatures in two distinct ways. Consider a message `ViewChange`(E, v) of a good replica R. As replica R signed this message, the new primary cannot tamper with this message when forwarding it as part of any `NewView` message. Hence, recipients of `NewView` messages have the guarantee that all g included `ViewChange` messages are untampered with and that at least $g - f$ of these messages are constructed by good replicas. Second, digital signatures play an important role in assuring that the at-most f `ViewChange` messages constructed by faulty replicas cannot claim to have prepared any proposals that conflict with the proposals that must be preserved. To see this, consider a message $ViewChange(E, v)$. In this message, E consists of a set of prepared certificates of the form $Prepare_R(m)$ that prove the claim that R prepared m. These prepared certificates consist of g signed `Prepare` message for some proposal $m := PrePrepare(\langle \tau \rangle_C, v, \rho)$. By Proposition 2.5, the existence of $Prepare_R(m)$ guarantees that *no* prepared certificate exists for any other proposal in round ρ of view v. Hence, if a faulty replica wants to construct a valid message $ViewChange(E, v)$, it either includes the prepared certificate $Prepare_R(m)$ or does not include any prepared certificate for round ρ of view v. Furthermore, the existence of $Prepare_R(m)$ guarantees that at least $g - f$ good replicas entered the *prepare phase* for m in round ρ, which they only do if round ρ was not preserved when changing to view v (and, hence, if no previous proposal needs to be preserved). Together, these two usages of digital signatures enable the preservation of proposals, as proven in Theorem 2.15.

In systems that do not use digital signatures, prepared certificates can no longer be exchanged. Consequently, good replicas cannot prove that they prepared or committed proposals, while faulty replicas can falsely claim that they prepared or committed proposals. Next, we will sketch a view-change algorithm based on *claims* of the proposals prepared and committed to by at-least-g replicas. Consider a proposal $m := PrePrepare(\langle \tau \rangle_C, v, \rho)$. We build the view-change algorithm using the following four crucial properties. First, a good replica only enters the prepare phase for m if it entered view v without preserving any proposal for round ρ (maintained by the view-change algorithm we will construct). Second, if a good replica prepared m, then $g - f$ good replicas must have entered the prepare phase for m (Line 18 of Figure 2.5). Third, if a good replica committed m, then at least $g - f$ good replicas prepared m (Line 21 of Figure 2.5). Fourth, if a good replica prepared m, then no replica can have prepared a proposal for any other request in round ρ of view v (Proposition 2.5).

Now consider a set of g replicas $R_1, \ldots, R_g$ such that the i-th replica, $1 \leq i \leq g$, claims to have entered the prepare phase for the set of proposals P_i and prepared the set of proposals C_i in round ρ. Although we do not know which of these replicas are good and which are faulty, we do know the following.

1. If there is a set S of $g - f$ good replicas that prepared m, then $S \cap \{R_1, \ldots, R_g\} \neq \emptyset$ and, hence, there must be at least a single good replica R_j, $1 \leq j \leq g$, with $m \in P_j$ and $m \in C_j$.

2. If there are two replicas R_i and R_j, $1 \leq i < j \leq g$, with $PrePrepare(\langle \tau_i \rangle_{C_i}, v, \rho) \in C_i$ and $PrePrepare(\langle \tau_j \rangle_{C_j}, v, \rho) \in C_j$, then—as a consequence of Proposition 2.5—either $\langle \tau_i \rangle_{C_i} = \langle \tau_j \rangle_{C_j}$ or there is a *claim conflict* in which case at-least one of the replicas must be faulty ($R_i \in \mathcal{F}$, or $R_j \in \mathcal{F}$, or both).

3. If $R_1, \ldots, R_g$ are all good and a replica R_i, $1 \leq i \leq g$, prepared m ($m \in C_i$), then at-least $g - f$ replicas R_j, $1 \leq j \leq g$, have entered the prepare phase for m ($m \in P_j$). In this case, we say that a prepared claim is *fully supported*.

Now consider a new primary P' that wants to determine the initial state for the new view $v + 1$. To determine the state of a particular round ρ, this primary will base itself upon a set of claims from g distinct replicas for proposals in round ρ. If the set has claim conflicts, as described in 2, then some of the claims are provided by faulty replicas. Hence, the primary P' awaits until additional claims of other replicas arrive.

As there are g good replicas and good replicas only make valid claims, P' eventually will receive a set of non-conflicting claims from g distinct replicas. Next, consider such a set of g non-conflicting claims and consider the case in which a replica R claims to have prepared $m :=$ $\texttt{PrePrepare}(\langle \tau \rangle_c, v, \rho)$. We distinguish two cases. First, the case in which at-most f replicas claim to have entered the prepare phase for m. In this case, the prepared claim by R and these f supporting claims can all be made by faulty replicas. Hence, it could be the case that this claim is *false* and the claim could even try to *overwrite* a previously committed and executed proposal $\texttt{PrePrepare}(\langle \tau' \rangle_{c'}, v', \rho)$ with $v' < v$. Therefore, in this case, we cannot trust the claim for m. Second, the case in which at-least $f + 1$ replicas claim to have entered the prepare phase for m. In this case, at least a single good replica Q claims to have entered the prepare phase for m in view v. Hence, when Q entered view v, it did not preserve anything for round ρ, indicating that there is no previously committed proposal for round ρ that should be preserved. In this case, we say that the prepared claim for m is *supported*

Now consider a prepared claim for m made by a good replica that is not supported. By 3, we know that there are $g - f \geq f + 1$ good replicas that must have entered the prepare phase for m. Hence, not all claims the new primary P' is working with are made by good replicas, and, again, P' can wait until it receives g claims without conflicts and in which all prepared claims are fully supported.

Finally, consider a set of g claims for round ρ without conflicts and in which all claims are supported. Based on these claims, there are two possible outcomes. First, the case in which no replica claimed to have prepared anything in round ρ. As described in 1, this can only happen if *no good replica* committed a proposal $\texttt{PrePrepare}(\langle \tau \rangle_c, v, \rho)$. Hence, in this case, the new primary P' proposes $\langle \text{nop} \rangle_{P'}$. Second, the case in which a replica claims to have prepared some $\texttt{PrePrepare}$ message. Let $m_1 := \texttt{PrePrepare}(\langle \tau_1 \rangle_{c_1}, w_1, \rho)$ be the message in the most-recent view w_1 that any replica claimed to have prepared. As the set of claims is non-conflicting, all other replicas that claim to have prepared, prepared to $\texttt{PrePrepare}(\langle \tau_2 \rangle_{c_2}, w_2, \rho)$ with $w_2 < w_1$ or with $\langle \tau_1 \rangle_{c_1} = \langle \tau_2 \rangle_{c_2}$. Furthermore, as all claims are fully supported, there are at least $g - f \geq$ $f + 1$ replicas that claim to have entered the prepare phase for m_1 in view w_1. Hence, at least one good replica supported m_1 in view w_1, which it only does if it did not have to preserve any proposals for round ρ in views before w_1.

1: {Replica R broadcasts a message ViewChange(P, C, v) to request a view-change in view v, in which P is the set of all proposals for which R entered the prepare phase at the end of view v (see Line 14 of Figure 2.5), and C is the set of the latest proposals m prepared in each round by R at the end of view v (R logged Prepare$_R(m)$).}

2: {The new primary P' broadcasts a message NewView($v + 1, V$) in which V is a set of **g** messages $m_i =$ ViewChange(P_i, C_i, v_i), $1 \le i \le$ **g**, such that no request in C_i *conflicts* with any request in C_j, $1 \le j \le$ **g**; every claim in C_i is *fully supported*; and v_i is the current view v.}

New view role (used by replica R to move into a new view) :

3: **event** R receives NewView($v + 1, V$) from P' such that:

    (i) v' follows the current view v ($v' > v$);

    (ii) $v' \bmod n = \text{id}(P')$; and

    (iii) NewView($v + 1, V$) is well-formed (see above)

  do

4:    $M := \{m \mid (\text{ViewChange}(P, C, v') \in V) \wedge (m \in C)\}$.

5:    $\rho_{\text{all}} := \{\rho \mid \text{PrePrepare}(\langle \tau \rangle_C, w, \rho) \in M\}$.

6:    **for** $\rho \in \{0, \ldots, \max(\rho_{\text{all}})\}$ **do**

7:      **if** PrePrepare($\langle \tau' \rangle_{C'}, w', \rho$) $\in M$ **then**

8:        Let $w = \max(\{w' \mid \text{PrePrepare}(\langle \tau \rangle_C, w', \rho) \in M\})$.

9:        Enter the commit phase for $m := \text{PrePrepare}(\langle \tau \rangle_C, w, \rho) \in M$.

10:        Resume the Byzantine commit algorithm of PBFT for m (Figure 2.5).

11:      **else**

12:        Construct $m := \text{PrePrepare}(\langle \text{nop} \rangle_{P'}, v', \rho)$.

13:        Enter the prepare phase for m as the first proposal for round ρ in view v'.

14:        Resume the Byzantine commit algorithm of PBFT for m (Figure 2.5).

15:      **end if**

16:    **end for**

17: **end event**

Figure 2.19: The local state update algorithm for PBFT without using digital signatures.

    The above, combined with the observation described in 1, are sufficient for an inductive proof in the spirit of the proof of Theorem 2.15 to show that, based on any set of **g** claims, any proposal will be preserved whenever a good replica committed it.

    Based on the above, the basic contours of a view-change algorithm can be derived: instead of ViewChange messages with prepared certificates, each replica constructs ViewChange messages with claims of the proposals they entered the prepare phase for and the proposals they prepared. Using the above rules, any good replica can choose a set of **g** of such ViewChange messages that provide non-conflicting claims of which all preparded claims are supported. From this set, one can deterministically derive the initial state of the next view. In Figure 2.19, we sketched the resulting rules determining the requests preserved in this next view.

    There is only one issue remaining in this setup, however: the new primary cannot simply forward a set of **g** ViewChange messages. As these messages do not carry signatures, any malicious new primary can easily tamper with these message or fabricate its own messages. To deal with this, we can use the same techniques as used to forward client requests: each replica treats its own `ViewChange` message as a client request and forwards it to all other replicas. Each replica then replies with acknowledgment messages. Finally, the new primary only picks those `ViewChange` message that received acknowledgment from at least **g** distinct replicas.

2.9 CONCLUDING REMARKS

This chapter lays the foundation for reaching consensus in a partially synchronous setting based on PBFT, a seminal work developed by Castro and Liskov in 1999 [55]. One may perceive PBFT as the means to agree on advancing the global time. Every newly generated sequence number by an orchestrator (the primary) can be seen as a clock tick if endorsed by the majority, a quorum of replicas (observers).[1] Furthermore, the causal event for the advancement of time is a client request that the orchestrator attributes to the clock tick. Hence, the quorum of observers not only have to endorse the clock tick but also agree on its cause, observing the same client request on the same clock tick—*the safety property*. Thus, as long as the system is sufficiently synchronized by a well-behaving quorum,[2] then the time advances—*the liveness property*. Reaching sufficient synchronization safely can only be achieved if a well-behaving quorum of replicas is available. The normal routine of the protocol is carried out in two simple steps.

- *Prepare Phase*: when a replica[3] observes that a quorum supported a clock tick for the same event (i.e., the replica enters the *prepared state* on the *prepared event*).

- *Commit Phase*: at least one honest replica observes[4] that a quorum of replicas reached the prepared state; hence, the honest replica enters the *committed state*.[5,6,7,8]

If a well-behaving quorum of replicas is unavailable or unreachable,[9] then simply no progress is made and the system stalls on the current clock tick; thus, safety is satisfied trivially

---

[1]It is further assumed that the majority of replicas in a quorum are honest. As a result, due to the *quorum intersection property*, any two quorums must share at least one common honest replica.

[2]We adopt the term *well-behaving* to signify that a malicious replica may choose to behave correctly.

[3]But not necessarily all replicas.

[4]To ensure there is at least one honest replica, at least **f** + 1 replicas must support the same claim.

[5]The *prepare phase* ensures that *each replica knows the majority have supported an event* while the *commit phase* ensures that *the majority of replicas know that the majority of replicas have supported an event*.

[6]Consider the following classroom analogy. We start by having all students sitting down. Each student privately receives endorsement messages from other students. When a student receives endorsements from a quorum, she stands (i.e., entering the *prepared state*). At this point, each student is only aware that he/she received the endorsement from the majority and unaware of the state of others. But if enough students stand, then each standing student will independently observe that a quorum of students has also received an endorsement from the majority (entering the *committed state*).

[7]If an honest replica observes a quorum, then the quorum is deemed as valid. If two honest replicas each observe a quorum, then, due to *quorum intersection property*, both quorums must agree on the causal event.

[8]The *prepare phase* ensures there is an agreement on the causal event within the same view while the *commit phase* ensures that the reached agreement persists across views.

[9]If the network delay is longer than expected, then it will have the same net effect as if a replica or the network becomes unavailable.

and liveness is lost. If reaching sufficient synchronization fails due to a faulty orchestrator, then, as long as a quorum of sufficiently well-behaving replicas is available, the liveness of the system can be restored. The recovery routine to elect a new orchestrator (*a new view*) is as follows.

- *View Change Phase*: a quorum of replicas raises a flag that the advancement of the global time has failed[10] for a sufficiently long enough period of time as observed locally in each replica.

- *New View Phase*: a quorum of replicas agrees upon the current global time and the means to attain it. This implies that the quorum agrees upon the causal event for every elapsed clock tick.

Depending on how messages were authenticates, the casual events of previous views can be derived from the quorum in the following two ways. If digital signatures using public-key (asymmetric) cryptography are used to sign messages, then either

- an honest replica claims that an event was endorsed by the majority and presents a signed *prepared certificate*,[11] or

- in absence of any *prepared certificate* given a quorum of replicas, the quorum agrees that no event was endorsed by the majority; hence, the casual event is a special *no-op*.

However, if authenticated communication via message authentication code (MAC) was used to authentic messages, then either

- there is (i) a quorum that provides non-conflicting support for a prepared event within a view (either replicas prepared that same event or prepared no event at all) along (ii) with at least an honest replica that claims the prepared event was proposed by an orchestrator in the same or later view,[12] or

- there is a quorum of replicas that agrees that no event was endorsed by the majority; hence, the casual event is a special *no-op*.

---

[10]Or if there is an outstanding client request for a sufficiently long-enough period.

[11]If an event was committed, then it was prepared by a quorum of replicas out of which the majority must be honest (greater than f). For the view change to take place, a quorum is needed, and due to the *quorum intersection property*, there must be a common honest replica between the prepared and view-change quorum. Thus, at least one honest prepared replica will always be present as part of the view change quorum. To prove its honesty, it simply presents a tamper-proof *prepared certificate* that consists of signed prepare messages that the replica received from the quorum.

[12]The commitment of an event proves that the event was prepared by a quorum of replicas, i.e., *an implicit prepared certificate*. Due to the *quorum intersection property*, at least one honest prepared replica will always be present as part of the view change quorum. Hence, it will result in a conflicting endorsement set (or results in the lack of support for proving that a previous orchestrator proposed the *presumably* prepared event) if any malicious replica claims a different event was prepared. To construct a non-conflicting endorsement set, a quorum of well-behaving replicas is needed, and the view change protocol will indefinitely fail unless a well-behaving replicas join the view change quorum. As a result, the liveness of the view change may only be guaranteed if all replicas (at least all the well-behaving or honest ones) are available.

If both *view change* and *new view* phases succeed, then the system is advanced to a new view, namely, the clock is restored and the orchestration by the new primary begins. If the *view change* phase fails, then the system stalls and no progress is made. If the *view change* is completed but the *new view* fails, then the *view change* is repeated with yet another new orchestrator.

In essence, at every step in the PBFT protocol, whether it is the normal or recovery routine, either (1) *sufficient quorum support exists allowing* PBFT *to progress safely* (i.e., the system is sufficiently synchronized within the timeout period) or (2) a *quorum is not formed in time and* PBFT *safely stalls indefinitely*. In the absence of a synchronized clock among replicas and an unknown network bound due to the partial synchrony assumption, replicas in PBFT are left with only a local timer that is rather powerful. The timer enables each replica to implement a timeout mechanism with an exponential back-off in order to gradually increase the timeout period longer than the unknown network delay which is necessary to construct a quorum; hence, re-establishing progress safely.

2.10   BIBLIOGRAPHIC NOTES

The original PBFT consensus protocol was proposed by Castro and Liskov in 1999 [55]. Furthermore, this paper also presented the application of PBFT in a Byzantine-fault-tolerant version of the Network File System [131] (an application we also discussed in Section 1.5 and Example 2.1). This Byzantine-fault-tolerant File System showed practical performance, underlining the practical nature of PBFT. Later publications focused on providing proactive recovery (which we discuss in the next chapter) and operating without using digital signatures [54, 56].

CHAPTER 3

Beyond the Design of PBFT

In the previous chapter, we presented a simplified version of the PBFT consensus protocol. Although this simplified protocol can easily serve as the workhorse in any deployment of a permissioned blockchain, there is still much room for improvement. In this chapter, we will take six steps to develop such improvements. First, we will formally model the performance of PBFT; then we focus on the typical *implementation techniques* that are applied to optimize the performance of PBFT (and of other primary-backup consensus protocols); third, we review common implementation techniques used to improve other primary-backup protocols; fourth, we explore the usage of trusted components; fifth, we consider the limitations of PBFT and other primary-backup consensus protocols and discuss techniques to deal with these limitations; and, finally, we examine how the resilience of practical consensus protocols can be further improved.

3.1 MODELING THE PERFORMANCE OF PBFT

The performance of any resilient system can be measured along five axes.

1. the *transaction throughput* of the system: the total number of transactions the system can accept per second;

2. the *transaction latency* of the system: the total duration between the primary proposing a transaction and the final execution of the transaction;

3. the *resource utilization* of the system: the total amount of computational power and network bandwidth required per transaction and the *imbalance* between resource utilized by the primary and by other replicas;

4. the *complexity* of the system: e.g., the complexity in the normal-case operations, of the recovery process, and of view-changes; and

5. the *failure model* used by the system.

As a final axis, one could also consider the *client latency*, the duration between a client requesting a transaction and the client learning of the outcome. Typically, client latency is a direct function of the transaction latency and, when the system is under heavy load, the transaction throughput.

The techniques to improve the performance of PBFT, and of resilient systems in general, will typically make trade-offs between these axes. To gain a good understanding of these trade-offs, we will model the performance impact of each of the techniques typically applied to primary-backup consensus protocols such as PBFT. As a first step, we study the performance of the simplified version of PBFT presented in the previous chapter.

3.1.1   DETERMINING THE PERFORMANCE VARIABLES

As a first step to modeling the performance of PBFT, we determine which variables contribute most to determining performance. The speed by which PBFT can complete consensus rounds and execute transactions is a function of four factors. First, the *number of replicas* in the system determines the total amount of messages that each replica will have to send and receive. Second, the *network bandwidth* determines how long it takes for a replica to send and receive these messages. Third, the *message delay* determines the delay between a replica completing sending a message and another replica starting receiving that message. Finally, the *computational speed* determines the speed by which replicas can interpret messages and perform the necessary steps of the protocol. Furthermore, the computational speed also determines the speed by which individual replicas can execute transactions after committing them.

In theory, the performance of any permissioned blockchain is ultimately upper-bounded by the computational speed: the speed by which individual replicas can execute transactions determines the maximum attainable throughput, this independent of the consensus protocol used. In most practical systems, the network costs for reaching consensus on transactions eclipses any computational costs for executing said transactions. Furthermore, most systems further hide computational costs by executing committed transactions in parallel with the consensus steps for future transactions. Hence, in the following, we will primarily investigate the performance of consensus as a function of the network bandwidth and the message delays.

3.1.2   THE SINGLE-ROUND COST OF PBFT

We assume consensus in a system with n replicas of which f are faulty and the remaining $g = n - f$ are good. The outgoing and incoming network bandwidth for each replica totals B, whereas messages take δ to arrive at their destination, e.g., if the system consists of replicas spread over North-America, then typical values for B and δ are $B = 100\,\text{MiB/s}$ and $\delta = 15\,\text{ms}$. In this setting, sending a message of $4\,\text{MiB}$ from replica R to replica Q will take at least $\frac{4}{B} + \delta = 55\,\text{ms}$. We notice that in geo-scale deployments of blockchains, in which replicas are spread over several continents, B could be as low as $B = 10\,\text{MiB/s}$ and δ could be as high as $\delta = 135\,\text{ms}$, in which case sending the same $4\,\text{MiB}$ message would take $535\,\text{ms}$. Finally, we assume that `PrePrepare` messages holding a single transaction have size s_t (in bytes), that message digests are used to reduce the size of `Prepare` and `Commit` messages (see Section 2.7.2), and that `Prepare` and `Commit` messages have size s_m (in bytes).

First, we will model the time it takes to complete a *single round* of PBFT in which each round is processed *in order*. Hence, the primary starts round $\rho + 1$ only after a proposal for round ρ is committed. We assume that redundant messages are eliminated (see Section 2.7.1).

At the start of round ρ, the primary choses a transaction and sends `PrePrepare` messages m proposing the chosen transaction to all $(n - 1)$ other replicas. Hence, the primary has to send $(n - 1)s_t$ bytes. As the network bandwidth for the primary is B, sending these messages will take $\frac{(n-1)s_t}{B}$ seconds. As it takes δ seconds for the last of these `PrePrepare` messages to be received by its receiving replica R_1, R_1 will only be able to prepare m at $\frac{(n-1)s_t}{B} + \delta$ seconds after the start of round ρ.

Next, all non-primary replicas, including replica R_1, will send `Prepare` messages for m to all $(n - 1)$ other replicas. Hence, R_1 has to send $(n - 1)s_m$ bytes, which will take $\frac{(n-1)s_m}{B}$ seconds, and R_1 will only be able to finish sending `Prepare` messages for m at $\frac{(n-1)s_t}{B} + \delta + \frac{(n-1)s_m}{B}$ seconds after the start of round ρ. As it takes δ seconds for the last of these `Prepare` messages to be received by its receiving replica R_2, R_2 will only be able to commit m at $\frac{(n-1)s_t}{B} + \delta + \frac{(n-1)s_m}{B} + \delta$ seconds after the start of round ρ.

Next, all replicas, including R_2, will send `Commit` messages for m to all $(n - 1)$ other replicas. Using a similar reasoning as for the `Prepare` messages, R_3 will only be able to finish sending `Commit` messages for m at $\frac{(n-1)s_t}{B} + 2\left(\delta + \frac{(n-1)s_m}{B}\right)$ seconds after the start of round ρ. Finally, as it takes δ seconds for the last of these `Commit` messages to be received by its receiving replica R_3, R_3 will only be able to reach the committed state for m at $\frac{(n-1)s_t}{B} + 2\left(\delta + \frac{(n-1)s_m}{B}\right) + \delta$ seconds after the start of round ρ. Based on the above, we conclude that each round takes at least

$$\Delta_{\text{PBFT}} = \frac{(n - 1)s_t}{B} + 2\left(\delta + \frac{(n-1)s_m}{B}\right) + \delta$$

seconds.

3.1.3   THE THROUGHPUT OF PBFT

We have seen that a single round of PBFT takes Δ_{PBFT} seconds. To determine the throughput, we simply determine how many such rounds one can complete per second. Hence, we have a best-case throughput of

$$T_{\text{PBFT}} = \frac{1}{\Delta_{\text{PBFT}}} = \frac{B}{(n - 1)s_t + 2(n - 1)s_m + 3B\delta}$$

transactions per second. We have plotted this throughput in Figure 3.1. As is clear from these figures, the simple PBFT protocol presented in the previous chapter has rather limited throughput, especially in environments with high latencies. In the next section, we shall explore how to improve this throughput significantly without changing the consensus protocol.

Remark 3.1   To simplify presentation, we only account for the time required by each replica to send messages, and we have not accounted for the time required to receive messages. This approach is valid in the best-case that we model here, as each replica R can receive any messages sent to it during the time it takes for the last message R send to arrive at its destination. In

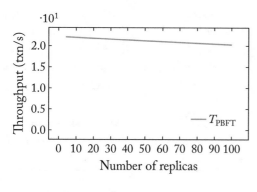 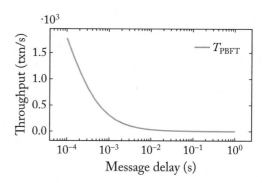

Figure 3.1: The maximum throughput for PBFT. In this figure, we use $B = 100\,\text{MiB/s}$, $s_t = 4048\,\text{B}$, and $s_m = 256\,\text{B}$. On the left, throughput as a function of the number for replicas, and we use $\delta = 15\,\text{ms}$. On the right, throughput as a function of the message delay, and we use $\mathbf{n} = 7$.

practice, each round will take longer than this best-case modeling we present here, as replicas in an asynchronous environment have little control over when messages exactly arrive. Furthermore, we only modeled the communication costs due to the normal-case consensus protocol, as we omitted the receipt of client requests by the primary, any checkpointing, and any `Inform` messages sent to the client. As these additional messages only account for a small fraction of all work in typical system, they would complicate the best-case performance model unnecessary.

3.2   IMPLEMENTATION TECHNIQUES FOR PBFT

As modeled in the previous section, a straightforward implementation of PBFT has a rather limited throughput of only a few dozen transactions per second in many realistic deployments. To improve performance, most resilient systems optimize their implementations of PBFT by utilizing *batching*, by utilizing *out-of-order processing*, and by *overlapping communication phases*. Next, we review these techniques in detail.

3.2.1   BATCHING OF CLIENT REQUESTS

We notice that the total communication cost of PBFT per client request is high. To see this, consider the replication of a single client request $\langle \tau \rangle_c$, as outlined in the previous section:

1. the primary broadcasts $\mathbf{n} - 1 = \mathcal{O}(\mathbf{n})$ `PrePrepare` messages of size s_t each and $\mathbf{n} - 1 = \mathcal{O}(\mathbf{n})$ `Commit` messages of size s_m each; and

2. all other replicas broadcast $\mathbf{n} - 1 = \mathcal{O}(\mathbf{n})$ `Prepare` and `Commit` messages of size s_m each.

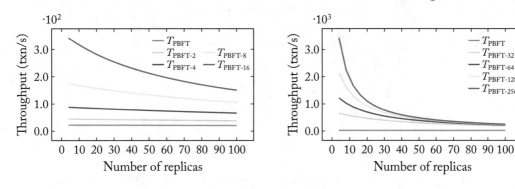

Figure 3.2: The maximum throughput for PBFT as a function of the number of replicas. In this figure, we use $B = 100\,\text{MiB/s}$, $\delta = 15\,\text{ms}$, $s_t = 4048\,\text{B}$, and $s_m = 256\,\text{B}$.

Hence, in total $2\mathbf{n}(\mathbf{n}-1)$ messages are sent with a total size of $\mathcal{O}(s_t\mathbf{n} + s_m\mathbf{n}^2)$. As such, the replication of a single requests costs a *quadratic* amount of communication.

Due to the usage of message digests, as outlined in Section 2.7.2, increasing the size of client requests *only affects* the size of the proposed `PrePrepare` messages and *not* the size of the other messages. We can use this to our advantage to reduce the overall communication cost to replicate a collection of client requests by grouping them into a single *batch* that is replicated by the primary via a single round of consensus.

To see the effectiveness of batching on throughput, consider a collection of m client requests with total size ms_t. If we replicate each request individually, then the throughput is T_{PBFT}. If we replicate per-group of m messages, then the throughput is

$$T_{\text{PBFT-}m} = m\left(\frac{B}{(\mathbf{n}-1)ms_t + 2(\mathbf{n}-1)s_m + 3B\delta}\right),$$

however. We have plotted this throughput in Figure 3.2. As is clear from the figure, batching provides a huge improvement on throughput.

Notice that by choosing the batch size sufficiently large, we can use batching to reduce the effective communication cost per client request to only *linear* in the number of replicas (instead of quadratic). To see this, consider the number of messages required to process a single batch with $m = \mathbf{n}$ requests. In total, we require $2\mathbf{n}(\mathbf{n}-1)$ messages with a total size of $\mathcal{O}(ms_t\mathbf{n} + s_m\mathbf{n}^2)$ to process this batch. As each batch has $\mathbf{n}$ requests, the cost *per client request* is only $\frac{2\mathbf{n}(\mathbf{n}-1)}{m} = 2(\mathbf{n}-1)$ messages with a total size of $\mathcal{O}(\frac{ms_t\mathbf{n}+s_m\mathbf{n}^2}{m}) = \mathcal{O}(s_t\mathbf{n} + s_m\mathbf{n})$.

Batching is a highly *effective* tool for increasing replication *throughput*—the number of client requests that can be replicated per time-unit—of a system utilizing PBFT-style replication. Unfortunately, batching does *not* resolve all communication issues, however. First, *batching* requires primaries to collect m client requests before replicating any of them. This delays replication of the first-arriving client request, thereby increasing the *latency*—the time it takes

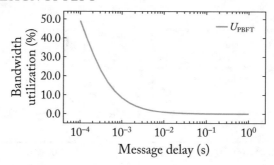

Figure 3.3: The network bandwidth utilization at the primary of PBFT as a function of the message delay. In this figure, we use $\mathbf{n} = 7$, $B = 100\,\mathrm{MiB/s}$, $s_t = 4048\,\mathrm{B}$, and $s_m = 256\,\mathrm{B}$.

for a client to get a response—for this request in situations where client requests arrive slowly. Furthermore, even though batching reduces overall communication costs for all replicas, the reduction at the primary is only moderate, as the cost of broadcasting the client replicas will dominate communication costs.

3.2.2   OUT-OF-ORDER PROCESSING

If one looks closer to the throughput, as modeled in the previous sections, then one can conclude that the throughput discussed is *not* fully determined by the network bandwidth: message delay has a significant impact. To illustrate this, consider the bandwidth utilization at the primary of PBFT as a function of the message delay. Remember that, in a single round of PBFT, the primary only sends out $(\mathbf{n} - 1)$ PrePrepare messages with a total size of $(\mathbf{n} - 1)s_t$, receives $(\mathbf{n} - 1)$ Prepare messages with a total size of $(\mathbf{n} - 1)s_m$, and sends and receives $(\mathbf{n} - 1)$ Commit messages with a total size of $2(\mathbf{n} - 1)s_m$. Hence, the primary uses $(\mathbf{n} - 1)(s_t + 3s_m)$ bytes per round and $T_{\mathrm{PBFT}}(\mathbf{n} - 1)(s_t + 3s_m)$ bytes per second out of the total bandwidth B. Hence, we have a bandwidth utilization of

$$U_{\mathrm{PBFT}} = \frac{T_{\mathrm{PBFT}}(\mathbf{n} - 1)(s_t + 3s_m)}{B} = \frac{(\mathbf{n} - 1)(s_t + 3s_m)}{(\mathbf{n} - 1)s_t + 2(\mathbf{n} - 1)s_m + 3B\delta}.$$

We have plotted this bandwidth utilization function in Figure 3.3. As is clear from this figure, the bandwidth utilization of PBFT is very low, especially when message delays are high.

To make throughput independent of the message delay, we need to maximize the utilization of the network bandwidth at the primary. To do so, we simply allow the primary to propose requests for future rounds before proposals for the current round are committed. We notice that the design of PBFT can handle such out-of-order proposing and processing of rounds, as it already has to deal with out-of-order message delivery (due to asynchronous communication). Indeed, PBFT only requires in-order processing of the execution step, which can be enforced by

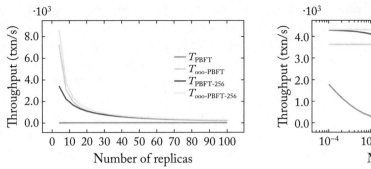
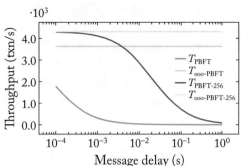

Figure 3.4: The maximum throughput for PBFT with *out-of-order processing*. In this figure, we use $B = 100\,\text{MiB/s}$, $s_t = 4048\,\text{B}$, and $s_m = 256\,\text{B}$. On the left, throughput as a function of the number for replicas, and we use $\delta = 15\,\text{ms}$. On the right, throughput as a function of the message delay, and we use $\mathbf{n} = 7$.

each replica independently. Finally, we remark that the view-change recovery protocol of PBFT already deals with cases in which primaries skip proposals for certain rounds.

The number of rounds that can be processed out-of-order is bounded in practice. First, out-of-order processing requires sufficient memory buffers to be able to store all intermediate state for each round that is being processed. Furthermore, one also needs to ensure that malicious primaries cannot exploit out-of-order processing to use up large ranges of round numbers.

To see the effectiveness of out-of-order processing on throughput, we build upon the throughput for PBFT. With out-of-order processing in place, the maximum throughput is completely determined by the bandwidth consumption at the primary. Per round, this primary sends out $\mathbf{n} - 1$ PrePrepare messages, receives $\mathbf{n} - 1$ Prepare messages, sends out $\mathbf{n} - 1$ Commit messages, and, finally, receives $\mathbf{n} - 1$ Commit messages. Hence, the maximum *out-of-order throughput of* PBFT is

$$T_{\text{ooo-PBFT}} = \frac{B}{(\mathbf{n} - 1)s_t + 3(\mathbf{n} - 1)s_m}$$

without batching and

$$T_{\text{ooo-PBFT-}m} = \frac{mB}{(\mathbf{n} - 1)ms_t + 3(\mathbf{n} - 1)s_m}$$

with batching. Notice that in both cases the message delay no longer plays a role in the maximum throughput. We have plotted this throughput in Figure 3.4. As is clear from the figure, out-of-order processing vastly improves performance of PBFT (and can even outperform PBFT implementations that already use batching).

We notice that out-of-order processing does not change the processing delay of PBFT: each individual round still takes at least Δ_{PBFT} to complete. It does sharply increase throughput, however. Hence, in high-load situations out-of-order processing will enable much faster response times for clients. Furthermore, we notice that out-of-order processing does not guarantee high throughput: high throughput can introduce other bottlenecks in the system, e.g., computational costs related to message signing and verification, the time it takes to execute transactions, and the available memory resources to maintain the relevant data to process many rounds in parallel. Consequently, high-performance systems that employ out-of-order processing typically require a heavily parallelized architecture to support maximum-throughput transaction processing on modern many-core processor architectures.

3.2.3   OVERLAPPING COMMUNICATION PHASES

We introduced batching and out-of-order processing to reduce communication costs and improve throughput. Unfortunately, batching increases latencies, while out-of-order processing increases the costs associated with consensus. As an alternative, one can eliminate communication by overlapping consecutive phases. Consider rounds ρ and $\rho + 1$ for non-primary replica R. As the last communication step of round ρ, R will send out Commit messages for some PrePrepare message m_ρ and, as the first communication step of round $\rho + 1$, R will send out Prepare messages for some PrePrepare message $m_{\rho+1}$. Instead, R can opt to send a combined CommitPrepare message that includes a Commit for m_ρ and a Prepare for $m_{\rho+1}$. Although this halves the number of messages sent by R, it does double the size of the messages sent by R. To further improve on the above idea, we can make proposals for round $\rho + 1$ refer to previous proposals such that a Prepare message of round $\rho + 1$ implicitly also indicates a Commit message for round ρ. In this way, non-primary replicas can reduce outgoing communication by half.

Unfortunately, overlapping consecutive phases of consecutive rounds of PBFT will introduce a strong dependence between consecutive rounds of PBFT. Consequently, reducing communication by overlapping phases will eliminate any opportunity to use out-of-order processing which, as we have seen in Section 3.2.2, is a major tool to maximize throughput in environments with high message delays. Still, overlapping communication does improve throughput compared to the baseline model of Section 3.1.3: as the last step of round ρ is overlapped with the first step of round $\rho + 1$, the effective duration of each round is reduced by $\delta + \frac{(n-1)s_m}{B}$ seconds. Hence, the best-case throughput of PBFT with overlapped phases is

$$T_{\text{op-PBFT}} = \frac{B}{(n-1)s_t + (n-1)s_m + 2B\delta}.$$

We have plotted this throughput in Figure 3.5. As is clear from these figures, overlapping phases in PBFT does help performance (this at little costs), but out-of-order processing is preferable in applications that require high throughputs.

A recent well-known example of a consensus protocol that overlaps communication phases is the event-based version of the four-phase HotStuff [249] consensus protocol. By overlap-

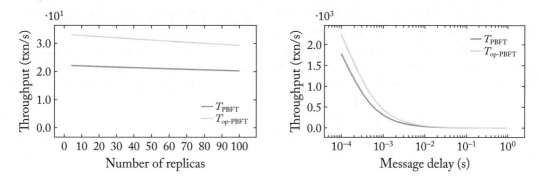

Figure 3.5: The maximum throughput for PBFT with and without overlapping phases. In this figure, we use $B = 100\,\text{MiB/s}$, $s_t = 4048\,\text{B}$, and $s_m = 256\,\text{B}$. On the left, throughput as a function of the number for replicas, and we use $\delta = 15\,\text{ms}$. On the right, throughput as a function of the message delay, and we use $\mathbf{n} = 7$.

ping communication phases, this protocol is able to process a single request per phase (even though fully processing a request takes four phases).

3.3   PRIMARY-BACKUP CONSENSUS BEYOND PBFT

In the previous section, we examined implementation techniques typically applied to PBFT. Although these techniques affect the performance of permissioned blockchains, they do not fundamentally change the working of the consensus protocol used to operate these systems. Next, we consider common technologies employed by PBFT-like primary-backup consensus protocols to further change the performance of permissioned blockchains. Specifically, we focus on *threshold signatures*, *optimistic execution*, and *speculative execution*.

3.3.1   THRESHOLD SIGNATURES

In the previous sections, we have examined several techniques to improve the throughput of PBFT and other primary-backup consensus protocols. Complementary to these techniques, there are also several techniques aimed at improving other aspects of PBFT. The first of these techniques we look at is the usage of *threshold signatures* to reduce overall network communication.

As outlined in Section 3.2.1, a single round of PBFT will cause the replicas to send a total of $2\mathbf{n}(\mathbf{n} - 1) = \mathcal{O}(\mathbf{n}^2)$ messages, a *quadratic amount*, as all replicas broadcast their Prepare and Commit messages to all other replicas. As an alternative, we can consider an all-to-one-to-all communication scheme that would reduce the number of messages to a *linear amount*. First, we apply this idea to the Commit messages. To do so, all replicas send their Commit messages to a dedicated *collector* replica C, which will then aggregate g matching `Commit` messages into a single *committed certificate*, and broadcast this certificate to all other replicas.

The naive way to do so, is to let C simply send a set of g `Commit` messages to each other replica. In this case, we have replaced the all-to-all broadcast step costing $n(n-1)$ `Commit` messages of size s_m each by an all-to-one communication step costing $n-1$ messages of size s_m and a one-to-all communication step costing $n-1$ messages of size gs_m each. As $g = \mathcal{O}(n)$, both approaches will use $\mathcal{O}(s_m n^2)$ bandwidth in total.

To truly reduce bandwidth usage, the collector C needs a way to aggregate the g messages into a single *constant-sized* message that can serve as a committed certificate. Here, *threshold signatures* come into play.

Definition 3.2   A $n : f$-threshold-signature scheme for public-key K consists of n public–private partial key pairs, one assigned to each replica, with the following properties:

1. each replica R can use its private partial key to produce a partial signature $\text{psign}(v, R)$ for any value v;

2. each replica Q can use the public partial key of R to verify the validity of partial signature $\text{psign}(v, R)$; and

3. only upon obtaining at least $n - f = g$ partial signatures $\text{psign}(v, R')$ of g distinct replicas R', can one produce a signature for v that can be verified using public-key K.

Threshold signature schemes exist for many public-key cryptosystems, including systems based on RSA [222] and on elliptic curves [20].

To employ threshold signatures, each replica R simply uses their private partial key to sign their `Commit` message. Next, R send the message and the partial signature to the collector. The collector can use the public partial key of R to verify the individual partial signature provided by R. After receiving valid partial signatures produced by g distinct replicas, the collector constructs the *threshold signature* for the `Commit` message and broadcasts this threshold signature to all replicas. Upon receiving such a threshold signature for a `Commit` message, each replica will use this signature as a *committed certificate*. In this way, the all-to-all communication step is replaced by a all-to-one-to-all communication step costing only $2(n-1)$ messages of size s_m each, thereby reducing communication to only a *linear amount*.

The same steps can also be applied to `Prepare` messages without much effort. To assure that sufficient partial signatures are produced to allow the construction of a threshold signature for the `Prepare` message, the primary needs to provide a partial signature too, however (e.g., as part of the `PrePrepare` message).

Using an aggregation scheme to reduce the communication costs of all-to-all communication has several disadvantages. First, we notice that any protocol must have recovery mechanisms to deal with the failure of the collector C. Second, most threshold signature schemes are rather expensive, and the computational costs involved for the collector can become a bottleneck. Finally, we notice that applying all-to-one-to-all communication to both the `Prepare` and `Commit` phase effectively adds *two* communication phases, each with message delay δ, to the consensus protocol, which negatively impacts the duration of each PBFT round. Using reasoning similar to that in Section 3.1.2, one can derive that each round in a threshold-signature version of PBFT takes at least

$$\Delta_{\text{ts-PBFT}} = \frac{(\mathbf{n}-1)s_{\text{t}}}{B} + 2\left(\delta + \frac{s_{\text{m}}}{B} + \delta + \frac{(\mathbf{n}-1)s_{\text{m}}}{B}\right) + \delta.$$

At the same time, aggregation can improve throughput by reducing communication involving the primary. By picking another replica as the collector, the primary will only receive a single `Prepare` message and send and receive only a single `Commit` message, this instead of sending and receiving $(\mathbf{n}-1)$ such messages. Hence, the maximum *out-of-order throughput of a threshold-signature version of* PBFT is

$$T_{\text{ts-PBFT}} = \frac{B}{(\mathbf{n}-1)s_{\text{t}} + 3s_{\text{m}}}$$

without batching and

$$T_{\text{ts-PBFT-}m} = \frac{mB}{(\mathbf{n}-1)ms_{\text{t}} + 3s_{\text{m}}}$$

with batching. We have plotted the round time and throughput of a threshold-signature version of PBFT in Figure 3.6. As is clear from this figure, aggregating messages has a drastic negative impact on the round duration, which will also negatively impact request latencies, while aggregating messages provides a minor improvement for maximum throughput.

Besides reducing overall communication costs, threshold signatures can also be used locally at each replica to reduce memory requirements for storing the ledger, prepared certificates, and committed certificates in a straightforward manner. This usage of threshold signatures can even be applied without resorting to an all-to-one-to-all scheme of communication.

Recently, there have been a flurry of protocols that proposed using threshold signatures to reduce overall communication, each with their own approaches to dealing with faulty collectors and with the high computational costs of threshold signatures. Examples include LinBFT [248], PoE [120], and SBFT [109]. A more thorough design that integrates threshold signatures not only in the normal-case operations of consensus, but also reworked and simplified the view-change methods is HotStuff. Unfortunately, the correctness of HotStuff [249] relies on multi-round reasoning (Section 3.2.3), which prevents application of any out-of-order processing, sharply limiting the performance of this, otherwise, simple and efficient consensus protocol. Finally, threshold signatures are also used to reduce global communication in geo-scale aware systems such as Steward [11] and GeoBFT [123] to enable aggregation of certificates of local decisions.

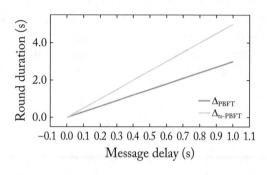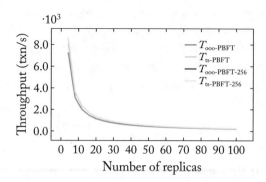

Figure 3.6: The performance of a threshold-signature version of PBFT. In this figure, we use $B = 100 \, \text{MiB/s}$, $s_\text{t} = 4048 \, \text{B}$, and $s_\text{m} = 256 \, \text{B}$. On the left, round duration as a function of the message delay and we use $\mathbf{n} = 7$. On the right, throughput as a function of the number of replicas.

3.3.2 SPECULATIVE EXECUTION

Many applications benefit from services that minimize the response times observed by clients. In a PBFT-based service, this response time is determined by three factors that we can try to improve, namely the time it takes for a client request to be sent from the client to the primary; the time it takes to start execution of the client request; and the time it takes for the client to receive sufficient responses to determine that its request was executed.

There is not much we can do to minimize the first and last factors besides placing the PBFT-based service physically close to clients. We can try to reduce the time it takes to start execution of the client request, however. The main determining factor in the time it takes to start execution is the number of communication phases used between initial proposal of a request via a `PrePrepare` message and execution of that request, e.g., using PBFT, we require three communication phases, due to which $\Delta_{\text{PBFT}} \geq 3\delta$, and in a threshold-signature version of PBFT, we require five communication phases, due to which $\Delta_{\text{ts-PBFT}} \geq 5\delta$.

Hence, one way to reduce response times for clients is by *expediting execution*. In PBFT, good replicas proceed with execution until *after* the commit phase, this to assure correctness of the protocol. Indeed, good replicas obtain a committed certificate during the commit phase, and the existence of this certificate guarantees that the request is always recoverable during a view-change. Hence, as soon as a client detects that a single good replica executed its transaction, the client can consider its transaction executed. As there are $\mathbf{f}$ faulty replicas, this means that the client must wait for at least $\mathbf{f} + 1$ replies.

Now consider execution before completing the commit phase. Such execution would provide less guarantees to good replicas and, consequently, such executions are required to be *spec-*

ulative in the sense that replicas might be forced to undo executions. To see this, consider the following two options.

1. Replicas can execute directly after the prepare phase. By Proposition 2.5, PBFT guarantees that in a single view, only a single request will finish the prepare phase per round. This does not mean that this single request can safely be executed: a future view-change might drop the request. To see this, consider a malicious primary in a system with $\mathbf{n} = 3\mathbf{f} + 1$ replicas. The malicious primary constructs conflicting PrePrepare messages $m_1 = \text{PrePrepare}(\langle \tau_1 \rangle_{c_1}, v, \rho)$ and $m_2 = \text{PrePrepare}(\langle \tau_2 \rangle_{c_2}, v, \rho)$. The primary then sends m_1 to good replica R and to $\mathbf{f}$ other good replicas, m_2 to the remaining $\mathbf{f}$ good replicas, and both m_1 and m_2 to the faulty replicas. The faulty replicas only send Prepare messages to R. Hence, R will receive $2\mathbf{f} + 1 = \mathbf{n} - \mathbf{f} = \mathbf{g}$ Prepare messages for m_1 and complete the prepare phase, while all other replicas detect failure and trigger a view-change.

   Such a view-change can be based upon the state of any $\mathbf{f} + 1$ good replicas (as up-to-$\mathbf{f}$ faulty replicas can provide ViewChange messages). In the worst case, the new view is based on information of $\mathbf{f}$ good replicas that received m_2, a single good replica other than R that received m_1 (but does not have a prepared certificate), while the faulty replicas can choose to behave as if they received nothing at all. Hence, the new primary can base the new-view on the combined state of $\mathbf{g} - \mathbf{f}$ good replicas that do not have a prepared certificate for m_1. Hence, the new-view can drop m_1, in which case R needs to undo its execution.

2. Replicas can execute directly after receiving PrePrepare messages. As malicious primaries can send conflicting PrePrepare messages to distinct replicas and this is only detected during the prepare phase, replicas can even end up executing conflicting requests.

As the above examples show, expedited execution within PBFT must necessarily be *speculative*, as malicious behavior of the primary can require some or all of the replicas to undo their execution upon detection of malicious behavior. Hence, clients can no longer rely on replies from a single good replica to determine that their requests are executed. This does not imply that execution cannot be expedited, however: one can change the conditions under which clients consider their requests to be executed to take into account the possibility of speculative execution. This notion is at the core of the *Proof-of-Execution* (PoE) consensus protocol [120] that we shall describe next.

At the core of PoE is the following observation on the operations of PBFT: whenever $\mathbf{g} - \mathbf{f}$ good replicas complete the prepare phase for some PrePrepare message m_1, then, due to Theorem 2.15, the normal PBFT view-change algorithm already guarantees that m_1 will be preserved during view-changes. Hence, if execution is performed after the prepare phase, then clients can consider their requests executed after detecting that $\mathbf{g} - \mathbf{f}$ good replicas executed the request. As there are $\mathbf{f}$ faulty replicas, this means that the client must wait for at least $\mathbf{g}$ replies. This will reduce the time from proposal to execution to two communication phases (three if threshold signatures are used).

We notice that when requests are executed speculatively after the prepare phase of PBFT, then the commit phase will only be used by replicas to determine whether a round is guaranteed to be recovered by future view-changes (and whether an execution can still be undone). This guarantee is *not essential* for correct operation in the eyes of clients: whenever a client detects execution of a request (as a result of **g** replies), the view-change algorithm will already guarantee that the executed request will be recovered. As the prepare phase is still performed, malicious primaries will not be able to force execution on several conflicting requests in the same round. Hence, the only malicious behavior that can affect replicas is that they are left in the dark for some rounds. This will prevent the affected replicas to execute requests in future rounds, which, if sufficient replicas are affected, will result in the primary being detected faulty. Hence, in PoE speculative execution after the prepare phase is used to drop the commit phase altogether. By dropping the commit phase in this way, one improves client response times, reduces overall communication (in the same way as overlapping phases does, see Section 3.2.3), while still allowing for out-of-order processing (see Section 3.2.2). For an out-of-order version of PoE, we have

$$\Delta_{\text{PoE}} = \frac{(\mathbf{n} - 1)s_t}{B} + \delta + \frac{(\mathbf{n} - 1)s_m}{B} + \delta,$$
$$T_{\text{PoE}} = \frac{B}{(\mathbf{n} - 1)s_t + (\mathbf{n} - 1)s_m},$$

and, when batching is enabled,

$$T_{\text{PoE-}m} = \frac{mB}{(\mathbf{n} - 1)ms_t + (\mathbf{n} - 1)s_m},$$

which we have plotted in Figure 3.7. As one can see, the throughput improvements compared to PBFT are minor (especially when batching is enabled), whereas the reduction in the round duration (and client response times) is significant.

The cost of the speculative design of PoE is an increase in complexity of the view-change algorithm: during the view-change, some replicas can be forced to *rollback execution* of transactions. We illustrate this next.

Example 3.3   Consider a system $\mathfrak{R}$ with good replica $\mathsf{R} \in \mathfrak{R}$. During round ρ, communication became unreliable, due to which only R received Prepare messages for $m :=$ PrePrepare($\langle \tau \rangle_C, v, \rho$). Consequently, R speculatively executes τ and informs the client C. During the view-change, all other replicas—none of which have a prepared certificate for m—provide their local state to the new primary, whom proposes a new-view that does not include round ρ. Hence, the first request the new primary proposes is $m' :=$ PrePrepare($\langle \tau' \rangle_{C'}, v + 1, \rho$), which gets accepted. Consequently, R needs to rollback execution of τ. Luckily, this is not an issue: the client C only got at-most $\mathbf{f} + 1 < \mathbf{n} - \mathbf{f}$ responses to its request and, consequently, does not yet consider τ executed.

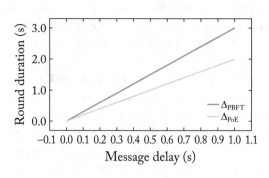
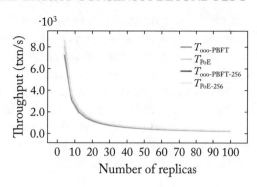

Figure 3.7: The maximum performance for PoE with *out-of-order processing*. In this figure, we use $B = 100\,\text{MiB/s}$, $s_t = 4048\,\text{B}$, and $s_m = 256\,\text{B}$. On the left, round duration as a function of the message delay, and we use $\mathbf{n} = 7$. On the right, throughput as a function of the number of replicas, and we use $\delta = 15\,\text{ms}$.

3.3.3   OPTIMISTIC EXECUTION

Speculative execution, as used in PoE, eliminates the commit phase of PBFT by executing transactions directly after the prepare phase and does not require special circumstances to work optimally. Consensus protocols with *optimistic execution* go one step further by optimizing for the case in which all replicas *behave good*. Consider, e.g., the design of ZYZZYVA [2, 3, 161–163]. This protocol performs *optimistic execution* directly after receiving a PrePrepare message and omits the prepare phase and commit phase.

Notice that with the view-change algorithm of PBFT, as outlined in Section 2.3, receiving PrePrepare message m provides *no guarantees* that m will ever be recovered: communication might become unreliable directly after receiving m, due to which no replica will ever construct the prepared certificates used by the view-change algorithm. Hence, if one wants to execute directly after receiving PrePrepare messages, then one also needs to completely redesign the view-change algorithm to provide a path to recovery for such executions.

One can design such a view-change algorithm by adding to the ViewChange messages a set of the most-recent PrePrepare message each replica has received in each round. Now, if no prepared certificates are provided for some round ρ by the $\mathbf{g}$ ViewChange messages on which a new view is based, and a majority of the ViewChange messages included an identical PrePrepare message m for round ρ (at least $\mathbf{g} - \mathbf{f}$ replicas), then the new primary chooses to repropose m in round ρ. As a new-view is based on the information of $\mathbf{g}$ replicas of which at-most $\mathbf{f}$ are faulty, this recovery path is only guaranteed to succeed if all $\mathbf{g}$ good replicas received the same PrePrepare message m from the primary (here, the optimistic execution assumption comes into play). Hence, if execution is performed after receiving a PrePrepare message, then clients can consider their requests executed after detecting that $\mathbf{g}$ good replicas executed the request. As there are **f** faulty replicas, this means that the client must wait for at least $\mathbf{g} + \mathbf{f} = \mathbf{n}$ replies. Consequently, ZYZZYVA requires that all replicas behave good to operate optimistically and to eliminate the prepare phase and commit phase, and ZYZZYVA falls back to a non-optimistic recovery path when this optimistic requirement does not hold.

By not performing the prepare phase, no replica of ZYZZYVA will learn anything about the state of other replicas, which makes it impossible for the replicas to determine malicious behavior by the primary (or by other replicas). Hence, several replicas can end up executing conflicting requests for the same round, which will go undetected by these replicas. To deal with this, ZYZZYVA requires *well-behaved clients* to aid in detecting malicious behavior (and, in general, in detecting whether the optimistic requirement holds) and to trigger the appropriate recovery paths.

Not all optimistic consensus protocols operate in a single preprepare phase. For example, the FAB protocol [2, 3, 182, 183] tries to perform consensus in two phases whenever the primary is good, but falls back into a three-phase recovery mode when irregularities are detected. Although optimistic execution promises great opportunities in reducing the cost of consensus whenever all replicas are good, optimistic execution also greatly complicates dealing with view-change and recovery. As such, optimistic protocols such as ZYZZYVA and FAB have shown critical weaknesses not shared by PBFT and PoE, especially in environments with unreliable communication (in which arbitrary messages can be dropped).

3.4   TRUSTED COMPONENTS

Up until now, we have presented PBFT and other consensus protocols in the standard fault model in which each replica is either good or is faulty. In this classification, good replicas are always reliable and behave exactly as prescribed by the protocols it is participating in, whereas faulty replicas act Byzantine (e.g., can crash, can omit, or can coordinate with an attacker for a targeted attack). We notice that this strict classification prohibits that replicas change classification: a good replica cannot get compromised and become faulty, while a faulty replica will always be considered faulty even after any recovery processes. This limitation is inherent to the reliability of the fault model, which we illustrate next.

Example 3.4   Consider a PBFT system that uses digital signatures. Hence, each replica has a public–private-key pair. Let R be a replica with private-key K. Originally, R behaves good and operates as prescribed. At some point, R gets compromised by an attacker. As part of this attack, the attacker makes key K public. At a later point, it is recognized that R is compromised and a recovery process is started. After recovery, R resumes its role. Unfortunately, the private-key K of R is now public and, hence, other replicas can impersonate R. Due to this impersonation, other good replicas can end up making decisions based on messages sent by malicious impersonators instead of messages sent by R.

In practice, every single replica is prone to faulty behavior, as each replica is prone to crashing eventually due to hardware failure. Furthermore, software bugs, failed software updates, and network disruptions also can prevent otherwise reliable replicas to behave good at all times. Consequently, one cannot expect that the set of faulty replicas is static and will never change, and practical systems need ways to recover faulty replicas and restore their operations to normal.

The two obvious solutions to deal with the failure of a replica R is by recovering the replica back to normal operations or to replace it with a fresh replica. Both solutions would require the replacement of the public–private-key pair of R with a new pair, this to deal with the situation of Example 3.4. Such replacement would in effect constitute the introduction of a new identity (new replica) to the system together with the removal of the old identity associated with R. Unfortunately, the introduction and removal of identities is outside of the scope of the typical fault model used by PBFT and other consensus techniques, and is itself a problem for which no practical solutions exist yet.

As an alternative solution, PBFT proposed the usage of *trusted components* to provide *proactive recovery*. Trusted components have also been proposed to provide other improvements. Next, we will examine what trusted components are and how they can be used to enhance the capabilities of consensus protocols such as PBFT.

3.4.1   SYSTEMS WITH TRUSTED COMPONENTS

In systems in which trusted components are used, each replica contains a local tamper-proof component that will perform its operations correctly and does not leak any sensitive information, even if the remainder of the system is compromised and under control of a malicious adversary. Hence, the trusted component will only *crash* (when the entire systems crashes) and never behave completely arbitrary. Typically, these tamper-proof components provide a small minimalistic set of functionality to aid building resilient systems that can deal with malicious behavior. For consensus protocols, examples of useful functionality are as follows.

1. The trusted component can provide *digital signing* of all messages with a private-key held within the component. Even if the replica gets compromised, this private-key is kept secret and secure. Hence, this usage prevents faulty replicas from publicizing their private-keys and from faulty replicas to impersonate each other.

2. The trusted component can append *secure counter values* to all messages, which prevents replicas from revoking messages or keeping other replicas in the dark.

3. Some trusted components provide *remote attestation* by which other replicas can determine what software the trusted component is running.

This kind of functionality can already be provided by *Trusted Platform Modules*, which have been integrated in systems for the last two decades. Recently, more flexible trusted software components (e.g., to provide trusted components within virtualized platforms) have been proposed and developed on top of CPU-specific instruction set extensions such as Intel SGX, ARM Trust-Zone, and AMD SEV.

We notice that the usage of trusted components complicates development, as the proper and secure utilization of a trusted component is non-trivial. Furthermore, relying on trusted components changes the failure model, as one requires more trust in some parts of the system. Finally, trusted components add addition points-of-failure in the design of a resilient system. Typically, these downsides are offset by minimizing the functionality provided by the trusted component and fully auditing this part of the system, after which the usage of the trusted component can reduce the complexity of the rest of the system.

In practice, trusted components are mainly used to provide proactive recovery and to improving failure resilience, both of which we shall detail next.

3.4.2   PROACTIVE RECOVERY

As hinted at before, PBFT can use trusted components to provide proactive recovery to enable recovery of faulty replicas. To provide proactive recovery, one can use the trusted component at replica R to securely store the private-key K of R and to sign any outgoing messages of R. By using the trusted component in this way, the private-key K of R will never leak to other replicas, not even if R is compromised. Securing the key K at R resolves the issue raised in Example 3.4, but does not yet provide full recovery.

To provide full recovery in simple systems, one can rely on manual intervention to recover the replica (e.g., by replacing broken parts and reinstalling all software). For large-scale complex deployments, manual intervention should be minimized, however. For such systems, proactive recovery proposed the usage of a *recovery manager* residing in *read-only memory* that reinitializes the system to an uncompromised good state on start up. (Here, we assume that this read-only memory is tamper-proof, which is easy to guarantee when attackers do not have physical access to the replica.) Finally, to provide proactive recovery, one simply forces the restart of faulty replicas that are detected. As faulty behavior is not always detectable, the recovery manager can periodically restart each system at random to trigger periodic recovery.

3.4.3   HIGH FAILURE RESILIENCE

To be able to deal with f faulty replicas, systems that use PBFT require are least $3f + 1$ replicas. This lower bound on the total number of replicas and upper bound on the number of faulty replicas is not specific to the design of PBFT, however, as it has been shown that these bounds follow from the fault model used by most consensus protocols (see Section 1.3.5).

Systems that utilize trusted components operate under a different fault model. Hence, this opens the possibility of providing higher resilience by requiring less than $3f + 1$ replicas to deal with f faulty replicas. Protocols such as 2FBC [71], A2M [63], CHEAPBFT [151], FASTBFT [174], and MINBFT [239] have shown that this is indeed the case: these protocols only require $2f + 1$ replicas to deal with f faulty replicas.

To understand the operations of these protocols, we first look back at *why* the design of PBFT requires $\mathbf{n} > 3\mathbf{f}$. A close look reveals the following usages.

1. In the normal-case operations of PBFT, the assumption that $\mathbf{n} > 3\mathbf{f}$ is used to assure that, in each round ρ of view v, good replicas only commit a single PrePrepare proposal $m = \texttt{PrePrepare}(\langle \tau \rangle_C, v, \rho)$ (Proposition 2.5).

2. In the view-change algorithm of PBFT, the assumption that $\mathbf{n} > 3\mathbf{f}$ is used to assure that future views always preserve PrePrepare proposal m if it has been executed by a good replica, which could be the case as soon as at least $\mathbf{g} - \mathbf{f}$ good replicas prepared and commit m (Theorem 2.15).

These two usages are at the basis for providing *non-divergence* and *termination*.

To illustrate how trusted components can be utilized to provide PBFT-style consensus when $\mathbf{n} > 2\mathbf{f}$, we will consider the minimalistic approach taken by MINBFT [239]. We assume that each replica uses a trusted component to *sign messages* and append a *secure counter value*. In the following, we write $\langle v \rangle_{\iota,R}$ to denote a value v signed by R and to which a secure counter value ι is added.

Instead of the three-phase preprepare-prepare-commit protocol of PBFT, MINBFT utilizes a two-phase preprepare-commit protocol in which the primary P broadcasts a PrePrepare proposal $m = \langle \texttt{PrePrepare}(\langle \tau \rangle_C, v, \rho) \rangle_{\iota,P}$. A good replica R will, after receiving m, *commit* m only if the following conditions hold:

1. m is well-formed and R is in view v;

2. m is the first (in terms of secure counter values) PrePrepare message R received for round ρ of view v; and

3. R received all messages from P with secure counter values less than ι.

When R commits m, it broadcasts a message $\langle \texttt{Commit}(m) \rangle_{\iota_R,R}$ to all other replicas. Finally, R will reach the *committed state* for m, execute τ, and inform C if the following conditions hold:

1. R receives Commit messages for m from $\mathbf{n} - \mathbf{f}$ distinct replicas; and

2. for each received message $\langle \texttt{Commit}(m) \rangle_{\iota_Q,Q}$ received from Q, R received all messages with secure counter values less than ι_Q from Q, none of which were ViewChange messages for view v.

Due to the reliance on secure counter values, we have the following replacement of Proposition 2.5.

Proposition 3.5   *Let $R_i \in \mathcal{G}$, $i \in \{1, 2\}$, be two good replicas. If $\mathbf{n} > 2\mathbf{f}$ and replica R_i, $i \in \{1, 2\}$, commit $m_i = \langle \texttt{PrePrepare}(\langle \tau_i \rangle_{C_i}, v, \rho) \rangle_{\iota_i,P}$, then $\langle \tau_1 \rangle_{C_1} = \langle \tau_2 \rangle_{C_2}$.*

Proof. Let $\iota = \min(\iota_1, \iota_2)$. As R_i commits m_i, R_i must have received all messages from P with secure counter values less than $\iota \leq \iota_i$. As R_i will commit to the first `PrePrepare` message R received for round ρ of view v, we must have $\iota = \iota_i$. Hence, $\iota_1 = \iota = \iota_2$. As the trusted component at P will only append ι to a single message, we must have $m_1 = m_2$. □

The usage of trusted components also impacts the view-change algorithm. In MINBFT, these changes affect both `ViewChange` messages and `NewView` messages. Specifically, replica R will broadcast `ViewChange` message $\langle\texttt{ViewChange}(M, v)\rangle_{\iota_\mathsf{R}, \mathsf{R}}$, with M the set of all messages sent by R with secure counter value less than ι_R, upon detection of the failure of the primary of view v.

In turn, the primary of view $v + 1$, the replica P' with $\text{id}(\mathsf{P}') = (v + 1) \bmod \mathbf{n}$, then constructs and broadcasts a `NewView` message $\langle\texttt{NewView}(v + 1, V)\rangle_{\iota_{\mathsf{P}'}, \mathsf{P}'}$ in which V is a set of $\mathbf{n} - \mathbf{f}$ well-formed `ViewChange` messages for view v. Finally, replica R will accept this `NewView` message if the following conditions hold:

1. V contains `ViewChange` messages for view v from $\mathbf{n} - \mathbf{f}$ distinct replicas;

2. for every $\langle\texttt{ViewChange}(M, v)\rangle_{\iota_\mathsf{R}, \mathsf{R}} \in V$, the set M contains all messages with secure counter value less than ι_R from R; and

3. R received all messages with secure counter values less than $\iota_{\mathsf{P}'}$ from P' and none of these messages were `NewView` messages for view $v + 1$.

We notice that, due to the last requirement, all replicas that receive a `NewView` message from $\iota_{\mathsf{P}'}$ must necessarily receive the same `NewView` message. Finally, each replica will upon acceptance of a well-formed `NewView` message update its local state by committing to all `PrePrepare` messages included in the `NewView` message it has not yet committed to. With this modified view-change algorithm in place, we have the following replacement of Proposition 2.12.

Proposition 3.6   *Let* $\langle\texttt{NewView}(v + 1, V)\rangle_{\iota_{\mathsf{P}'}, \mathsf{P}'}$ *be a well-formed* `NewView` *message. If* $\mathbf{n} > 2\mathbf{f}$ *and a single good replica committed* $m = \langle\texttt{PrePrepare}(\langle\tau\rangle_C, v, \rho)\rangle_{\iota, \mathsf{P}}$, *then there exists a message* $\langle\texttt{ViewChange}(M, v)\rangle_{\iota, \mathsf{Q}} \in V$ *with* $\langle\texttt{Commit}(m)\rangle_{\iota, \mathsf{Q}} \in M$.

Proof. Any good replica only committed m after it received `Commit` messages for m from $\mathbf{n} - \mathbf{f}$ distinct replicas. We assume that a good replica R accepted m based on the `Commit` messages received from a set T of $\mathbf{n} - \mathbf{f}$ distinct replicas. Next, consider a replica that entered view $v + 1$ based upon $\langle\texttt{NewView}(v + 1, V)\rangle_{\iota_{\mathsf{P}'}, \mathsf{P}'}$, and let S be the set of replicas that constructed the `ViewChange` messages in V.

First, we will prove that $S \cap T \neq \emptyset$, this by contradiction. We assume $S \cap T = \emptyset$. Hence, we have $|S \cap T| = 0$. By construction, we also have $|T| = \mathbf{n} - \mathbf{f}$, $|S| = \mathbf{n} - \mathbf{f}$, and $|S \cup T| \leq \mathbf{n}$. As $|S \cap T| = 0$, we must have $|S \cup T| = |T| + |S| = 2(\mathbf{n} - \mathbf{f})$. Hence, $2(\mathbf{n} - \mathbf{f}) \leq \mathbf{n}$, and rearrangement of terms yields $\mathbf{n} \leq 2\mathbf{f}$, a contradiction, and we conclude $S \cap T \neq \emptyset$.

Now let $Q \in (S \cap T)$. Replica Q must have send a $\texttt{Commit}$ message $m_c = \langle \texttt{Commit}(m) \rangle_{\iota_1, Q}$ to R and a $\texttt{ViewChange}$ message $m_{vc} = \langle \texttt{ViewChange}(M, v) \rangle_{\iota_2, Q}$ to the new primary P'. Next, we prove that $\iota_1 < \iota_2$ and $m_c \in M$ must hold in all cases. If Q is good, then it will have constructed and broadcasted m_c before m_{vc}, and $\iota_1 < \iota_2$ and $m_c \in M$ hold.

Now consider the case in which Q is faulty. First, we prove $\iota_1 < \iota_2$ by contradiction. Assume $\iota_1 \geq \iota_2$ holds. We notice that R only uses m_c to decide accept if it received all messages with secure counter value less than ι_1 from Q. Hence, R must have received m_{vc}. As m_{vc} is a $\texttt{ViewChange}$ message, R would not have used m_c when accepting m and $Q \notin (S \cap T)$, a contradiction. Hence, $\iota_1 < \iota_2$ must hold.

By construction, $\langle \texttt{NewView}(v + 1, V) \rangle_{\iota_{P'}, P'}$ is well-formed and, as $m_{vc} \in V$, also m_{vc} must be well-formed. As $\iota_1 < \iota_2$, we conclude that m_{vc} is only well-formed if $m_c \in M$, completing the proof. □

In a similar manner as to how Proposition 2.12 is used to prove Theorem 2.15, Proposition 3.6 can be used to prove the following.

Theorem 3.7   *Let $Q \in \mathcal{G}$ be a good replica that committed $m = \langle \texttt{PrePrepare}(\langle \tau \rangle_C, v, \rho) \rangle_{\iota, P}$, and let $\langle \texttt{NewView}(w, V) \rangle_{\iota_{P'}, P'}$ be a well-formed $\texttt{NewView}$ message with $w > v$. If $\mathbf{n} > 2\mathbf{f}$, then any good replica $R \in \mathcal{G}$ will commit to m when updating its local state.*

As with PBFT, MINBFT additionally uses periodic checkpoints to enable recovery of replicas that are left in the dark and to limit the size of $\texttt{ViewChange}$ messages.

3.5   LIMITATIONS OF PRIMARY-BACKUP CONSENSUS

In Section 3.2, we have seen how to use batching and out-of-order processing to assure high resource utilization at the primary and improve throughput, this independent of the message delay δ. These techniques do little to improve resource utilization at other replicas, however. Indeed, one can easily observe a huge discrepancy between resource utilization at the primary and at other replicas. To see this, consider the out-of-order processing of m batched client requests.

1. The primary will send $\texttt{PrePrepare}$ messages and $\texttt{Commit}$ messages to all $(\mathbf{n} - 1)$ other replicas and will receive $\texttt{Prepare}$ and $\texttt{Commit}$ messages from all $(\mathbf{n} - 1)$ other replicas, which totals to a bandwidth usage of $(\mathbf{n} - 1)(m s_t + 3 s_m)$.

2. All other replicas will receive a single $\texttt{PrePrepare}$ message, send out $\texttt{Prepare}$ and $\texttt{Commit}$ messages to all $(\mathbf{n} - 1)$ other replicas, and receive an equal number of $\texttt{Prepare}$ and $\texttt{Commit}$ messages in return, which totals to a bandwidth usage of only $m s_t + 4(\mathbf{n} - 1) s_m$.

Hence, the ratio between bandwidth usage for the primary and for all other replicas is

$$R_{\text{PBFT}} = \frac{(\mathbf{n} - 1)(m s_t + 3 s_m)}{m s_t + 4(\mathbf{n} - 1) s_m}.$$

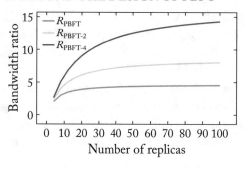
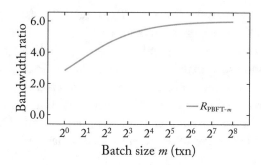

Figure 3.8: The ratio between the bandwidth usage of the primary and of other replicas in PBFT. In this figure, we use $B = 100 \, \text{MiB/s}$, $\delta = 15 \, \text{ms}$, $s_t = 4048 \, \text{B}$, and $s_m = 256 \, \text{B}$. On the left, the ratio as a function of the number of replicas with $m = 16$. On the right, the ratio as a function of the batch size with $\mathbf{n} = 7$.

We have plotted this ratio in Figure 3.8. As one can see from the figure, the resource utilization at the primary is several times higher than the resource utilization at the other replicas. This is especially true when scaling to many replicas or when the `PrePrepare` messages are big (e.g., large batch size).

Based on the above, one can conclude that the throughput of PBFT is bound by the resources available to the *primary*, whereas the other replicas have little influence on throughput. This observation is not tied to specific details of PBFT: any primary-backup consensus protocol in which the primary broadcasts *large* messages, while the other replicas exchange small messages will show similar discrepancies between resource utilization by the primary and by other replicas. To further underline this, one can compare the performance of PBFT with large messages to the performance of the simplest primary-backup replication protocol possible: one in which the primary only broadcasts proposals and other replicas only receive these proposals. Such a protocol would be a *maximum-throughput primary-backup protocol* and will have a throughput of

$$T_{\max} = \frac{B}{(\mathbf{n} - 1)s_t}.$$

We have plotted this throughput in Figure 3.9. As is clear from this figure, the throughput of PBFT with out-of-order processing ($T_{\text{ooo-PBFT}}$) is already close to the maximum throughput $T_{\max}$, and if we also use batching ($T_{\text{ooo-PBFT-256}}$), then the throughput is practically indistinguishable from the maximum throughput $T_{\max}$.

This observation puts a hard limit of $T_{\max}$ on the throughput of primary-backup consensus protocols. Furthermore, as is clear from this limit, primary-backup consensus protocols are *not* scalable: adding replicas will always reduce maximum throughput. This has fueled several approaches toward lifting these hard limits on throughput and toward supporting systems that require higher throughputs than $T_{\max}$. Examples include utilizing *gossip protocols* for communi-

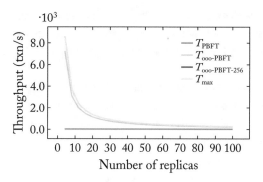

Figure 3.9: The maximum throughput for primary-backup protocols with out-of-order processing as a function of the number of replicas. In this figure, we use $B = 100\,\mathrm{MiB/s}$, $s_t = 4048\,\mathrm{B}$, and $s_m = 256\,\mathrm{B}$.

cation, restricting consensus to a *replica subset*, introducing *sharding*, and introducing *concurrent consensus*. Next, we shall consider each of these approaches in a bit more detail.

3.5.1   GOSSIP PROTOCOLS

In traditional primary-backup protocols, the primary broadcasts requests to all other replicas. Consequently, the throughput is ultimately limited by the bandwidth available to the primary. To lift this limitation, one can replace the traditional direct communication model (in which each replica can directly communicate with all other replicas) with communication via some *gossip protocol* that ensures that the cost of broadcasting messages from the primary to all other replicas is distributed more evenly across the network.

In typical gossip protocols, e.g., as used in peer-to-peer networks, some replicas are *relays* that are responsible for forwarding any message they receive to some set of *replicas*. With such a setup, the primary only has to send its proposals to some relays, which, in turn, will forward the proposals to all other replicas (possibly via additional relay steps). This setup will obviously reduce bandwidth costs for the primary, but this comes at the price of longer consensus rounds (and, hence, higher latencies for clients). Indeed, in a system in which some messages have to traverse r relays when sending a message from one replica to another, the effective message delay δ is increased by a factor at-least r.

Employing a gossip protocol in a Byzantine environment is not trivial, however. As seen in Section 1.3.6, the consensus problem fundamentally requires a highly connected network in which pairs of nodes are always able to communicate via many distinct paths. In practice, this means that the gossip protocol needs to be hardened to take into account replicas that refuse to forward messages, only forward some messages, or forward corrupted messages, which itself can require significant resources. To offset these costs due to malicious behavior, one can utilize aggregation at relays to reduce communication costs for individual relays: relays can collect several messages (e.g., `Prepare` or `Commit` messages for the same proposal) and aggregate them into a single message before forwarding them (e.g., using a threshold signature scheme, see Section 3.3.1).

An example of a consensus protocol that utilizes gossiping is FastBFT [174]. Furthermore, the distinction between local and global communication in geo-aware consensus protocols such as GeoBFT [123] (see Section 4.4) and Steward [11] can be seen as an application of a hierarchical location-based gossip-network.

3.5.2   CONSENSUS VIA A SUBSET OF REPLICAS

In traditional primary-backup protocols, all replicas participate in each round of the protocol, thereby forcing the primary to send proposals to all these replicas. One way to reduce this cost is by reducing the set of replicas that participate in each round of the protocol. Selecting a subset of replicas that participate in a particular round is tricky in a Byzantine environment, however. First, all replicas need to agree on which replicas participate in each round. Second, one needs to deal with subsets that consists of mainly faulty replicas. Finally, one needs a mechanism by which replicas outside the selected subset reliably learn all made decisions.

One way to deal with these issues is by relying on cryptographic primitives and probabilistic arguments for round success, Algorand [107] being the prime example of this approach. Algorand relies on verifiable random functions, a cryptographic primitive, to deterministically select a verifiable set of replicas in each round, and uses probabilistic arguments to show that there is a high-enough probability to select sufficient good replicas to provide reliable consensus.

Another approach is taken by geo-scale aware systems such as GeoBFT [123] (see Section 4.4) and Steward [11]. These systems statically partition all replicas based on location and assume that each location has sufficient good replicas. Each such location-based part only performs consensus on transactions requested by local clients, whereas a global primitive is used to distribute and order these transactions among the other locations. In Steward, global ordering is done by a single *primary* location, whereas GeoBFT uses a decentralized approach with one concurrent instance per location-based part. In this manner, these systems are able to reduce global communication—which typically has lower bandwidth and higher message delays—in favor of cheaper local communication.

3.5.3   SHARDING

Sharding is one of the fundamental techniques utilized to make data and transaction processing *scalable*. In a sharded system, the data is partitioned over individual shards, and each shard only processes transactions that affect data in that shard. To enable such a design, sharded systems require coordination between shards to deal with transactions that affect data in multiple shards. Several approaches toward combining sharding and consensus have been proposed, each with their own trade-offs. We will study sharding techniques in Chapter 4.

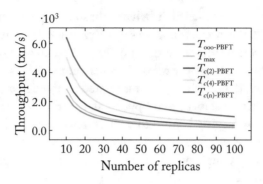

Figure 3.10: The maximum throughput for concurrent-PBFT with out-of-order processing as a function of the number of replicas. In this figure, we use $B = 100 \, \text{MiB/s}$, $s_t = 4048 \, \text{B}$, and $s_m = 256 \, \text{B}$.

3.5.4   CONCURRENT CONSENSUS

As illustrated in Figure 3.8, the primary performs a lot more work than other replicas. Hence, we can easily assign the other replicas additional tasks. One way to do so is by employing several consensus instances concurrently, e.g., by making several replicas *primaries*, each proposing requests concurrently. To see the benefits of such an approach, we consider a *concurrent*-PBFT with $\mathbf{n}$ replicas of which $1 \leq z \leq \mathbf{n}$ are primaries. In every round of such a concurrent-PBFT, each of the z primaries will:

1. send a `PrePrepare` message for some request to $(\mathbf{n} - 1)$ replicas, receive $(\mathbf{n} - 1)$ `Prepare` messages for this request from all other replicas, and send and receive $(\mathbf{n} - 1)$ `Commit` messages for this request; and

2. participate as a backup while processing the $z - 1$ `PrePrepare` messages of the other primaries. Hence, receive $z - 1$ `PrePrepare` messages and send and receive $(z - 1)(\mathbf{n} - 1)$ `Prepare` and `Commit` messages.

Hence, the maximum throughput of such a concurrent system (assuming out-of-order processing) will be

$$T_{c(z)-\text{PBFT}} = \frac{zB}{(\mathbf{n} - 1)s_t + 3(\mathbf{n} - 1)s_m + (z - 1)(s_t + 4(\mathbf{n} - 1)s_m)}.$$

We have plotted this throughput in Figure 3.10. As one can see from the figure, concurrent consensus has the potential to significantly improve performance beyond the hard primary-backup throughput limit T_{max}.

At its basis, concurrent consensus is a simple idea with huge potential to improve performance and scalability. Designing and implementing a concurrent consensus system that operates correctly, even during crashes and malicious behavior of some replicas and clients, is challenging, however. Indeed, concurrent consensus operates in a Byzantine environment in which malicious behavior by both replicas and clients can target any throughput benefits of concurrent consensus. For example, concurrent consensus only maximizes performance if each primary is able to propose distinct requests (such that no throughput is wasted on duplicate requests), and concurrent consensus needs to deal with instances that operate at significantly different speeds than other instances (e.g., by purposely lagging behind to disrupt execution).

Several protocols have proposed novel solutions to these challenges, thereby providing consensus protocols with very high practical throughputs. Prime examples are protocols such as EBAWA [238], GeoBFT [123], MirBFT [225], Omada [90, 91], RCC [121, 122], and Sarek [171], which all build concurrent consensus on top of PBFT-like instances. To further understand the challenges of implementing concurrent consensus, we shall take an in-depth look at the design of the RCC paradigm [121, 122].

The design goals of RCC   RCC is a paradigm that can turn any primary-backup consensus protocol into a concurrent consensus protocol. At its basis, RCC makes every replica a primary of a consensus-instance that replicates transactions among all replicas. Furthermore, RCC provides the necessary coordination between these consensus-instances to coordinate execution and deal with faulty primaries. To assure resilience and maximize throughput, RCC has the following design goals.

D1. RCC provides *consensus* among replicas on the client transactions that are to be executed and the order in which they are executed.

D2. Clients can interact with RCC to force execution of their transactions and learn the outcome of execution.

D3. RCC is a design paradigm that can be applied to any primary-backup consensus protocol, turning it into a concurrent consensus protocol.

D4. In RCC, consensus-instances with good primaries are *always* able to propose transactions at maximum throughput (with respect to the resources available to any replica), this independent of faulty behavior by any other replica.

D5. In RCC, dealing with faulty primaries does not interfere with the operations of other consensus-instances.

Combined, design goals D1 and D2 specify that RCC is a practical consensus protocol (Definition 2.3), and design goals D4 and D5 imply that instances with good primaries can propose transactions *wait-free*: transactions are proposed concurrent to any other activities and does not require any coordination with other instances. Finally, design goal D3 states that RCC can be applied to any (PBFT-like) primary-backup consensus protocol, resulting in a highly flexible approach toward concurrent consensus.

The design of RCC Next, we study the design of RCC in detail. Consider a primary-backup consensus protocol P that utilizes Byzantine commit algorithm BCA (e.g., the Byzantine commit algorithm of PBFT presented in Section 2.2). At the core of applying our RCC paradigm to P is running **m**, $1 \leq \mathbf{m} \leq \mathbf{n}$, instances of BCA *concurrently*, while providing sufficient coordination between the instances to deal with any malicious behavior. To do so, RCC makes BCA *concurrent* and uses a checkpoint protocol for per-instance recovery of in-the-dark replicas). Instead of view-changes, RCC uses a novel wait-free mechanism that does not involve replacing primaries, to deal with detectable primary failures.

To enable design goal D3, which states that RCC can be applied to any (PBFT-like) primary-backup consensus protocol, RCC makes some basic assumptions on P and BCA running in a system with **n** replicas, $\mathbf{n} > 3\mathbf{f}$.

A1. If no failures are detected in round ρ of BCA (the round is *successful*), then at least $\mathbf{g} - \mathbf{f}$ good replicas have *committed* a proposed transaction in round ρ.

A2. If a good replica *committed* a proposed transaction τ in round ρ of BCA, then all other good replicas that committed a proposed transaction, committed τ.

A3. If a good replica *committed* a proposed transaction τ, then τ can be recovered from the state of any subset of $\mathbf{g} - \mathbf{f}$ good replicas.

A4. If the primary is good and communication is reliable, then all good replicas will reach the committed state for a proposal in round ρ of BCA.

With minor fine-tuning, these assumptions are met by PBFT and many other primary-backup consensus protocols, meeting design goal D3.

RCC operates in rounds. In each round, RCC replicates **m** (batches of) client transactions, one for each instance. We write $\mathcal{I}_i$ to denote the i-th instance of BCA. To enforce that each instance is coordinated by a distinct primary, the i-th replica $\mathcal{P}_i$ is assigned as the primary coordinating $\mathcal{I}_i$. Initially, RCC operates with $\mathbf{m} = \mathbf{n}$ instances. In RCC, instances can fail and be *stopped*, e.g., when coordinated by malicious primaries or during periods of unreliable communication. Each round ρ of RCC operates in three steps.

1. *Concurrent* BCA. First, each replica participates in **m** instances of BCA, in which each instance is proposing a transaction requested by a client among all replicas.

2. *Ordering.* Then, each replica collects all successfully replicated client transactions and puts them in the same—deterministically determined—*order*.

3. *Execution.* Finally, each replica *executes* the transactions of round ρ in order and informs the clients of the outcome of their requested transactions.

Figure 3.11 sketches a high-level overview of running **m** *concurrent instances of* BCA.

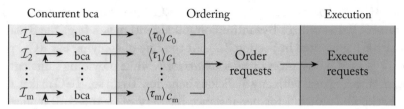

Figure 3.11: A high-level overview of RCC running at replica R. Replica R participates in **m** concurrent instances of BCA (that run independently and continuously output transactions). The instances yield **m** transactions, which are executed in a deterministic order.

To maximize performance, RCC forces every instance to propose distinct transactions, such that every round results in **m** distinct transactions.

To meet design goal D4 and D5, individual BCA instances in RCC can operate out-of-order and continuously propose and replicate transactions: ordering and execution of the transactions replicated in a round by the **m** instances is done *in parallel* to the proposal and replication of transactions for future rounds. Consequently, good primaries can utilize their entire outgoing network bandwidth for proposing transactions, even if other replicas or primaries are acting malicious.

First, we examine how RCC orders and executes transactions in a single round. Let $\langle \tau_i \rangle_{C_i}$ be the transaction τ_i requested by C_i and proposed by P_i in round ρ. After all **m** instances complete round ρ, each replica can collect the set of transactions $S = \{\langle \tau_i \rangle_{C_i} \mid 1 \leq i \leq \mathbf{m}\}$. By Assumption A2, all good replicas will obtain the same set S. Next, all replicas choose an order on S and execute all transactions in that order. As a direct consequence of Assumption A4, we have the following.

Proposition 3.8   *Consider* RCC *running in a system with* **n** *replicas,* **n** > 3**f**. *If all* **m** *instances have good primaries and communication is reliable, then, in each round, all good replicas will reach the committed state on the same set of* **m** *transactions and execute these transactions in the same order.*

As all good replicas will execute each transaction $\langle \tau_i \rangle_{C_i} \in S$, there are **g** distinct good replicas that can inform the client of the outcome of execution. As all good replicas operate deterministically and execute the transactions in the same order, client C_i will receive identical outcomes of **g** > **f** replicas, guaranteeing that this outcome is correct. In the above, we described the normal-case operations of RCC. As in normal primary-backup protocols, individual instances in RCC can be subject to both *detectable* and *undetectable* failures. Next, we sketch how RCC deals with these two types of failures.

Dealing with detectable failures   Consensus-based systems typically operate in an environment with asynchronous communication: messages can get lost, arrive with arbitrary delays, and in arbitrary order. As we have seen in Example 2.8, this environment makes it impossible to distinguish between on the one hand, a primary that is malicious and does not send out proposals and, on the other hand, a primary that does send out proposals that get lost in the network.

To be able to deal with failures, RCC assumes that *any failure* of good replicas to receive proposals from a primary $\mathcal{P}_i$, $1 \leq i \leq \mathbf{m}$, is due to *failure* of $\mathcal{P}_i$, and we design the recovery process such that it can also recover from failures due to unreliable communication. Furthermore, in accordance with the wait-free design goals D4 and D5, the recovery process will be designed so that it does not interfere with other BCA instances or other recovery processes. Now assume that primary $\mathcal{P}_i$ of $\mathcal{I}_i$, $1 \leq i \leq \mathbf{m}$, fails in round ρ. The recovery process consists of three steps.

1. All good replicas need to detect failure of the primary $\mathcal{P}_i$.

2. All good replicas need to reach agreement on the state of $\mathcal{I}_i$: which transactions have been proposed by $\mathcal{P}_i$ and have been committed in the rounds up-to-ρ.

3. To deal with unreliable communication, all good replicas need to determine the round in which $\mathcal{P}_i$ is allowed to resume its operations.

To reach agreement on the state of $\mathcal{I}_i$, RCC relies on a separate instance of the consensus protocol P that is only used to coordinate agreement on the state of $\mathcal{I}_i$ during failure. This coordinating consensus protocol P replicates $\mathtt{stop}(i; E)$ operations, in which E is a set of $\mathbf{g}$ `Failure` messages sent by $\mathbf{g}$ distinct replicas from which all committed proposals in instance $\mathcal{I}_i$ can be derived (in PBFT, these would be the `ViewChange` messages). We notice that P is—itself—an instance of a primary-backup protocol that is coordinated by some primary $\mathcal{L}_i$ (based on the current view in which the instance of P operates), and RCC use the standard machinery of P to deal with failures of that leader. Next, we shall describe how the recovery process is initiated. The details of this protocol can be found in Figure 3.12.

When a replica R detects failure of instance $\mathcal{I}_i$, $0 \leq i < \mathbf{m}$, in round ρ, it broadcasts a message $\mathtt{Failure}(i, \rho, P)$, in which P is the state of R in accordance to Assumption A3 (Line 1 of Figure 3.12). To deal with unreliable communication, R will continuously broadcast this `Failure` message with an exponentially-growing delay until it learns on how to proceed with $\mathcal{I}_i$. To reduce communication in the normal-case operations of P, one can send the full message $\mathtt{Failure}(i, \rho, P)$ to only $\mathcal{L}_i$, while sending $\mathtt{Failure}(i, \rho)$ to all other replicas.

If a replica receives $\mathbf{f} + 1$ `Failure` messages from distinct replicas for a certain instance $\mathcal{I}_i$, then it received at least one such message from a good replica. Hence, it can detect failure of $\mathcal{I}_i$ (Line 6 of Figure 3.12). Finally, if a replica R receives $\mathbf{g}$ `Failure` messages from distinct replicas for a certain instance $\mathcal{I}_i$, then we say there is a *confirmed failure*, as R has the guarantee that eventually—within at most two message delays—also the primary $\mathcal{L}_i$ of P will receive $\mathbf{g}$ `Failure` messages (if communication is reliable). Hence, at this point, R sets a timer based on some internal timeout value (that estimates the message delay) and waits on the leader $\mathcal{L}_i$ to propose a valid $\mathtt{stop}$-operation or for the timer to run out. In the latter case, replica R detects

---

Recovery request role (used by replica R) :

1: **event** R detects failure of the primary Pi, $1 \le i \le$ **m**, in round ρ **do**
2:     R halts $\mathcal{I}_i$.
3:     Let P be the state of R in accordance to Assumption A3.
4:     Broadcast Failure(i, ρ, P) to all replicas.
5: **end event**
6: **event** R receives **f** + 1 messages $m_j = $ Failure(i, ρ_j, P_j) such that:

   (i) these messages are sent by a set S of $|S| = $ **f** + 1 distinct replicas;

   (ii) all **f** + 1 messages are well-formed; and

   (iii) ρ_j, $1 \le j \le $ **f** + 1, comes after the round in which $\mathcal{I}_i$ started last

   do
7:     R detects failure of Pi (if not yet done so).
8: **end event**

Recovery leader role (used by leader $\mathcal{L}_i$ of P) :

9: **event** $\mathcal{L}_i$ receives **g** messages $m_j = $ Failure(i, ρ_j, P_j) such that

   (i) these messages are sent by a set S of $|S| = $ **f** + 1 distinct replicas;

   (ii) all **g** messages are well-formed; and

   (iii) ρ_j, $1 \le j \le $ **f** + 1, comes after the round in which $\mathcal{I}_i$ started last

   do
10:     Propose stop$(i; \{m_1, \ldots, m_\mathbf{g}\})$ via P.
11: **end event**

State recovery role (used by replica R) :

12: **event** R committed a proposal for stop$(i; E)$ from $\mathcal{L}_i$ via P **do**
13:     Recover the state of $\mathcal{I}_i$ using E in accordance to Assumption A3.
14:     Determine the last round ρ for which $\mathcal{I}_i$ committed a proposal.
15:     Set $\rho + 2^f$, with f the number of committed stop$(i; E')$ operations, as the next valid round number for instance $\mathcal{I}_i$.
16: **end event**

Figure 3.12: The *recovery algorithm* of RCC.

failure of the leader $\mathcal{L}_i$ and follows the steps of a view-change in P to (try to) replace $\mathcal{L}_i$. When the leader $\mathcal{L}_i$ receives **g** Failure messages, it can and must construct a valid stop-operation and reach consensus on this operation (Line 9 of Figure 3.12). After reaching consensus, each replica can recover to a common state of $\mathcal{I}_i$:

Theorem 3.9   *Consider RCC running in a system with* **n** *replicas. If* **n** > 3**f***, an instance* $\mathcal{I}_i$*,* $0 \le i < $ **m***, has a confirmed failure, and the last proposal of* $\mathcal{P}_i$ *committed by a good replica was in round* ρ*, then—whenever communication becomes reliable—the recovery protocol of Figure 3.12 will assure* *that all good replicas will recover the same state, which will include all proposals committed by good replicas before-or-at round ρ.*

An important property of this sketched recovery process is that recovery only affects the capabilities of the BCA instance that is stopped. All other BCA instances can concurrently propose transactions for current and for future rounds. Hence, the recovery algorithm adheres to the wait-free design goals D4 and D5. Furthermore, we reiterate that RCC uses separate instance of the coordinating consensus protocol for each instance $\mathcal{I}_i$, $1 \leq i \leq \mathbf{m}$. Hence, recovery of several instances can happen concurrently, which minimizes the time it takes to recover from several simultaneous primary failures and, consequently, minimizes the delay before a round can be executed during primary failures.

Confirmed failures not only happen due to malicious behavior. Instances can also fail due to periods of unreliable communication. To deal with this, we eventually restart any stopped instances. To prevent malicious primaries from continuously causing recovery of their instances, every failure will incur an exponentially growing restart penalty (Line 15 of Figure 3.12). The exact round in which an instance can resume operations can be determined deterministically from the history of committed stop-requests. When all instances have round failures due to unreliable communication (which can be detected from the history of stop-requests), any instance is allowed to resume operations in the earliest available round (after which all other instances are also required to resume operations).

Dealing with undetectable failures   As stated in Assumption A1, a malicious primary $\mathcal{P}_i$ of a BCA instance $\mathcal{I}_i$ is able to keep up-to-$\mathbf{f}$ good replicas in the dark without being detected. In normal primary-backup protocols, this is not a huge issue: at least $\mathbf{g} - \mathbf{f} > \mathbf{f}$ good replicas still committed transactions, and these replicas can execute and reliably inform the client of the outcome of execution. This is not the case in RCC and other forms of concurrent consensus, however, as seen in the following.

Example 3.10   Consider a system with $\mathbf{n} = 3\mathbf{f} + 1 = 7$ replicas. Assume that primaries $\mathcal{P}_1$ and $\mathcal{P}_2$ are malicious, while all other primaries are good. We partition the good replicas into three sets A_1, A_2, and B with $|A_1| = |A_2| = \mathbf{f}$ and $|B| = 1$. In round ρ, the malicious primary $\mathcal{P}_i$, $i \in \{1, 2\}$, proposes transaction $\langle \tau_i \rangle_{c_i}$ to only the good replicas in $A_i \cup B$. This situation is sketched in Figure 3.13. After all concurrent instances of BCA finish round ρ, we see that the replicas in A_1 have committed the proposal for $\langle \tau_1 \rangle_{c_1}$, the replicas in A_2 have committed the proposal for $\langle \tau_2 \rangle_{c_2}$, and only the replica in B has committed proposals for both $\langle \tau_1 \rangle_{c_1}$ and $\langle \tau_2 \rangle_{c_2}$. Hence, only the single replica in B can proceed with execution of round ρ. Notice that, due to Assumption A1, we consider all instances as finished successfully. If $\mathbf{n} \geq 10$ and $\mathbf{f} \geq 3$, this example attack can be generalized such that also the replica in B is missing at least a single client transaction.

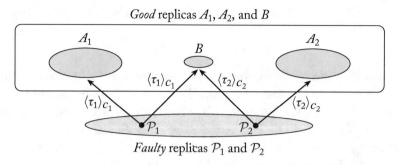

Figure 3.13: An attack possible when parallelizing BCA: malicious primaries can prevent good replicas from learning all client requests in a round, thereby preventing timely round execution. The faulty primary $\mathcal{P}_i$, $i \in \{1, 2\}$, does so by only letting good replicas $A_i \cup B$ participate in instance $\mathcal{I}_i$.

To deal with *in-the-dark* attacks of Example 3.10, we can run a standard checkpoint algorithm for each BCA instance (e.g., the checkpoint algorithm of Section 2.4.1 if using the Byzantine commit algorithm of PBFT): if the system does not reach confirmed failure of $\mathcal{P}_i$ in round ρ, $1 \le i \le \mathbf{m}$, then, by Assumptions A1 and A2, at-least-$\mathbf{g} - \mathbf{f}$ good replicas have committed the same transaction τ in round ρ of $\mathcal{I}_i$. Hence, by Assumption A3, a standard checkpoint algorithm that exchanges the state of these at-least-$\mathbf{g} - \mathbf{f}$ good replicas among all other replicas is sufficient to assure that all good replicas eventually reach the committed state for a proposal τ. We notice that these checkpoint algorithms can be run concurrently with the operations of BCA instances, thereby adhering to the wait-free design goals D4 and D5.

To reduce the cost of checkpoints, typical consensus systems only perform checkpoints after every x-th round for some system-defined constant x (see Section 2.4). Due to in-the-dark attacks, applying such a strategy to RCC means choosing between execution latency and throughput. Consequently, RCC performs checkpoints on a dynamic *per-need basis*: if replica R receives $\mathbf{g} - \mathbf{f}$ claims of failure of primaries (via the Failure messages of the recovery protocol) in round ρ and R itself finished round ρ for all its instances, then it will participate in any attempt for a checkpoint for round ρ. Hence, if an in-the-dark attack affects more than $\mathbf{f}$ distinct good replicas in round ρ, then a successful checkpoint will be made and all good replicas recover from the attack, reach the committed state for all transaction proposals in round ρ, and execute all these transactions.

Using Theorem 3.9 to deal with detectable failures and using checkpoint protocols to deal with replicas in-the-dark, we conclude that RCC adheres to design goal D1.

Theorem 3.11   *Consider RCC running in a system with $\mathbf{n}$ replicas. If $\mathbf{n} > 3\mathbf{f}$, then RCC provides consensus in periods in which communication is reliable.*

Client interactions with RCC   To maximize performance, it is important that every instance proposes distinct client requests, as proposing the same client requests several times would reduce throughput. RCC is designed with faulty clients in mind, hence RCC cannot expect cooperation of clients to assure that they send their requests to only a single primary.

To assure that every instance proposes distinct client requests, the design of RCC is optimized for the case in which there are always many more concurrent clients than replicas in the system. In this setting, RCC assigns every client C to a single primary $\mathcal{P}_i$, $1 \leq i \leq \mathbf{m} = \mathbf{n}$, such that only instance $\mathcal{I}_i$ can propose client requests of C. For this design to work in *all cases*, RCC needs to solve two issues, however RCC needs to deal with situations in which primaries do not receive client requests (e.g., during downtime periods in which only few clients make requests), and RCC needs to deal with faulty primaries that refuse to propose requests of some clients.

First, if there are less concurrent clients than replicas in the system, e.g., when demand for services is low, then RCC still needs to process client requests correctly, but it can do so without optimally utilizing resources available, as this would not impact throughput in this case due to the low demands. If a primary $\mathcal{P}_i$, $1 \leq i \leq \mathbf{m}$, does not have requests to propose in any round ρ and $\mathcal{P}_i$ detects that other BCA instances are proposing for round ρ (e.g., as it receives proposals), then $\mathcal{P}_i$ proposes a small no-op-request instead.

Second, to deal with a primary $\mathcal{P}_i$, $1 \leq i \leq \mathbf{m}$, that refuses to propose requests of some clients, RCC takes a two-step approach. First, RCC incentivizes malicious primaries to *not refuse* services, as otherwise they will be detected faulty and loose the ability to propose requests altogether. To detect failure of $\mathcal{P}_i$, RCC uses standard techniques to enable a client C to *force* execution of a transaction τ (see Section 2.5). Second, RCC needs to deal with primaries that are unwilling or incapable of proposing requests of C, e.g., when the primary crashes. To do so, C can request to be reassigned to another instance $\mathcal{I}_j$, $1 \leq j \leq \mathbf{m}$, and RCC is designed to deal with any attempts of malicious clients that try to get assigned to several instances at once.

3.6   IMPROVING RESILIENCE

As long as communication is sufficiently reliable, PBFT and many other primary-backup consensus protocols are able to provide consensus in a Byzantine environment even if the current primary is malicious. This does not imply that consensus protocols such as PBFT are immune to malicious behavior, however.

Traditional primary-backup consensus protocols rely heavily on the operations of their primary. Although these protocols are designed to deal with primaries that *completely fail* proposing client requests, they are not designed to deal with many other types of malicious behavior. We consider two types of such malicious behavior: *throttling attacks* and *ordering attacks*.

3.6.1   THROTTLING ATTACKS

A prime example of malicious behavior by primaries that is not detected by traditional primary-backup consensus are attempts to maliciously throttle throughput. The primary sets the pace at which the system processes transactions by setting the pace by which it proposes `PrePrepare` messages. By the results of the previous sections, we already know that a consensus round of PBFT on a proposal takes at least Δ_{PBFT} to complete. Hence, good replicas must use *time-outs* substantially larger than Δ_{PBFT} to detect malicious behavior of the primary and trigger view-changes. Say that the replicas use a time-out of $c\Delta_{\text{PBFT}}$, $c > 1$. To minimize throughput, the primary can throttle the pace by which it proposes `PrePrepare` messages so that a single round is completed every $c\Delta_{\text{PBFT}} - \epsilon$, for some small value ϵ (e.g., $\epsilon = 0.1$ ms), resulting in a throughput of

$$T_{\text{PBFT-throttled}} = \frac{1}{c\Delta_{\text{PBFT}} - \epsilon} \approx \frac{T_{\text{PBFT}}}{c}.$$

By doing so, the throughput is severely reduced (and, furthermore, out-of-order processing is completely prevented).

There are two common approaches toward dealing with throttling attacks. First, one can use *concurrent consensus* (see Section 3.5.4) to reduce the impact of any particular primaries and, at the same time, enable detection of throttling primaries. In an environment in which multiple consensus instances operate on the same replicas, each instance has the same resources available and, hence, should achieve roughly the same throughput when sufficient requests are available. Hence, any malicious primary that throttles its instance can be detected in doing so by comparing its throughput with the other instances. This approach is put in practice by RBFT [17, 19] and RCC [121, 122]. In RBFT, concurrent consensus is *not* used to improve maximum throughput, however, but is only used to enable performance monitoring of the main primary and, in this way, enable detection of throttling primaries. The RCC paradigm goes one step further by utilizing the concurrent consensus instances not only for performance monitoring, but also for improving maximum throughput, this at the cost of the complexity of concurrent consensus.

Second, one can use *primary rotation* in which the primary is frequently replaced by the next primary (e.g., after every r consensus rounds). Such primary rotation will *not* prevent or reduce malicious behavior by faulty primaries, but will limit the time in which faulty primaries are in control. Indeed, as typical consensus-based systems have $\mathbf{n} > \mathbf{3f}$, primary rotation assures that at least two-thirds of the rounds are proposed by good primaries (which try to maintain maximum throughput). Primary rotation is much easier to implement than concurrent consensus, as it can be implemented on top of any primary-backup consensus protocol without further changes. This simplicity comes at a cost, however: primary rotation requires handing over control from one primary to the next, which necessitates a *view-change step* in which the next primary is able to derive the state of the system at the start of its view. Consequently, primary rotation introduces dependencies between consecutive views, thereby sharply reducing the ability to employ out-of-order processing to only within the r consecutive rounds of each single view. Furthermore, we notice that primary rotation will—over time—evenly spread out the cost of consensus over all replicas, but, due to the dependencies between consecutive views, only one primary will be active at any time. Hence, primary rotation will not resolve the limitations of primary-backup consensus, as discussed in Section 3.5. Rotating primaries are part of several consensus protocols, including HOTSTUFF [249] and SPINNING [237].

In practice, throttling performance can even happen with good primaries. As argued in Sections 3.2.2 and 3.5, the primary requires much more network resources than the other replicas and, hence, the throughput of a primary-backup consensus system is mainly determined by the network resources available to the primary. Attackers can use this observation by targeting the primary via a *denial-of-service*-style attack, e.g., by sending spurious messages to the primary. Even if the primary recognizes such an attack, it has spent resources (network bandwidth, computational power, and memory) to do so, thereby reducing throughput. Notice that—in the worst case—this can even lead to failure of a good primary to propose transactions in a timely manner. Preventing or alleviating denial-of-service attacks is hard at the level of the consensus protocol, as large-scale attacks require measures at the network level to alleviate. A properly spread-out deployment of replicas can reduce the effectiveness (or increase the costs) of such attacks, however. By spreading out replicas in a high-bandwidth wide-area-network, an attack on a single replica might take that replica out of the system (by making its communication unreliable), but should not impact communication for other replicas. In this sense, consensus-based systems can provide *some* resilience against denial-of-service.

3.6.2   ORDERING ATTACKS

Primaries not only determine the throughput of consensus, but also completely determine the order in which client requests are processed. Under normal operations, good primaries will simply choose an arbitrary ordering (e.g., based on the arrival time of requests). A malicious primary can choose an ordering that best fits its own interests.

Example 3.12   We extend Example 2.29. We consider client requests of the form:

$$\text{transfer}(A, B, n, m) := \text{if } \text{amount}(A) > n \text{ then } \text{withdraw}(A, m); \text{ deposit}(B, m).$$

Let $\tau_1 = \text{transfer}(\text{Alice}, \text{Bob}, 500, 200)$ and $\tau_2 = \text{transfer}(\text{Bob}, \text{Eve}, 400, 300)$. Before processing these requests, the balance for Alice is 800, for Bob 300, and for Eve 100. If τ_1 is executed before τ_2, then Bob will receive sufficient funds from Alice to enable a transfer from Bob to Eve. Otherwise, if τ_2 is executed before τ_1, then Bob will not have sufficient funds and no transfer from Bob to Eve is performed. In Figure 3.14, we summarize the results of either first executing τ_1 or first executing τ_2.

As is clear from the above example, the order of execution of requests influences the outcome of execution. As primaries choose the ordering of requests, a malicious primary can choose an ordering whose outcome benefits its own interests, e.g., formulate targeted attacks to affect the execution of requests of some clients.

To reduce the effectiveness of ordering attacks, one needs to reduce the influence faulty primaries have on the order in which requests are executed. One way to do so is by utilizing

	Initial Balance	First τ_1, Then τ_2		First τ_2, Then τ_1	
		After τ_1	After τ_2	After τ_2	After τ_1
Alice	800	600	600	800	600
Bob	300	500	200	300	500
Eve	100	100	400	100	100

Figure 3.14: Illustration of the influence of execution order on the outcome: switching around requests affects the transfer of τ_2.

concurrent consensus, as proposed by the RCC paradigm [121, 122]. Remember from Section 3.5.4 that RCC operates **m** Byzantine commit algorithms concurrently. If **m** > **f**, then at least a single of these instances will be good and, hence, at least a single request per concurrent round will be proposed by a good replica. RCC uses this information to select a different permutation of the order of execution in every round in such a way that this ordering is practically impossible to predict or influence by faulty replicas. Note that for any sequence S of $k = |S|$ requests, there exist $k!$ distinct permutations. We write $P(S)$ to denote these permutations of S. To deterministically select one of these permutations, we construct a function that maps an integer $h \in \{0, \dots, k! - 1\}$ to a unique permutation in $P(S)$. Then we discuss how replicas will uniformly pick h. As $|P(S)| = k!$, we can construct the following bijection $f_S : \{0, \dots, k! - 1\} \to P(S)$:

$$f_S(i) = \begin{cases} S & \text{if } |S| = 1; \\ f_{S \setminus S[q]}(r) || S[q] & \text{if } |S| > 1, \end{cases}$$

in which $q = i \operatorname{div} (|S| - 1)!$ is the quotient and $r = i \bmod (|S| - 1)!$ is the remainder of integer division by $(|S| - 1)!$. Using induction on the size of S, we can prove the following.

Lemma 3.13 f_S *is a bijection from* $\{0, \dots, |S|! - 1\}$ *to all possible permutations of* S.

Let S be the sequence of all transactions accepted in round ρ, ordered on increasing instance. The replicas uniformly pick $h = \operatorname{digest}(S) \bmod (k! - 1)$, in which $\operatorname{digest}(S)$ is a *strong cryptographic hash function* that maps an arbitrary value v to a numeric digest value in a bounded range such that it is practically impossible to find another value S', $S \neq S'$, with $\operatorname{digest}(S) = \operatorname{digest}(S')$. When at least one primary is non-malicious (**m** > **f**), the final value h is only known after completion of round ρ and it is practically impossible to predictably influence this value. After selecting h, all replicas execute the transactions in S in the order given by $f_S(h)$.

To the best of our knowledge, only RCC partially mitigates ordering attacks using the above approach, although similar methods can be applied to other concurrent consensus protocols and primary rotation protocols.

3.7 CONCLUDING REMARKS

In the previous chapters, we provided an in-depth explanation of PBFT. The normal-case of PBFT consists of a *prepare* phase, during which the primary assigns a sequence number to a single client request and replicas reach agreement on this assignment, and a *commit* phase, which ensures the agreed-upon sequence number and client request survive view changes and primary replacement. In this chapter, we analyzed the key design choices that affect PBFT's performance, complexity, and resiliency. Communication bandwidth and latency[1] dictates the performance profile of any PBFT-like consensus protocol that heavily relies on all-to-all communication for reaching an agreement. The latency determines how fast we can assign a sequence number, while the bandwidth determines how many sequence numbers can be assigned per unit of time.

PBFT is a three-phase protocol *preprepare-prepare-commit* and the message delay prolongs each phase resulting in a long sequential pipeline. A simple way to amortize the delay is to achieve consensus in batches, namely, in each round of PBFT, a batch of consecutive sequence number is agreed upon as opposed to generating one sequence number at a time [124]. Nevertheless, batching neither solves the problem of sequential consensus, nor addresses the underlying challenge of underutilized pipeline bandwidth. For any primary-backup consensus protocol with a stable leader (those without primary rotation), a new round of consensus can begin without the need to wait for the completion of the last round, referred to as *out-of-order processing*. In theory, this may provide full utilization of the network bandwidth of replicas. But despite replicas being homogeneous, their assigned tasks are not [124]. The primary is given the task of creating batches of messages and, more importantly, to forward the content of the client's message to all replicas while the subsequent *prepare* and *commit* phases only include a digest of the message. Forwarding the client's message quickly saturates the bandwidth of the primary, thereby leaving the bandwidth of the other replicas underutilized.

One approach to improve the average utilization of replica bandwidth is by adopting primary rotation (e.g., as in HotStuff [249]), which may come at the cost of losing out-of-order processing, thus, enforcing sequential consensus. This sequential choice not only increases the latency, but it also results in loss of bandwidth. Instead, one can conceive a *concurrent design* in which every replica serves as primary to assign sequence numbers in their pre-determined slice of time. Concurrent consensus designs do in fact solve the underutilized bandwidth problem at the cost of a more complex recovery algorithm that must deal with new kinds of attacks such as collusion of primaries (cf. RCC [121, 122], MirBFT [225]). A notable approach is RCC, a resilient concurrent consensus paradigm that transforms any single-leader BFT protocol into a multi-primary concurrent design. The hallmark of RCC is a wait-free design such that the detection and recovery of any failed consensus instances do not hinder the progress of concurrent instances. The independent instance recovery in RCC rests upon a simple yet powerful idea of

---

[1]A communication channel may be visualized as a pipe, in which bandwidth translates to the diameter of the pipe (how much fluid can be pushed in a unit of time), while latency translates to the length of pipe (how much time it takes to push water from source to destination).

only *temporariliy stopping* and *not replacing* the primary of a failed instance, which is carried out by invoking a separate consensus instance.

Another effective approach to address the communication limitation is to exploit the topological hierarchy in a global-scale network by distinguishing between global and local communication. We can adopt a model in which a full-fledged consensus is only carried out locally and only the result of consensus is reliably communicated globally (cf. GEoBFT [123]). Another toolkit to reduce communication is to adopt more advanced cryptographic methods such as threshold signature to reliably aggregate and broadcast messages to avoid quadratic all-to-all communication (cf. PoE, [120], HotStuff [249], SBFT [109]).

The next step to reduce communication is to rethink the need of having all three phases of PBFT. We considered two complementary approaches: speculative and optimistic executions. The speculation may occur at either the *preprepare* or *prepare* phases without waiting until after the *commit* phase. Normally, when the non-speculative execution happens after the *commit* phase, it is known that at least a quorum of replicas has passed through the *prepare* phase so any committed messages can always be recovered. Thus, as long as a single honest replica reaches a committed state then that message can be announced as *committed*. This would require the client to observe $f + 1$ such commitments to ensure the existence of at least one honest replica. But if the execution occurs speculatively after the *prepare* phase (dropping the *commit* phase) then to simulate the same outcome as the non-speculative case, the client would need to observe $n - f \geq 2f + 1$ prepared states (cf. PoE [120]). Essentially, this translates to having an honest replica reaching the committed state, satisfying the commitment criteria of PBFT. Now, we can push speculation to the extreme, albeit resulting in an unsafe protocol, by performing speculation after the *preprepare* phase and without knowing the state of any other replicas. In such scenarios, clients must unanimously observe endorsement from all $n \geq 3f + 1$ replicas, and we further must assume that clients are trusted and non-malicious, weakening the PBFT's fault model (cf. Zyzzyva [2, 3, 161–163]). Furthermore, opportunistic protocols may offer two paths: first attempting a fast optimistic path (e.g., one that speculatively executes directly after the preprepare phase) and only resorting to a slower multi-phase path if the optimistic path failed (cf. FaB [2, 3, 182, 183], SBFT [109], and Zyzzyva).

A final optimization discussed in this chapter is to increase resiliency and reduce message complexity by employing trusted component to sign messages, *ensuring replica's private-keys are not stolen, shared, or leaked,* and assign sequence number, *ensuring the assignment of the sequence number cannot be tampered with and no two client requests can be assigned to the same sequence number.* Through the use of trusted hardware, PBFT would only require $n \geq 2f + 1$ replicas without the need of having the *prepare* phase because no two client requests can be assigned to the same sequence number within a view (cf. MinBFT [239], CheapBFT [151]).

3.8   BIBLIOGRAPHIC NOTES

There are many different approaches toward consensus protocols, both in the literature and in use in real-worlds systems. Consequently, we can only scratch the surface and as such we provided a high-level overview of the techniques consensus protocols employ and the trade-offs they make. Next, we provide an overview of the techniques we explored and consensus protocols utilizing these techniques.

Batching, out-of-order processing, and overlapping communication phases are all considered in the original design of PBFT [54–56]. Threshold signatures have been considered in many consensus protocols, e.g., GEOBFT [123], HOTSTUFF [249], LINBFT [248], PoE [120], SBFT [109], and STEWARD [10, 11]. Specific threshold signature schemes have been developed for popular public-key cryptography schemes such as RSA [222] and elliptic-curves [20].

Speculative execution is pioneered in the recently-proposed design of PoE [120], whereas optimistic execution is a core part of protocols such as ALIPH [17, 18, 113], FaB [2, 3, 182, 183], and ZYZZYVA [2, 3, 161–163]. Although optimistic execution and speculative execution seem related, this is not the case. On the one hand, speculative execution works in all situations (even if replicas are faulty), while, on the other hand, optimistic execution distinguishes between an optimistic path (when replicas are good) and a fallback path when replicas are faulty. Unfortunately, distinguishing between an optimistic path and a fallback path makes recovery of failures tricky and, consequently, optimistic protocols are vulnerable to subtle issues [2, 3].

Trusted components and proactive recovery have been used in PBFT [54–56], whereas protocols such as 2FBC [71], A2M [63], CHEAPBFT [151], FASTBFT [174], and MINBFT [239] use trusted components to improve resilience.

Gossiping has been used in FASTBFT [174] to reduce communication costs and gossiping has also been used in Byzantine broadcast protocols, e.g., the protocol of Guerraoui et al. [114]. Furthermore, GEOBFT [123] and STEWARD [10, 11] both use hierarchical location-based communication. The ALGORAND protocol proposed to use only a subset of the replicas for consensus in a uniform environment [59, 107], whereas GEOBFT [123] and STEWARD [10, 11] restrict consensus to location-aware subsets of the replicas. Variations of concurrent consensus have been used by many protocols, including EBAWA [238], MIRBFT [225], OMADA [90, 91], RCC [121, 122], RBFT [17, 19], and SAREK [171]. Finally, primary rotation has been used in protocols such as HOTSTUFF [249] and SPINNING [237].

In this and the previous chapter, we primarily focused on primary-backup consensus protocols based on the influential design of PBFT, which allowed us to explore many different techniques and consensus protocols in practical use. Not all consensus protocols are based on PBFT or share a similar primary-backup design, however. The literature has many other techniques and consensus protocols with aims that we did not address, some of which can certainly find their place in future systems. Next, we shall provide a brief overview.

Crash-fault tolerance   Consensus-based systems are resilient to many types of failures that not only includes simple crashes (e.g., replica failure, network failure), but also includes Byzantine behavior (e.g., sending incorrect messages due to software error or due to malicious behavior). As we have seen, this resilience does not come for free: PBFT and other consensus protocols are complex and need considerable resources to provide high transaction throughputs. Applications that do not require such high levels of resilience can opt to settle for less-resilient systems, e.g., systems that can only deal with replica or network crashes. Such systems can employ PBFT or other consensus protocols to provide transaction replication and ordering, but these systems can also use specialized *crash-fault tolerant consensus protocols*. Choosing for crash-fault tolerance greatly simplifies the problem of consensus: typical crash-fault tolerant systems can tolerate f faulty replicas with only $n > 2f$ replicas (see Section 1.3.5), while not requiring any costly cryptographic primitives or trusted components.

A well-known crash-fault tolerant consensus protocol is PAXOS [165, 166], which itself has inspired a large family of crash-fault tolerant consensus protocols (e.g., [42, 180, 190, 252, 252]). Many of the techniques discussed in this chapter have also been applied to variants of PAXOS. Examples include EPAXOS [190], which explores *concurrent consensus*, and MENCIUS [180], which explores *primary rotation*. A few works study consensus in mixed failure models in which not all faulty replicas behave fully arbitrarily (e.g., can only crash or only try to prevent non-divergence). A recent example of such a consensus protocol is FLEXIBLE BFT [177].

Synchronous communication   Another direction toward simplifying consensus is by assuming *synchronous communication* in which all messages are always reliably delivered within a bounded time. Designing for synchronous communication simplifies the problem of consensus drastically, as replicas can rely on message delay assumptions to determine whether messages have been sent to them. Consequently, synchronous consensus can tolerate f faulty replicas with only $f + 1$ replicas, while not requiring any trusted components (most practical systems still require $n > 2f$ replicas, as otherwise clients have no way to determine whether they are served by faulty or good replicas; see also Section 1.3.5). Furthermore, synchronous communication can enable consensus with very low communication costs [156]. Unfortunately, synchronous communication is rather impractical in most deployments of replicated systems, as networks naturally have to deal with message loss and delays. Recent examples of consensus protocols that aim at environments with forms of synchronous communication include SYNC HOTSTUFF [5] and FLEXIBLE BFT [177].

Asynchronous communication   Most practical consensus protocols, including PBFT, provide weak consensus and operate in a *partial synchronous* environment: these consensus protocols can operate in an asynchronous environment while guaranteeing non-divergence, but require sufficiently reliable communication to provide termination. By utilizing such partial synchrony, these systems can provide consensus in practical environments under normal network conditions, this without the complications of dealing with all forms of asynchronous communication.

As the alternative, one can design fully *asynchronous consensus protocols*. A recent example is HONEYBADGERBFT [186], a consensus protocol that is designed explicitly for asynchronous communication without relying on explicit timing assumptions to guarantee termination. As HONEYBADGERBFT is fully asynchronous, it is a probabilistic protocol that has a high probability of success. Even though HONEYBADGERBFT shares little similarities with primary-backup consensus protocols such as PBFT, we still see common design themes. First, HONEYBADGERBFT strongly relies on *batching* to reduce communication complexity and uses *concurrent consensus*—in which all replicas propose transactions—to both improve performance and improve resilience. Furthermore, HONEYBADGERBFT relies on *threshold signatures* to prevent ordering attacks. To do so, all replicas in HONEYBADGERBFT have access to a common public-key K, which can be used to encrypt and hide their transactions τ. While reaching agreement on such an encrypted transaction $E(\tau)$, the replicas exchange their local decryption share. Only after reaching agreement, will each replica have sufficient decryption shares to decrypt the proposal and obtain τ. This approach helps to hide transactions until after agreement is reached, which will also prevent interference by malicious replicas to affect execution order.

Design-wise, HONEYBADGERBFT is the composition of several distributed protocols. More recent works have build upon this design by proposing consensus protocols obtained by replacing some of these components, e.g., the BEAT family [86] of consensus protocols and the Dumbo consensus protocol [115].

Concurrent execution   To model the performance of PBFT and other primary-backup consensus protocols in Section 3.1, we assumed that computational resources are abundant and that the practical throughput is upper-bounded by network resources. This assumption does typically hold when individual transactions are small or network resources are scarce. In systems that execute complex transactions and that are employed in high-performance networks, the sequential execution of transactions can become a bottleneck.

On modern many-core systems, the main way to deal with bottlenecks due to the sequential execution of transactions is by parallelizing execution. Unfortunately, parallelizing transaction execution is a complex problem on itself as the individual operations of transactions can interfere with each other. Such interference even happens in non-replicated systems and to deal with unwanted interference, such systems typically use elaborate *concurrency control* mechanisms. In fully replicated systems, parallel execution is further complicated, as the parallel execution of transactions at distinct replicas can result in these replicas ending up executing transactions in different orders, due to which they can end up maintaining distinct states (see Example 3.12).

A promising approach toward parallel execution in consensus-based systems is proposed by EVE [152]. EVE processes transactions in batches. At each replica, each batch of transactions is processed by a *mixer* that analyzes the transactions and partitions them into per-thread batches. This partitioning is deterministic, ensuring that all replicas end up with the same partitioning. Next, these per-thread batches are executed in parallel, and the transactions in each per-thread batch are executed sequentially by some thread. If the mixer is *perfect*, then the partitioning of the batch of transactions will yield per-thread batches that are independent of each other in the sense that execution of transactions in one batch do not affect the execution of transactions in any other batch. For example, in a banking application, transactions can be partitioned based on the accounts they affect. With a perfect mixer, each replica will end up with the same final state after executing all transactions in the batch.

For many use cases, it is hard or even impossible to construct a perfect mixer, however. In these use cases, replicas in EVE can end up with distinct final states after execution. To deal with this, EVE proposes to perform a *verification* round after execution, in which the replicas attempt to reach agreement on the final state after execution of the batch. To enable practical verification of state, EVE proposes a Merkle-tree based representation of state updates that allows for a concise representation of the updates performed by executing a batch. Finally, the verification round can have two outcomes: either the mixer was perfect-enough to assure a majority of all good replicas reached the same final state, in which case this state is transferred to all other replicas, or the mixer failed, in which case the system falls back to a deterministic sequential execution of the batch.

Quorum-based systems Although consensus is a powerful general-purpose tool to build resilient systems, not all applications require the guarantees provided by the fully replicated nature of consensus. For some less-demanding applications, quorum systems—in which the majority of all replicas hold the same written values—already suffice. On the one hand, quorum operations are simpler than the fully replicated ordered state-machine replication provided by consensus-based systems due to which quorum operations can typically be implemented with much lower cost than consensus. On the other hand, quorum operations do not provide the strong guarantees of consensus and their usage in applications requires careful design (e.g., to deal with concurrent reads and writes). To enable quorum systems in a byzantine environment, many distinct highly efficient Byzantine quorum protocols have been proposed and applied in real-world complex systems [1, 23, 73, 178, 179, 184].

CHAPTER 4

Toward Scalable Blockchains

In the previous two chapters we reviewed the basic technologies necessary to operate a permissioned blockchain. First, we consider PBFT, a practical and efficient consensus protocol. Then, we investigated clever engineering and implementation techniques that can be applied to PBFT (and other consensus protocols) to yield systems that can process tens-of-thousands transactions per second within a data center.

Although these results are a promising starting point for the development of permissioned blockchains, they are not sufficient for the development of scalable high-performance systems. Indeed, a close inspection of the traditional fully replicated design of permissioned blockchains shows that this design lacks *scalability*. First, permissioned blockchains lack *storage scalability*, as all replicas in the blockchain store the entire ledger. Second, permissioned blockchains lack *throughput scalability*, as there is no way to increase throughput beyond the limitations of individual replicas as adding replicas to a permissioned blockchain will increase the cost of consensus and always decrease performance.

This rules out the usage of traditional fully replicated PBFT-style permissioned blockchains for applications that deal with large amounts of data and transactions. In this chapter, we identify techniques to deal with these scalability issues. Specifically, we shall consider the following.

1. First, we will examine the fully replicated design of permissioned blockchains and show that the non-scalable fully replicated storage of the *ledger* can be replaced by a scalable fault-resilient storage of the ledger using *information dispersal* [137].

2. Next, we will explain how to improve scalability for read-only workloads by either reducing the cost of consensus for such workloads (small read-only transactions) or by splitting these workloads off to independent systems (large read-only workloads that affect most data).

3. Then, to truly tackle scalability, we will introduce *cluster-sending* [135, 136, 139], a core technique that enable *independent permissioned blockchains* to reliably communicate with each other. Such communication enables cooperation and coordinate between blockchains.

4. As the first application of cluster-sending, we will present the design of RESILIENTDB [123], a fully replicated system designed to operate in an environment where replicas are operated in geo-aware clusters that are dispersed over geologically large distances.

5. Finally, as the second application of cluster-sending, we will apply to *sharding architectures* for permissioned blockchain systems in which each shard is operated as an independent permissioned blockchain.

4.1 TOWARD SCALABLE LEDGER STORAGE

State-of-the-art blockchain systems use fully replicated designs in which every replica R maintains a full copy of the ledger $\mathcal{L}_R$. For most applications, replicas only need the current state to execute transactions, however, and do not need access to the full history of all transactions stored in $\mathcal{L}_R$.

Example 4.1 Consider a federated inventory management system used by several companies to keep track of their inventories and of transactions between them. To decide upon updates on the data, replicas only need to be able to validate updates, e.g., a transfer of ownership from company A to company B of a product is only a valid update if A originally owned the product. Hence, for validation, it is not necessary that replicas maintain full copies of the journal ledger, they only need the status of the current inventory, a much smaller dataset.

To further illustrate the necessity of storage scalability in blockchains, we only have to examine the permissionless Bitcoin blockchain. Although bitcoin has a low transaction throughput of only a handful of transactions per second, the size of the Bitcoin *ledger* is currently already exceeding 283 GB and has grown by 31 GB over the last half year. As we have seen in the previous chapter, the permissioned blockchains our work focusses on can easily process hundreds to thousands transactions per second. Hence, the size of the ledger maintained by permissioned blockchains can grow even more rapidly.

In this section, we shall show how storage of the ledger can be made scalable without changing the resilience of the system against Byzantine failures [137]. We make ledger storage scalable using an *information dispersal algorithm*. First, in Section 4.1.1, we introduce information dispersal. Then, in Section 4.1.2, we introduce the rules by which replicas determine what portion of the ledger they need to store. Next, in Section 4.1.3, we describe *brute-force* techniques by which (parts of) the original ledger can be reconstructed, even in the presence of faulty replicas. Finally, in Section 4.1.4, we describe computationally efficient reconstruction techniques that only introduce a minor storage overhead to the presented scalable ledger storage scheme.

4.1.1 INFORMATION DISPERSAL

We use an *information dispersal algorithm* that is able to *encode* any value v with storage size $\|v\|$ into $\mathbf{n}$ pieces v_i, $0 \le i < \mathbf{n}$, such that v can be *decoded* from every set of $\mathbf{g}$ distinct pieces. We say that an information dispersal algorithm is *optimal* when each piece v_i has size $\|v_i\| \le \left\lceil \frac{\|v\|}{\mathbf{g}} \right\rceil$. Hence, the minimal number of pieces necessary for recovering v by decoding, $\mathbf{g}$ pieces, have a combined storage size of $\mathbf{g} \left\lceil \frac{\|v\|}{\mathbf{g}} \right\rceil \approx \|v\|$. The information dispersal algorithm (IDA) of Rabin provides these properties [8, 9, 213].

We assume that each good replica R has a unique identifier $0 \leq \mathrm{id}(\mathsf{R}) < \mathbf{n}$ and is equipped with IDA. We write $\mathrm{slice}_\mathsf{R}(v)$, for any value v, to denote the $\mathrm{id}(\mathsf{R})$-th piece $v_{\mathrm{id}(\mathsf{R})}$ obtained by encoding v. With these assumptions and notations, we have $\|\mathrm{slice}_\mathsf{R}(v)\| \leq \left\lceil \frac{\|v\|}{\mathbf{g}} \right\rceil$.

Example 4.2 Consider replicas $\mathsf{R}_0, \mathsf{R}_1, \mathsf{R}_2$, and B such that B is faulty. Hence, $\mathbf{g} = 3$ and $\mathbf{f} = 1$. Let v be a piece of data. When using the encode step of IDA, we obtain pieces v_0, v_1, v_2, v_3 with $\|v_0\| = \|v_1\| = \|v_2\| = \|v_3\| = \left\lceil \frac{\|v\|}{3} \right\rceil$. Consequently, $\mathrm{slice}_{\mathsf{R}_0}(v) = v_0$, $\mathrm{slice}_{\mathsf{R}_1}(v) = v_1$, $\mathrm{slice}_{\mathsf{R}_2}(v) = v_2$, and, finally, $\mathrm{slice}_\mathsf{B}(v) = v_3$.

Now consider any outside observer. Upon obtaining any three valid and distinct pieces, the observer can use the decode step of IDA to reconstruct v. As the replicas $\mathsf{R}_0, \mathsf{R}_1$, and R_2 are good, the observer will always be able to obtain v_0, v_1, and v_2. Hence, the observer can reconstruct v. We notice that $\|v_0\| + \|v_1\| + \|v_2\| = 3 \left\lceil \frac{\|v\|}{3} \right\rceil \approx \|v\|$.

4.1.2 ENCODING THE LEDGER

We will use IDA to encode the ledger and assign each replica only a single piece of this encoded ledger. To assure that IDA will encode parts of the ledger into pieces of $\frac{1}{\mathbf{g}}$-th the size, we need to assure that we encode large-enough parts of the ledger. To do so, every replica R is instructed to collect blocks of $\mathbf{n}$ ledger updates, encode each such block $\mathbb{B}$, and store only the resulting slice $\mathrm{slice}_\mathsf{R}(\mathbb{B})$. Notice that each replica will store only a single slice (of size $\left\lceil \frac{\|\mathbb{B}\|}{\mathbf{g}} \right\rceil$): the replica R will store only the $\mathrm{id}(\mathsf{R})$-th piece resulting from the information dispersal encoding step. The pseudo-code for this encoding step can be found in Figure 4.1. We refer to Figure 4.5 for a schematic representation of how the ledger is stored.

To allow reconstruction of $\mathbb{B}$ and to validate the correctness of such a reconstructed block, replicas will include a *checksum* of $\mathbb{B}$. The exact type of checksum used determines the computational complexity of decoding and the storage complexity of these checksums: in Section 4.1.3, we describe decoding using checksums with a size of $\mathcal{O}(1)$ that requires worst-case $\binom{\mathbf{n}}{\mathbf{g}}$ IDA-decoding steps, and in Section 4.1.4, we describe decoding using checksums with a size of $\mathcal{O}(\log \mathbf{n})$ that requires worst-case only one IDA-decoding step.

Theorem 4.3 *Consider the storage scheme of Figure 4.1 running at replica R after R appends the ρ-th decision, $\rho \geq 1$, to $\mathcal{L}_\mathsf{R}$. After this step, R stores $\lfloor \frac{\rho}{\mathbf{n}} \rfloor$ slices with a total size of $\mathcal{O}(c(\frac{\rho}{\mathbf{n}}) + \frac{\|\mathcal{L}_\mathsf{R}\|}{\mathbf{g}})$, in which c is the size of a checksum.*

Proof. Notice that R only stores slices after every i-th append to the ledger, $i \geq 1$ and $i \mod \mathbf{n} = 0$. Hence, after the ρ-th decision, R will have stored $m = \lfloor \frac{\rho}{\mathbf{n}} \rfloor$ slices. Now consider the j-th

```
1: event R appends a new decision to L_R do
2:    if L_R ≠ [ ] and |L_R| mod n = 0 then
3:       B := L_R[|L_R| − n : |L_R|].
4:       s, c := slice_R(B), checksum_R(B).
5:       Discard B and store (s, c).
6:    end if
7: end event
```

Figure 4.1: The IDA step used to store the ledger at good replica R.

block of $\mathbf{n}$ appended transactions, the block $\mathbb{B} = \mathcal{L}_R[(j-1)\mathbf{n} : j\mathbf{n}]$, $1 \leq j \leq m$. For this block, replica R will store the pair $(\texttt{slice}_R(\mathbb{B}), \texttt{checksum}_R(\mathbb{B}))$. We assume that $\texttt{checksum}_R(\mathbb{B})$ has size $\gamma = \Theta(c)$ and we conclude that the m pairs stored by R have size σ at most

$$
\begin{aligned}
\sigma &\leq \sum_{1 \leq i \leq m} (\gamma + \|\texttt{slice}_R(\mathcal{L}_R[(i-1)\mathbf{n} : i\mathbf{n}])\|) \\
&\leq \gamma m + \sum_{1 \leq i \leq m} \left\lceil \frac{\|\mathcal{L}_R[(i-1)\mathbf{n} : i\mathbf{n}]\|}{\mathbf{g}} \right\rceil \leq \gamma m + \sum_{1 \leq i \leq m} \left(1 + \frac{\|\mathcal{L}_R[(i-1)\mathbf{n} : i\mathbf{n}]\|}{\mathbf{g}}\right) \\
&\leq \gamma m + m + \frac{\|\mathcal{L}_R[0 : \mathbf{n}m]\|}{\mathbf{g}} \leq m(\gamma + 1) + \frac{\|\mathcal{L}_R\|}{\mathbf{g}} = \mathcal{O}(c(\frac{\rho}{\mathbf{n}}) + \frac{\|\mathcal{L}_R\|}{\mathbf{g}}). \qquad \square
\end{aligned}
$$

4.1.3   RECONSTRUCTING THE LEDGER (SIMPLE CHECKSUMS)

In the previous section, we showed how IDA can be used to store a ledger in a scalable manner. This IDA-based storage scheme is only of use if the original ledger can be reconstructed, however. Next, we show how one can reliably reconstruct the ledger from only the encoded pieces stored at the replicas.

To deal with faulty replicas, we will use *simple checksums* $\texttt{checksum}_R(\mathbb{B}) = \text{digest}(\mathbb{B})$ to verify whether reconstructed blocks are valid. In this, $\text{digest}(\cdot)$ is a *collision-resistant hash function* that maps an arbitrary value v to a numeric value $\text{digest}(v)$ in a bounded range. We assume that it is practically impossible to find another value v', $v \neq v'$, such that $\text{digest}(v) = \text{digest}(v')$. These simple checksums have a constant size independent of $\mathbf{n}$ or $\mathbf{g}$.

Proposition 4.4   *Consider the information stored at replicas after they appended the ρ-th transaction to their ledgers. If $\mathbf{g} > \mathbf{f}$ and simple checksums are used, then any outside observer can reconstruct (with very high probability) the first $\mathbf{n}\lfloor\frac{\rho}{\mathbf{n}}\rfloor$ transactions appended to the ledger using at most $\binom{\mathbf{n}}{\mathbf{g}}\lfloor\frac{\rho}{\mathbf{n}}\rfloor$ IDA decode steps per $\mathbf{n}$ transactions.*

Proof. Let $i = \mathbf{n}\lfloor\frac{\rho}{\mathbf{n}}\rfloor$ be the last round after which replicas appended to their ledgers. We assume that the observer already reconstructed the first $(i-1)\mathbf{n}$ update decisions, and we show how the observer can reconstruct the block $\mathbb{B}$ containing update decisions $(i-1)\mathbf{n}, \ldots, i\mathbf{n} - 1$, this independent of the behavior of any faulty replicas. To initiate reconstruction of $\mathbb{B}$, the observer will collect pairs (s_j, c_j) from replicas R_j with $\mathrm{id}(\mathsf{R}_j) = j$, which all good replicas will eventually provide. Hence, eventually the observer will receive $\mathbf{g}$ such pairs. Next, the observer can start reconstruction of $\mathbb{B}$ by decoding the pieces contained in the received pairs

Faulty replicas can send invalid pairs (s', c'), however, which complicates reconstruction of $\mathbb{B}$ from the pairs received. The observer does not a-priori know which replicas are faulty. Hence, the observer needs to verify whether any block reconstructed from pairs collected from $\mathbf{g}$ distinct replicas is equivalent to $\mathbb{B}$. The first step in this verification process is to determine the checksum $\mathrm{digest}(\mathbb{B})$. Consider the first $z > \mathbf{f}$ messages received. We distinguish two cases.

1. At least $\mathbf{f} + 1$ messages have identical checksum c. In this case, at least one such message must be sent by a good replica. Hence, we have $c = \mathrm{digest}(\mathbb{B})$.

2. At most, $\mathbf{f}$ messages have identical checksums. In this case, some of the messages received have been sent by faulty replicas. As the observer will eventually receive $\mathbf{g} > \mathbf{f}$ messages from good replicas and all these messages will contain the same checksum $\mathrm{digest}(\mathbb{B})$, the observer can wait until more messages are received to determine the checksum $\mathrm{digest}(\mathbb{B})$.

After determining $\mathrm{digest}(\mathbb{B})$, the observer can simply reconstruct $\mathbb{B}$ by trying to decode every combination of pieces received from $\mathbf{g}$ distinct replicas, this until eventually a block b is constructed with $\mathrm{digest}(b) = \mathrm{digest}(\mathbb{B})$. In the worst case, the observer will have to wait until it receives pairs from all $\mathbf{n}$ replicas, before it receives $\mathbf{g}$ uncorrupted pairs, in which case it will have to try to decode $\binom{\mathbf{n}}{\mathbf{g}}$ combinations of $\mathbf{g}$ pieces.

The only way for faulty replicas to subvert the reconstruction step is by finding a value $w, w \neq \mathbb{B}$, with $\mathrm{digest}(w) = \mathrm{digest}(\mathbb{B})$. As we assumed that $\mathrm{digest}(\cdot)$ is a *collision-resistant hash function*, it is exceedingly hard for the faulty replicas to find such a value w. Hence, assuming reasonable limits on the computational resources, the faulty replicas are unable to subvert the learning step with high probability. Finally, in the unlikely case in which the faulty replicas are able to mount a collision-based attack, this attack can always be detected: the attack will yield at least two sets of $\mathbf{g}$ pieces that decode to values w and $\mathbb{B}$ with $w \neq \mathbb{B}$ and $\mathrm{digest}(w) = \mathrm{digest}(\mathbb{B})$. $\qquad\qquad\qquad\qquad\qquad\qquad\qquad\qquad\qquad\qquad\qquad\qquad\qquad\qquad\qquad$ $\square$

Notice that if the system only tolerates crash or omit failures (and no Byzantine failures), then the checksums can be omitted entirely, as no replica will ever send an invalid pair (s', c'). To conclude, we notice that faulty replicas that provide invalid pairs are easily detectable by outside observers. Hence, after an observer decoded $\mathbf{g}$ pieces into a valid block $\mathbb{B}$, it can simply re-encode this block and determine the exact value of each encoded piece a replica should have sent. Consequently, after trying to subvert reconstruction, all faulty replicas can be recognized and be eliminated from future considerations.

4.1.4   RECONSTRUCTING THE LEDGER (TREE CHECKSUMS)

In the previous section, we have shown how observers can reliably reconstruct the ledger in the presence of faulty replicas. In theory, that approach has a high computational overhead due to the worst-case combinatorics involved. Next, we explore a different checksum scheme via which observers can recognize invalid information provided by faulty replicas and easily discard such information with minimal effort. Consequently, an observer can directly select the fault-free information and perform only a single information dispersal decode step to reconstruct a block from the ledger. We base this checksum scheme on *Merkle trees* [185].

Definition 4.5   Consider a block $\mathbb{B}$ of $\mathbf{n}$ transactions. The replica R with $\mathrm{id}(\mathsf{R}) = i$, $0 \leq i < \mathbf{n}$, should produce the i-th encoded piece $\mathbb{B}_i = \mathtt{slice}_\mathsf{R}(\mathbb{B})$. To simplify the presentation, we assume that the total number of such pieces is a power-of-two (otherwise, we simply add $\mathtt{null}$-pieces until we have a power-of-two number of pieces). A *Merkle tree* build over these pieces is a balanced binary tree constructed as follows.

1. The i-th leaf of the tree has the value $\mathrm{digest}(\mathbb{B}_i)$.

2. The value of an internal node of which the left-child has value w_1 and the right-child has value w_2 is $\mathrm{digest}([w_1, w_2])$.

Notice that this construction is deterministic. Hence, every good replica will construct exactly the same Merkle tree for $\mathbb{B}$. The *tree checksum* we propose for the i-th piece $\mathbb{B}_i$, $\mathtt{checksum}_\mathsf{R}(\mathbb{B})$, consists of the value of the root of the Merkle tree and the values of the sibling of each node on the path from the root to the i-th leaf.

We illustrate this further in the following example.

Example 4.6   Assume $\mathbf{n} = 8$ and consider a block $\mathbb{B}$ that encodes into pieces $\mathbb{B}_0, \ldots, \mathbb{B}_7$. The Merkle tree for $\mathbb{B}$ can be found in Figure 4.2. The tree checksum $\mathtt{checksum}_\mathsf{R}(\mathbb{B})$ is obtained as follows. First, the path from the root of the tree to the 5th leaf visits the nodes with values h_{4567}, h_{45}, and h_5. The node with value h_{4567} has the sibling with value h_{0123}; the node with value h_{45} has the sibling with value h_{67}; and, finally, the node with value h_5 has the sibling with value h_4. The root of the tree has value $h_{01234567}$. Hence, $\mathtt{checksum}_\mathsf{R}(\mathbb{B}) = [h_{01234567}, h_{0123}, h_{67}, h_4]$.

Next, we show that these tree checksums are sufficient to recognize messages corrupted by Byzantine replicas.

Proposition 4.7   *Consider the information stored at replicas after they appended the ρ-th transaction to their ledgers. If $\mathbf{g} > \mathbf{f}$ and tree checksums are used, then any outside observer can reconstruct (with very high probability) the first $\mathbf{n}\lfloor \frac{\rho}{\mathbf{n}} \rfloor$ transactions appended to the ledger using at most a single IDA decode step per $\mathbf{n}$ transactions.*

Proof. Let $i = \mathbf{n}\lfloor \frac{\rho}{\mathbf{n}} \rfloor$ be the last round after which replicas appended to their ledgers. We assume that the observer already reconstructed the first $(i-1)\mathbf{n}$ update decisions, and we show how

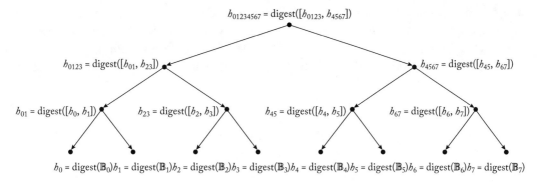

Figure 4.2: A *Merkle tree* over eight data pieces $\mathbb{B}_0, \ldots, \mathbb{B}_7$. The leaf nodes are each labeled with the hash of a data piece, while every internal node is labeled with the hash of the value of its two children. The *tree checksum* for $\mathbb{B}_5$ of R_5 is $\mathsf{checksum}_{\mathsf{R}_5}(\mathbb{B}) = [h_{01234567}, h_{0123}, h_{67}, h_4]$.

the observer can reconstruct the block $\mathbb{B}$ containing update decisions $(i-1)\mathbf{n}, \ldots, i\mathbf{n} - 1$, this independent of the behavior of any faulty replicas. Every pair (s, c) provided by a good replica will include a valid tree checksum. Each of these checksums is constructed over the same Merkle tree. Consequently, each of these checksums share the same value for the root of the Merkle tree. Hence, using the reasoning of Proposition 4.4, the observer can reliably determine the root value r of the Merkle tree after receiving at least $\mathbf{f}+1$ messages with identical root values in their checksum.

Now consider the pair (s_j, c_j) received from the replica R with $\mathsf{id}(\mathsf{R}) = j$. To determine whether this pair is valid and uncorrupted, we first check whether the root value in c_j matches r. If this check fails, we can already discard the message. Next, we compute $\mathsf{digest}(s_j)$ to obtain the value of the j-th leaf in the Merkle tree. We observe that c_j contains the value of the sibling of the j-th leaf. Hence, we can construct the value of the parent p of the j-th leaf. This can be repeated: for any ancestor of the j-th leaf, c_j also contains the value of the sibling of this ancestor. Hence, one can recompute the value of every ancestor of the j-th leaf based on the value s_j. When done, one will obtain the root value r when the message is valid and uncorrupted. If any other value is obtained, then the message must be corrupted and one can discard the message.

As with the simple checksums, the only way in which faulty replicas can subvert the reconstruction step is by finding hash collisions. Hence, assuming reasonable limits on the computational resources, the faulty replicas are unable to subvert the reconstruction step with high probability. □

To further clarify the verification of messages, we illustrate how the verification process of the proof of Proposition 4.7 works.

Example 4.8   Consider the situation of Example 4.6 and consider an observer that already determined that the root value is $h_{01234567}$. At some point, the observer receives a pair $(\mathbb{B}'_5, [w_1, w_2, w_3, w_4])$ from replica R with $id(R) = 5$. The observer checks whether $w_1 = h_{01234567}$, as otherwise the message is discarded. We assume $w_1 = h_{01234567}$. Next, the observer computes

$$h'_5 = digest(\mathbb{B}'_5);$$
$$h'_{45} = digest([w_4, h'_5]);$$
$$h'_{4567} = digest([h'_{45}, w_3]);$$
$$h'_{01234567} = digest([w_2, h_{4567}]).$$

If $\mathbb{B}'_5 = \mathbb{B}_5$, $w_4 = h_4$, $w_3 = h_{67}$, and $w_2 = h_{0123}$, then $h'_{01234567} = h_{01234567}$ and the message received from R is valid and uncorrupted. In any other case, the resulting value $h'_{01234567}$ will not match $h_{01234567}$ with high probability and the message is discarded.

In Proposition 4.7, we analyzed the computational complexity of reconstructing the ledger with tree checksums in terms of the number of IDA decode steps. As we show in Example 4.8, one also needs to validate the correctness of each message via its tree checksum, for which $\log(\mathbf{n})$ hashes need to be computed. In practice, the IDA decode steps are much more costly than these validation steps (this is especially true when using modern processors that provide hardware acceleration for hashing). Hence, in our analysis, we only focus on the number of information dispersal decode steps.

4.1.5   SCALABLE STORAGE USING INFORMATION DISPERSAL

Finally, we are ready to put the results of the previous three sections together. With the storage scheme described in Section 4.1.2, each replica R ends up storing a single pair $(\texttt{slice}_R(\mathbb{B}), \texttt{checksum}_R(\mathbb{B}))$ per $\mathbf{n}$ transactions in which $\|\texttt{slice}_R(\mathbb{B})\| = \left\lceil \frac{\|\mathbb{B}\|}{g} \right\rceil$. The simple checksums described in Section 4.1.3 have a constant size independent of $\mathbb{B}$, hence, $\|\texttt{checksum}_R(\mathbb{B})\| = \Theta(1)$. Finally, the tree checksums described in Section 4.1.4 have an $\mathbf{n}$-logarithmic size independent of $\mathbb{B}$, hence, $\|\texttt{checksum}_R(\mathbb{B})\| = \Theta(\log(\mathbf{n}))$. We combine these observations with Theorem 4.3, Proposition 4.4, and Proposition 4.7 to conclude the following.

Theorem 4.9   *Let R be a good replica with ledger $\mathcal{L}_R$, current state S, and in which only S is necessary to make update decisions. If $\mathbf{g} > \mathbf{f}$ and $\|B\|$ is the maximum size of any set of up-to-$\mathbf{n}$ transactions, then the storage scheme of Figure 4.1 can provide storage scalability with these guarantees.*

1. *If simple checksums are used, then the storage cost per replica R is reduced from $\mathcal{O}(\|\mathcal{L}_R\| + \|S\|)$ to $\mathcal{O}(\frac{\|\mathcal{L}_R\|}{g} + \|S\| + \|B\|)$. The first ρ transactions in the ledger can be reconstructed using at-most $\binom{\mathbf{n}}{\mathbf{g}} \frac{\rho}{\mathbf{n}}$ IDA decode steps.*

2. *If tree checksums are used, then the storage cost per replica* R *is reduced from* $\mathcal{O}(\|\mathcal{L}_R\| + \|S\|)$ *to* $\mathcal{O}(\frac{\|\mathcal{L}_R\|}{g} + \frac{|\mathcal{L}_R|}{n} \log(n) + \|S\| + \|B\|)$. *The first ρ transactions in the ledger can be reconstructed using at-most $\frac{\rho}{n}$* IDA *decode steps.*

4.2 SCALABILITY FOR READ-ONLY WORKLOADS

In Chapter 3, we discussed implementation techniques to maximize throughput of permissioned blockchains without specializing for any specific workload. In many practical transaction processing systems, a distinction can be made between read-only transactions and transactions that modify state: only transactions that modify state need to be executed by all relevant replicas (e.g., via a commit protocol) to assure that all replicas maintain a consistent state. This provides room for such systems to improve performance and scalability when dealing with read-only workloads. Here, we will focus on two such approaches. First, in Section 4.2.1, we explore how one can optimize for processing individual read-only transactions. Then, in Section 4.2.2, we focus on how to optimize for performing large-scale read-only analytics on the state maintained by a system.

4.2.1 OPTIMISTIC READ-ONLY TRANSACTION PROCESSING

In practical transaction processing systems, individual read-only transactions are typically executed by only a single replica, preferably a replica that is closest to the client. If the majority of the workload consists of such read-only transactions, then this approach improves throughput scalability significantly, as read-only transactions can be processed in parallel by individual replicas.

Unfortunately, scalability via such read-only optimizations are not possible in fault-tolerant blockchains: to assure that the response to read-only transactions is valid and not tampered with by faulty replicas, blockchains need to assure that at least $f + 1$ good replicas execute each transaction. Consequently, most blockchains treat all participating replicas and all transactions equally: all replicas will process all transactions in the same order. This approach is at the basis of maintaining a consistent state among all replicas and returning consistent results to all clients when dealing with faulty replicas. One can improve on this situation, however, by providing an optimistic optimized execution path for read-only transactions. We have sketched such an optimistic path in Figure 4.3.

As with the normal consensus protocol, the client $\mathcal{C}$ will accept any response it receives from $f + 1$ distinct replicas. In this case, the client $\mathcal{C}$ has the guarantee that at least one of those replicas is good and, hence, that the response is valid. This optimistic read-only path does not *guarantee* a result, however. As replicas do not agree on a unique order in which to execute τ, each replica can end up executing τ on a different local state and return different responses, due to which the client cannot determine the result. This only happens when τ queries state that

---

Client-role (used by client C to request a read-only transaction τ) :

1: Broadcast $\langle\tau\rangle_C$ to all replicas.
2: Await receipt of messages $\texttt{InformRO}(\langle\tau\rangle_C, r)$ from up-to-g replicas.
3: **if** C received $\mathbf{f} + 1$ identical messages $\texttt{InformRO}(\langle\tau\rangle_C, r)$ **then**
4:     Considers τ read-only executed with result r.
5: **end if**

Replica-role (running at every replica $\mathsf{R} \in \mathfrak{R}$) :

6: **event** R receives message $\langle\tau\rangle_C$ **do**
7:   **if** τ is read-only **then**
8:       Execute τ and let r be any (optional) result of execution.
9:       Send $\texttt{InformRO}(\langle\tau\rangle_C, r)$ to C.
10:   **else**
11:       Process τ via the normal consensus protocol.
12:   **end if**
13: **end event**

Figure 4.3: A read-only optimistic path for consensus-based systems.

is modified by concurrent transactions, however. Hence, when an application has workloads in which such concurrent modifications are rare, this optimization can result in a sharp reduction of the number of transactions on which (expensive) consensus needs to be reached, thereby increasing the throughput and reducing the latency for read-only transactions drastically.

We notice that we can prevent any issues between read-only transactions and concurrent modifications by relying on the primary to *soft-order* read-only transactions. We can allow the primary to instruct all replicas to execute a read-only transaction after completion of some modifications in a specified round. If the primary is good, then all replicas will receive the same instructions, execute the read-only transaction, and successfully inform the client, this without any consensus. If the primary is faulty, however, it can give conflicting instructions to various replicas, which can result in the client being unable to determine the result.

We notice that this *read-only optimization* does reduce the cost of read-only transactions. It does not make processing such transactions scalable, however. Even with these read-only optimizations, one still requires that at-least-$\mathbf{f} + 1$ good replicas execute the transaction. This is in sharp contrast with traditional systems that do *not* tolerate Byzantine failures: in such systems, the client can simply send its read-only transactions to only the closest replica (or even to a read-only proxy) for a quick response.

4.2.2   ROLE-SPECIALIZATION VIA LEARNERS

In many practical transaction processing systems, there is also a need for costly read-only workloads such as data analytics, data provenance, machine learning, and data visualization. These read-only workloads are computationally complex and require access to large portions of the

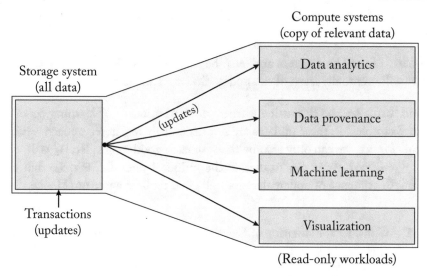

Figure 4.4: Schematic overview of *hierarchical* transaction processing. At the core is a *cluster* that manages and stores all data. The managed data is used by many *independent read-only partici-pants*, e.g., for analytics, data provenance, machine learning, and visualization. To do so, these participants do not need to partake in managing and storing the data, they only need to *learn the data*.

state managed by the transaction processing system. To deal with such workloads, these work-loads are typically split off to specialized systems that operate on a copy of the data. This enables the usage of a specialized system optimized for the intended workload, e.g., equipped with spe-cialized hardware accelerators to aid in the tasks at hand. Such a *hierarchical design* in which a central system manages the data by processing transactions and specialized systems perform their operations on copies of the managed data is sketched in Figure 4.4.

This hierarchical design not only supports data-hungry and compute intensive read-only workloads (e.g., analytics, data provenance, machine learning, and data visualization), but also enables deployment of read-only proxies close to the end user. In this capacity, this hierarchical design can provide end-users with high performance, low latency, read-only access to the data managed by the system.

To apply such a *hierarchical design* to a blockchain-based system, we need a way for the specialized systems to reliably learn all the data held by the blockchain system. The easy way would be to let these specialized systems retrieve all data via read-only transactions. In the pre-vious section, we have seen that even with read-only optimizations, processing these read-only transactions is costly and not scalable. Hence, we need a better approach. To do so, we formalize the specialized systems as *learners* that want to learn the set of *update decisions* maintained by the blockchain (in the form of transactions stored in the ledger). In this setting, we need to solve the following problem:

Definition 4.10   Let $\mathfrak{R}$ be a system and let L be a learner. The *Byzantine learner problem* states that a learner will eventually learn of the update decisions made by $\mathfrak{R}$.

We will formalize the Byzantine learner problem in terms of learning *ledger updates*. As illustrated in Example 2.4, these updates are not necessarily registered at each replica at exactly the same time. Hence, we can only assume that, for each good replica $R_1, R_2 \in \mathfrak{R}$, either $\mathcal{L}_{R_1} \preceq \mathcal{L}_{R_2}$ or $\mathcal{L}_{R_2} \preceq \mathcal{L}_{R_1}$. We write $\mathcal{L}_{\mathfrak{R}}$ to denote the unique ledger $\mathcal{L}_R$, $R \in \mathfrak{R}$, that contains the maximum-length sequence of update decisions all good replicas agree on. Hence, $\mathcal{L}_{\mathfrak{R}} \preceq \mathcal{L}_{R'}$ for all good replicas $R' \in \mathfrak{R}$.

Example 4.11   Consider the situation of Example 2.4. The three good replicas share the update journal $\mathcal{L}_{\mathfrak{R}} = [\tau_1, \tau_2, \tau_3, \tau_4, \tau_5, \tau_6]$.

Next, we refine Definition 4.10 in terms of ledger updates:

Definition 4.12   Let $\mathfrak{R}$ be a system. For every i, $0 \leq i < |\mathcal{L}_{\mathfrak{R}}|$, the *Byzantine learner problem* states that any learner L will eventually learn of the i-th update decision $\mathcal{L}_{\mathfrak{R}}[i]$. At the same time, no faulty replica $B \in \mathcal{F}$ can convince L that any other update was the i-th update decision made.

Notice that we only specified the data model of replicas. We did not specify how the learners store data or process transactions, we only specified that the learners will receive *all* updates (in the form of transactions) decided upon by the replicas. Indeed, the specifics of what a learner does with the transactions received depend on the workload for which the learner is designed.

Example 4.13   Consider the system from Example 2.4. A learner L will be able to learn the updates τ_0, τ_1, τ_2, τ_3, τ_4, τ_5, and τ_6. The learner will not yet be able to learn τ_7, as this update is still being processed by some good replicas in $\mathfrak{R}$. Replica B will never be able to convince the learner that the updates τ_3' or τ_4' happened, as B is Byzantine. The learner L can store the updates it learned in a temporal database view that provides access to historical data, e.g., for in-depth analysis.

As a simple solution to the *Byzantine learner problem*, learners can request the transactions appended to the ledger via read-only transactions. As discussed before, this approach is not scalable. Using an *information dispersal algorithm*, as described in Section 4.1, we can solve the Byzantine learner problem much more efficient, however.

To do so, we assume that each learner L can register itself with the system. Using the information dispersal step, each replica R can obtain pairs $(\texttt{slice}_R(\mathbb{B}), \texttt{checksum}_R(\mathbb{B}))$ (Line 4

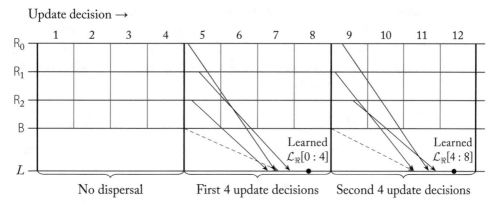

Figure 4.5: A schematic representation of the interactions between a system $\mathfrak{R} = \{R_0, R_1, R_2, B\}$ and a learner L participating in information dispersal. The replica B is faulty and sends invalid messages. The other replicas repeatedly send a valid message encoding 4 decisions from their update journal. After receiving these messages, L is able to reconstruct (learn) the update decisions made by the system. Specifically, after the $\mathbf{n} = 4$th update decision, L will start receiving messages from which it can reconstruct the first four update decisions.

of Figure 4.1) that encode its share of every block $\mathbb{B}$ of $\mathbf{n}$ transactions that are appended to the ledger. After registration of learner L, each replica R will send only its own share of each block $\mathbb{B}$, the pair ($\texttt{slice}_R(\mathbb{B}), \texttt{checksum}_R(\mathbb{B})$), to learner L. Finally, learner L can use the reconstruction techniques of Sections 4.1.3 and 4.1.4 to reconstruct the full ledger of transactions. We refer to Figure 4.5 for a schematic representation of the interactions between replicas and a learner due to these information dispersal steps.

We notice that information dispersal is a *push-based* algorithm that pushes the ledger to all learners without any coordination. Additionally, the total communication cost of information dispersal is shared equally among all participating replicas, independent of the behavior of any faulty replicas. This is in sharp contrast with simple and naive *pull-based* approaches using read-only transactions. Using the results of Theorem 4.9, it is straightforward to show that information dispersal is a scalable approach toward Byzantine learning.

Corollary 4.14   *Consider a learner L and replica R. If $\mathbf{g} > \mathbf{f}$, then information dispersal steps with tree checksums guarantee that*

1. *L will learn the update journal $\mathcal{L}_{\mathfrak{R}}$;*

2. *L will receive at most $|\mathcal{L}_{\mathfrak{R}}|$ messages with a total size of $\mathcal{O}(\|\mathcal{L}_{\mathfrak{R}}\|(\frac{\mathbf{n}}{\mathbf{g}}) + |\mathcal{L}_{\mathfrak{R}}|\log(\mathbf{n}))$;*

3. *L will only need at most $\frac{|\mathcal{L}_{\mathfrak{R}}|}{\mathbf{n}}$ IDA decode steps; and*

4. *R will sent at most $\frac{|\mathcal{L}_{\mathfrak{R}}|}{\mathbf{n}}$ messages to L with a total size of $\mathcal{O}(\frac{\|\mathcal{L}_{\mathfrak{R}}\|}{\mathbf{g}} + (\frac{|\mathcal{L}_{\mathfrak{R}}|}{\mathbf{n}})\log(\mathbf{n}))$.*

We notice that we can also implement the information dispersal steps with simple check-sums, which would decrease message complexity slightly, while increasing the computational cost for L to reconstruct the transactions. As is clear form Corollary 4.14, information dispersal is scalable: by adding replicas to the system, we decrease the overall communication cost per replica to keep the learners up-to-date.

4.3   COORDINATION BETWEEN BLOCKCHAINS

In the previous sections, we presented techniques to improve performance of a system that operates a single permissioned blockchain by reducing the costs for the blockchain to service read-only workloads. Although the presented read-only techniques can provide a welcome performance boosts to blockchain systems, they do not lift the performance limitations imposed by using only a single blockchain. Specifically, read-only optimizations do not provide unlimited scalability for read-only workloads, while also not improving throughput for non-read-only workloads consisting of transactions that update state.

In many practical distributed transaction processing systems, scalability is achieved using *sharding*. In a traditional sharded design, the data is partitioned among the replicas such that each replica holds only a fragment of the data. Consequently, sharded designs provide *storage scalability* as adding replicas increases overall storage capacity [125, 127, 217]. To also provide *throughput scalability*, sharded systems are designed to process transactions in *parallel* whenever these parallel transactions do not affect the same data.

To illustrate throughput scalability, consider the *geo-scale aware* sharded system sketched in Figure 4.6. We assume that this system manages bank accounts. The sharded systems is divided in four regions (Africa, America, Asia, and Europe); and in each region a single replica (a shard) is placed managing the accounts of customers from that region. Now consider transactions of the form:

$$\tau_{X,Y} = \text{Transfer money from a customer in region } X \text{ to a customer in region } Y.$$

Now, the transactions $\tau_{\text{Africa,Africa}}$, $\tau_{\text{America,America}}$, $\tau_{\text{Asia,Asia}}$, and $\tau_{\text{Europe,Europe}}$ can all be processed in parallel within their respective regions. Hence, by increasing the number of regions, one can increase the maximum total throughput. Furthermore, if the data can be split between regions such that most transactions only involve data from a single region, then using a sharded design will also increase practical throughput significantly.

Sharding introduces complications for transaction processing, however. To process *multi-shard transactions* that affect several regions in a consistent manner, one will require significant coordination between the shards. With a proper design and sufficient coordination, sets of multi-shard transactions that do not affect the same data can still be processed in parallel, e.g., the transactions $\tau_{\text{Africa,America}}$ and $\tau_{\text{Asia,Europe}}$.

The crucial component in achieving a highly scalable sharded design is the way in which data is partitioned (this to assure that most transactions can be handled by a single or by only a

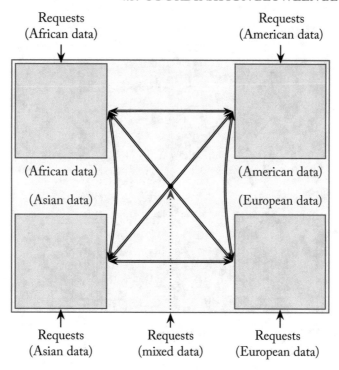

Figure 4.6: A *geo-scale aware sharded* design in which four replicas each hold only a part of the data, e.g., in a banking system, each region can hold account information of customers in that region only.

few shards) and the way in which multi-shard transactions are processed (this to maximize the number of transactions that are processed in parallel). As effective data partitioning is mainly determined by the requirements of individual applications, we focus on techniques that enable multi-shard transaction processing in a Byzantine environment.

The concept of sharding is a major departure from the fully replicated design of blockchains. Next, we will discuss sharded architectures that still can provide the fault-resilience of blockchains. A conceptually simple way to do so, is by taking a sharded system and replacing each replica (shard) by an independent blockchain that operates as a single fault-resilient replica. We have sketched this design in Figure 4.7. In this design, the individual shards can be operated via normal consensus (e.g., PBFT). To further enable such a sharded design, we do require techniques beyond consensus, however. Foremost, we need a way to enable coordination between shards, which can be provided by a *reliable cross-blockchain communication primitive*. In this section, we will formalize such communication via the *Byzantine cluster-sending problem* and study the fundamental nature of cluster-sending [135, 136, 139]. In the next two sections, we will

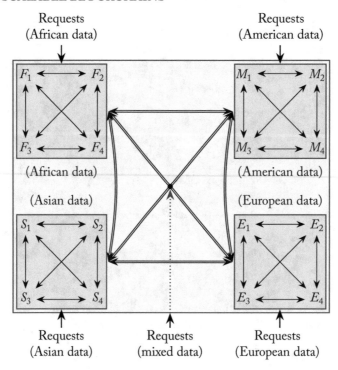

Figure 4.7: A *geo-scale aware sharded* design in which four shards, each consisting of a four-replica blockchain, hold only a part of the data. Local decisions within a shard are made via *consensus* (⟵⟶), whereas multi-shard transaction processing requires coordination between shards (⟵⟶).

study in-depth two ways in which sharding can be used in blockchains. First, we explore geo-scale aware blockchains that utilize location-based sharding to improve scalability of consensus. Then, we examine how consensus and cluster-sending are used to realize sharded blockchain architectures.

4.3.1   FORMALIZING CLUSTER-SENDING

Up till now, all systems we considered consisted of a single fully replicated blockchain represented by a single set of replicas. Next, we will consider systems consisting of several independent-operating blockchains represented by distinct sets of replicas. We refer to each such a blockchain consisting of a distinct set of replicas as a *cluster*. Let $\mathcal{C}$ be a cluster (consisting of a set of replicas). We write $\mathcal{F}(\mathcal{C}) \subseteq \mathcal{C}$ to denote the set of *faulty replicas* in $\mathcal{C}$ and $\mathcal{G}(\mathcal{C}) = \mathcal{C} \setminus \mathcal{F}(\mathcal{C})$ to denote the set of *good replicas* in $\mathcal{C}$. We write $\mathbf{n}_{\mathcal{C}} = |\mathcal{C}|$, $\mathbf{f}_{\mathcal{C}} = |\mathcal{F}(\mathcal{C})|$, and $\mathbf{g}_{\mathcal{C}} = |\mathcal{G}(\mathcal{C})|$ to denote the number of replicas, faulty replicas, and good replicas in the cluster,

	Ping round-trip times (ms)						Bandwidth (Mbit/s)					
	O	I	M	B	T	S	O	I	M	B	T	S
Oregon (O)	≤1	38	65	136	118	161	7998	669	371	194	188	136
Iowa (I)		≤1	33	98	153	172		10004	752	243	144	120
Montreal (M)			≤1	82	186	202			7977	283	111	102
Belgium (B)				≤1	252	270				9728	79	66
Taiwan (T)					≤1	137					7998	160
Sydney (S)						≤1						7977

Figure 4.8: Real-world inter- and intra-cluster communication costs in terms of the ping round-trip times (which determines *latency*) and bandwidth (which determines *throughput*).

respectively. We extend the notations $\mathcal{F}(\cdot)$, $\mathcal{G}(\cdot)$, $\mathbf{n}(\cdot)$, $\mathbf{f}(\cdot)$, and $\mathbf{g}(\cdot)$ to arbitrary sets of replicas. We assume that all replicas in each cluster have a predetermined order (e.g., on identifier or on public address), which allows us to deterministically select any number of replicas in a unique order from each cluster.

A *cluster system* over a set of replicas $\mathfrak{R}$ is a set of clusters obtained by partitioning $\mathfrak{R}$. In the following, we shall specifically look at geo-scale aware systems in which communication between replicas in a cluster is *local* and communication between clusters is *non-local*. We assume that there is no practical bound on local communication (e.g., within a single data center rack), while global communication is limited, costly, and to be avoided (e.g., between data centers in different continents). If $C_1, C_2 \subset \mathfrak{R}$ are distinct clusters, then we assume that $C_1 \cap C_2 = \emptyset$: no replica is part of two distinct clusters. Our abstract model of a cluster system—in which we distinguish between unbounded local communication and costly global communication— is supported by practice; see, e.g., the ping round-trip time and bandwidth measurements in Figure 4.8. These measurements imply that message latencies between clusters are at least 33–270 times higher than within clusters, while the maximum throughput is 10–151 times lower, both implying that communication between clusters is *up-to-two orders of magnitude* more costly than communication within clusters.

Definition 4.15 Let $\mathfrak{R}$ be a set of replicas and let $C_1, C_2 \subset \mathfrak{R}$ be two distinct clusters over $\mathfrak{R}$ with good replicas ($\mathcal{G}(C_1) \neq \emptyset$ and $\mathcal{G}(C_2) \neq \emptyset$). The *cluster-sending problem* is the problem of sending a value v from C_1 to C_2 such that:

1. all good replicas in C_2 *receive* the value v;

2. all good replicas in C_1 *confirm* that the value v was received by all good replicas in C_2; and

3. good replicas in C_2 can only receive a value v if all good replicas in C_1 *agree* upon sending v.

The cluster-sending problem is a generic problem and not specifically tied to enabling sharded blockchain architectures. Indeed, cluster-sending also enables other scalable architectures, e.g., *service-oriented blockchain architectures*. In such a service-oriented blockchain architecture, many *independently operating* blockchains each provide simple services. Due to their singular focus on providing only a limited set of simple services, each such blockchain can be optimized toward providing only that service. To implement complex services, one takes the simple services provided by these independent blockchains, and composes them together. In such a design, cluster-sending can be used as the glue between the independent blockchains that allows service composition.

Cluster-sending can easily be solved using *message broadcasting*. Let C_1 be a cluster in which the good replicas have reached *agreement* on sending a value v to a cluster C_2, e.g., via a consensus protocol. In our first cluster-sending protocol, we assume that all good replicas in C_1 have already reached agreement on sending v. To prove this agreement to a replica $R_2 \in C_2$, R_2 only needs to determine that it received v from a good replica in C_1. To do so, $R_2 \in C_2$ needs to receive at-least $f_{C_1} + 1$ messages of distinct replicas in C_1. Only after receiving at least f_{C_1} messages, does R_2 have the guarantee that at least one of these messages came from a good replica in C_1 and, hence, can be trusted and that agreement was reached on sending v. To assure that R_2 will receive these $f_{C_1} + 1$ messages from good replicas, we need to instruct a set $S_1 \subseteq C_1$ of $n_{S_1} = 2f_{C_1} + 1$ replicas to send to R_2, as at-most f_{C_1} replicas in S_1 could be faulty.

To assure that all replicas in C_2 receive v, good replicas in C_2 broadcast the messages they receive to all other replicas in C_2. Hence, to force receipt, C_1 only needs to assure that a single good replica in C_2 receive at-least $f_{C_1} + 1$ messages from good replicas. To so do, we simply choose a set of $S_2 \subseteq C_2$ of $n_{S_2} = f_{C_2} + 1$ replicas that will receive messages from the replicas in S_1. The pseudo-code for this *reliable broadcast* cluster-sending protocol (RB-RS) can be found in Figure 4.9. Next, we prove correctness of this protocol.

Proposition 4.16   *Let $\mathfrak{R}$ be a system and let $C_1, C_2 \subset \mathfrak{R}$. If $n_{C_1} > 2f_{C_1}$ and $n_{C_2} > f_{C_2}$, then RB-RS satisfies Definition 4.15. The protocol sends $(2f_{C_1} + 1) \cdot (f_{C_2} + 1)$ messages, of size $\mathcal{O}(\|v\|)$ each, between C_1 and C_2.*

Proof. Choose $S_1 \subseteq C_1$ and $S_2 \subseteq C_2$ in accordance with RB-RS (Figure 4.9). We have $n_{S_1} = 2f_{C_1} + 1$ and $n_{S_2} = f_{C_2} + 1$. By construction, we have $g_{S_1} \geq f_{C_1} + 1$ and $g_{S_2} \geq 1$. Due to Line 6, each replica $R_2 \in \mathcal{G}(S_2)$ will receive messages v from every replica in $R_1 \in \mathcal{G}(S_1)$. Hence, R_2 will meet the condition at Line 9 for each such message v and broadcast these messages to all replicas in C_2. As $g_{S_2} \geq 1$ and $g_{S_1} \geq f_{C_1} + 1$, each replica $R'_2 \in \mathcal{G}(C_2)$ will meet the condition at Line 12, proving *receipt* and *confirmation*. To prove *agreement*, we show that only values agreed upon by C_1 will be considered received by good replicas in $\mathcal{G}(C_2)$. Consider a value v' not agreed upon by C_1. Hence, only the replicas in $\mathcal{F}(C_1)$ will sign v'. Due to non-forgeability of signatures, the only signatures constructed for v' are constructed by replicas $R_1 \in \mathcal{F}(C_1)$. Consequently, each replica

Sending-role (for the sending cluster C_1) :

1: All replicas in $\mathcal{G}(C_1)$ agree on v.
2: Choose replicas $S_1 \subseteq C_1$ with $\mathbf{n}_{S_1} = 2\mathbf{f}_{C_1} + 1$.
3: Choose replicas $S_2 \subseteq C_2$ with $\mathbf{n}_{S_2} = \mathbf{f}_{C_2} + 1$.
4: **for** $\mathsf{R}_1 \in S_1$ **do**
5:     **for** $\mathsf{R}_2 \in S_2$ **do**
6:         R_1 sends v to R_2.
7:     **end for**
8: **end for**

Receiving-role (for the receiving cluster C_2) :

9: **event** $\mathsf{R}_2 \in \mathcal{G}(C_2)$ receives w from $\mathsf{R}_1' \in C_1$ **do**
10:     Broadcast w to all replicas in C_2.
11: **end event**
12: **event** $\mathsf{R}_2' \in \mathcal{G}(C_2)$ receives $\mathbf{f}_{C_1} + 1$ messages w:

    1. each message is sent by a replica in C_2;
    2. each message carries the same value w; and
    3. each message has a distinct signature from a replica $\mathsf{R}_1' \in C_1$

   do
13:     R_2' considers w *received*.
14: **end event**

Figure 4.9: RB-RS, the reliable broadcast cluster-sending protocol that sends a value v from C_1 to C_2. In this protocol, replicas in C_1 digitally sign their messages.

in C_2 can only receive and broadcast up-to-$\mathbf{f}_{C_1}$ distinct signed messages for v'. We conclude that no good replica will meet the conditions for v' at Line 12. □

In RB-RS, each replica in C_2 needs to receive at least $\mathbf{f}_{C_1} + 1$ copies of v to determine that agreement was reached in C_1 on sending v. In many environments, individual replicas in C_1 are also able to prove agreement on sending v via some *agreement certificate* cert(v, C_1). For example, if consensus was reached using PBFT, then each replica can present a *committed certificate* (see Section 2.2). If C_1 uses threshold signatures (see Section 3.3.1), then this committed certificate can be represented by a constant-sized signature. Finally, if consensus was reached in a system without malicious replicas, e.g., a PAXOS-based system [165, 166] that can deal with only crashes, then any claim of *agreement* by a replica in C_1 is automatically proven.

Now assume that C_1 reached agreement on sending v and that each good replica in C_1 has a certificate cert(v, C_1). Now any replica in C_2 only needs to receive a *single* message $(v, \text{cert}(v, C_1))$ from a good replica in C_1 to have the guarantee that this message can be trusted and agreement was reached on sending v. To assure that at least one such message is sent, we still need to instruct at least $\mathbf{f}_{C_1} + 1$ replicas in C_1. Hence, by using certificates, we can reduce the size of set S_1 in RB-RS from $2\mathbf{f}_{C_1} + 1$ to $\mathbf{n}_{S_1} = \mathbf{f}_{C_1} + 1$. Likewise, replicas in C_2 that receive a message

$(v, \mathrm{cert}(v, C_1))$ forwarded by another replica in C_2 only need one such message. Applying this certification logic to RB-RS results in RB-CS, and we have the following.

Corollary 4.17 *Let $\mathfrak{R}$ be a system and let $C_1, C_2 \subset \mathfrak{R}$. If $n_{C_1} > 2f_{C_1}$ and $n_{C_2} > f_{C_2}$, then RB-CS satisfies Definition 4.15. The protocol sends $(f_{C_1} + 1) \cdot (f_{C_2} + 1)$ messages, of size $\mathcal{O}(\|v\| + \|\mathrm{cert}(v, C_1)\|)$ each, between C_1 and C_2.*

4.3.2 LOWER BOUNDS FOR CLUSTER-SENDING

In the previous section, we formalized the cluster-sending problem and showed that this problem can be solved intuitively using *message broadcasting*. Unfortunately, broadcast-based protocols have a high communication cost that, in the worst case, is quadratic in the size of the clusters involved. To determine whether we can do better than broadcasting, we will show in this section the *lower bound* on the communication cost for any protocol solving the cluster-sending problem. In the following section, we show that the lower bounds we establish are strict, this by providing *optimal algorithms* to perform cluster-sending in an asynchronous environment with reliable communication.

First, we consider systems with only crash failures, in which case we can lower bound the number of messages exchanged. Any lower bound on the number of messages exchanged is determined by the maximum number of messages that can get *lost* due to crashed replicas that do not send or receive messages. In situations in which some replicas need to send or receive *multiple* messages, as is the case for the reliable broadcast protocols of the previous section, the capabilities of crashed replicas to lose messages is likewise multiplied. For example, when the number of senders outnumbers the receivers, some receivers then must receive multiple messages. As these receivers could have crashed, they could cause loss of multiple messages each, as the following example illustrates.

Example 4.18 Consider a system $\mathfrak{R}$ with clusters $C_1, C_2 \subset \mathfrak{R}$ such that $n_{C_1} = 15$, $f_{C_1} = 7$, $n_{C_2} = 5$, and $f_{C_2} = 2$. We assume that $\mathfrak{R}$ only has crash failures and that the cluster C_1 wants to send value v to C_2. We will argue that any correct cluster sending protocol P needs to send at least 14 messages in the worst case, as we can always assure that up-to-13 messages will get lost by crashing f_{C_1} replicas in C_1 and f_{C_2} replicas in C_2, this independent as to whom sends and receives these messages.

Consider the messages of a protocol P that wants to send only 13 messages from C_1 to C_2, e.g., the run in Figure 4.10. Notice that $13 > n_{C_2}$. Hence, the run of P can only send 13 messages to replicas in C_2 if some replicas in C_2 will receive several messages. Neither P nor the replicas in C_1 know which replicas in C_2 have crashed. Hence, in the worst case, the $f_{C_2} = 2$ replicas in C_2 that received the most messages have crashed. As we are sending 13 messages and $n_{C_2} = 5$, the 2 replicas that received the most messages must have received at least 6 messages in total. Hence, out of the 13 messages sent, at least 6 can be considered lost. In the run of Figure 4.10, this loss would happen if $R_{2,1}$ and $R_{2,2}$ crash.

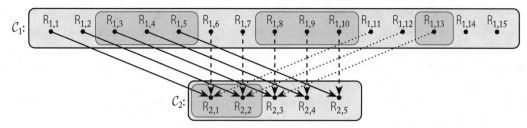

Figure 4.10: A run of a protocol P that sends messages from C_1 and C_2. The protocol P sends 13 messages, which is one message short of guaranteeing successful cluster-sending. Hence, to thwart this particular run we can crash (highlighted using a red background) $\mathbf{f}_{C_1} = 7$ and $\mathbf{f}_{C_2} = 2$ replicas in C_1 and C_2, respectively, to assure that cluster-sending does not happen.

Consequently, at most $13 - 6 = 7$ messages will arrive at good replicas. Unfortunately, these messages are sent by at most 7 distinct replicas. As $\mathbf{f}_{C_1} = 7$, all these sending replicas could have crashed. In the run of Figure 4.10, this loss would happen if $R_{1,3}$, $R_{1,4}$, $R_{1,5}$, $R_{1,8}$, $R_{1,9}$, $R_{1,10}$, and $R_{1,13}$ crash. Hence, we can thwart any run of P that intends to send 13 messages by crashing $\mathbf{f}_{C_1}$ replicas in C_1 and $\mathbf{f}_{C_2}$ replicas in C_2. Consequently, none of the messages of the run will be sent and received by good replicas, assuring that cluster-sending does not happen.

We already argued that at least $\mathbf{f}_{C_1} + 1$ replicas in C_1 need to send messages to good replicas in $\mathbf{f}_{C_2}$, this to assure that at least a *single* such message is sent by a good replica in $\mathcal{G}(C_1)$ and, hence, is guaranteed to arrive. We combine this with a thorough analysis along the lines of Example 4.18, resulting in the following lower bounds.

Theorem 4.19 *Let $\mathfrak{R}$ be a system with crash failures, let $C_1, C_2 \subset \mathfrak{R}$, and let $\{i, j\} = \{1, 2\}$ such that $\mathbf{n}_{C_i} \geq \mathbf{n}_{C_j}$. Let*

$$q_i = (\mathbf{f}_{C_i} + 1) \operatorname{div} \mathbf{g}_{C_j}; \qquad\qquad r_i = (\mathbf{f}_{C_i} + 1) \bmod \mathbf{g}_{C_j};$$
$$\sigma_i = q_i \mathbf{n}_{C_j} + r_i + \mathbf{f}_{C_j} \operatorname{sgn} r_i,$$

in which sgn r_i *is the sign function that evaluates to 1 if $r_i > 0$ and 0 otherwise. Any protocol that solves the cluster-sending problem in which C_1 sends a value v to C_2 needs to exchange at least σ_i messages.*

Proof. Before we prove the theorem, we look at how σ_i is obtained. As Example 4.18 showed, we can reduce the impact of faulty replicas by minimizing the number of messages each replica exchanges. Let $\mathbf{n}_{C_1} > \mathbf{n}_{C_2}$. If the number of messages sent to $\mathbf{n}_{C_2}$ is not a multiple of $\mathbf{n}_{C_2}$, then minimizing the number of messages received by each replica in $\mathbf{n}_{C_2}$ means that some replicas in $\mathbf{n}_{C_2}$ will receive *one* more message than others. Specifically, the theorem claims that each replica in $\mathbf{n}_{C_2}$ will need to receive at least q_1 messages, while the term $r_1 + \mathbf{f}_{C_2} \operatorname{sgn} r_1$ specifies the minimum number of replicas in $\mathbf{n}_{C_2}$ that will need to receive at least $q_1 + 1$ messages.

Next, we will prove the theorem. The proof uses the same reasoning as Example 4.18: if a protocol sends at most $\sigma_i - 1$ messages, then we can choose $\mathbf{f}_{C_1}$ replicas in C_1 and $\mathbf{f}_{C_2}$ replicas in C_2 that will crash and thus assure that each of the $\sigma_i - 1$ messages is either sent by a crashed replica in C_1 or received by a crashed replica in C_2. We assume $i = 1$, $j = 2$, and $\mathbf{n}_{C_1} \geq \mathbf{n}_{C_2}$. The proof is by contradiction. Hence, assume that a protocol P can solve the cluster-sending problem using at most $\sigma_1 - 1$ messages. Consider a run of P that sends messages M. Without loss of generality, we can assume that $|M| = \sigma_1 - 1$. Let R be the top $\mathbf{f}_{C_2}$ receivers of messages in M, let $S = C_2 \setminus R$, let $M_R \subset M$ be the messages received by replicas in R, and let $N = M \setminus M_R$. We notice that $\mathbf{n}_R = \mathbf{f}_{C_2}$ and $\mathbf{n}_S = \mathbf{g}_{C_2}$.

First, we prove that $|M_R| \geq q_1 \mathbf{f}_{C_2} + \mathbf{f}_{C_2} \operatorname{sgn} r_1$, this by contradiction. Assume $|M_R| = q_1 \mathbf{f}_{C_2} + \mathbf{f}_{C_2} \operatorname{sgn} r_1 - v$, $v \geq 1$. Hence, we must have $|N| = q_1 \mathbf{g}_{C_2} + r_1 + v - 1$. Based on the value r_1, we distinguish two cases. The first case is $r_1 = 0$. In this case, $|M_R| = q_1 \mathbf{f}_{C_2} - v < q_1 \mathbf{f}_{C_2}$ and $|N| = q_1 \mathbf{g}_{C_2} + v - 1 \geq q_1 \mathbf{g}_{C_2}$. As $q_1 \mathbf{f}_{C_2} > |M_R|$, there must be a replica in R that received at most $q_1 - 1$ messages. As $|N| \geq q_1 \mathbf{g}_{C_2}$, there must be a replica in S that received at least q_1 messages. The other case is $r_1 > 0$. In this case, $|M_R| = q_1 \mathbf{f}_{C_2} + \mathbf{f}_{C_2} - v < (q_1 + 1)\mathbf{f}_{C_2}$ and $|N| = q_1 \mathbf{g}_{C_2} + r_1 + v - 1 > q_1 \mathbf{g}_{C_2}$. As $(q_1 + 1)\mathbf{f}_{C_2} > |M_R|$, there must be a replica in R that received at most q_1 messages. As $|N| > q_1 \mathbf{g}_{C_2}$, there must be a replica in S that received at least $q_1 + 1$ messages. In both cases, we identified a replica in S that received more messages than a replica in R, a contradiction. Hence, we must conclude that $|M_R| \geq q_1 \mathbf{f}_{C_2} + \mathbf{f}_{C_2} \operatorname{sgn} r_1$ and, consequently, $|N| \leq q_1 \mathbf{g}_{C_2} + r_1 - 1 \leq \mathbf{f}_{C_1}$. As $\mathbf{n}_R = \mathbf{f}_{C_2}$, all replicas in R could have crashed, in which case only the messages in N are actually received. As $|N| \leq \mathbf{f}_{C_1}$, all messages in N could be sent by replicas that have crashed. Hence, in the worst case, no message in M is successfully sent by a good replica in C_1 and received by a good replica in C_2, implying that P fails. $\qquad \square$

Notice that the above lower bounds guarantee the delivery of at least one message. Next, we consider systems with Byzantine failures and replica signing. As we have seen in RB-RS, at least $2\mathbf{f}_{C_1} + 1$ replicas in C_1 need to send a signed message to good replicas in C_2 to assure that at least $\mathbf{f}_{C_1} + 1$ such signed messages are send by good replicas and, hence, are guaranteed to arrive. A thorough analysis similar to the one of Theorem 4.19 reveals the following lower bounds.

Theorem 4.20   *Let $\mathfrak{R}$ be a system with Byzantine failures, let $C_1, C_2 \subset \mathfrak{R}$, and let $\{i, j\} = \{1, 2\}$ such that $\mathbf{n}_{C_i} \geq \mathbf{n}_{C_j}$. Let*

$$q_1 = (2\mathbf{f}_{C_1} + 1) \operatorname{div} \mathbf{g}_{C_2}; \qquad\qquad r_1 = (2\mathbf{f}_{C_1} + 1) \operatorname{mod} \mathbf{g}_{C_2};$$
$$\tau_1 = q_1 \mathbf{n}_{C_2} + r_1 + \mathbf{f}_{C_2} \operatorname{sgn} r_1,$$

and let

$$q_2 = (\mathbf{f}_{C_2} + 1) \operatorname{div} (\mathbf{g}_{C_1} - \mathbf{f}_{C_1}); \qquad\qquad r_2 = (\mathbf{f}_{C_2} + 1) \operatorname{mod} (\mathbf{g}_{C_1} - \mathbf{f}_{C_1});$$
$$\tau_2 = q_2 \mathbf{n}_{C_1} + r_2 + 2\mathbf{f}_{C_1} \operatorname{sgn} r_2,$$

in which sgn r_i *is the sign function that evaluates to* 1 *if* $r_i > 0$ *and* 0 *otherwise. Any protocol that solves the cluster-sending problem in which* C_1 *sends a value* v *to* C_2 *needs to exchange at least* τ_i *messages signed by replicas in* C_1.

Proof. Before we prove the theorem, we look at how τ_i, $i \in \{1, 2\}$, is obtained. There is a huge similarity to how σ_i is obtained: the main difference being that not *a single* but at least $\mathbf{f}_{C_1} + 1$ *messages* must arrive at C_2 (and, hence, be sent by good replicas). Furthermore, we observe that tolerating Byzantine failures using only digital signatures leads to an asymmetry between the sending cluster C_1 and C_2: the sending cluster needs at least $2\mathbf{f}_{C_1} + 1$ sending replicas, whereas the receiving cluster C_2 needs at least $\mathbf{f}_{C_2} + 1$ receiving replicas. We have seen a similar asymmetry in the cluster-sending protocol RB-RS. Due to this asymmetry, we end up with two distinct cases based on the relative cluster sizes.

First, we prove the case for $\mathbf{n}_{C_1} \geq \mathbf{n}_{C_2}$ using contradiction. Assume that a protocol P can solve the cluster-sending problem by sending at-most-$\tau_1 - 1$ signatures from C_1 to C_2. Consider a run of P that sends messages C, each message representing a single signature, with $|C| = \tau_1 - 1$. Following the proof of Theorem 4.19, one can show that, in the worst case, at most $\mathbf{f}_{C_1}$ signed messages are sent by good replicas in C_1 and received by good replicas in C_2. Now consider the situation in which the faulty replicas in C_1 mimic the behavior in C by sending signed messages for another value v' to the same receivers. For the replicas in C_2, the two runs behave the same, as in both cases at-most-$\mathbf{f}_{C_1}$ signatures for a value, possibly signed by distinct replicas, are received. Hence, either both runs successfully send values, in which case v' is received by C_2 without agreement, or both runs fail to send values. In both cases, P fails to solve the cluster-sending problem.

Next, we prove the case for $\mathbf{n}_{C_2} \geq \mathbf{n}_{C_1}$ using contradiction. Assume that a protocol P can solve the cluster-sending problem by sending at-most-$\tau_2 - 1$ signatures from C_1 to C_2. Consider a run of P that sends messages C, each message representing a single signature, with $|C| = \tau_2 - 1$. Let R be the top $2\mathbf{f}_{C_1}$ signers of messages in C, let $C_R \subset C$ be the messages signed by replicas in R, and let $D = C \setminus C_R$. Via a contradiction argument similar to the one used in the proof of Theorem 4.19, one can show that $|C_R| \geq 2q_2\mathbf{f}_{C_1} + 2\mathbf{f}_{C_1}$ sgn r and $|D| \leq q_2(\mathbf{g}_{C_1} - \mathbf{f}_{C_1}) + r - 1 = \mathbf{f}_{C_2}$. As $|D| \leq \mathbf{f}_{C_2}$, all replicas receiving these messages could have crashed. Hence, the only messages that are received by C_2 are in C_R. To complete the proof, we partition C_R into two sets of messages $C_{R,1}$ and $C_{R,2}$ such that both sets contain messages signed by at most $\mathbf{f}_{C_1}$ distinct replicas. As the messages in $C_{R,1}$ and $C_{R,2}$ are signed by $\mathbf{f}_{C_1}$ distinct replicas, one of these sets can contain only messages signed by Byzantine replicas. Hence, either $C_{R,1}$ or $C_{R,2}$ could represent a non-agreed upon value v', while only the other set represents v. Consequently, the replicas in C_2 cannot distinguish between receiving an agreed-upon value v or a non-agreed-upon-value v'. We conclude that P fails to solve the cluster-sending problem. $\square$

Sending-role (for the sending cluster C_1) :

1: All replicas in $\mathcal{G}(C_1)$ agree on v and construct $\text{cert}(v, C_1)$.
2: Choose replicas $S_1 \subseteq C_1$ with $\mathbf{n}_{S_1} = \mathbf{f}_{C_1} + \mathbf{f}_{C_2} + 1$.
3: Choose replicas $S_2 \subseteq C_2$ with $\mathbf{n}_{S_2} = \mathbf{f}_{C_1} + \mathbf{f}_{C_2} + 1$.
4: Choose a bijection $b : S_1 \to S_2$.
5: **for** $\mathsf{R}_1 \in S_1$ **do**
6:     R_1 sends $(v, \text{cert}(v, C_1))$ to $b(\mathsf{R}_1)$.
7: **end for**

Receiving-role (for the receiving cluster C_1) :

8: **event** $\mathsf{R}_2 \in \mathcal{G}(C_2)$ receives $(w, \text{cert}(w, C_1))$ from $\mathsf{R}_1 \in C_1$ **do**
9:     Broadcast $(w, \text{cert}(w, C_1))$ to all replicas in C_2.
10: **end event**
11: **event** $\mathsf{R}'_2 \in \mathcal{G}(C_2)$ receives $(w, \text{cert}(w, C_1))$ from $\mathsf{R}_2 \in C_2$ **do**
12:     R'_2 considers w *received*.
13: **end event**

Figure 4.11: BS-cs, the bijective sending cluster-sending protocol that sends a value v from C_1 to C_2. We assume Byzantine failures and a system that provides agreement certificates.

4.3.3   CLUSTER-SENDING VIA BIJECTIVE SENDING

In the previous section, we explored lower bounds for the cluster-sending problem. Close inspection shows that these lower bounds are only linear in the size of the clusters involved, which is much better than the quadratic complexity of the protocols presented in Section 4.3.1. Next, we develop *bijective sending*, a powerful technique that allows the design of highly efficient cluster-sending protocols that matches the established lower bounds.

First, we present a bijective sending protocol for systems with Byzantine failures and using agreement certificates. Let C_1 be a cluster in which the good replicas have reached *agreement* on sending a value v to a cluster C_2 and each has access to an agreement certificate $\text{cert}(v, C_1)$. Let $C_i, i \in \{1, 2\}$, be the cluster with the most replicas. To assure that at least a single good replica in C_1 sends a message to a good replica in C_2, we use the lower bound of Theorem 4.19: we choose σ_i distinct replicas $S_1 \subseteq C_1$ and distinct replicas $S_2 \subseteq C_2$ and instruct each replica in $S_1 \subseteq C_1$ to send v to a distinct replica in C_2. By doing so, we guarantee that at least a single message is sent and received by good replicas and, hence, guarantee successful cluster-sending. To be able to choose S_1 and S_2 with $\mathbf{n}_{S_1} = \mathbf{n}_{S_2} = \sigma_i$, we need $\sigma_i \leq \min(\mathbf{n}_{C_1}, \mathbf{n}_{C_2})$, in which case we have $\sigma_i = \mathbf{f}_{C_1} + \mathbf{f}_{C_2} + 1$. The pseudo-code for this *bijective sending* protocol (BS-cs), can be found in Figure 4.11. Next, we illustrate bijective sending, the underlying technique utilized by BS-cs.

Example 4.21   Let $\mathfrak{R}$ be a system and let $C_1, C_2 \subset \mathfrak{R}$ with

$$C_1 = \{\mathsf{R}_{1,1}, \ldots, \mathsf{R}_{1,8}\}, \qquad \mathcal{F}(C_1) = \{\mathsf{R}_{1,1}, \mathsf{R}_{1,3}, \mathsf{R}_{1,4}\},$$
$$C_2 = \{\mathsf{R}_{2,1}, \ldots, \mathsf{R}_{2,7}\}, \qquad \mathcal{F}(C_2) = \{\mathsf{R}_{2,1}, \mathsf{R}_{2,3}\}.$$

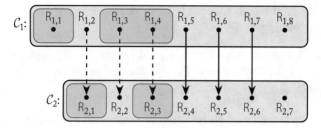

Figure 4.12: Bijective sending from C_1 to C_2. The faulty replicas are highlighted using a red background. The edges connect replicas $R \in C_1$ with $b(R) \in C_2$. Each solid edge indicates a message sent and received by good replicas. Each dashed edge indicates a message sent or received by a faulty replica.

We have $f_{C_1} + f_{C_2} + 1 = 6$ and we choose $S_1 = \{R_{1,2}, \ldots, R_{1,7}\}$, $S_2 = \{R_{2,1}, \ldots, R_{2,6}\}$, and $b = \{R_{1,i} \mapsto R_{2,i-1} \mid 2 \leq i \leq 7\}$. In Figure 4.12, we sketched this situation. Replica $R_{1,2}$ sends a valid message to $R_{2,1}$. As $R_{2,1}$ is faulty, it might ignore this message. Replicas $R_{1,3}$ and $R_{1,4}$ are faulty and might not send a valid message. Additionally, $R_{2,3}$ is faulty and might ignore any message it receives. The messages sent from $R_{1,5}$ to $R_{2,4}$, from $R_{1,6}$ to $R_{2,5}$, and from $R_{1,7}$ to $R_{2,6}$ are all sent by good replicas to good replicas. Hence, these messages all arrive correctly.

Having illustrated the concept of bijective sending, as employed by BS-cs, we are now ready to prove correctness of BS-cs.

Proposition 4.22 *Let $\mathfrak{R}$ be a system and let $C_1, C_2 \subset \mathfrak{R}$. If $\mathbf{n}_{C_1} > 2\mathbf{f}_{C_1}$, $\mathbf{n}_{C_2} > \mathbf{f}_{C_2}$, $\mathbf{n}_{C_1} > \mathbf{f}_{C_1} + \mathbf{f}_{C_2}$, and $\mathbf{n}_{C_2} > \mathbf{f}_{C_1} + \mathbf{f}_{C_2}$ then BS-cs satisfies Definition 4.15. The protocol sends $\mathbf{f}_{C_1} + \mathbf{f}_{C_2} + 1$ messages, of size $\mathcal{O}(\|v\| + \|\text{cert}(v, C_1)\|)$ each, between C_1 and C_2.*

Proof. Choose $S_1 \subseteq C_1$ and $S_2 \subseteq C_2$ in accordance with BS-cs (Figure 4.11). We have $\mathbf{n}_{S_1} = \mathbf{n}_{S_2} = \mathbf{f}_{C_1} + \mathbf{f}_{C_2} + 1$. Let $T = \{b(R) \mid R \in \mathcal{G}(S_1)\}$. By construction, we have $\mathbf{g}_{S_1} = \mathbf{n}_T \geq \mathbf{f}_{C_2} + 1$. Hence, we have $\mathbf{g}_T \geq 1$. Due to Line 6, each replica in $\mathcal{G}(T)$ will receive the message $(v, \text{cert}(v, C_1))$ from a distinct replica in $\mathcal{G}(S_1)$ and broadcast $(v, \text{cert}(v, C_1))$ to all replicas in C_2. As $\mathbf{g}_T \geq 1$, each replica $R'_2 \in \mathcal{G}(C_2)$ will receive $(v, \text{cert}(v, C_1))$ from a replica in C_2 and meet the condition at Line 11, proving *receipt* and *confirmation*. Finally, we have *agreement*, as $\text{cert}(v, C_1)$ is non-forgeable. □

We can also apply bijective sending when we only have signed messages. To do so, we replace the sender-role in RB-rs with a bijective sender-role. To assure that at least $\mathbf{f}_{C_1} + 1$ good replicas in C_1 send signed messages to good replicas in C_2, we choose sets of replicas $S_1 \subseteq C_1$ and $S_2 \subseteq C_2$ with $\mathbf{n}_{S_1} = \mathbf{n}_{S_2} = \tau_j$. To be able to choose S_1 and S_2 with $\mathbf{n}_{S_1} = \mathbf{n}_{S_2} = \tau_i$, we need $\tau_i \leq \min(\mathbf{n}_{C_1}, \mathbf{n}_{C_2})$, in which case we have $\tau_i = 2\mathbf{f}_{C_1} + \mathbf{f}_{C_2} + 1$. For the resultant protocol BS-RS, we have the following.

Corollary 4.23 *Let $\mathfrak{R}$ be a system and let $C_1, C_2 \subset \mathfrak{R}$. If $\mathbf{n}_{C_1} > 2\mathbf{f}_{C_1} + \mathbf{f}_{C_2} + 1$ and $\mathbf{n}_{C_2} > 2\mathbf{f}_{C_1} + \mathbf{f}_{C_2} + 1$, then BS-RS satisfies Definition 4.15. The protocol sends $2\mathbf{f}_{C_1} + \mathbf{f}_{C_2} + 1$ messages, of size $\mathcal{O}(\|v\|)$ each, between C_1 and C_2.*

Consider two clusters C_1 and C_2 in a highly structured multi-blockchain system, e.g., in a sharded fault-resilience system. In such environments, clusters typically have the same size, hence, $\mathbf{n}_{C_1} = \mathbf{n}_{C_2}$. Furthermore, each cluster operates via a practical high-performance consensus protocol such as PBFT, which implies that $\mathbf{n}_{C_1} > 3\mathbf{f}_{C_1}$ and $\mathbf{n}_{C_2} > 3\mathbf{f}_{C_2}$. In this situation, we always have $\mathbf{n}_{C_1} > 2\mathbf{f}_{C_1} + \mathbf{f}_{C_2} + 1$ and $\mathbf{n}_{C_2} > 2\mathbf{f}_{C_1} + \mathbf{f}_{C_2} + 1$. As such, both RB-CS and RB-RS can be applied to provide highly-efficient communication between the blockchains in these systems.

4.3.4 OPTIMAL CLUSTER-SENDING VIA PARTITIONING

The bijective sending techniques introduced in the previous section have optimal communication complexity. Unfortunately, bijective sending is in practice limited to communication between similar-sized clusters, as it places unrealistic requirements on clusters that vastly differ in size.

Example 4.24 Consider a system $\mathfrak{R}$ with Byzantine failures. The cluster $C_1 \subset \mathfrak{R}$ wants to send value v to $C_2 \subset \mathfrak{R}$ with $\mathbf{n}_{C_1} \geq \mathbf{n}_{C_2}$. To do so, BS-CS requires $\sigma_1 \leq \mathbf{n}_{C_2}$, in which case we have $\mathbf{f}_{C_1} + \mathbf{f}_{C_2} < \mathbf{n}_{C_2}$. Hence, when using BS-CS, the number of faulty replicas in C_1 is upper-bounded by $\mathbf{g}_{C_2} \leq \mathbf{n}_{C_2}$, this independent of the size of C_1.

Next, we show how to generalize bijective sending to arbitrary-sized clusters. We do so by *partitioning* the larger-sized cluster into a set of smaller clusters, and then letting sufficient of these smaller clusters participate independently in bijective sending. First, we introduce the relevant partitioning notation.

Definition 4.25 Let $\mathfrak{R}$ be a system, let $\mathcal{P} \subset \mathfrak{R}$ be a set of replicas in $\mathfrak{R}$, let $c > 0$ be a constant, let $q = \mathbf{n}_P \operatorname{div} c$, and let $r = \mathbf{n}_P \operatorname{mod} c$. A *c-partition* $\operatorname{partition}(\mathcal{P}) = \{P_1, \ldots, P_q, P'\}$ of $\mathcal{P}$ is a partition of the set of replicas $\mathcal{P}$ into sets $P_1, \ldots, P_q, P'$ such that $\mathbf{n}_{P_i} = c$, $1 \leq i \leq q$, and $\mathbf{n}_{P'} = r$.

Example 4.26 Let $\mathfrak{R}$ be a system, let $C = \{R_1, \ldots, R_{11}\} \subset \mathfrak{R}$, and let $\mathcal{F}(C) = \{R_1, \ldots, R_5\}$. The set $\{P_1, P_2, P'\}$ with

$$P_1 = \{R_1, \ldots, R_4\}, \quad P_2 = \{R_5, \ldots, R_8\}, \quad P' = \{R_9, R_{10}, R_{11}\}$$

is a 4-partition of C. The cluster C and the partition $\operatorname{partition}(C) = \{P_1, P_2, P'\}$ are illustrated in Figure 4.13. We have $\mathcal{F}(P_1) = P_1$, $\mathcal{G}(P_1) = \emptyset$, and $\mathbf{n}_{P_1} = \mathbf{f}_{P_1} = 4$. Likewise, we have $\mathcal{F}(P_2) = \{R_5\}$, $\mathcal{G}(P_2) = \{R_6, R_7, R_8\}$, $\mathbf{n}_{P_2} = 4$, and $\mathbf{f}_{P_2} = 1$.

Cluster $\mathcal{C}$:

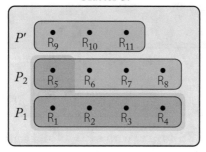

Figure 4.13: An example of a 4-partition of a cluster $\mathcal{C}$ with 11 replicas, of which the first five are faulty. The three partitions are grouped in blue boxes, the faulty replicas are highlighted using a red background.

Having introduced partitioning, we are ready to apply partitioning to BS-cs. Let $\mathcal{C}_1$ be a cluster in which the good replicas have reached agreement on sending a value v to a cluster $\mathcal{C}_2$ and constructed $\mathrm{cert}(v, \mathcal{C}_1)$. First, we consider the case $\mathbf{n}_{\mathcal{C}_1} \geq \mathbf{n}_{\mathcal{C}_2}$. In this case, we choose a set $P \subseteq \mathcal{C}_1$ of σ_1 replicas in $\mathcal{C}_1$ to send v to replicas in $\mathcal{C}_2$. To minimize the number of values v received by faulty replicas in $\mathcal{C}_2$, we minimize the number of values v send to each replica in $\mathcal{C}_2$. Conceptually, we do so by constructing a $\mathbf{n}_{\mathcal{C}_2}$-partition of the σ_1 replicas in P and instruct each resultant set in the partition to perform bijective sending of $(v, \mathrm{cert}(v, \mathcal{C}_1))$ to $\mathcal{C}_2$. The pseudo-code for the resultant *sender-partitioned bijective sending* protocol for systems that provide agreement certificates, named SPBS-(σ_1, cs), can be found in Figure 4.15. In a similar fashion, we can also apply partitioning to BS-rs, in which case we instruct τ_1 replicas in $\mathcal{C}_1$ to send a signed message holding v to replicas in $\mathcal{C}_2$, which yields the *sender-partitioned bijective sending* protocol SPBS-(τ_1, rs) for systems that provide replica signing. Next, we illustrate sender-partitioned bijective sending.

Example 4.27   We build on the situation of Example 4.18: we have clusters

$$\mathcal{C}_1 = \{\mathsf{R}_{1,1}, \ldots, \mathsf{R}_{1,15}\}, \qquad\qquad \mathcal{C}_2 = \{\mathsf{R}_{2,1}, \ldots, \mathsf{R}_{2,5}\}$$

with faulty replicas

$$\mathcal{F}(\mathcal{C}_1) = \{\mathsf{R}_{1,3}, \mathsf{R}_{1,4}, \mathsf{R}_{1,5}, \mathsf{R}_{1,8}, \mathsf{R}_{1,9}, \mathsf{R}_{1,10}, \mathsf{R}_{1,13}\}, \qquad \mathcal{F}(\mathcal{C}_2) = \{\mathsf{R}_{2,1}, \mathsf{R}_{2,2}\}.$$

We apply sender-partitioned bijective sending. We have $\mathbf{n}_{\mathcal{C}_1} > \mathbf{n}_{\mathcal{C}_2}$, $q_1 = 8 \operatorname{div} 3 = 2$, $r_1 = 8 \bmod 3 = 2$, and $\sigma_1 = 2 \cdot 5 + 2 + 2 = 14$. We choose the replicas $\mathcal{P} = \{\mathsf{R}_{1,1}, \ldots, \mathsf{R}_{1,14}\} \subseteq \mathcal{C}_1$ and we choose the $\mathbf{n}_{\mathcal{C}_2}$-partition $\mathrm{partition}(\mathcal{P}) = \{P_1, P_2, P'\}$ with

$$P_1 = \{\mathsf{R}_{1,1}, \mathsf{R}_{1,2}, \mathsf{R}_{1,3}, \mathsf{R}_{1,4}, \mathsf{R}_{1,5}\},$$
$$P_2 = \{\mathsf{R}_{1,6}, \mathsf{R}_{1,7}, \mathsf{R}_{1,8}, \mathsf{R}_{1,9}, \mathsf{R}_{1,10}\},$$
$$P' = \{\mathsf{R}_{1,11}, \mathsf{R}_{1,12}, \mathsf{R}_{1,13}, \mathsf{R}_{1,14}\}.$$

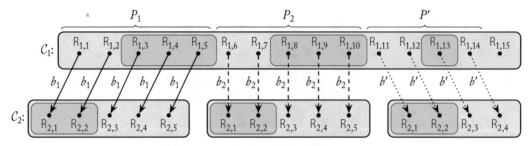

Figure 4.14: An example of SPBS-(σ_1,cs) with $\sigma_1 = 14$ and partition$(\mathcal{P}) = \{P_1, P_2, P'\}$. Notice that only the instance of bijective sending with the replicas in P' and bijection b' will succeed in cluster-sending.

Hence, SPBS-(σ_1,cs) will perform three rounds of bijective sending. In the first two rounds, we will send to all replicas in $\mathcal{C}_2$. In the last round, we will send to the replicas $Q = \{\mathsf{R}_{2,1}, \mathsf{R}_{2,2}, \mathsf{R}_{2,3}, \mathsf{R}_{2,4}\}$. We choose bijections

$$b_1 = \{\mathsf{R}_{1,1} \mapsto \mathsf{R}_{2,1}, \ldots, \mathsf{R}_{1,5} \mapsto \mathsf{R}_{2,5}\},$$
$$b_2 = \{\mathsf{R}_{1,6} \mapsto \mathsf{R}_{2,1}, \ldots, \mathsf{R}_{1,10} \mapsto \mathsf{R}_{2,5}\},$$
$$b' = \{\mathsf{R}_{1,11} \mapsto \mathsf{R}_{2,1}, \ldots, \mathsf{R}_{1,14} \mapsto \mathsf{R}_{2,4}\}.$$

In the rounds of bijective sending for P_1 and P_2, we have $\mathbf{f}_{P_1} + \mathbf{f}_{\mathcal{C}_2} = \mathbf{f}_{P_2} + \mathbf{f}_{\mathcal{C}_2} = 3 + 2 = 5 = \mathbf{n}_{\mathcal{C}_2}$. Due to the particular choice of bijections b_1 and b_2, these rounds will fail cluster-sending. In the last round, we have $\mathbf{f}_{P'} + \mathbf{f}_Q = 1 + 2 = 3 < \mathbf{n}_{P'} = \mathbf{n}_Q$. Hence, for these two sets of replicas, we satisfy the conditions of BS-cs, can successfully apply bijective sending, and, as we have proven in Proposition 4.22, we will have successful cluster-sending (as the good replica $\mathsf{R}_{1,14} \in \mathcal{C}_1$ will send v together with an agreement certificate $\mathrm{cert}(v, \mathcal{C}_1)$ to the good replica $\mathsf{R}_{2,4} \in \mathcal{C}_2$). We have illustrated the described working of SPBS-(σ_1,cs) in Figure 4.14.

Having illustrated the working of sender-partitioned bijective sending, we now prove the correctness of these instances of sender-partitioned bijective sending.

Proposition 4.28   *Let $\mathfrak{R}$ be a system, let $\mathcal{C}_1, \mathcal{C}_2 \subset \mathfrak{R}$, let σ_1 be as defined in Theorem 4.19, and let τ_1 be as defined in Theorem 4.20.*

1. *If $\mathfrak{R}$ has agreement certificates and $\sigma_1 \leq \mathbf{n}_{\mathcal{C}_1}$, then SPBS-$(\sigma_1,\mathrm{cs})$ satisfies Definition 4.15. The protocol sends σ_1 messages, of size $\mathcal{O}(\|v\| + \|\mathrm{cert}(v, \mathcal{C}_1)\|)$ each, between $\mathcal{C}_1$ and $\mathcal{C}_2$.*

2. *If $\tau_1 \leq \mathbf{n}_{\mathcal{C}_1}$, then SPBS-$(\tau_1,\mathrm{RS})$ satisfies Definition 4.15. The protocol sends τ_1 messages, of size $\mathcal{O}(\|v\|)$ each, between $\mathcal{C}_1$ and $\mathcal{C}_2$.*

Sending-role (for the sending cluster C_1) :

1: The agreement step of BS-ζ for value v.
2: Choose replicas $\mathcal{P} \subseteq C_1$ with $\mathbf{n}_\mathcal{P} = \alpha$.
3: Choose a $\mathbf{n}_{C_2}$-partition partition$(\mathcal{P})$ of $\mathcal{P}$.
4: **for** $P \in$ partition$(\mathcal{P})$ **do**
5:    Choose replicas $Q \subseteq C_2$ with $\mathbf{n}_Q = \mathbf{n}_P$.
6:    Choose a bijection $b : P \to Q$.
7:    **for** $\mathsf{R}_1 \in P$ **do**
8:       Send v from R_1 to $b(\mathsf{R}_1)$ via the send step of BS-ζ.
9:    **end for**
10: **end for**

Receiving-role (for the receiving cluster C_1) :

11: See the protocol for the receiving cluster in BS-ζ.

Figure 4.15: SPBS-(α,ζ), $\zeta \in \{\text{cs, rs}\}$, the sender-partitioned bijective sending cluster-sending protocol that sends a value v from C_1 to C_2. We assume the same system properties as BS-ζ.

Proof. Let $\beta = (\mathbf{f}_{C_1} + 1)$ when using agreement certificates (SPBS-(σ_1,cs)) and let $\beta = (2\mathbf{f}_{C_1} + 1)$ when using only signed messages (SPBS-(τ_1,rs)). Let $q = \beta$ div $\mathbf{g}_{C_2}$ and $r = \beta \bmod \mathbf{g}_{C_2}$. We have $\alpha = q\mathbf{n}_{C_2} + r + \mathbf{f}_{C_2} \operatorname{sgn} r$. Choose $\mathcal{P}$ and choose partition$(\mathcal{P}) = \{P_1, \ldots, P_q, P'\}$ in accordance with SPBS-(α,ζ) (Figure 4.15). For each $P \in \mathcal{P}$, choose a Q and b in accordance with SPBS-(α,ζ), and let $z(P) = \{\mathsf{R} \in P \mid b(\mathsf{R}) \in \mathcal{F}(Q)\}$. As each such b has a distinct domain, the union of them is a surjection $f : \mathcal{P} \to \mathbf{n}_{C_2}$. By construction, we have $\mathbf{n}_{P'} = r + \mathbf{f}_{C_2} \operatorname{sgn} r$, $\mathbf{n}_{z(P')} \leq \mathbf{f}_{C_2} \operatorname{sgn} r$, and, for every i, $1 \leq i \leq q$, $\mathbf{n}_{P_i} = \mathbf{n}_{C_2}$ and $\mathbf{n}_{z(P_i)} = \mathbf{f}_{C_2}$. Let $V = \mathcal{P} \setminus \left(\bigcup_{P \in \text{partition}(\mathcal{P})} z(P) \right)$. We have

$$\mathbf{n}_V \geq \mathbf{n}_\mathcal{P} - (q\mathbf{f}_{C_2} + \mathbf{f}_{C_2} \operatorname{sgn} r) = (q\mathbf{n}_{C_2} + r + \mathbf{f}_{C_2} \operatorname{sgn} r) - (q\mathbf{f}_{C_2} + \mathbf{f}_{C_2} \operatorname{sgn} r) = q\mathbf{g}_{C_2} + r = \beta.$$

Let $T = \{f(\mathsf{R}) \mid \mathsf{R} \in \mathcal{G}(V)\}$. By construction, we have $\mathbf{g}_T = \mathbf{n}_T$. To complete the proof, we consider agreement certificates and signed messages separately. First, the case when using agreement certificates. As $\mathbf{n}_V \geq \beta = \mathbf{f}_{C_1} + 1$, we have $\mathbf{g}_V \geq 1$. By construction, the replicas in $\mathcal{G}(T)$ will receive the messages $(v, \text{cert}(v, C_1))$ from the replicas $\mathsf{R}_1 \in \mathcal{G}(V)$. Hence, analogous to Proposition 4.22, we can prove *receipt*, *confirmation*, and *agreement*. Finally, the case when using only signed messages. As $\mathbf{n}_V \geq \beta = 2\mathbf{f}_{C_1} + 1$, we have $\mathbf{g}_V \geq \mathbf{f}_{C_1} + 1$. By construction, the replicas in $\mathcal{G}(T)$ will receive the messages $(v, \text{cert}(v, \mathsf{R}_1))$ from each replica $\mathsf{R}_1 \in \mathcal{G}(V)$. Hence, analogous to Corollary 4.23, we can prove *receipt*, *confirmation*, and *agreement*. $\square$

Finally, we consider the case $\mathbf{n}_{C_1} \leq \mathbf{n}_{C_2}$. In this case, we apply partitioning to BS-cs by choosing a set P of σ_2 replicas in C_2, constructing a $\mathbf{n}_{C_1}$-partition of P, and instruct C_1 to perform bijective sending with each set in the partition. The pseudo-code for the resultant *receiver-partitioned bijective sending* protocol for systems that provide agreement certificates,

Sending-role (for the sending cluster C_1) :

1: The agreement step of BS-ζ for value v.
2: Choose replicas $\mathcal{P} \subseteq C_2$ with $\mathbf{n}_\mathcal{P} = \alpha$.
3: Choose a $\mathbf{n}_{C_1}$-partition partition$(\mathcal{P})$ of $\mathcal{P}$.
4: **for** $P \in$ partition$(\mathcal{P})$ **do**
5:     Choose replicas $Q \subseteq C_1$ with $\mathbf{n}_Q = \mathbf{n}_P$.
6:     Choose a bijection $b : Q \to P$.
7:     **for** $\mathsf{R}_1 \in Q$ **do**
8:         Send v from R_1 to $b(\mathsf{R}_1)$ via the send step of BS-ζ.
9:     **end for**
10: **end for**

Receiving-role (for the receiving cluster C_1) :

11: See the protocol for the receiving cluster in BS-ζ.

Figure 4.16: RPBS-(α,ζ), $\zeta \in \{\text{CS}, \text{RS}\}$, the receiver-partitioned bijective sending cluster-sending protocol that sends a value v from C_1 to C_2. We assume the same system properties as BS-ζ.

named RPBS-(σ_2,cs), can be found in Figure 4.16. In a similar fashion, we can also apply partitioning to BS-RS, which yields the *receiver-partitioned bijective sending* protocol RPBS-(τ_2,RS) for systems that provide replica signing. Next, we prove the correctness of these instances of receiver-partitioned bijective sending.

Proposition 4.29   *Let $\mathfrak{R}$ be a system, let $C_1, C_2 \subset \mathfrak{R}$, let σ_2 be as defined in Theorem 4.19, and let τ_2 be as defined in Theorem 4.20.*

1. *If $\mathfrak{R}$ has agreement certificates and $\sigma_2 \leq \mathbf{n}_{C_2}$, then RPBS-$(\sigma_2,\text{cs})$ satisfies Definition 4.15. The protocol sends σ_2 messages, of size $\mathcal{O}(\|v\| + \|\text{cert}(v, C_1)\|)$ each, between C_1 and C_2.*

2. *If $\tau_2 \leq \mathbf{n}_{C_2}$, then RPBS-$(\tau_2,\text{RS})$ satisfies Definition 4.15. The protocol sends τ_2 messages, of size $\mathcal{O}(\|v\|)$ each, between C_1 and C_2.*

Proof. Let $\beta = \mathbf{g}_{C_1}$ and $\gamma = 1$ when using agreement certificates (RPBS-(σ_2,cs)) and let $\beta = (\mathbf{g}_{C_1} - \mathbf{f}_{C_1})$ and $\gamma = 2$ when using only signed messages (RPBS-(τ_2,RS)). Let $q = (\mathbf{f}_{C_2} + 1) \operatorname{div} \beta$ and $r = (\mathbf{f}_{C_2} + 1) \operatorname{mod} \beta$. We have $\alpha = q\mathbf{n}_{C_1} + r + \gamma \mathbf{f}_{C_1} \operatorname{sgn} r$. Choose $\mathcal{P}$ and choose partition$(\mathcal{P}) = \{P_1, \ldots, P_q, P'\}$ in accordance with RPBS-(α,ζ) (Figure 4.16). For each $P \in \mathcal{P}$, choose a Q and b in accordance with RPBS-(α,ζ), and let $z(P) = \{\mathsf{R} \in P \mid b^{-1}(\mathsf{R}) \in \mathcal{F}(Q)\}$. As each such b^{-1} has a distinct domain, the union of them is a surjection $f^{-1} : \mathcal{P} \to \mathbf{n}_{C_1}$. By construction, we have $\mathbf{n}_{P'} = r + \gamma \mathbf{f}_{C_1} \operatorname{sgn} r$, $\mathbf{n}_{z(P')} \leq \mathbf{f}_{C_1} \operatorname{sgn} r$, and, for every i, $1 \leq i \leq q$,

$\mathbf{n}_{P_i} = \mathbf{n}_{C_1}$ and $\mathbf{n}_{z(P_i)} = \mathbf{f}_{C_1}$. Let $T = \mathcal{P} \setminus \left(\bigcup_{P \in \text{partition}(\mathcal{P})} z(P) \right)$. We have

$$\mathbf{n}_T \geq \mathbf{n}_{\mathcal{P}} - (q\mathbf{f}_{C_1} + \mathbf{f}_{C_1} \operatorname{sgn} r) = (q\mathbf{n}_{C_1} + r + \gamma \mathbf{f}_{C_1} \operatorname{sgn} r) - (q\mathbf{f}_{C_1} + \mathbf{f}_{C_1} \operatorname{sgn} r) =$$
$$q\mathbf{g}_{C_1} + r + (\gamma - 1)\mathbf{f}_{C_1} \operatorname{sgn} r.$$

To complete the proof, we consider agreement certificates and signed messages separately.

First, the case when using agreement certificates. We have $\beta = \mathbf{g}_{C_1}$ and $\gamma = 1$. Hence,

$$\mathbf{n}_T \geq q\mathbf{g}_{C_1} + r + (\gamma - 1)\mathbf{f}_{C_1} \operatorname{sgn} r = q\beta + r = \mathbf{f}_{C_2} + 1.$$

We have $\mathbf{g}_T \geq \mathbf{n}_T - \mathbf{f}_{C_2} \geq 1$. Let $V = \{f^{-1}(\mathsf{R}) \mid \mathsf{R} \in \mathcal{G}(T)\}$. By construction, we have $\mathbf{g}_V = \mathbf{n}_V$ and we have $\mathbf{g}_V \geq 1$. Consequently, the replicas in $\mathcal{G}(T)$ will receive the messages $(v, \text{cert}(v, C_1))$ from the replicas $\mathsf{R}_1 \in \mathcal{G}(V)$. Analogous to Proposition 4.22, we can prove *receipt*, *confirmation*, and *agreement*.

Finally, the case when using only signed messages. We have $\beta = \mathbf{g}_{C_1} - \mathbf{f}_{C_1}$ and $\gamma = 2$. Hence,

$$\mathbf{n}_T \geq q\mathbf{g}_{C_1} + r + (\gamma - 1)\mathbf{f}_{C_1} \operatorname{sgn} r = q(\beta + \mathbf{f}_{C_1}) + r + \mathbf{f}_{C_1} \operatorname{sgn} r =$$
$$(q\beta + r) + q\mathbf{f}_{C_1} + \mathbf{f}_{C_1} \operatorname{sgn} r = (\mathbf{f}_{C_2} + 1) + q\mathbf{f}_{C_1} + \mathbf{f}_{C_1} \operatorname{sgn} r.$$

We have $\mathbf{g}_T \geq q\mathbf{f}_{C_1} + \mathbf{f}_{C_1} \operatorname{sgn} r + 1 = (q + \operatorname{sgn} r)\mathbf{f}_{C_1} + 1$. As there are $(q + \operatorname{sgn} r)$ non-empty sets in partition($\mathcal{P}$), there must be a set $P \in \mathcal{P}$ with $\mathbf{n}_{P \cap \mathbf{g}_T} \geq \mathbf{f}_{C_1} + 1$. Let b be the bijection chosen earlier for P and let $V = \{b^{-1}(\mathsf{R}) \mid \mathsf{R} \in (P \cap \mathbf{g}_T)\}$. By construction, we have $\mathbf{g}_V = \mathbf{n}_V$ and we have $\mathbf{g}_V \geq \mathbf{f}_{C_1} + 1$. Consequently, the replicas in $\mathcal{G}(T)$ will receive the messages $(v, \text{cert}(v, \mathsf{R}_1))$ from each replica $\mathsf{R}_1 \in \mathcal{G}(V)$. Hence, analogous to Corollary 4.23, we can prove *receipt*, *confirmation*, and *agreement*. □

The bijective sending cluster-sending protocols, the sender-partitioned bijective cluster-sending protocols, and the receiver-partitioned bijective cluster-sending protocols each deal with differently sized clusters. By choosing the applicable protocols, we have the following.

Theorem 4.30   *Let $\mathfrak{R}$ be a system, let $C_1, C_2 \subset \mathfrak{R}$, let σ_1 and σ_2 be as defined in Theorem 4.19, and let τ_1 and τ_2 be as defined in Theorem 4.20. Consider the cluster-sending problem in which C_1 sends a value v to C_2.*

1. *If $\mathbf{n}_C > 3\mathbf{f}_C$, $C \subset \mathfrak{R}$, and $\mathfrak{R}$ has only crash failures or omit failures, then BS-cs, SPBS-(σ_1, cs), and RPBS-(σ_2, cs) are a solution to the cluster-sending problem with optimal message complexity. These protocols solve the cluster-sending problem using $\mathcal{O}(\max(\mathbf{n}_{C_1}, \mathbf{n}_{C_2}))$ messages, of size $\mathcal{O}(\|v\|)$ each.*

2. *If $\mathbf{n}_C > 3\mathbf{f}_C$, $C \subset \mathfrak{R}$, and $\mathfrak{R}$ has agreement certificates, then BS-cs, SPBS-(σ_1, cs), and RPBS-(σ_2, cs) are a solution to the cluster-sending problem with optimal message complexity (in the number of messages). These protocols solve the cluster-sending problem using $\mathcal{O}(\max(\mathbf{n}_{C_1}, \mathbf{n}_{C_2}))$ messages, of size $\mathcal{O}(\|v\| + \|\text{cert}(v, C_1)\|)$ each.*

3. *If $n_C > 4f_C$, $C \subset \mathfrak{R}$, and $\mathfrak{R}$ use signed messages, then* BS-RS, SPBS-$(\tau_1,$RS$)$, *and* RPBS-$(\tau_2,$RS$)$ *are a solution to the cluster-sending problem with optimal usage of message signatures. These protocols solve the cluster-sending problem using* $\mathcal{O}(\max(n_{C_1}, n_{C_2}))$ *messages, of size* $\mathcal{O}(\|v\|)$ *each.*

We notice that the above cluster-sending protocols require reliable communication: if messages can get lost, then the above protocols do not always work. To deal with message loss, one can incorporate a message acknowledgment mechanism in which C_2 cluster-sends a receipt-message back to C_1. Next, C_1 will repeat cluster-sending of v until such a receipt message is received.

4.4   GEO-SCALE AWARE CONSENSUS

For our first application of *cluster-sending*, we consider the problem of deploying a fully replicated blockchain with replicas spread out over large geographic distances. Due to the high message complexity of consensus, as discussed in Chapter 3, and the high communication costs in a wide-area network (see Figure 4.8), most state-of-the-art blockchain systems will have only limited throughput when replicas are spread out.

To enable the geo-scale deployment of a permissioned blockchain system, it is necessary that the underlying consensus protocol used distinguish between *local* and *global* communication. Several consensus protocols have proposed novel solutions toward such geo-scale awareness. Prime examples are protocols such as GEOBFT [123] and STEWARD [11]. Next, we illustrate such protocols by taking an in-depth look at the design of GEOBFT [123].

The Geo-Scale Byzantine Fault-Tolerant consensus protocol GEOBFT [123] is a consensus protocol that uses topological information to group all replicas in a single region into a single cluster and favors communication within a cluster over communication between clusters. Likewise, GEOBFT assigns each client to a single cluster. This clustering is used to achieve high throughput and scalability in geo-scale deployments. GEOBFT operates in rounds and in each round every cluster will be able to propose a single client request for execution (or, if batching is enabled, a single batch fo client requests). Hence, GEOBFT uses *geo-aware sharding* with respect to consensus decisions, even though the system remains fully replicated. Next we sketch the high-level working of such a round of GEOBFT. Each round consists of three steps: *local replication*, *inter-cluster sharing*, and *ordering and execution*.

1. At the start of each round, each cluster chooses a single transaction of a local client. Next, the cluster will *locally replicate* this transaction in a Byzantine fault-tolerant manner using PBFT. At the end of successful local replication, PBFT guarantees that each good replica can prove successful local replication via a *committed certificate*.

2. Next, each cluster shares the locally-replicated transaction together with its committed certificate with all other clusters. To minimize inter-cluster communication, GEOBFT

uses a novel *optimistic cluster-sending protocol* to perform this *inter-cluster sharing* step. This optimistic cluster-sending protocol has a global phase in which clusters exchange locally-replicated transactions, followed by a local phase in which clusters distribute any received transactions locally among all local replicas. To deal with failures, the global sharing protocol utilizes a novel remote view-change algorithm.

3. Finally, after receiving all transactions that are locally replicated in other clusters, each replica in each cluster will deterministically *order* all these transactions and then proceed with *executing* them. After execution, the replicas in each cluster inform only local clients of the outcome of execution of their transactions (e.g., confirm execution or return any execution results).

In Figure 4.17, we have sketched the working of a single round of GEOBFT in a setting of two clusters with four replicas each.

To perform the inter-cluster sharing step, GEOBFT relies on a novel optimistic cluster-sending protocol to exchange committed certificates between clusters. Next, we provide a detailed description of this optimistic cluster-sending protocol. Then, in Section 4.4.2, we explore in more detail at how GEOBFT orders and executes transactions of each cluster. Finally, in Section 4.4.3, we conclude on the geo-scale performance of GEOBFT.

4.4.1   OPTIMISTIC INTER-CLUSTER SENDING

After a cluster C chooses a client request $\langle \tau \rangle_C$ by reaching local consensus on PrePrepare message m in round ρ—enabling construction of the committed certificate for m that proves local consensus—C needs to exchange this client request and the accompanying proof with all other clusters. This exchange step requires global inter-cluster communication, which we want to minimize while retaining the ability to reliably detect failure of the sender. This is not as straightforward as it sounds, as the following example illustrates.

Example 4.31   Consider two clusters C_1, C_2 and the simple global communication protocol in which a message m is sent from C_1 to C_2 by letting the primary P_{C_1} of C_1 send m to the primary P_{C_2} of C_2 (which can then disseminate m in C_2). In this protocol, the replicas in C_2 will be unable to determine what went wrong if they do not receive any messages. We distinguish two cases.

1. P_{C_1} is Byzantine and behaves correctly toward every replica, except that it never sends messages to P_{C_2}, while P_{C_2} is good.

2. P_{C_1} is good, while P_{C_2} is Byzantine and behaves correctly toward every replica, except that it drops all messages sent by P_{C_1}.

In both cases, the replicas in C_2 do not receive any messages from C_1, while both clusters see correct behavior of their primaries with respect to local consensus. Indeed, with this little amount

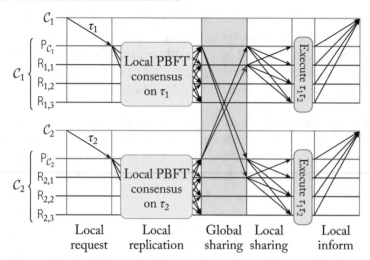

Figure 4.17: Representation of the normal-case algorithm of GEOBFT running on two clusters. Clients C_i, $i \in \{1, 2\}$, request transactions τ_i from their local cluster C_i. The primary $P_{C_i} \in C_i$ replicates this transaction to all local replicas using PBFT. At the end of local replication, the primary can produce a committed certificate to prove replication of τ_i. These certificates are shared with other clusters via inter-cluster communication, after which all replicas in all clusters can execute τ_i and C_i can inform C_i.

of communication, it is impossible for replicas in C_2 to determine whether P_{C_1} is faulty (and did not send any messages) or P_{C_2} is faulty (and did not forward any received messages from C_1).

The optimistic cluster-sending protocol of GEOBFT alleviate the detection issue illustrated in Example 4.31, while still optimizing for the case in which the sending primary is good. In Example 4.31, we already showed that sending only a single message is not sufficient. Sending $f + 1$ messages is sufficient, however.

Let $(m, \text{Commit}_{P_{C_1}}(m))$ be the message C_1 needs to send to C_2 consisting of a `PrePrepare` message m and a committed certificate $\text{Commit}_{P_{C_1}}(m)$. Based on the observations made above, we propose the following two-phase normal-case global sharing protocol. In the *global phase*, the primary P_{C_1} of C_1 sends $(m, \text{Commit}_{P_{C_1}}(m))$ to $f + 1$ replicas in C_2. In the *local phase*, any good replica $R \in C_2$ that receives a well-formed message $(m, \text{Commit}_{P_{C_1}}(m))$ with valid signatures will forward $(m, \text{Commit}_{P_{C_1}}(m))$ to all replicas in C_2. We have sketched this normal-case sending protocol in Figure 4.18 and the detailed pseudo-code for this protocol can be found in Figure 4.19.

Proposition 4.32 *Let $\mathfrak{R}$ be a system, let $C_1, C_2 \subset \mathfrak{R}$ be two clusters, and let $(m, \text{Commit}_{P_{C_1}}(m))$ be the message C_1 sends to C_2 using the normal-case global sharing protocol of Figure 4.19, in which*

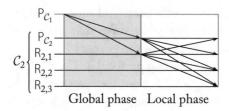

Figure 4.18: A schematic representation of the normal-case working of the global sharing protocol used by C_1 to send $(m, \text{Commit}_{P_{C_1}}(m))$ to C_2.

The global phase (used by the primary P_{C_1} of C_1) :

1: Choose a set S of $\mathbf{f}+1$ replicas in C_2.
2: Send $(m, \text{Commit}_{P_{C_1}}(m))$ to each replica in S.

The local phase (used by replicas $\mathsf{R} \in C_2$) :

3: **event** receive $(m, \text{Commit}_{P_{C_1}}(m))$ from a replica $\mathsf{Q} \in C_1$ **do**
4:     Broadcast $(m, \text{Commit}_{P_{C_1}}(m))$ to all replicas in C_2.
5: **end event**

Figure 4.19: The normal-case global sharing protocol used by C_1 to send $(m, \text{Commit}_{P_{C_1}}(m))$ to C_2, in which m is a PrePrepare message and $\text{Commit}_{P_{C_1}}(m)$ a committed certificate for m.

m is a PrePrepare *message for round ρ of C_1 and* $\text{Commit}_{P_{C_1}}(m)$ *a committed certificate for m. We have the following.*

1. *If the primary* P_{C_1} *of C_1 is good and communication is reliable, then every replica in C_2 will eventually receive v.*

2. *Replicas in C_2 will only accept m for round ρ of C_1.*

Proof. If P_{C_1} is good and communication is reliable, then $\mathbf{f}+1$ replicas in C_2 will receive v. At least a single out of these $\mathbf{f}+1$ receiving replicas in C_2 is good and will forward this message to all replicas in C_2, proving the first statement.

The committed certificate $\text{Commit}_{P_{C_1}}(m)$ cannot be forged by faulty replicas. Hence, the message m itself proves intent of C_1 to send m even after m is forwarded by replicas in C_2. Any other PrePrepare message m' for round ρ must also contain a committed certificate. By Theorem 2.15, only one such a certificate can exist for round ρ of C_1. Hence, $m = m'$, proving the second statement.   □

We notice that there are two cases in which replicas in C_2 do not receive $(m, \text{Commit}_{P_{C_1}}(m))$ from C_1: either P_{C_1} is faulty and did not sent $(m, \text{Commit}_{P_{C_1}}(m))$ to $\mathbf{f}+1$

replicas in C_2, or communication is unreliable and messages are delayed or lost. In both cases, GEOBFT provides a *remote view-change algorithm* that replicas in C_2 can use to force primary replacement in C_1 (causing replacement of the primary P_{C_1}).

The optimistic inter-cluster sending protocol of GEOBFT provides *cluster-sending*. In the optimistic case, it does so *more efficiently* than the (partitioned) bijective cluster sending techniques of Section 4.3. Furthermore, the optimistic inter-cluster sending protocol can deal with *unreliable communication* as it has a recovery path via remote view-changes. The downside of the optimistic inter-cluster sending protocol is that the recovery path is rather expensive when compared to the (partitioned) bijective cluster sending techniques of Section 4.3. Finally, we notice that the optimistic inter-cluster sending protocol of GEOBFT resembles the RB-cs protocol [135, 136] of Section 4.3.1. Specifically, the optimistic case of the inter-cluster sending protocol is equivalent to cluster-sending using reliable broadcasts in an environment (assuming that the sending cluster is fault-free).

4.4.2   ORDERING AND EXECUTION

After each cluster has chosen a client request for execution and has received all client requests chosen by other clusters, replicas are ready for the final step: ordering and executing these client requests. Notice here the conceptual resemblance between GEOBFT and *concurrent consensus* (see Section 3.5.4): both provide full replication by letting several independent parties propose transactions for each round. As such, the ordering and execution approach of RCC [121, 122] can easily be applied to GEOBFT (see Section 3.6.2). In practice, GEOBFT is designed with only geo-scale aware scalability in mind, and, hence, uses a rather simple ordering and execution scheme. Assume that GEOBFT is operating over $\mathbf{m}$ clusters, $C_1, \ldots, C_{\mathbf{m}}$ and let

$$S_\rho = \{(\langle \tau_i \rangle_{C_i} \mid (1 \leq i \leq \mathbf{m}) \wedge (C_i \text{ a client of cluster } C_i)\}$$

be the set of $\mathbf{m}$ client requests received by each replica.

The last step is to put these client requests in a unique order, execute them, and inform the clients of the outcome. To do so, GEOBFT simply uses a strict pre-defined ordering on the clusters. E.g., it will execute the transactions in the order $[\tau_1, \ldots, \tau_{\mathbf{m}}]$. Finally, each replica $R \in C_i$, $1 \leq i \leq \mathbf{m}$, will inform the client C_i after execution of τ_i (e.g., confirmation of execution or the result of execution). As all good replicas behave deterministic, execution will yield the same state and execution results across all good replicas, and the client C_i can determine the outcome by simply checking for at least $\mathbf{f}_{C_i}$ identical outcomes.

4.4.3   ON THE GEO-SCALE PERFORMANCE OF GEOBFT

To see the impact of the geo-scale aware design of GEOBFT, we will model the normal-case performance (when communication is reliable and all primaries are good) and compare it with PBFT. Consider running GEOBFT in a system with $\mathbf{m}$ clusters, each having $\mathbf{n}$ replicas of which $\mathbf{f}$ are faulty ($\mathbf{n} > 3\mathbf{f}$). Hence, we have $\mathbf{mn}$ replicas in total.

First, we consider a single round of PBFT in a system with $\mathbf{mn}$ replicas. A primary will send PrePrepare messages to all other replicas (of size s_t). Then, this primary will receive Prepare messages from all other replicas, send commit messages to all other replicas, and receive commit messages from all other replicas (each of size s_m). Only $(\mathbf{n}-1)$ other replicas are local, while the remaining $(\mathbf{m}-1)\mathbf{n}$ replicas are non-local. Hence, in total, the primary will send and receive $4(\mathbf{n}-1)$ local messages with a total size of $(s_t + 3s_m)(\mathbf{n}-1)$ and send and receive $4(\mathbf{m}-1)\mathbf{n}$ non-local messages with a total size of $(s_t + 3s_m)(\mathbf{m}-1)\mathbf{n}$. As we have seen in Chapter 3, the communication by the primary is typically higher than any other replica and, hence, will be the bottleneck in a geo-scale system.

In a single round of GEOBFT, each cluster will perform the local replication step independently. To do so, each cluster performs PBFT locally to decide on a transaction. The primary of each cluster does so by sending and receiving $4(\mathbf{n}-1)$ local messages with a total size of $(s_t + 3s_m)(\mathbf{n}-1)$. Next, each cluster performs inter-cluster sharing. To do so, the primary of each cluster performs global sharing, during which it sends $\mathbf{f}+1$ non-local messages, with a size of s_t each, to every other cluster. During global sharing, each primary can also receives at most $\mathbf{m}-1$ non-local messages with a total size of $s_t(\mathbf{m}-1)$. Hence, global sharing results in at-most $\mathbf{f}+\mathbf{m}$ non-local messages send and received per primary with a total size of $s_t(\mathbf{f}+\mathbf{m})$ (assuming committed certificates are represented using threshold signatures). Finally, each cluster performs local sharing, during which the primary will send and receive at-most $(\mathbf{m}-1)(\mathbf{n}-1)$ local messages with a total size of $s_t(\mathbf{m}-1)(\mathbf{n}-1)$.

As GEOBFT uses $\mathbf{m}$ primaries that are accepting transactions per round, this means each primary will send and receive at most $\frac{4(\mathbf{n}-1)+(\mathbf{m}-1)(\mathbf{n}-1)}{\mathbf{m}}$ local messages with a total size of $\frac{(s_t+3s_m)(\mathbf{n}-1)+s_t(\mathbf{m}-1)(\mathbf{n}-1)}{\mathbf{m}}$ per transaction, and only $\frac{\mathbf{f}+\mathbf{m}}{\mathbf{m}}$ non-local messages with a total size of $\frac{s_t(\mathbf{f}+\mathbf{m})}{\mathbf{m}}$ per transaction. We notice that $\frac{\mathbf{f}+\mathbf{m}}{\mathbf{m}}$ non-local messages with a total size of $\frac{s_t(\mathbf{f}+\mathbf{m})}{\mathbf{m}}$ exchanged by GEOBFT per transaction is much less than the $4(\mathbf{m}-1)\mathbf{n}$ non-local messages with a total size of $(s_t + 3s_m)(\mathbf{m}-1)\mathbf{n}$ used by PBFT. We have sketched the difference in the number of global messages in Figure 4.20. As one can see, the amount of non-local communication per transactions is much higher for PBFT than for GEOBFT, showcasing the scalability of GEOBFT in a geo-scale aware environment.

Remark 4.33 GEOBFT and other geo-aware consensus protocols such as STEWARD [11] assume $\mathbf{m}$ clusters with $\mathbf{n} > 3\mathbf{f}$ replicas each. Hence, $\mathbf{n} = 3\mathbf{f} + j$ for some $j \geq 1$. This failure model differs from the more-general failure model utilized by PBFT. On the one hand, PBFT can tolerate the failure of up-to-$\lfloor \frac{\mathbf{mn}}{3} \rfloor = \lfloor \frac{(3\mathbf{fm}+\mathbf{m}j)}{3} \rfloor = \mathbf{fm} + \lfloor \frac{\mathbf{m}j}{3} \rfloor$ replicas, even if more than $\mathbf{f}$ of these failures happen in a single cluster. On the other hand, GEOBFT can only tolerate $\mathbf{fm}$ failures, of which $\mathbf{f}$ in a single cluster. For example, if $\mathbf{n} = 13$, $\mathbf{f} = 4$, and $\mathbf{m} = 7$, then GEOBFT can tolerate $\mathbf{fm} = 28$ replica failures in total, whereas PBFT can tolerate 30 replica failures. The failure model GEOBFT uses enables the efficient geo-scale aware design of GEOBFT, this without facing the well-known communication bounds outlined in Section 1.3.6.

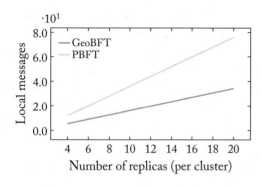
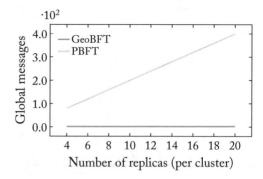

Figure 4.20: The geo-scale performance of GᴇᴏBFT using six clusters in terms of the total number of local (*left*) and global messages exchanged by the primary per accepted transaction.

4.5   GENERAL-PURPOSE SHARDED BLOCKCHAINS

In Section 4.3, we introduced the idea of combining sharding with blockchains and argued that such sharding would require cross-blockchain communication. To provide such communication, we introduced cluster-sending. As the next step toward sharded blockchains, we will now further examine the challenges and opportunities of sharded blockchain architectures. To understand how sharding affects the design of resilient distributed systems, we first summarize the operations of traditional permissioned blockchains that can deal with *Byzantine* behavior (e.g., replicas that crash, behave faulty, or act malicious). Then, we indicate which parts are affected when introducing sharding, thereby showing the complexity involved with sharded blockchain architectures. Finally, we discuss several proposed sharded blockchain architectures and show how they deal with these complexities.

4.5.1   TRADITIONAL PERMISSIONED BLOCKCHAINS

Typical permissioned blockchains are build on top of traditional fully replicated resilient distributed systems. At the core of these systems are *consensus protocols* that coordinate the operations of individual replicas in the system, e.g., a Byzantine fault-tolerant system driven by PBFT or a crash fault-tolerant system driven by Pᴀxᴏs [165, 166]. As these systems are fully replicated, each replica holds exactly the same data. To simplify discussion, we assume that this data is represented by a *sequence of transactions*, the ledger, and a *current state*.

Consensus is expensive: in an environment with a message delay of 10 ms, it will take PBFT at least 30 ms to make a single consensus decision (see Section 3.1 of Chapter 3). To assure that all good replicas have *the same state*, transactions are executed in the linearizable

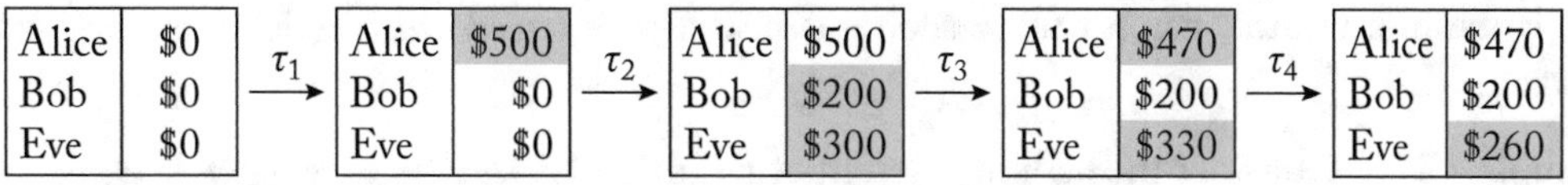

Alice	$0		Alice	$500		Alice	$500		Alice	$470		Alice	$470
Bob	$0	$\xrightarrow{\tau_1}$	Bob	$0	$\xrightarrow{\tau_2}$	Bob	$200	$\xrightarrow{\tau_3}$	Bob	$200	$\xrightarrow{\tau_4}$	Bob	$200
Eve	$0		Eve	$0		Eve	$300		Eve	$330		Eve	$260

Figure 4.21: Evolution of the *current state* while executing the sequence of transactions of Example 4.34.

order determined via consensus and must be *deterministic* in the sense that execution must always produce exactly the same results given identical inputs.

Example 4.34   Consider a banking system in which each transaction changes the balance of one or more accounts. The *current state* is the current balance of each account and can be obtained from the initial state by performing the sequence of transactions in-order, e.g., if the transactions are

$\tau_1 =$ "add $500 to the balance of *Alice*";
$\tau_2 =$ "add $200 to the balance of *Bob* and $300 to the balance of *Eve*";
$\tau_3 =$ "move $30 from the balance of *Alice* to the balance of *Eve*";
$\tau_4 =$ "remove $70 from the balance of *Eve*";

then, after executing of these transactions, the current state evolves as illustrated in Figure 4.21.

To process a transaction τ of a client C, a fault-tolerant system needs to perform five distinct steps.

1. First, transaction τ needs to be *received* by the system.

2. Second, transaction τ must be reliably *replicated* among all replicas.

3. Third, the replicas need to agree on an *execution order* for the transaction τ.

4. Fourth, the replicas each need to *execute* the transaction τ and *update* their current state accordingly.

5. Finally, the client C needs to be *informed* about the result of execution.

Here, we assume that transactions are always replicated and executed as a whole. To deal with *non-applicable transactions* of which certain preconditions do not hold, we can include *abort* as a legitimate execution outcome (that does not affect the current state). This assumption is essential to reliably deal with Byzantine behavior: all decisions—including the decision that a transaction is not-applicable—need to be made by *all good replicas* (via consensus), this to ensure that Byzantine replicas cannot force such a decision or interfere with reliably making such a decision.

Example 4.35 Consider the banking system of Example 4.34. After execution of $\tau_1, \tau_2, \tau_3, \tau_4$, Alice has a balance of \$470. Now consider the transaction

$$\tau_5 = \text{"move \$500 from the balance of \textit{Alice} to the balance of \textit{Bob}"}.$$

If the system does not support *negative* balances, then τ cannot be successfully executed after τ_4. Hence, if after replication and determining an execution order, it is scheduled for execution right after τ_4, then the transaction *aborts* and the client is informed of this abort.

Fully replicated resilient systems operate in rounds, and in each round a single transaction is *replicated* via consensus. The round in which a transaction is replicated also determines a linearizable *execution order*. Hence, replication of a transaction and agreeing on an execution order are *a single consensus step*. As all replicas maintain exactly the same current state and, using consensus, replicate exactly the same transactions and determine exactly the same execution order, each replica can *execute* each transaction and *update* their current state fully independent (without any further need to exchange information). Hence, in a fully replicated resilient system, transaction processing can be reduced to the *single* problem of ordered transaction replication, which is solved by off-the-shelf consensus protocols (independent of the data and transaction model supported by the system).

In fully replicated systems running traditional primary-backup consensus protocols, a transaction τ of client C is *typically* received by the system when it is sent by C to an arbitrary good replica. This replica can then forward τ to the primary, which will take care of replicating τ. As outlined in Chapter 2, typical consensus protocols can provide ways to deal with situations in which this process fails, e.g., when the primary is faulty. After execution, the client is informed by all good replicas and—as all good replicas will maintain the same state—the client will receive identical information of each of these replicas. In typical systems, the good replicas outnumber the faulty replicas. Hence, by simply counting the number of identical responses the client receives, the client can determine whether a response is valid.

4.5.2 PROCESSING MULTI-SHARD TRANSACTIONS

In the previous section, we outlined *five* steps resilient systems perform to process transactions in a *Byzantine environment* and showed that all necessary coordination and communication is restricted to the *replication step*, which is handled via consensus. Next, we revisit these transaction processing steps for transactions in a sharded system in which each shard is an independent blockchain. Before we continue, we make a distinction between *single-shard transactions* that only affect data in a single shard and *multi-shard transactions* that affect data in multiple shards.

Example 4.36 Consider a banking system similar to that of Example 4.34. This time, however, the system is *sharded* into twenty-six shards $\mathcal{S} = \{\mathcal{S}_a, \dots, \mathcal{S}_z\}$ such that shard $\mathcal{S}_i, i \in \{a, \dots, z\}$, holds accounts of people whose name starts with an i. Now reconsider the transaction of Example 4.34. Clearly, τ_1 can be processed by $\mathcal{S}_a$ only and is *single-shard*, whereas processing τ_2 requires cooperation between $\mathcal{S}_b$ and $\mathcal{S}_e$ and is *multi-shard*.

In well-designed sharded blockchain architectures, single-shard transactions can be completely processed within a shard using traditional consensus. Hence, in the following, we focus on how to process multi-shard transactions. Let τ be such a multi-shard transaction. As a first step toward understanding the complexity of multi-shard transaction processing in a fault-tolerant system, we walk over the steps necessary to process a transaction, as outlined in Section 4.5.1.

1. *First, transaction τ needs to be* received *by the system.*

We want to limit the number of replicas involved in processing τ. At the same time, all shards involved in processing τ need to receive τ. Hence, eventually τ should be received by only all shards affected by τ. Furthermore, clients need to be able to determine to which shard(s) it needs to send its transactions to assure execution.

2. *Second, transaction τ must be reliably* replicated *among all replicas.*

After each shard affected by τ receives τ, replication within each shard can be done via a shard-specific *consensus protocol* that enforces a shard-specific replication order for the transaction.

3. *Third, the replicas need to agree on an* execution order *for the transaction τ.*

In traditional non-sharded systems, the execution order is determined by the replication order. This is no longer the case in a sharded system, as different shards can receive transactions, locally replicate transactions, and execute transactions in a different ordering.

Typically, sharded systems provide a single service to the outside world that mimics the behavior of a simple non-sharded system that executes all transactions in a single unique order. By doing so, sharded systems can hide the complexities of parallel transaction processing and can provide a simple-to-use and simple-to-understand transaction processing service to their users. To assure that sharded systems can provide such services, sharded systems enforce a *serializable* execution order among all shards. Such a serializable execution order exists if one can globally order all transactions processed by the sharded system such that all shards execute transactions (that affect them) in an order that is consistent with this global order.

4. *Fourth, the replicas each need to* execute *the transaction τ and* update *their current state accordingly.*

Within traditional systems, individual replicas can independently execute transactions and update their state accordingly. This no longer holds for multi-shard transactions: for the execution of these transactions, shards need to exchange information. Hence, some coordination is required to assure that all information exchange is reliable and not affected by Byzantine replicas in the involved shards. As coordination in a Byzantine fault-tolerant setting requires costly communication, e.g., via consensus steps, the data and transaction model should be designed such that the amount of coordination is minimized.

5. *Finally, the client C needs to be* informed *about the result of execution.*

At least a single shard needs to be assigned to reliably inform the client. If a single such shard S can be derived from the transaction, then this shard can simply require that all good replicas in S inform the client. As is the case in traditional fault-tolerant systems, the client can then determine the valid response on their transaction by simply counting the number of identical responses the client receives.

As one can see, adding sharding to a fault-tolerant system increases the amount of coordination necessary: not only do we need to coordinate between replicas to *replicate* a transaction in a fault-tolerant manner, we also need additional coordination between shards to determine an execution order and to perform the execution. Next, we further illustrate the need for cross-shard coordination during execution of a multi-shard transaction.

Example 4.37   Consider the sharded banking system of Example 4.36 and consider the following transaction:

$$\tau = \text{``if } Alice \text{ has \$500 and } Bob \text{ has \$200}$$
$$\text{move \$300 from } Alice \text{ to } Eve\text{''}.$$

This transaction affects three shards, S_a, S_b, and S_e. Assume τ is replicated among all replicas of these shards and that all replicas start execution at the same time. During execution, the state of replicas at S_b will remain unchanged. If the account of Bob, maintained at shard S_b, has at least \$200, then execution of τ can modify accounts in S_a and S_e. Hence, during execution the replicas in S_a and S_e need to learn whether *Bob* has \$200 from S_b. Likewise, the replicas in S_e need to learn whether *Ana* has \$500.

Next, consider the following three transactions:

$$\tau_1 = \text{``if } Alice \text{ has \$500, move \$200 from } Alice \text{ to } Bob\text{''};$$
$$\tau_2 = \text{``if } Bob \text{ has \$500, move \$200 from } Bob \text{ to } Cecile\text{''};$$
$$\tau_3 = \text{``if } Cecile \text{ has \$500, move \$200 from } Cecile \text{ to } Alice\text{''}.$$

The transaction τ_1 affects S_a and S_b, τ_2 affects S_b and S_c, and τ_3 affects S_a and S_c. Now consider the shards executing these transactions in the following order:

$$S_a\text{: first } \tau_1, \text{ then } \tau_3; \quad S_b\text{: first } \tau_2, \text{ then } \tau_1; \quad S_c\text{: first } \tau_3, \text{ then } \tau_2.$$

Say—for simplicity—that each shard starts with their first transaction and waits until the other affected shard confirms execution. It is clear that each shard will be waiting on the other shards, as none of the shards are operating on the same transaction. Hence, such execution will fail. Furthermore, we observe that no ordering of τ_1, τ_2, τ_3 is consistent with these per-shard execution orders. Hence, these per-shard orderings are not serializable. If we change the execution ordering of $\mathcal{S}_c$, the resulting per-shard execution order is consistent with the global order τ_1, τ_2, τ_3 and, hence, is serializable. With such a serializable execution order, the simple execution scheme proposed—in which each shard confirms execution of each transaction with all other shards affected by the transaction—will be able to successfully execute all transactions.

4.5.3   PRACTICAL SHARDING IN A BYZANTINE ENVIRONMENT

In the previous section, we outlined the complexities of applying sharding to a blockchain-based system. Several practical sharded architectures have been proposed to deal with these complexities, each having their own trade-off between the type of transactions they can process, the amount of coordination required, and the maximum performance and performance scalability they can offer. Before we discuss these architectures, we first introduce some notation.

We model a *sharded system* as a partitioning of $\mathfrak{R}$ into a set of z shards shards$(\mathfrak{R}) = \{\mathcal{S}_1, \ldots, \mathcal{S}_z\}$. For every shard $\mathcal{S}$, we assume $\mathbf{n}_\mathcal{S} > 3\mathbf{f}_\mathcal{S}$, a minimal requirement to deal with Byzantine behavior within a single shard in practical settings. Let τ be a transaction. We write shards$(\tau) \subseteq$ shards$(\mathfrak{R})$ to denote the shards that are affected by τ (the shards that contain data that τ reads or writes). Finally, τ is a *single-shard transaction* if $|\text{shards}(\tau)| = 1$ and a *multi-shard transaction* otherwise.

Before we can discuss sharded blockchain architectures, we have to consider how we determine *correctness* of these sharded architectures. Let τ be a transaction processed by a sharded blockchain system. Processing of τ does not imply execution: the transaction could be invalid (e.g., a syntax error if it is an SQL query, the client did not have sufficient authorization, and so on). Or the transaction could affect data that no longer exists. We say that the system *commits* to τ if it decides to execute τ and apply the modifications prescribed by τ, and we say that the system *aborts* τ if it decides to not do so. Using this terminology, we put forward the following requirements for any sharded fault-tolerant system.

1. *Validity.* The system must only processes valid transactions requested by some client.

2. *Shard-involvement.* The shard $\mathcal{S}$ only processes transaction τ if $\mathcal{S} \in$ shards(τ).

3. *Shard-applicability.* Let $D(\mathcal{S})$ be the dataset maintained by shard $\mathcal{S}$ at time t. The shards shards(τ) only commit to execution of transaction τ at t if the input of τ is available. Hence, the input of τ is a subset of $\{D(\mathcal{S}) \mid \mathcal{S} \in \text{shards}(\tau)\}$.

4. *Cross-shard-consistency.* If shard $\mathcal{S}$ commits (aborts) transaction τ, then all shards $\mathcal{S}' \in$ shards(τ) eventually commit (abort) τ.

5. *Service.* If client C is well-behaved and wants to request a valid transaction τ, then the sharded system will eventually *process* $\langle\tau\rangle_C$. If τ is shard-applicable, then the sharded system will eventually *execute* $\langle\tau\rangle_C$.

6. *Confirmation.* If the system processes $\langle\tau\rangle_C$ and C is well-behaved, then C will eventually learn whether τ is committed or aborted.

We notice that these requirements mirror the practical requirements we put on consensus in Definition 2.3. Furthermore, we notice that shard-involvement is a *local requirement*, as individual shards can determine whether they need to process a given transaction. In the same sense, shard-applicability and cross-shard-consistency are *global* requirements, as assuring these requirements requires coordination between the shards affected by a transaction. Next, we shall outline three possible architectures for sharding in a Byzantine environment.

Centralized multi-shard transaction coordination A simple way to provide multi-shard transaction processing is by assigning one *central shard* the task to globally order all multi-shard transactions. As this central shard determines a global order on all multi-shard transactions, we always end up with a serializable order of execution, even if multi-shard transactions are executed in parallel. Next, we formalize such centralized coordination. Let $S^c \in \text{shards}(\mathfrak{R})$ be the central shard and let $\langle\tau\rangle_C$ be a transaction requested by C. For now, we assume that the client C can determine $\text{shards}(\tau)$ and, hence, can determine whether τ is single-shard or multi-shard.

If τ is a single-shard transaction with $\text{shards}(\tau) = \{S'\}$, then C simply sends τ to the blockchain operating S'. For example, if S' is operated using PBFT, then C sends τ to the primary $\mathsf{P}_{S'}$ of S' (or, when C determines that this primary $\mathsf{P}_{S'}$ is faulty, it can request all replicas in S' to enforce execution). In return, S' will append τ to its ledger, execute τ, and inform C.

If τ is a multi-shard transaction, then C sends τ to S^c. Upon receipt of τ, S^c appends τ to its ledger. We assume that τ is added as the ρ-th transaction, indicating that τ is the ρ-th multi-shard transaction that needs to be executed, thereby determining the global order of execution of τ with respect to all other multi-shard transactions. Next, S^c does *not* execute τ, but instead informs all shards $S \in \text{shards}(\tau)$ that τ can be executed. To do so, S^c cluster-sends to $S \in \text{shards}(\tau)$ a triple (τ, ρ, j) with $j \leq \rho$ the round of the *previous* multi-shard transaction that affected S. Finally, S will eventually append τ to its own ledger, execute τ, and inform C. To enforce a serializable execution, S is only allowed to do so after it has successfully executed the j-th multi-shard transaction, however.

Example 4.38 Consider the banking system of Example 4.36 and the following transactions:

$\tau_1 =$ "move \$200 from the balance of *Alice* to the balance of *Ana*";
$\tau_2 =$ "move \$100 from the balance of *Ana* to the balance of *Bob*";
$\tau_3 =$ "move \$75 from the balance of *Benne* to the balance of *Dan*";
$\tau_4 =$ "move \$125 from the balance of *Eve* to the balance of *Emma*";
$\tau_5 =$ "move \$150 from the balance of *Eve* to the balance of *Alice*";
$\tau_6 =$ "move \$25 from the balance of *Dan* to the balance of *Dalia*";
$\tau_7 =$ "move \$75 from the balance of *Alice* to the balance of *Dalia*".

We have $\text{shards}(\tau_1) = \{S_a\}$, $\text{shards}(\tau_2) = \{S_a, S_b\}$, $\text{shards}(\tau_3) = \{S_b, S_d\}$, $\text{shards}(\tau_4) = \{S_e\}$, $\text{shards}(\tau_5) = \{S_a, S_e\}$, $\text{shards}(\tau_6) = \{S_d\}$, and $\text{shards}(\tau_7) = \{S_a, S_d\}$. Hence, τ_1, τ_4, and τ_6 are single-shard, while τ_2, τ_3, τ_5, and τ_7 are multi-shard.

The central shard S^c appends all multi-shard transactions to its ledger, resulting in

$$\mathcal{L}_{S^c} = [\tau_2, \tau_3, \tau_5, \tau_7],$$

which determines the order in which these transactions can appear in all affected shards. The shards S_a, S_b, S_c, and S_e append their single-shard transactions and multi-shard transactions to their ledgers and arrive at

$$\mathcal{L}_{S_a} = [\tau_1, \tau_2, \tau_5, \tau_7];$$
$$\mathcal{L}_{S_b} = [\tau_2, \tau_3];$$
$$\mathcal{L}_{S_d} = [\tau_3, \tau_6, \tau_7];$$
$$\mathcal{L}_{S_e} = [\tau_4, \tau_5],$$

and each shard executes all multi-shard transactions they are affected by in an order that is consistent with the order prescribed by $\mathcal{L}_{S^c}$. We have visualized this execution order in Figure 4.22, *left*. We notice that single-shard transactions can easily be executed in any other order. For example, for S_a, the following ledger would also be valid

$$\mathcal{L}_{S_a} = [\tau_2, \tau_5, \tau_1, \tau_7],$$

which results in the execution order visualized in Figure 4.22, *right*. Notice that in both execution orders visualized in Figure 4.22 multiple transactions (even multi-shard transactions) can be executed at the same time (in parallel).

In the above, we assumed that clients can determine the shards affected by their transactions. In most systems, clients are unable to do so. Instead, clients simply send their requests to a replica they *trust*, which can then forward the transaction to the responsible replicas. When the replica chosen by the client is unable (or unwilling) to facilitate execution, the client can always resend its transactions to an other replica.

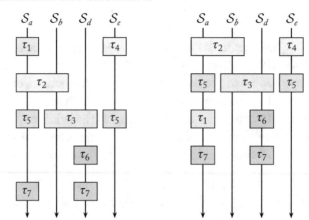

Figure 4.22: Two possible execution orders at each shard that are consistent with the global ordering defined by $\mathcal{S}^c$.

We have not yet discussed what it actually means for a multi-shard transaction to be executed, we only presented the way in which centralized coordination can assure that the affected shards execute multi-shard transactions in a serializable manner. Unfortunately, the way in which a multi-shard transaction is executed is highly application-specific, which prevents us from going too much into detail. Instead, we illustrate execution with an example.

Example 4.39   Consider again the transaction

$$\tau = \text{"if } Alice \text{ has \$500 and } Bob \text{ has \$200}$$
$$\text{move \$300 from } Alice \text{ to } Eve\text{"}$$

of Example 4.37. We have shards$(\tau) = \{\mathcal{S}_a, \mathcal{S}_b, \mathcal{S}_e\}$. Notice that this transaction affects the three shards in distinct ways: only $\mathcal{S}_a$ and $\mathcal{S}_e$ might update their state while executing τ, while $\mathcal{S}_b$ will never update state while executing τ. This already indicates that each shard needs to execute a different set of steps. In Figure 4.23, we have sketched the individual low-level *programs* executed by the affected shards in parallel to execute τ.

First, notice that this execution only puts a single shard, $\mathcal{S}_e$, in charge of informing the client of the outcome. This is sufficient for the client to derive an outcome. Furthermore, the execution involves several cluster-sending steps to exchange the necessary information between the shards. Consider, e.g., the cluster-sending steps at $\mathcal{S}_b$ (Line 8 of Figure 4.23). These steps happen as a consequence of the consensus-step that appended τ to the ledger in $\mathcal{S}_b$. Hence, due to this consensus-step, the replicas in $\mathcal{S}_b$ already reached agreement on performing this cluster-sending step, and this step can be performed without further steps to reach agreement in $\mathcal{S}_b$.

$\mathcal{S}_a$-**role** (used by replicas in $\mathcal{S}_a$ to execute τ) :

1: $a :=$ the balance of *Alice*.
2: Send (τ, ρ, a) to shard $\mathcal{S}_e$ (via cluster-sending).
3: Receive (τ, ρ, b) from shard $\mathcal{S}_b$ (via cluster-sending).
4: **if** $a \geq \$500$ **and** $b \geq \$200$ **then**
5:    The balance of *Alice* $:= a - 300$.
6: **end if**

$\mathcal{S}_b$-**role** (used by replicas in $\mathcal{S}_b$ to execute τ) :

7: $b :=$ the balance of *Bob*.
8: Send (τ, ρ, b) to shards $\mathcal{S}_a$ and $\mathcal{S}_e$ (via cluster-sending).

$\mathcal{S}_c$-**role** (used by replicas in $\mathcal{S}_c$ to execute τ) :

9: Receive (τ, ρ, a) from shard $\mathcal{S}_a$ (via cluster-sending).
10: Receive (τ, ρ, b) from shard $\mathcal{S}_b$ (via cluster-sending).
11: **if** $a \geq \$500$ **and** $b \geq \$200$ **then**
12:    $e :=$ the balance of *Eve*.
13:    The balance of *Eve* $:= e + 300$.
14:    Inform the client of *transfer*.
15: **else**
16:    Inform the client of *no transfer*.
17: **end if**

Figure 4.23: A possible multi-shard execution of a conditional transfer of money from Alice to Eve. The central coordinator has added τ to its ledger as the ρ-th transaction.

Although we have illustrated the working of centralized coordination using per-shard consensus primitives and cluster-sending, not all systems employing centralized coordination use these primitives. Instead, most existing systems utilize system-specific protocols to enable communication between the central shard $\mathcal{S}^c$ and affected shards and to exchange any information necessary for transaction execution.

Centralized coordination is a rather simple approach toward providing multi-shard transaction processing. For simple workloads with mainly single-shard transactions, a system with centralized coordination will be able to drastically improve performance (compared to a single blockchain). Furthermore, centralized coordination can guarantee validity, shard-applicability, cross-shard-consistency, service, and confirmation. Unfortunately, due the reliance on a central coordinator for *all* multi-shard transaction centralized coordination does not provide shard-involvement. Furthermore, this reliance on a central coordinator is a major bottleneck for processing multi-shard transactions. This, in turn, limits the scalability of centralized coordination, as scaling the number of shards will increase the percentage of multi-shard transactions for complex workloads.

Decentralized multi-shard transaction coordination   In the previous, we reviewed central-ized coordination, a simple approach toward multi-shard transaction processing that provides excellent performance for single-shard transactions, but does not provide scalability for multi-shard transactions. To deal with these limitations of centralized coordination, several sharded blockchain architectures use fully decentralized multi-shard transaction coordination. Many such decentralized approaches use a multi-shard consensus protocol that partly depends on specific assumptions on the data model or on the type of transactions executed to reduce the costs of their protocol and to simplify the way in which they deal with failures or malicious behavior. As we do not want to complicate our presentation or bind it to a single data and transaction model, we illustrate decentralized multi-shard transaction coordination using the Pessimistic-CERBERUS protocol (PCERBERUS) [134], which does not rely on such assumptions.

The core aim of PCERBERUS is to minimize and fully decentralize the coordination necessary for multi-shard ordering and execution of transactions, while assuring that any malicious behavior within a shard can be dealt with within that shard. PCERBERUS does so by using the following high-level three-step approach toward processing any multi-shard transaction τ.

1. *Local inputs.* First, every affected shard $S \in \text{shards}(\tau)$ locally determines whether all data affected by τ in S is available.

2. *Cross-shard exchange.* Then, every affected shard $S \in \text{shards}(\tau)$ exchanges all available data affected by τ to all other shards in $\text{shards}(\tau)$, thereby pledging to use this data in the execution of τ.

3. *Decide outcome.* Finally, every affected shard $S \in \text{shards}(\tau)$ decides to commit τ if all affected shards were able to provide all data affected by τ. When τ is committed, all replicas in all affected shards have received all affected data and, hence, can fully execute the transaction independently.

Next, we describe how these three high-level steps are implemented in PCERBERUS using normal consensus and cluster-sending steps. Let shard $S \in \text{shards}(\mathfrak{R})$ receive client request $\langle \tau \rangle_C$. The good replicas in S will first determine whether τ is valid and applicable. If τ is not valid or $S \notin \text{shards}(\tau)$, then the good replicas discard τ. Otherwise, if τ is valid and $S \in \text{shards}(\tau)$, then the good replicas utilize *consensus* to force the primary P_S to propose in some consensus round ρ the message $m(S, \tau)_\rho = (\langle \tau \rangle_C, A(S, \tau), P(S, \tau))$, in which $A(S, \tau)$ is all data in S affected by τ and $P(S, \tau) \subseteq A(S, \tau)$ is all data in S that is available and is pledged to the execution of τ.

The acceptance of $m(S, \tau)_\rho$ in round ρ by all good replicas completes the *local inputs* step. Before cross-shard exchange, the replicas in S fully pledge the data in $P(S, \tau)$ to τ until the commit or abort decision. Then, S performs cross-shard exchange by broadcasting $m(S, \tau)_\rho$ to all other shards in $\text{shards}(\tau)$, while the replicas in S wait until they receive messages $m(S', \tau)_{\rho'} = (\langle \tau \rangle_C, A(S', \tau), P(S', \tau))$ from all other shards $S' \in \text{shards}(\tau)$.

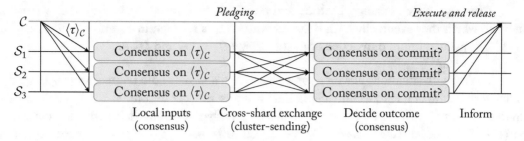

Figure 4.24: The message flow of PCERBERUS for a three-shard client request $\langle \tau \rangle_C$ that is committed.

After cross-shard exchange comes the final *decide outcome* step. After S receives $m(S', \tau)_{\rho'}$ from all shards $S' \in \text{shards}(\tau)$, the replicas force a *second consensus step* that determines the round ρ^* at which S decides *commit* (whenever $A(S', \tau) = P(S', \tau)$ for all $S' \in \text{shards}(\tau)$) or *abort*. If S decides commit, then, in round ρ^*, all good replicas in S execute τ on the data $\bigcup_{S' \in \text{shards}(\tau)} P(S', \tau)$, update their local state accordingly, and release all data pledged to τ. If S decides abort, then, in round ρ^*, all good replicas in S simply release all data pledged to τ.

Finally, each good replica informs C of the outcome of execution. If C receives, from every shard $S' \in \text{shards}(\tau)$, identical outcomes from $\mathbf{g}_{S'} - \mathbf{f}_{S'}$ distinct replicas in S', then it considers τ to be successfully executed. In Figure 4.24, we sketched the working of PCERBERUS.

We notice that processing a multi-shard transaction via PCERBERUS requires *two* consensus steps per shard. In some cases, we can eliminate the second step, however. First, if τ is a multi-shard transaction with $S \in \text{shards}(\tau)$ and the replicas in S accept $(\langle \tau \rangle_C, I(S, \tau), D(S, \tau))$ with $A(S, \tau) \neq P(S, \tau)$, then the replicas can immediately abort whenever they accept $(\langle \tau \rangle_C, A(S, \tau), P(S, \tau))$. Second, if τ is a single-shard transaction with $\text{shards}(\tau) = \{S\}$, then the replicas in S can immediately decide commit or abort whenever they accept $(\langle \tau \rangle_C, A(S, \tau), P(S, \tau))$. Hence, in both cases, processing of τ at S only requires a single consensus step at S.

Next, we illustrate how PCERBERUS deals with concurrent transactions.

Example 4.40   Consider distinct transactions $\langle \tau_1 \rangle_{C_1}$ and $\langle \tau_2 \rangle_{C_2}$ that both affect objects O_a in S_a and O_b in S_b. We assume that S_a processes τ_1 first and S_b processes τ_2 first. Shard S_a will start by sending $m(S, \tau_1)_{\rho_1} = (\langle \tau_1 \rangle_{C_1}, \{O_a\}, \{O_a\})$ to S_b, after which all replicas in S_a have pledged object O_a to τ_1. Next, S_a will wait, during which it receives τ_2. At the same time, S_b follows similar steps for τ_2 and sends $m(S, \tau_2)_{\rho_2} = (\langle \tau_2 \rangle_{C_2}, \{O_b\}, \{O_b\})$ to S_a.

After sending $m(S, \tau_1)_{\rho_1}$, S_a receives τ_2 and starts processing of τ_2. Shard S_a directly determines that O_a is already pledged to τ_1. Hence, it sends $(\langle \tau_2 \rangle_{C_2}, \{O_a\}, \emptyset)$ to S_b. Likewise, S_b will start processing of τ_1, sending $(\langle \tau_1 \rangle_{C_1}, \{O_b\}, \emptyset)$ to S_a as a result.

After the above exchange, both S_a and S_b conclude that transactions τ_1 and τ_2 must be aborted, which they eventually both do, after which O_a is released in S_a and O_b is released in S_b. Consequently, future transactions can still utilize O_a in S_a and O_b in S_b.

To deal with situations in which some shards $S \in \text{shards}(\tau)$ did not receive $\langle \tau \rangle_C$ (e.g., due to network failure or due to a faulty client that fails to send $\langle \tau \rangle_C$ to some shards), we allow each shard to learn τ from any other shard. Specifically, any shard $S \in \text{shards}(\tau)$ will start consensus on $\langle \tau \rangle_C$ after receiving *cross-shard exchange* related to $\langle \tau \rangle_C$. Next, we prove the correctness of PCerberus.

Theorem 4.41 *If, for all shards S^*, $g_{S^*} > 3f_{S^*}$, then Pessimistic-Cerberus guarantees validity, shard-involvement, shard-applicability, cross-shard-consistency, service, and confirmation.*

Proof. Let τ be a transaction. As good replicas in S discard τ if it is invalid or if $S \notin \text{shards}(\tau)$, PCerberus provides *validity* and *shard-involvement*. Next, *shard-applicability* follow directly from the decide outcome step.

If a shard S commits or aborts transaction τ, then it must have completed the decide outcome and cross-shard exchange steps. As S completed cross-shard exchange, all shards $S' \in \text{shards}(\tau)$ must have exchanged the necessary information to S. By relying on cluster-sending for cross-shard exchange, S' requires cooperation of all good replicas in S' to exchange the necessary information to S. Hence, we have the guarantee that these good replicas will also perform cross-shard exchange to any other shard $S'' \in \text{shards}(\tau)$. Hence, every shard $S'' \in \text{shards}(\tau)$ will receive the same information as S, complete cross-shard exchange, and make the same decision during the decide outcome step, providing *cross-shard consistency*.

A client can force service on a transaction τ by choosing a shard $S \in \text{shards}(\tau)$ and sending τ to all good replicas in S. By doing so, the normal mechanisms of consensus can be used by the good replicas in S to force acceptance on τ in S and, hence, bootstrapping acceptance on τ in all shards $S' \in \text{shards}(\tau)$. Due to cross-shard consistency, every shard in $\text{shards}(\tau)$ will perform the necessary steps to eventually inform the client. As all good replicas $R \in S$, $S \in \text{shards}(\tau)$, will inform the client of the outcome for τ, the majority of these inform-messages come from good replicas, enabling the client to reliably derive the true outcome. Hence, PCerberus provides *service* and *confirmation*. □

The presented Pessimistic-Cerberus protocol provides single-shard transaction processing with minimal cost, while also providing a scalable solution toward processing multi-shard transactions as long as the workload mainly consists of transactions that do not affect the same data (as, otherwise, many transactions can end up aborted). Furthermore, as PCerberus essentially utilizes *locks*, PCerberus can provide serializable execution for all committed transactions. Finally, as PCerberus is built using basic consensus primitives, all techniques of Chapter 3 to improve these consensus steps can be applied.

There are many variations on decentralized coordination with different trade-offs than PCerberus, however. First, we notice that PCerberus utilizes *two* local consensus steps and a *single* cluster-sending step per multi-shard transaction. The Optimistic-Cerberus design has shown that this can be reduced to only a single consensus step per shard at the cost of a complex multi-shard view-change and recovery algorithm. Furthermore, there are several systems that try to minimize the number of consensus steps by employing a system-specific multi-shard consensus protocol that involves all replicas of all affected shards. Unfortunately, such multi-shard consensus designs come with their own complicated view-change algorithms and their own challenges with respect to out-of-order processing.

Emulation of traditional sharding   The development of sharded blockchain systems is still in its infancy and the few existing sharded blockchain architectures that have seen the light are each fully optimized toward a singular purpose. This is reflected by the specialized nature of the multi-shard transaction techniques utilized, as current sharded blockchain systems either use a variation on the centralized coordination or decentralized coordination in the form of a system-specific single-purpose protocol that provides a singular way to process transactions.

This is in sharp contrast with transaction processing in traditional systems, which typically provide much more flexible general-purpose ACID-compliant data and transaction processing mechanisms, e.g., by using *two-phase commit* to reach agreement between shards on executing transactions and by using *two-phase locking* to guarantee a serializable execution.

One way to extend such general-purpose capabilities to sharded blockchains is by implementing mechanisms such as two-phase commit and two-phase locking on top of the fault-tolerant primitives provided by a sharded blockchain system. Specifically, operations that need to be performed at a shard can be implemented via consensus steps, while communication between shards can be implemented via cluster-sending steps. Unfortunately, such implementations are limited by the high costs of operating blockchains via consensus steps, as we have seen in Section 3.1. Hence, any attempt to implement traditional multi-shard transaction processing mechanisms on top of sharded blockchains requires the minimization of the consensus and cluster-sending steps involved. Fortunately, typical mechanisms to process multi-shard transactions can often be implemented using at-most two consensus steps per shard.

4.6   CONCLUDING REMARKS

In the past two chapters, we focused on the design and optimization of consensus protocols. In this chapter, we re-examine consensus from a broader perspective to effectively scale a blockchain beyond a single data center, aiming towards a global deployment that is operated over partially or independently maintained ledgers. We envision the emergence of an array of new resilient consensus paradigm as meta-protocols that are BFT-agnostic (e.g., [121–123, 225]) and are built upon novel basic primitives (e.g. [135–137]). Examples of two such primitives are (1) *Byzantine learner problem* [137] and (2) *cluster sending problem* [135, 136].

In the *Byzantine learner problem*, the goal is to expand application space to support efficient read-only analytical workloads. This allows feeding the ledger into the analytical engines reliably without requiring active participation in the consensus itself. The analytics is modeled as a *learner* that lazily learn the outcome of consensus through a fault-tolerant delayed replication protocol [137]. The delayed replication employs information dispersal theory to reliably encode and transmit recent ledger updates with almost linear communication (reduced from quadratic complexity) accompanied by an efficient reconstruction scheme using Merkle-tree proofs. The key intuition is to allow each replica to only encode and send a chuck of recent updates, and as long as a quorum of well-behaving replicas sends a set of distinct chunks, the information can be reconstructed reliably tolerating the failures of up to f replicas. Other notable applications of the leaner problem are efficient checkpointing and recovery routines needed in any fault-tolerant setting.

The next step to scale blockchain is the ability to maintain a global ledger spanning geographically dispersed data centers over a set of independently maintained local ledgers, each maintained in a data center (or a cluster). This is reminiscent of the classical sharding problem in databases. Thus, the central question arises as to *whether it is possible to maintain a fault-tolerant globally consistent ledger through strictly local consensus along with provably minimal global communication?* This motivates the need to facilitate reliable cross-blockchain or inter-cluster communication conceptualized as a basic primitive for communicating among any two clusters. It is formalized as Byzantine *cluster sending problem* [135, 136]: *the problem of sending a message reliably from one cluster to another.* To ensure the reliable communication of a message, we must ensure that at least one honest replica from the source cluster sends the message to another honest replica in the destined cluster. This simple realization establishes the lower-bound linear message complexity, for which it is shown there is an optimal bijective cluster sending algorithm such that with $2f + 1$ pairwise communications it *ensures a message is sent and received by an honest replica* [135, 136].[1]

The general concept of sharding can be conceived as geo-aware partitioning of the transactional workload or the ledger data or a combination of both. For example, GEoBFT [123] is a fully replicated design, in which the workload is partitioned based on the network topology and the client's proximity to each cluster. As a result, the problem of global consensus is reduced to an efficient local consensus followed by a cluster sending step to propagate the local decision globally. The cluster sending step is further optimized, on the optimistic ground, by assuming the sender's primary of each cluster is honest and sends the local decision to $f + 1$ replicas in remote clusters. If no decision is received by any remote replicas, a remote view change is invoked to replace the misbehaving primary.[2]

Going a step further, the ledger itself can be partitioned among clusters. This gives rise to a partially replicated design, in which each cluster (or a shard) holds only a slice of the data. Thus,

---

[1]For simplicity, here we are assuming equal size clusters, the general setting is covered in Section 4.3.
[2]Similar to PBFT, an honest primary may also be replaced due to an unreliable network.

the execution of a single transaction may span multiple shards, which requires a centralized or decentralized coordination mechanism among shards. For example, AHL [75] introduces the notion of reference committee (a set of replicas) as a centralized coordination entity to essentially run a fault-tolerant two-phase commit protocol. In contrast, CERBERUS [134] adopts a decentralized design, in which each shard independently reach consensus on a fragment of the transaction for which it is responsible and communicate the local decision to all involved shards using a cluster sending step. Thus, each shard can unilaterally decide the faith of the transaction once it receives decisions from all involved shards. Consequently, a global view change is triggered to deal with misbehaving clusters and network unreliability.

4.7   BIBLIOGRAPHIC NOTES

There is abundant literature on making distributed systems and distributed databases scalable via the usage of sharding and other technologies (e.g., [199, 229, 235]).

The information dispersal algorithm IDA, used for scalable storage and role-specialization, was proposed by Rabin [213] to provide reliable load-balanced storage and communication in a distributed setting. Alon et al. [8, 9] expanded IDA toward recovery by incorporating *fingerprints* in the design of IDA. More recently, Hellings et al. [137] showed how to utilize IDA to provide both role-specialization and scalable storage in a Byzantine environment with no overhead.

The cluster-sending problem was first formalized by Hellings et al. [135, 136]. Furthermore, they showed lower bounds on the complexity of cluster-sending, and introduced bijective sending for optimal cluster-sending. In recent work, the same authors also showed that cluster-sending can be solved using an expected-constant number of messages (and worst-case optimal number of messages) using probabilistic methods [139]. Several other works provide protocols that can be used for cluster-sending in specific situations. For example, GEOBFT and the RESILIENTDB system [123] utilize a special-purpose optimistic primitive for communication between clusters that will have lower communication costs than the optimal cluster-sending protocol of Hellings et al. whenever the primary of the sending cluster is good.

Several architectures designed for geo-aware scalability have been proposed, the most notable being STEWARD and RESILIENTDB. STEWARD [10, 11] approaches geo-awareness only by reducing overall communication of PBFT by replacing replica-to-replica communication with cluster-to-cluster replication. Unfortunately, STEWARD utilizes a centralized design in which a central cluster eventually drives all consensus decision. RESILIENTDB [123] improves on this significantly by utilizing the GEOBFT consensus protocol that utilizes concurrent consensus on a per-cluster level to improve consensus throughput beyond what any single customer can provide.

Sharded permissioned blockchains are still in their infancy, although a few approaches have already been proposed such as AHL [75], BYSHARD [138], CAPER [12], CERBERUS [134], CHAINSPACE [6], and SHARPER [13]. AHL is a good example of centralized coordination and follows a design similar as outlined in this work. The decentralized coordination approach presented in this book is based on CERBERUS. The systems CAPER, CHAINSPACE, and SHARPER each follow a variation of decentralized coordination. Finally, the recently introduced BYSHARD work proposes to build a flexible general-purpose ACID-compliant approach toward multi-shard transaction processing by showing how to implement (variations of) traditional mechanisms such as two-phase commit and two-phase locking with a minimal amount of consensus steps, resulting in eighteen different multi-shard transaction protocols, each with their own trade-off between throughput, latency, communication costs, and provided isolation level.

In parallel to the development of traditional resilient systems and permissioned blockchains, there has been promising work on sharding in permissionless blockchains. Examples include techniques for enabling reliable inter-chain communication (similar to cluster-sending) and transaction coordination, e.g., via sidechains, blockchain relays, and atomic swaps [94, 96, 141, 164, 245]. There are also a few specialized high-performance permissionless blockchain designs that use some form of sharding, e.g., CONFLUX [172], ELASTICO [176], MESHCASH [27], MONOXIDE [243], NIGHTSHADE [223], OMNILEDGER [159], RAPIDCHAIN [250], and SPECTRE [224]. Finally, we also see the development of read-only participants in the form of light clients. Unfortunately, these permissionless techniques are several orders of magnitudes slower than comparable techniques for traditional resilient systems, making them unsuitable for systems that aim at high-performance transaction processing.

CHAPTER 5

Permissioned Blockchains

Until now, we looked at the design of different BFT protocols that can help achieve consensus among a set of replicas. A key use case for these protocols is a permissioned blockchain fabric, which, unlike a permissionless blockchain application, expects the identities of the participants to be known a priori. Permissioned blockchains have found applications in several domains such as healthcare, food production, energy trading, and financial trades [80, 150, 215, 231]. These permissioned blockchains have also laid down paths that ease transition of a traditional database into blockchain databases [94, 106, 123, 124, 195].

In this chapter, we take a dive into the design of a permissioned blockchain fabric. We study key principles that help in realizing a BFT protocol into practice. To achieve these goals, we discuss the characteristics of two of the well-known permissioned blockchain systems. Specifically, we shall look at the following.

1. First, we analyze the design of HYPERLEDGER Fabric, which is often regarded as the first permissioned blockchain fabric [14, 231]. HYPERLEDGER Fabric presents a flexible architecture that supports different degrees of resilience.

2. Next, we illustrate the architecture of RESILIENTDB [116–119, 123, 124, 214], which facilitates scaling permissioned blockchain systems to large setups and prioritizes designing an optimal system-centric design rather than a protocol-centric framework.

5.1   HYPERLEDGER FABRIC

HYPERLEDGER [231] was launched as an open-source Linux Foundation project with 30 founding member organizations. The key aim of this project is to design an enterprise-grade permissioned blockchain fabric that can provide blockchain support for business transaction. HYPERLEDGER targets business that do not want to rely on the open-access model of Bitcoin [193] and Ethereum [244], but want to provide their users access to a secure decentralized ledger. Under the HYPERLEDGER organization there are several projects such as Hyperledger Fabric, Hyperledger Sawtooth, Hyperledger Burrow, Hyperledger Indy, and so on. [14, 231] that serve distinct use cases. In this section, we analyze the design of Hyperledger Fabric [14] that aims to provide access to a permissioned blockchain ledger. In the rest of this section, we use the term HYPERLEDGER to refer to Hyperledger Fabric.

5.1.1   MOTIVATION

Existing blockchains and BFT systems adhere to the *order-execute* architecture. In an order-execute architecture, all the replicas order each client transaction prior to its execution. This architecture ensures that each replica only executes a transaction once it has been confirmed by the majority of non-faulty replicas. HYPERLEDGER introduces a distinct *execute-order-verify* architecture, which promotes replicas to execute the transaction prior to its ordering.

To understand why HYPERLEDGER adopts the execute-order-verify, we need to look at the issues raised by HYPERLEDGER community.

- *Execution-by-All.* Each transaction fed to a blockchain system is executed at all the replicas. If the transaction runs for a large amount of time, then it can impact the system throughput. In fact, an adversary can perform a *denial-of-service* (DoS) attack by sending a smart-contract that runs infinitely. To cope with this problem, systems that permit smart-contracts or complex transaction, such as Ethereum, need to set a time-limit on the total time spent on executing the corresponding transaction. Further, these systems require each user to pay for the total time taken by its transaction to execute. Such a requirement is not feasible in a permissioned system.

- *Non-deterministic Execution.* Existing blockchains require each transaction or smart-contract to be deterministic, that is, on identical inputs, all the replicas produce identical outputs [55]. The key issue with this requirement is the onus to design such a transaction lies on the untrusted user, which can either lack sufficient knowledge to detect non-determinism in its code, or can act malicious with the aim of disrupting the system. To avoid such issues, some blockchains require users to write smart-contracts in a specific language [244]. First, this solution reduces programmability as a restricted programming language lacks expressiveness. Second, this solution places the onus on the programmer to learn another new language.

- *Lack of Confidentiality.* As existing blockchains require each smart-contract to be executed at all the replicas, this prevents keeping any user data confidential. It is possible that a user may want its smart-contract to be executed by only a subset of replicas. However, existing blockchains, such as Tendermint [230], Quorum [68] and Multi-Chain [64], do not support such a design.

5.1.2   ARCHITECTURE

We use Figure 5.1 to illustrate the execute-order-verify architecture of HYPERLEDGER. Through this figure, we analyze the steps a client smart-contract undergoes in HYPERLEDGER. Notice that the HYPERLEDGER community refers to a smart-contract as *chaincode*. Each chaincode is deployed by some user to run an application logic.

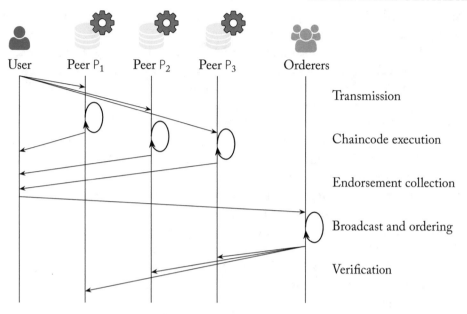

Figure 5.1: An illustration of how the execute-order-verify architecture of HYPERLEDGER processes a smart-contract.

HYPERLEDGER defines an *endorsement policy*, which helps a user set the number of peers to endorse its chaincode. This endorsement policy cannot be set by any user, but is available as a static library, which can be parameterized to state the endorsement policy. To validate identities of all the participants, HYPERLEDGER employs a *Membership Service Provider* to generate a unique identity for each participant.

Each client that wishes to execute some chaincode, creates and signs a transaction, and sends it to all the endorsers. Any endorsing peer that receives a chaincode can check the chaincode's endorsement policy to ensure it is one of the designated set of endorsers. Next, each endorser executes the chaincode against its local blockchain. Specifically, there is no communication/synchronization among the endorsers prior to execution. On executing the chaincode, each endorser produces a *write-set* that represents updates to the blockchain state, and a *read-set* that represents all the inputs and dependencies for successful chaincode execution. Next, each endorser sends these *read-set* and *write-set* to the client. Notice that an endorser has not applied the *write-set* updates to its local blockchain. These updates will only be applied post successful verification.

Each client waits for responses from all the endorsers specified in the endorsement policy. Specifically, a client assumes its chaincode's execution as complete once it receives identical *read-set* and *write-set* from all the stated endorsers. Next, this client creates a transaction that includes the chaincode and the identical responses from the endorsers, and forwards this transaction to the *ordering-service*.

The ordering-service runs the underlying consensus protocol to generate an order for this chaincode. HYPERLEDGER provides a modular architecture where each blockchain application developer can employ a BFT protocol of its own choice for the ordering service. Further, the ordering-service does not maintain the state of the blockchain, which facilitates fairness. Once a transaction is ordered, it is transmitted to the peers for verification.

During the verification phase, each peer performs three tasks. First, it verifies the endorsement policy and ensures the execution result has sufficient endorsers. Next, it checks the *read-set* for the chaincode to ensure it is unchanged since its execution. Finally, it updates the state of the blockchain by applying the corresponding *write-set*. Notice that a peer only updates the state if both the preceding steps are successful. Otherwise, the transaction is discarded.

This execute-order-verify architecture of HYPERLEDGER Fabric allows it to process non-deterministic transaction as each non-deterministic transaction will only update the blockchain state if there are sufficient number of identical responses. Further, by stating an endorsement policy, each user has the freedom to specify its own fault-tolerance model, and limiting the number of matching responses.

5.2   RESILIENTDB

RESILIENTDB [120–124, 138, 214] is an academic permissioned blockchain fabric, which is designed with the aim of fostering academic and industrial research. The key aim behind the development of RESILIENTDB is to illustrate that the design and architecture of the underlying system are as important as optimizing BFT consensus. RESILIENTDB raises a simple yet intriguing question: *can a well-crafted system-centric architecture based on a classical* BFT *protocol outperform a protocol-centric architecture?*

We use Figure 5.2 to illustrate such a possibility. This figure compares the throughput of system-centric design of RESILIENTDB against a permissioned blockchain framework that adopts a protocol-centric design. Even though RESILIENTDB makes use of the slow PBFT protocol, it outperforms the protocol-centric permissioned blockchain system that adopts practices suggested in BFTSmart [31] and employs the fast ZYZZYVA protocol. Notice that the PBFT protocol requires three-phase of communication among its replicas, of which two phases necessitate quadratic communication complexity, while the ZYZZYVA protocol requires a single linear-phase of communication.

There are several key *factors* that affect the throughput and increase the latency of a blockchain system. Prior to discussing the architecture of RESILIENTDB, we look at some of these factors.

- **Single-threaded Monolithic Design.** There are ample opportunities available in the design of a permissioned blockchain application to extract parallelism. Several existing permissioned systems provide minimal to no discussion on how they can benefit from

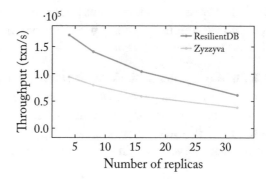

Figure 5.2: Two permissioned blockchains employing distinct BFT consensus protocols (80K clients used for each experiment).

the underlying hardware or cores [12, 75, 250]. Due to the sustained reduction in hardware cost (as a consequence of Moore's Law [188]), it is easy for each replica to have at least *eight* cores. Hence, by parallelizing the tasks across different threads and pipelining several transactions, a blockchain application can highly benefit from the available computational power.

- **Successive Consensuses.** Several works advocate the benefits of performing consensus on one request at a time [12, 145], while others promote aggregating client requests into large batches [14, 193]. We believe there is a communication and computation trade-off that needs to be analyzed before reaching such a decision. Hence, an optimal batching limit needs to discovered that can help reduce the costs associated with successive consensuses.

- **Decoupling Ordering and Execution.** On receiving a client request, each replica of a permissioned blockchain application has to order and execute that request. Although these tasks share a dependency, it is a useful design practice to separate them at the physical or logical level. At the physical level, distinct replicas can be used for execution. However, such an approach would incur additional communication costs. At the logical level, distinct threads can be asked to process requests in parallel, but additional hardware cores would be needed to facilitate such parallelism [211, 212]. Specifically, a single entity performing both ordering and execution loses an opportunity to gain from inherent parallelism.

- **Strict Ordering.** Permissioned blockchains rely on BFT protocols, which necessitate ordering of client requests in accordance with linearizability [143]. Although linearizability helps in guaranteeing a safe state across all the replicas, it is an expensive property to achieve. Hence, we need an approach that can provide linearizability but is inexpensive. We observe that permissioned blockchains can benefit from delaying the ordering of client requests until execution. This delay permits processing several client requests in parallel, while they are executed in order.

- **Off-Memory Chain Management.** Blockchains work on a large set of records or data. Hence, they require access to databases to store these records. There is a clear trade-off when system store data in-memory or on an off-the-shelf database. Off-memory storage requires several CPU cycles to fetch data [140]. Hence, employing in-memory storage can ensure faster access, which in turn can lead to high system throughput.

- **Expensive Cryptographic Practices.** Blockchains expect the exchange of several messages among the participating replicas and the clients, of which some may be byzantine. Hence, each blockchain application requires strong cryptographic constructs that allow a client or a replica to validate any message. As discussed earlier, these cryptographic constructs find a variety of uses in a blockchain application: (i) to sign a message; (ii) to verify an incoming message; (iii) to generate the digest of a client request; and (iv) to hash a record or data.

  To sign and verify a message, a blockchain application can employ either symmetric-key cryptography or asymmetric-key cryptography. Although symmetric-key signatures, such as Message Authentication Code (MAC), are faster to generate than asymmetric-key signatures, such as Digital Signature (DS), DS offer the key property of non-repudiation, which is not guaranteed by MACs. Hence, several works suggest using DSs [12, 14, 75, 250]. However, a cleverly designed permissioned blockchain system can skip using DS for a majority of its communication, which in turn will help increase its throughput. For generating digests or hash, a blockchain application needs to employ standard Hash functions, such as SHA256 or SHA3, which are secure.

Any blockchain application that takes into account these design principles can yield high system throughputs. Next, we illustrate the design of RESILIENTDB that aims to incorporate these principles into its design.

5.2.1   ARCHITECTURE

In Figure 5.3, we illustrate the overall architecture of RESILIENTDB, which lays down a client-server architecture. At the *application layer*, RESILIENTDB allows multiple clients to co-exist, each of which creates its own requests. For this purpose, they can either employ an existing benchmark suite or design a *Smart Contract* suiting to the active application. Next, clients and replicas use the *transport layer* to exchange messages across the network. RESILIENTDB provides support for communication through TCP/IP sockets and RDMA. RESILIENTDB also provides a *storage layer* where all the metadata corresponding to a request and the blockchain is stored. At each replica, there is an *execution layer* where the underlying consensus protocol is run on the

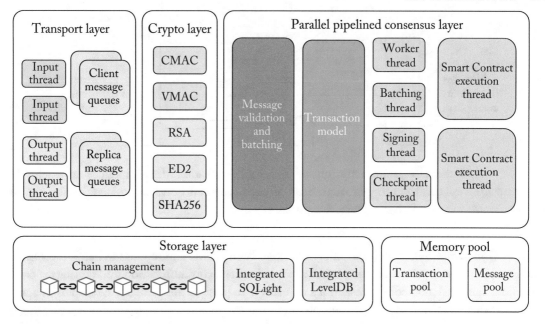

Figure 5.3: RESILIENTDB Architecture.

client request, and the request is ordered and executed. During ordering, the *secure layer* provides cryptographic support.

For the sake of explanation, we assume RESILIENTDB employs the PBFT protocol for reaching consensus among the replicas. However, the succeeding insights also apply to other BFT protocols, such as PoE, RCC, and GEOBFT.

Multi-Threaded Deep Pipeline. PBFT follows the primary-backup model, where one replica is designated as the primary and other replicas act as backups. On receiving a client request, the primary replica must initiate PBFT consensus among all the backup replicas and ensure all the replicas execute this client request in the same order. Note that depending on the choice of underlying BFT consensus protocol, RESILIENTDB can be molded to adopt a different model (e.g., leaderless architecture or clustered design).

In Figure 5.4, we illustrate the threaded-pipelined architecture of RESILIENTDB replicas. RESILIENTDB permits increasing (or decreasing) the number of threads of each type. With each replica, RESILIENTDB associate multiple *input* and *output* threads. Some of these input-threads are dedicated toward receiving requests from the clients, while the remaining input-threads collect messages sent by other replicas. RESILIENTDB also balances the task of transmitting messages between the output-threads by assigning equal clients and replicas to each output-thread. To facilitate this division, RESILIENTDB associates a distinct *queue* with each output-thread.

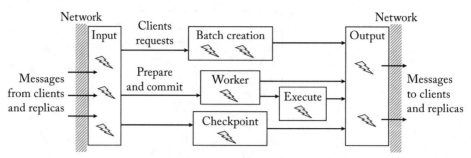

Figure 5.4: Schematic representation of the multi-threaded deep-pipelines at each RE-SILIENTDB replica. The number of threads of each type can be varied depending on the requirements of the underlying consensus protocol.

Transaction Batching. RESILIENTDB allows both clients and replicas to batch their transactions. Using an optimal batching policy can help mask communication and consensus costs. A client can send a burst of transactions as a single request to the primary. Examples of applications where a client may batch multiple transactions are stock-trading, monetary-exchanges, and service level-agreements. The primary replica can also aggregate client requests together to significantly reduce the number of times a consensus protocol needs to be run among the replicas.

Modeling a Primary Replica. To facilitate efficient batching of requests, RESILIENTDB associates multiple *batch-threads* with the primary replica. When the primary replica receives a batch of requests from the client, it treats it as a single request. The input-thread at the primary assigns a monotonically increasing sequence number to each incoming client request and enqueues it into the common queue for the batch-threads. To prevent contention among the batch-threads, RESILIENTDB implements the common queue as *lock-free*. This common queue ensures that any enqueued request is consumed as soon as any batch-thread is available.

Each batch-thread also performs the task of verifying the signature of the client request. If the verification is successful, then it creates a batch and names it as the PrePrepare message. PBFT also requires the primary replica to generate the digest of the client request and send this digest as part of the PrePrepare message. This digest helps in identifying the client request in future communication. Hence, each batch-thread also hashes a batch and marks this hash as a digest. Finally, the batch-thread signs and enqueues the corresponding PrePrepare message into the queue for an output-thread.

Apart from the client requests, the primary replica receives Prepare and Commit messages from backup replicas. As the system is partially asynchronous, the primary replica P may receive both the Prepare and Commit messages from a backup replica R1 before it receives a Prepare message from another backup R2. *How is this possible?* The replica R1 can receive sufficient number of Prepare messages before P receives Prepare from replica R2 (total number of replicas are $\mathbf{n} \geq 3\mathbf{f} + 1$). In such a case, R1 would proceed to the next phase and broadcast a Commit message. To prevent any resource contention, RESILIENTDB has only one *worker-thread* to process the Prepare and Commit messages.

When the input-thread receives a Prepare message, it enqueues that message in the *work-queue*. The worker-thread dequeues a message and verifies the signature on this message. If the verification is successful, then it records this message and continues collecting Prepare messages corresponding to a PrePrepare message until its count reaches $\mathbf{g}$. Once it reaches this count, then it creates a Commit message, signs and broadcasts this message. The worker-thread follows similar steps for a Commit message, and once it has received $\mathbf{g}$ Commit messages, it requests the *execute-thread* to execute the client requests.

Modeling a Backup Replica. As a backup replica does not batch client requests, RESILIENTDB assigns it fewer threads. When the input-thread at a backup replica receives a PrePrepare message from the primary, then it enqueues it in the work-queue. The worker-thread at a backup dequeues a PrePrepare message and checks if the message has a valid signature of the primary. If this is the case, then the worker-thread creates a Prepare message, signs this message, and enqueues it in the queue for output-thread. Notice that this Prepare message includes the digest from the PrePrepare message and the sequence number suggested by the primary. The output-thread broadcasts this Prepare message on the network. Similar to the primary, each backup replica also waits for $\mathbf{g}$ Prepare messages, creates and broadcasts a Commit message, collects $\mathbf{g}$ Commit messages, and informs the execute-thread.

Efficient Ordered Execution. Although RESILIENTDB attempts to pipeline different phases of the underlying consensus, it ensures execution happens in order. For instance, if primary P proposed a request $\mathbf{m}_1$ before $\mathbf{m}_2$, then $\mathbf{m}_1$ and $\mathbf{m}_2$ are executed in that order, irrespective of the order their consensuses are completed (possible due to Out-of-order processing discussed in Section 3.2.2). To ensure a single order of execution, RESILIENTDB includes a separate *execution-thread* for executing the requests. Clearly, execution-thread has to manage the overhead of tracking the requests and executing them in the correct order.

RESILIENTDB requires the worker-thread to create an Execute message and place this message in the *appropriate* queue once it receives $\mathbf{g}$ Commit messages. This Execute message includes the identifier for the starting and ending transactions of the corresponding batch. These identifiers help to locate the *correct* queue for enqueuing the message. Specifically, RESILIENTDB associate a large set of queues with the execution-thread. To determine the number of required queues for the execution-thread, we use the parameter QC:

$$QC = 2 \times Num\_Clients \times Num\_Req.$$

Here, *Num_Clients* represent the total number of clients in the system, while *Num_Req* represents the maximum number of requests a client can send without waiting for any response. We assume both of these parameters to be finite. Although QC can be very large, the queues are logical. So, the space complexity remains almost the same as for a single queue.

Using this design the execute-thread can deterministically select the queue to dequeue. If k was the sequence number for last executed request, the execute-thread calculates $r = (k + 1)$ mod QC and waits for an Execute message to be enqueued in its r-th queue. This design helps reduce several dequeues and enqueues on the same queue until the arrival of the next request in order. Once the execution is complete, the execution-thread creates a Response message and enqueues it in the queue for output-threads, to send to the client.

Block Generation. Following execution, the execution-thread creates a block representing the corresponding batch of requests. As the execute-thread has access to the previous block in the chain, so it can easily hash this previous block and store this hash in the new block. Notice that this step provides another opportunity for parallelism where the execute-thread can delegate the task of creating a new block to another thread.

Checkpointing. RESILIENTDB also require replicas to periodically generate and exchange *checkpoints*. These checkpoints serve *two* purposes: (1) help a failed replica to recover itself to the current state; and (2) facilitate clearing of old requests, messages, and blocks. RESILIENTDB deploys a separate *checkpoint-thread* at each replica to collect and process incoming Checkpoint messages. These checkpoint messages simply include all the blocks generated since the last checkpoint. Specifically, a Checkpoint message is sent only after a replica has executed Δ requests. Once execute-thread completes executing a batch, it checks if the sequence number of the batch is a *multiple of* Δ. If such is the case, it sends a Checkpoint message to all the replicas. When a replica receives g identical Checkpoint messages from distinct replicas, then it marks the checkpoint and clears all the data before the previous checkpoint [55, 161].

Message Pool Management. RESILIENTDB provides access to a *base class* API for creating newer message types. This base class provides the schema for all the messages that are exchanged across clients and replicas. Any developer can inherit this base class to create new messages that facilitate exchange of its desired data. To create a new message type, a developer can simply inherit this base class and add required properties. Although on delivery to the network, each message is simply a buffer of characters, this typed representation allows RESILIENTDB to easily manipulate the required properties. Similarly, RESILIENTDB includes a *base class* to represent all client transactions. An object of this transaction class includes: transaction identifier, client identifier, and transaction data, among many other properties.

When a message arrives in the system, a replica needs to allocate some space for that message. Similarly, when a replica receives a client request, it needs to allocate corresponding transaction objects. When the lifetime of a message ends (or a new checkpoint is established), then the memory occupied by the corresponding message (or transactions object) needs to be released. To avoid such frequent allocations and de-allocations, RESILIENTDB adheres to the standard practice of maintaining a set of *buffer pools*. During the system initialization phase (or warmup stage), RESILIENTDB create a large pool of empty objects representing the messages and transactions. So, when a thread needs to allocate some memory, it pulls an empty object from the pool, and once the lifetime of that object ends, it is placed back in the pool.

5.2.2 EXPERIMENTAL ANALYSIS

We now experimentally analyze the architecture of RESILIENTDB fabric. Specifically, we employ the graphs presented by Gupta et al. [124], and discuss some of the factors that affect the throughput and latency of a Permissioned Blockchain system.

Evaluation Setup. Each experiment that we discuss in this section is run on the Google Cloud infrastructure at Iowa region. All the RESILIENTDB replicas, are deployed on c2 machines with an 8-core Intel Xeon Cascade Lake CPU running at 3.8 GHz and having 16 GB memory, while the clients use c2 4-core machines. Each experiment is run for 180 s, and the results are averaged over *three* runs.

Clients generate workload using the YCSB benchmark, which is part of the Blockbench suite [69, 81]. For creating a request, each client indexes a YCSB table with an active set of 600K records. In these experiments, each client request contains only write accesses, as a majority of blockchain requests are updates to the existing data. At the time of initialization, each replica has an identical copy of the table. Each client YCSB request is generated from a uniform Zipfian distribution.

Unless *explicitly* stated otherwise, each experiment uses the following setup: Each consensus is run among 16 replicas and up to 80K clients are deployed on 4 machines to send reqests. For efficiency, clients send a batch of 100 requests at a time instead of a single request. For any communication between clients and replicas, digital signatures based on ED25519 help to authenticate the messages, while a combination of CMAC and AES helps to authenticate communication between replicas [153]. At each replica, the threaded-pipeline comprises of one worker-thread, one execute-thread and two batch-threads.

Effect of Threading and Pipelining. In this section, we analyze the benefits of a threaded-pipelined architecture. For this study, the system parameters are varied in two dimensions: (i) the number of replicas participating in the consensus are increased from 4 to 32; and (ii) the pipeline is gradually expanded to balance the load among parallel threads.

To reiterate the claim that a well-crafted system can lead to high throughputs, these experiments lay down a comparison between two well-known consensus protocols, PBFT and ZYZZYVA. These experiments start with a bare-bones architecture and gradually move toward the RESILIENTDB architecture of Figure 5.4. We denote the number of execution-threads with symbol E, and batch-threads with symbol B. In all these experiments, only *one* worker-thread is employed. In Figure 5.5, we illustrate the effects of this gradual increase. The key intuition behind these plots is to continue expanding the stages of pipeline and the number of threads, until system can no longer increase its throughput. In this manner, it would be easy to observe design choices that could make even PBFT outperform ZYZZYVA.

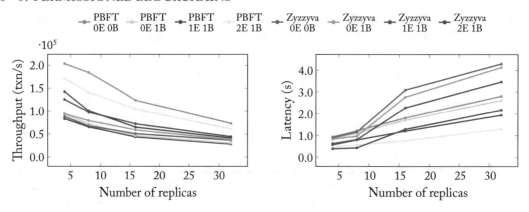

Figure 5.5: System throughput (*left*) and latency (*right*), on varying the number of replicas participating in the consensus. Here, E denotes number of execution-threads, while B denotes batch-threads.

On close observation of Figure 5.5, it is trivial to highlight the benefits of a good implementation. These plots help to illustrate the resulting gains due a multi-threaded pipelined architecture over a single-threaded design. Next, we explain the methodology for gradual changes.

The initial variant of RESILIENTDB (denoted as 1E 0B) has no additional threads to perform the tasks of execution and batching, that is, all tasks are done by one worker-thread. On scaling this system, it was evident that the worker-thread was getting fully utilized. Hence, the load is partially divided by having an execute-thread (1E 0B). However, we again observe that the worker-thread at the primary is getting completely utilized. This creates an opportunity to introduce a separate thread to create batches (1E 1B). Now, although the worker-thread is no longer saturating, the single batch-thread is overloaded due to the task of creating batches. Hence, the task of batching client requests is further divided among multiple batch-threads (1E 2B), which ensured none of the batch-threads are fully utilized. We use Figure 5.6 to illustrate this utilization level for different threads at a replica.

In this figure, we mark 100% as the maximum utilization for any thread. Using the bar for *cumulative utilization*, helps to present a summation of the utilization for all the threads, for any experiment. Notice that for PBFT 1E 2B, the worker-thread at backup replicas has nearly saturated. But, as the architecture at the non-primary is following the base design, so no new threads are introduced in the system to further balance the load.

From these figures, it is evident that if PBFT is given benefit of RESILIENTDB's standard pipeline (1E 2B), then it can attain higher throughput than all but one ZYZZYVA implementations. The only ZYZZYVA implementation (1E 2B) that outperforms PBFT is the one that employs RESILIENTDB's standard threaded-pipeline. Further, even the simpler implementation

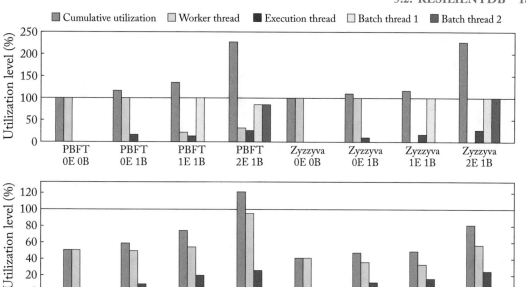

Figure 5.6: Utilization level of different threads at a replica: the primary replica (*top*) and backup replica (*bottom*). The mean is at 100%, which implies the thread is completely utilized.

for PBFT (1E 1B) attains higher throughput than Zyzzyva's 0E 0B and 1E 0B implementations.

Effect of Cryptographic Signatures. In this section, we study the impact of different cryptographic signature schemes. The key intuition behind these experiments is to determine which signing scheme helps a permissioned blockchainn fabric achieve the highest throughput while preventing byzantine attacks. For this purpose, we run four different experiments to measure the system throughput and latency when: (i) no signature scheme is used, (ii) everyone uses digital signatures based on ED25519, (iii) everyone uses digital signatures based on RSA, and (iv) all replicas use CMAC+AES for signing, while clients sign their message using ED25519.

We use Figure 5.7 to illustrate the throughput attained and latency incurred by Re-silientDB for different configurations. It is evident that any system will attain maximum throughput when no signatures are employed. However, such a system does not fulfill the minimal requirements expected of a permissioned blockchain system. An alternate strategy is to employ digital signatures for signing messages, which is clearly not the best practice. An optimal configuration would require clients to sign their messages using digital signatures, while replicas can communicate using message authentication codes.

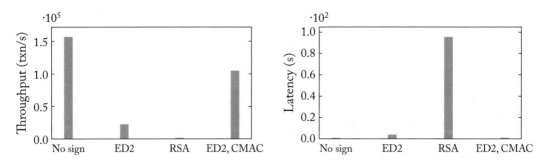

Figure 5.7: System throughput (*left*) and latency (*right*) with different signature schemes. Here, 16 replicas participate in consensus.

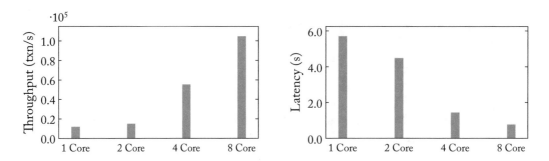

Figure 5.8: System throughput (*left*) and latency (*right*) on varying the number of hardware cores. Here, 16 replicas participate in consensus.

Effect of Hardware Cores. We now analyze the effects of a deployed hardware on a permissioned blockchain hardware application. In this experiment, RESILIENTDB replicas are deployed on different Google Cloud machines having 1, 2, 4, and 8 cores. We use Figure 5.8 to illustrate the throughput and latency attained by RESILIENTDB system on different machines. In all these experiments, a total of 16 replicas participate in the consensus. These figures affirm our claim that if replicas run on a machine with fewer cores, then the overall system throughput will be reduced (and higher latency will be incurred). As our architecture (refer to Figure 5.4) requires several threads, so on a machine with fewer cores our threads face resource contention. Hence, RESILIENTDB attains maximum throughput on the 8-core machines.

5.3   CONCLUDING REMARKS

Building scalable systems demand more than just an optimized protocol, and blockchains are no exception. In this chapter, we shift our focus from studying consensus protocols to fundamental design principles necessary in architecting resilient systems in the context of permissioned blockchains. In particular, we focused on two representative systems, namely, (1) HYPERLEDGER Fabric, an industry incubation part of Linux Foundation [14, 231] and (2) RESILIENTDB, an academic initiative born at the University of California, Davis [117–124, 134–138, 214].

HYPERLEDGER offers a wide range of toolkit along with sophisticated smart contract support necessary to build and deploy industrial-strength blockchain applications. Arguably what sets apart HYPERLEDGER Fabric is their unique architecture in how the fault-tolerant consensus protocols are incorporated as a plug-and-play ordering service into the larger execution runtime. The traditional design has been first to order transactions or smart contracts then execute them serially. This *order-execute* design assumes that the execution is deterministic such that an identical outcome is always produced independently on all replicas. In contrast, HYPERLEDGER Fabric introduced an *execute-order-verify* architecture together with a flexible *endorsement policy* to allow the client to decide the faith of the smart contract especially when there is inherent non-determinism or uncertainty in the contract. For instance, when the smart contact entails probabilistic computation (e.g., machine learning models) or relies on external measurements (e.g., sensor readings). After the smart contract is executed (albeit tentatively) by a set of endorsers, each endorser reports the outcome of their execution (i.e., the read and write sets) to the client. If there is a discrepancy among endorsers, then the client may choose to ignore outliers or opt to average the results, for example. Once the client's endorsement policy is satisfied, then the smart contract is sequenced by the ordering service and enters the verification phase before committing and appending the contract to the ledger. It is noteworthy that the execution is tentative contingent upon the stability of the endorsers' snapshot of the ledger at the time of execution. Therefore, verifiers must ensure that the endorsed read set of the contract has not changed by any newly committed and conflicting transactions since the time of the tentative execution; otherwise, the contract is aborted.

RESILIENTDB calls for a holistic system view in building permissioned blockchain by re-examining the entire fabric through a scale-centric lens. This is a sharp deviation from the recent trends that heavily focuses on a developing system based on yet more sophisticated and optimized BFT protocols. Thus, it raises a basic fundamental question: *can a well-crafted system-centric architecture based on a classical* BFT *protocol outperform a protocol-centric architecture?* In exploring this tenet, RESILIENTDB has re-architected and developed a modular system design from scratch that embeds parallelism and deep pipelining at every layer to fully exploit modern hardware and cloud infrastructure globally. Broadly speaking, it aims to pioneer a resilient data platform at scale, a distributed ledger centered around a democratic and decentralized model.

5.4   BIBLIOGRAPHIC NOTES

Apart from the HYPERLEDGER project, several other blockchain systems displayed a surge in adoption of the permissioned blockchain technology [64, 68, 70, 230]. Corda [70] provides a set of blockchain APIs for enterprise use. It supports a pluggable consensus architecture where a set of nodes designated as the notaries work together to order client transactions. Quorum [68] also provides support permissioned blockchain APIs, but it is targeted toward developers that want to work on top of Ethereum Virtual Machine. Tendermint [230] provides its user access to the Tendermint Core APIs, which can be employed by any blockchain platform to achieve consensus among its set of replicas. Tendermint Core follows the design pioneered by the PBFT protocol to safely order the transaction.

Several permissioned blockchain systems are also working toward providing support for a native cryptocurrency [80, 132]. *Hedera* [132] represents its monetary unit as HBAR, which can be used by two or more users to make payments in exchange for any commodities. To order all the incoming client transactions, Hedera introduces a hashgraph algorithm that facilitates consensus among a set of governing nodes. Further, Hedera also provides APIs that can be used by an enterprise to build its own blockchains. *Libra* [80] aims to develop efficient financial solutions that can serve as a global payment system. To achieve consensus on the order of client transactions, Libra runs the LibraBFT protocol, which is a variant of HotStuff [249] protocol. Further, Libra allows its users to write and publish smart contracts on its blockchain using the Move programming language.

CHAPTER 6

Permissionless Blockchains

The rise of Bitcoin [193] and other cryptocurrencies [57, 244] led to the research and design of several new BFT consensus protocols. These protocols were designed with following two goals in mind: (1) running BFT consensus among a massively large set of replicas and (2) protecting identities of the participating replicas. The former goal is a consequence of PBFT's design, which necessitates multiple phases of quadratic communication among the replicas. Hence, even though PBFT is safe, it cannot be scaled to large distributed applications. The latter goal is a *key* ingredient for expressing permissionless blockchains [126, 251].

Permissionless blockchains inspired by the design of Bitcoin allow any user, node, or machine to act as a replica. Further, these systems permit these replicas to participate in the consensus at any point in time. Hence, the identities of the participants may often be unknown. This attribute is in sharp contrast with traditional BFT protocols, where the identities of the participating replicas need to be known a priori.

To achieve aforementioned goals, permissionless blockchains employ consensus based on *Proof-of-X* protocols. We use the symbol X as a placeholder for different terms such as work, stake, and capacity [126]. In this chapter, we take a deep dive and understand the design of three distinct *Proof-of-X* protocols that are employed by *well-known* permissionless blockchains to achieve consensus among their replicas. Specifically, we shall look at the following.

1. First, we will lay down the principles of *Proof-of-Work* algorithm and show how to employ these principles to achieve the consensus among a set of replicas.

2. Then, we will study the design of an authenticated data-structure that not only eliminates the need for exchanging large messages, but also facilitates efficient verification of the data stored in a blockchain.

3. Next, we will illustrate a well-known permissionless blockchain application of *Proof-of-Work* algorithm and efficient authenticated data-structure—Bitcoin.

4. Following the description of *Proof-of-Work* protocol, we will study the design of two *energy-aware* Proof-of-X protocols. Specifically, prior works have shown that consensus based on *Proof-of-Work* protocol requires massive energy to guarantee safety [76, 196, 241]. Hence, we present the design of *Proof-of-Stake* and *Proof-of-Space* protocols.

5. Finally, we conclude this chapter by presenting another permissionless blockchain that plans to adopt the *Proof-of-Stake* protocol in the future—Ethereum.

6.1 PROOF-OF-WORK CONSENSUS

The design of *Proof-of-Work* (henceforth referred to as PoW) protocol lies at the core of a fundamentally intriguing question, "What is mathematically hard to compute but easy to verify?" Hence, the consensus based on PoW [87, 146] protocol revolves around this *trapdoor*.

Prior to the introduction of blockchain technology, the distributed systems community employed PoW protocol to control spam, allocate resources, prevent denial-of-service-attacks, and in many other situations [87, 105, 147]. Leaning on the definition from [52], PoW can be stated as an uncheatable benchmark that can only be computed in one direction. Specifically, the PoW protocol prevents fraudulent claims as only a *prover* who has actually performed the required computation can produce a verifiable result.

6.1.1 CORE ALGORITHM

Our above description of PoW requires the computation to be expensive, that is, it should deplete some resources of the prover. This depletion prevents invalid proofs and safeguards the system against adversaries. Essentially, PoW requires a computationally expensive function. In computing, several computationally hard problems exist, such as Diophantine Equation, RSA Factorization, Fermat's Last Theorem, One-way Hash Functions, and so on. Among these hard problems, Bitcoin opted for the computation based on *one-way hash functions*. Since then, hash functions have been employed by blockchain application designers for their deployments of PoW-based consensus. We now present a definition for PoW protocol that employs hash functions for its hardness.

Definition 6.1   Let S be a system consisting of a prover P and a verifier V. Assume both P and V have access to a collision-resistant hash function digest(). Given a challenge y, the prover P needs to find the input x to digest() such that $y = \text{digest}(x)$. When P finds x, it sends x to V, which can easily verify whether $y = \text{digest}(x)$ holds.

Definition 6.1 helps us to illustrate how replicas can use the PoW protocol to reach consensus. In a blockchain that employs PoW for achieving consensus among its replicas, the tasks of a P and V are taken up by one or more replicas. In such a system, each replica can alternate between the roles of a prover and a verifier. Achieving consensus in such a blockchain system requires generating a challenge y for which finding the corresponding input x is non-trivial. Once the system determines the value of y, it broadcasts this value on the network. Each replica on receiving y can decide if it wishes to act as a prover[1] and if so, it attempts to find x. Once a replica R finds x, it broadcasts this value on the network. Finally, each replica that *receive x* from R acts as a verifier and checks the validity of x. If the x is valid, then the verifying replicas conclude that R indeed solved the required PoW computation.

---

[1]Blockchains like Bitcoin and Ethereum use the term "miner" to denote a prover.

For reaching a safe consensus among a set of replicas, the PoW protocol adheres to the following properties.

1. ***Collision-Resistant Hashing.*** PoW protocol requires all the replicas to have access to a collision-resistant hash function [153]. Specifically, given $y = \text{digest}(x)$, an adversary should not be able to find a x' such that $\text{digest}(x) = \text{digest}(x')$. Hence, collision-resistance provides V an assurance that P could not have cheated. Existing blockchains employ SHA3 or SHA256 to achieve collision-resistance.

2. ***Resource Intensive.*** PoW protocol also requires the P to do some expensive task that depletes its resources. If the P can perform the required task instantaneously, then it can create multiple fake identities to gain profit. Such fake identities are a *threat* to the safe execution of the system. For example, each byzantine-fault tolerant or blockchain system expects the majority of its replicas to be non-faulty. If each malicious replica can somehow create multiple fake identities, then the system will no longer meet the standard requirements, and such a system will be termed as compromised. Hence, blockchain systems that employ PoW for consensus need to ensure that the prover's task is computationally expensive.

3. ***Non-Boundedness.*** If a prover is given enough time and resources, then it will always be able to provide the valid proof for a given challenge. Specifically, if there are unbounded resources, then eventually any prover can yield a solution. Hence, most systems that employ PoW protocol for consensus only await the arrival of first valid proof. Once they receive a proof, they mark the consensus on that request as complete.

4. ***Pre-Computations.*** The hardness of a PoW computation is determined by the inability of the prover to successfully predict the result. If a prover P can make a valid guess about the challenge y, then it can perform pre-computations, which can expedite the process of determining x. Hence, y needs to be selected at random, and its difficulty needs to be increased if there is an increase in the prover's computational ability, which can be determined by the rate of receiving responses.

Attacks and Critiques Against Proof-of-Work

Prior works [98, 99] have observed several attacks on the PoW-based blockchains. Further, some of these works have also raised questions on the impact of PoW-based blockchains on the environment. We now discuss some of these questions and illustrate common attacks associated with PoW protocol.

High Energy Consumption. Earlier in this chapter, we noted several essential properties expected from the PoW consensus. A key property in this list requires the PoW protocol to be *resource-intensive*. Specifically, each prover wastes its computational resources in the process of finding the correct solution. Prior works have shown that Bitcoin—a well-known blockchains—employs PoW protocol to achieve consensus among its replicas, and hence, Bitcoin consumes a massive amount of energy [76, 196, 241]. In fact, Bitcoin's carbon footprint is greater than the energy consumed by some of the developed European nations [126].

51% Dilemma. The security of any blockchain that employs the PoW protocol is bounded by the fact that the majority of miners are honest. Specifically, PoW-based systems expect that at least 51% of the computing power is in control with the non-faulty replicas. If this is not the case, then malicious replicas can pool their resources and perform a series of PoW computations during the time required by a single replica to solve a single PoW computation. *Why is this an issue?* In the case of blockchains, a 51% attack essentially centralizes the system. Moreover, a 51% attack can lead to other attacks such as *selfish mining* [99] and *double-spending* [126], where malicious miners attempt to rollback committed transaction.

6.1.2   MERKLE TREE HASHING

We now digress a little and discuss design of an important data-structure that facilitates efficient verification and exchange of data. Specifically, we now present a discussion on Merkle Trees [185]. Later, in this section, we show how blockchains based on PoW consensus use these Merkle trees to reduce communication and verification costs.

To amortize latency and to increase throughput, blockchains permit *batching* multiple client requests in a single block. By employing batching, replicas can achieve consensus on multiple client requests in fewer communication steps. In Section 2.7.2, while discussing the PBFT protocol, we illustrated that the primary replica optimizes the cost due to large `PrePrepare` messages by employing small bounded-size digests. If batching is employed, then one block would contain multiple client requests. Hence, it would have to carry several digests. Although the size of an individual digest is smaller than the corresponding client request, the combined size of digests of a batch of requests consumes too much space, which in turn makes the communication expensive.

Merkle trees act as a resolve to this problem. Using Merkle trees, it is easy to combine multiple hashes into a single hash, which can be used for both verification and identification. In Figure 6.1, we represent a simple Merkle tree of four client requests T_1, T_2, T_3, and T_4. The hash of each of these transactions acts as the leaves of this tree. As we go up the tree, the hash of the *concatenation* of the hashes of child nodes results in the parent node. For example, H_{12} is a result of first concatenating H_1 and H_2, and then taking a hash of the concatenated string, digest($H_1||H_2$). Similarly, the root of this Merkle tree is generated, which is a cryptographic combination of all the leaf transactions.

Verification. As a Merkle root is a hash of the cryptographic combination of all the transactions is a block, it can help to detect any attacks or failures. For instance, in Figure 6.1, an adversary tries to modify the content of transaction T_3. This modification would result in a com-

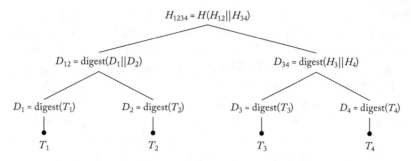

Figure 6.1: Application of Merkle Tree Hashing algorithm on a set of four transactions T_1, T_2, T_3, and T_4. At the end of the algorithm, H_{1234} is outputted as the Merkle root.

pletely different Merkle root, even if the modification is of just one bit. *Why is this the case?* Any change in transaction T_3 would result in a massive change in the generated hash (a guarantee offered by collision-resistant hash functions). Further, this change would propagate up the root and would result in distinct Merkel root. In practice, replicas can use this property of Merkle trees to pin-point the contention transaction.

6.2   BITCOIN

Bitcoin [193] is popularly regarded as the first realization of blockchain technology. Invented by Nakamoto, Bitcoin aimed at establishing a decentralized payment system between two or more parties. To meet this goal, Nakamoto designed a peer-to-peer money transfer system that employed a *crypto-currency* known as Bitcoin.

Each user participating in the Bitcoin subsystem uses Bitcoin to acquire, exchange, or provide services. As Bitcoin necessitates decentralized access, so multiple replicas participate and record the transactions that take place in the system. These records are maintained in an immutable ledger, also known as blockchain. Bitcoins are generated through a process of *mining* where each replica that wants to propose the next block to be added to the chain needs to provide a proof of the work it has done and earns Bitcoins in exchange.[2]

In Bitcoin, any node that wishes to mine is termed as a miner. Each miner also needs to verify the user transactions, which it wishes to add to the next block. As any node can participate to be a miner, so Bitcoin's design is termed as permissionless or open membership.

6.2.1   GENERAL WORKING

When a node wishes to participate as a miner, it needs to first install one of the many available *Bitcoin mining softwares* such as Bitcoin Miner [112], BTCMiner [198], CGMiner [160],

---

[2]Not every user has to perform mining to own Bitcoins. Users can acquire Bitcoins through trading-exchanges, investments, or through commodity exchange. The discussion of these mechanisms is outside the scope of this book.

and GUIMiner [157]. The choice of a Bitcoin software depends on the expected features, and its compatibility with the underlying hardware, that is, some of these are specialized to outperform others on specific hardware. For instance, GUIMiner provides miners with graphical frontend and facilitates mining on both CPU and GPU platforms, BTCMiner provides support for ZTEX USB-FPGA modules, and BFGMiner provides supports for ASICs.

To increase randomness, Bitcoin miners perform a double hash computation during the PoW protocol. Specifically, to find the *nonce* that solves the challenge, Bitcoin miners have to hash each value x twice (two computations of SHA256 algorithm). Clearly, if each node R mines alone, it would require R a significant amount of time to perform all such computations and to find the valid nonce x. This would result in extremely low system throughput and would require miners to perform massive investments in computational resources that can help solve the challenge. Hence, Bitcoin rewards its miners with incentives if they are successful in finding the valid nonce (refer to Section 6.2.3).

Although the existence of incentives can excite miners to invest their resources, it does not solve the issue of double SHA256 calculations requiring a massive amount of time to compute. To ensure regular flow of incentives, Bitcoin miners often work in groups, that is, they end up joining *mining pools* where several miners work together to find the nonce that helps to meet the PoW target (refer to Section 6.2.5).

Mining pools can be categorized as *centralized* or *decentralized*. Centralized mining pools are maintained by an administrator, while decentralized pools expect a collaborative effort. A key reason several miners prefer decentralized pools is because they prevent attacks by the administrator, which could be hard to detect.

In a decentralized pool, when a miner finds a new *share* with lower difficulty, it forwards that share to all the other miners. This share should include the information regarding the payouts for other miners. Once some miner finds a share with the same difficulty as Bitcoin target, then every miner is paid in proportion to their work. MultiPool [74] and P2Pool [240] are examples of two such decentralized mining pools.

Centralized mining pools require an administrator, which operates the pool and takes a fee to do the same. Some of the famous centralized mining pools used by Bitcoin miners, among many others, are AntPool [66], F2Pool [100], BTCC [48], and Poolin [209]. These pools are also among the major Bitcoin block creators.

Prior to mining any Bitcoins, each miner also needs to setup a secure *wallet*. This wallet is used by the miner to store and receive Bitcoins. As Bitcoins are not a tangible currency so its storage and handling is also digital. Specifically, each Bitcoin is located at some *address*. These addresses are stored in a Bitcoin wallet.

Each Bitcoin address in its vanilla form is a *public-key*. Bitcoin users employ asymmetric-key cryptography to generate unique pairs of *public- and private-keys*, of which public-keys are distributed to receive Bitcoins while private keys are kept secret and help the receiver in proving its claim. Specifically, these bitcoin address act as a bank account number where anyone can send

Field	Size	Description
Version (v)	Integer (4B)	Version of block format
PrevHash	Unsigned integer (32B)	Hash of the previous block header
MerkleRoot ($\mathcal{M}$)	Unsigned integer (32B)	Root of the Merkle Tree
Timestamp (t)	Unsigned integer (4B)	Time of block creation
Target (T_D)	Hexadecimal (4B)	Target string for block creation
Nonce (n)	Unsigned integer (4B)	Discovered input for challenge

Figure 6.2: Components of a PoW challenge string used by replicas in Bitcoin.

money. If a user wants to prevent its activity being tracked, Bitcoin advises each user to associate a different address for each transaction.

6.2.2 CHALLENGE STRING

Each Bitcoin miner runs the PoW protocol on a *challenge string*, which corresponds to the header of a new block that this miner wishes to propose. Specifically, this challenge string comprises of the following: (1) version of the block format, (2) Merkle root of all the transactions in the new block, (3) hash of the previous block in the chain, (4) timestamp marking the block creation time, (5) current PoW target for miners, and (6) nonce to be discovered by miners [197].

We use Figure 6.2 to illustrate the components of the challenge string. For the sake of explanation, we assume that the new block will be the i-th block in the blockchain.

- *Version* v corresponds to the version of block format. For example, in Bitcoin, the latest version introduced is 4 [210].
- *PrevHash* H_{i-1} is the hash of the previous block in the chain, which is calculated by taking hash of the corresponding components of the previous block, as follows:

$$\text{digest}(v||H_{i-2}||\mathcal{M}||t||T_D||n). \qquad (6.1)$$

As all of these components are available to a miner, so calculating H_{i-1} is trivial.
- *Timestamp* t is fixed at the start of block generation process.
- *Target* T_D is the puzzle for which a miner competes in PoW protocol. As this target is also a hash, it is often represented in *hexadecimal* format.
- *Nonce* n is the solution to the PoW challenge, which helps to meet the target.

Notice that in this challenge string, the nonce n is the variable component, which a miner keeps on changing until the hash of this challenge is equal to T_D.

MINING DIFFICULTY AND TARGET

PoW protocol expects miners to find a valid *nonce* that helps to meet the current *target*. Specifically, Bitcoin miners repeatedly do the following: (i) pick a nonce and append it to the challenge string and (ii) *double hash* the appended string and check if it is lower than the target. To ensure that the *target* is not easily attainable by the miners, Bitcoin keeps on automatically updating the *difficulty* parameter. Specifically, difficulty helps to measure the necessary effort needed to reach the target. Every 2016 blocks, the difficulty parameter is updated [43]. If Bitcoin, the desired rate for block creation is 10 minutes. This implies that creating 2016 blocks should take two weeks. If the previous set of 2016 blocks takes more than two weeks, then difficulty is reduced and vice-versa in other case. As Bitcoin target (T_D) is a 256-bit number,[3] so difficulty (D) can be calculated using the following formula:

$$D = \text{base-difficulty}/T_D.$$

In Bitcoin, the value of base-difficulty is set as a hash whose leading 32 bits are zero and remaining bits are set to one. Another faster way to calculate difficulty is based on Taylor series for logarithm. Note that the minimum difficulty is *one*, when the target is set at maximum permissible value.

6.2.3   CONSENSUS AND MINER INCENTIVES

From the preceding sections, it became clear that Bitcoin employs a slight variation of the PoW protocol described in Section 6.1. We now describe this variation, which will also act as a base for discussing succeeding protocols.

Each client that wants its request to be processed transmits it to all the replicas. Prior to computing the PoW challenge, each replica validates each incoming request. Next, this replica packages all the valid request as a *block*, generates a Merkle root of these requests, and hashes the previous block in the chain. Each miner also creates the challenge string and initiates the PoW protocol. Each miner aims to find a nonce that helps it to reach the target. Specifically, the miner tries different nonce until it computes a hash that is less than the target. Once the miner finds such a hash, then it broadcasts the new block. Any other replica can use the nonce in the new block to verify the proof-of-work.

Incentivization. It is evident that the PoW protocol requires miners to dedicate their resources to calculate a computationally expensive hash. Hence, PoW-based systems need to reward their participating miners for their expenses. To promote block creation, each miner is given a fixed reward once they successfully generate a new block. Note that the mere existence of a rewarding policy has natural trade-offs. On the one hand, it promotes mining, which increases participation in the consensus protocol. On the other hand, it attracts adversaries, which for the sake of profits, could indulge in malicious practices.

---

[3]Although Bitcoin target is packed in a 4 byte representation, it is expanded into a 256-bit format during calculations.

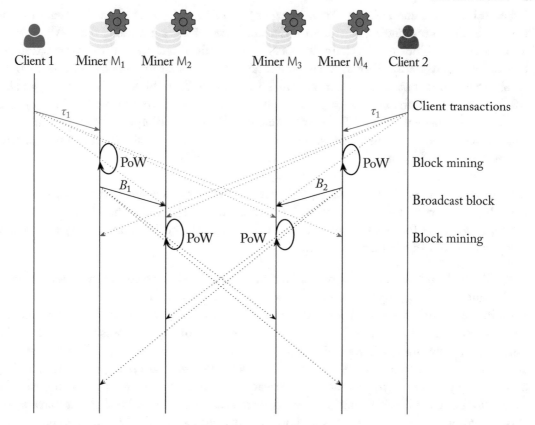

Figure 6.3: An illustration of how Bitcoin faces forks in the blockchain. Clients 1 and 2 broadcast their transactions on the network. Miners M_1 and M_4 attempt to propose the next block each with different transaction. Once they resolve the challenge, they broadcast their respective blocks. Due to network delay in block reception, miners M_2 and M_3 are extending distinct chains.

The introduction of incentives into the PoW protocol has paved the path for a profitable system. Specifically, a lot of miners are dedicating their resources in the hope of earning high rewards. A negative result of this reward-based design is that it has increased the probability of occurrence of *chain-forks*. Notice that PoW protocol is essentially leaderless as any miner can propose the next block. As all the miners are attempting to generate the next block, so multiple miners may end up proposing the next block for the chain at nearly the same time. Moreover, due to network delays and distance between the miners, the order in which different miners receive these new blocks may not be the same. Hence, disjoint set of miners may waste their resources by doing the same work as only one block will be designated as the next block while other blocks are discarded. We illustrate this in the following example.

Example 6.2   Assume a system $\mathfrak{R}$ consisting of four miners M_1, M_2, M_3, and M_4 (refer to Figure 6.3 for the corresponding illustration). Each of these miners are running the PoW protocol to propose a new block for the chain. Say each miner needs to include only one transaction per block. Due to arbitrarily delay in the network, say miner M_1 first receives transaction T_1 from Client 1 while miner M_4 receives transaction T_2 from Client 2. In this scenario, both M_1 and M_4 will start mining for the next block in the chain where the block from M_1 will include T_1, and the block from M_4 will include T_2. Now assume that both M_1 and M_4 end up solving the challenge string at the same time, that is, they concurrently propose blocks B_1 and B_2 containing transactions T_1 and T_2, respectively, and broadcast them on the network.

Assume miner M_2 receives B_1 from M_1 before it receives B_2 from M_4, while miner M_3 receives B_2 before B_1. In this case, M_2 will start mining for a new block with transaction T_2, while M_3 will start mining for a new block with transaction T_1. Notice that the previous block for M_2 is B_1 while for M_3, the previous block is B_2. Hence, both the miners M_2 and M_3 are working on two distinct chains or forks.

The issue in Example 6.2 arises as no miner wants to either wait or retract their blocks. Each miner wants to propose the next block as soon as possible to maximize its rewards. As a result, the original blockchain forks and miners start working on distinct forks of the chain. The key issue with the forks is that at some point in time, one of the forks will gain over the others (or become larger) when a majority of miners start working on that fork. This implies that all the resources spent to manage the other forks will get *wasted*. Moreover, the mere existence of forks imply that neither a miner can be rewarded as soon as it creates a block, nor can the transactions in a new block be considered valid, instantaneously. Hence, blockchains that employ PoW protocol require their users to wait for a block to reach a specific *depth*, before considering their transaction complete or rewarding the miner.

6.2.4   BITCOIN TRANSACTIONS

Bitcoin transactions are categorized under two heads: *Regular* and *Coinbase*. Regular transactions are employed by the users of Bitcoin to send and receive Bitcoins from other users, while the Coinbase transactions help to track the newly minted coins. Both of these transactions share similar fields, which we explain next.

Regular Transactions

Regular transactions are submitted by clients or users of Bitcoin ecosystem to exchange Bitcoins. Figure 6.4a illustrates different components of a regular transaction.

- *Version* corresponds to the version of transaction format.

- *nInputs* tracks the total number of inputs for this transaction.

- *Inputs* stores all the inputs of this transaction.

Field	Type	Description
Version	Integer	Version of format
nInputs	Variable integer	Number of inputs
Inputs	Array	Inputs
nOutputs	Variable integer	Number of outputs
Outputs	Array	Outputs
LockTime	Unsigned integer	Transaction recording time

(a) Fields of a regular transaction

Field	Description
Hash	Hash of a past transaction
Id	Index of transaction output
SignLen	Length of Sign field
Sign	Spending condition
Sequence	Transaction sequence

(b) Inputs of a regular transaction

Field	Description
Value	Amount of Bitcoins
PubkeyLen	Length of Pubkey field
Pubkey	Claiming condition

(c) Outputs of a regular transaction

Figure 6.4: Regular transaction.

- *nOutputs* tracks the total number of outputs for this transaction.

- *Outputs* stores all the outputs for this transaction.

- *LockTime* states the time beyond which a transaction needs to be included in a block. LockTime is used in conjunction with the *Sequence* field (Figure 6.4b) and is ignored if the latter is set.

Inputs to any regular transaction are the source of Bitcoins. Specifically, these inputs refer to one or more past transactions (e.g., coinbase transactions) which the client uses to make payments. Figure 6.4b lists some of the fields for these inputs.

- *Hash* of the past transaction.

- *Id* is the identifier of the specific output in the past transaction.

- *Sign* is the signature computed over the transaction.

- *SignLen* is the length of this signature.

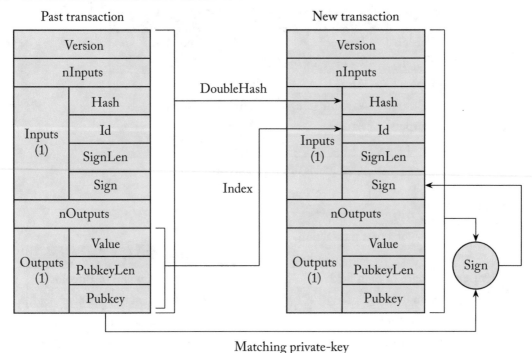

Figure 6.5: Structure of a regular transaction in Bitcoin. For the sake of illustration, assume that each of these transactions has a single input and output. Each new transaction relies on one or more past transactions for its inputs. Further, the private-key matching to the public-key (Pubkey) helps in generating the signature (Sign).

Outputs of any regular transactions are the sink of Bitcoins. Note that there can be multiple sinks. These outputs represent the users who will receive Bitcoins from a client. Figure 6.4c lists some of the fields for these outputs.

- *Value* is the number of Bitcoins that the sender wants to give this receiver.

- *Pubkey* is the address of the receiver.

- *PubkeyLen* is the length of Pubkey.

A simple illustration of a *new* regular transaction is presented in Figure 6.5. In Bitcoin, every regular transaction has a set of *inputs* and *outputs*. If a Bitcoin user wants to transfer some Bitcoins to another user, then it needs to first prove that it owns required Bitcoins. We know that a user could have either generated Bitcoins (*coinbase* transactions) or received Bitcoins (*regular* transactions). These transactions include an array of *Outputs*, which are simply the addresses of the Bitcoins. Specifically, each element of the *Outputs* array specifies the *public-key* of a receiver of some Bitcoins. As the Outputs field is an array, so a single transaction may transfer Bitcoins to multiple distinct users. Notice that to securely identify a past transaction, the sender also includes its hash and an index in the *Outputs* array (public-key corresponding to the Bitcoins that will be transferred).

As Bitcoin transactions are available to every replica (or miner), a malicious replica may attempt to lay claim on an output from a past transaction. Such an attempt will always be unsuccessful as each output is essentially a public-key, and is associated with a unique *private-key*. To lay claim to any output from a past transaction, each sender needs to sign its transaction with the private-key corresponding to that output and include this signature in the Sign field. This helps in validating the identity of each Bitcoin spender.

At a first glance this seems confounding as the sender is trying to obtain a signature on a transaction, of which some fields are still missing. Specifically, to compute a signature on the current transaction, Bitcoin permits some fields to be empty. Depending on the signing scheme (SIGHASH_ALL, SIGHASH_NONE, and SIGHASH_SINGLE), the number of empty fields can vary [197].

So how does this signature defend against malicious attacks? As every replica has knowledge of the claimed output (public-key), they can use this public-key to verify if the signature is valid or not. Only the owner of matching private-key can create a valid signature.

For denotational purposes, Bitcoin users employ the symbol *BTC*. To allow users to transfer Bitcoins in fractional denominations, the smallest unit of exchange in Bitcoin is denoted as a *Satoshi*, which is equivalent to $10^{-8}BTC$. Note that in some implementations, transactions with outputs less than a specified threshold are considered as *dust transactions*.

Coinbase Transactions

A Coinbase transaction is used to specify a miner's reward. When a miner succeeds in finding the nonce that solves the challenge, it includes a coinbase transaction in the current block that states its rewards. Specifically, a coinbase transaction introduces new coins to the Bitcoin ecosystem. The coinbase transaction is recorded in the new block itself as the first transaction of the block. The structure of the coinbase transaction is similar to a regular transaction with some minor changes.

Each coinbase transaction has only one transactional input. As it does not refer to any previous transaction so the *Hash* and *Id* field are set to some constant value. The *Sign* field is now referred to as *Coinbase* and stores information about the height of the block (block number) in the existing blockchain. The *Coinbase* field also provides space for storing any other arbitrary block specific data. The *Outputs* field records the reward for the miner and any block generation fees. Note that there is a restriction on the amount a miner can claim as a reward and gets halved every 210,000 blocks.

6.2.5   POOLED MINING

The concept of gaining incentives by mining new blocks has promoted miners to work in groups. Prior works [99, 216] have observed that for a lone miner (miner working alone), the probability of completing the PoW challenge and proposing the new block is very low. In fact, for some of the PoW-based blockchains, the variance is so low that, on average, it may take a miner at least three months to earn any reward [216]. Further, as most of the permissionless blockchain systems are memoryless, that is, as soon as a miner proposes a new block, all the miners switch to creating the next block, so the efforts of a lone miner end up as a waste. Hence, a lone miner may have an indefinite wait time before it can propose the next block. Note that for any PoW-based blockchain, which rewards its miners for their efforts, the probability of a lone miner proposing the next block decreases with time.

The approach of pooled mining allows multiple miners to combine their resources together to solve the cryptographic challenge and to propose the next block. By working in groups, miners increase their probability of adding the next block to the chain and agree to share the rewards among themselves. Although the sharing of rewards reduces the actual incentive received per block, it ensures a regular flow of incentives. Hence, pooling resources significantly reduces the variance in the payout of an individual miner. A key observation at this stage is that the concept of pooled mining makes the underlying system *centralized*, which is in clear opposition with the *decentralized* paradigm that the blockchain technology advocates.

Miner pools are usually maintained by an administrator, who generally takes a fixed fee for managing the pools and distributes the remaining incentives among all the miners. In pooled mining, a miner receives incentives in proportion to the work it has done. To illustrate this practice and other common pooling strategies, we use the following notations. Let I be the incentive rewarded on creating a new block, and σ be the fees (in percentage) of the administrator. Further, we term the process of finding one PoW challenge as a *round*.

Proportional

To earn an incentive, each miner has to submit *shares*. Each share is a hash of the challenge string under the assumption of reduced *difficulty* of reaching the target. Note that the target for PoW is unchanged, so each miner tries to submit more shares in an attempt to find the right nonce to reach the target. If a pool is successful in proposing the next block, then miners receive rewards *in proportion* to the number of valid shares they had submitted. Clearly, this mechanism favors those miners, who have more computational resources to expend. Assume during a successful block, a miner submitted s shares, out of a total of S shares, then this miner would receive $\frac{s}{S}(1 - \sigma)I$ as incentive payout.

Pay-Per-share

The Pay-per-share approach is used to significantly reduce the high variance in payout of a miner [37, 216]. In this approach the administrator bears all the variance and ensures each miner receives a fixed payment for each of his shares. This scheme is optimal for miners as their payments are no longer dependent on the ability of the pool to propose a block and percentage of total shares they submit. Although this approach allows the operator to keep a large share of incentive for himself by rewarding each miner with only a small amount for its hash, the operator can face huge losses if its pool is unable to find new blocks for a long period.

Slush's Method

The proportional and pay-per-share approach benefit those miners who have submitted more shares than others. Although this practice rewards those who have done more work, it discourages miners who have started a little late than others. This practice, in addition to the problem of *pool-hopping* [24], makes the existing pooling approaches undesirable.

Any miner that indulges in pool-hopping jumps from one pool to another, in an attempt to gain more rewards. A pool-hopper tends to predict the remaining length of an ongoing round for a pool and decides if it wants to invest its resources in this pool in this round. For each pool, based on the number of shares already generated in a round, probabilistically, it is possible to determine the remaining length of the round. A pool-hopper uses this information to determine if it is the right stage to invest in this pool or should it wait till the next round. If a round has stretched too long, then it indicates that a large percentage of the total shares have already been generated. Hence, it is more beneficial for a pool-hopper to participate in a pool, which is at an early stage of resolving the PoW challenge.

The slush pooling approach [45, 216] attempts at eliminating the factors leading up to the *pool-hopping* practice, that is, reduces the impact of old shares if a round has stretched too long. Instead of tracking the number of shares submitted by each miner, slush pooling awards a *score* to each share. Slush pooling uses an exponential function to associate a score to each share submitted in a round. Specifically, if τ is the time at which a miner submitted his share and β is a constant, then a miner's score is s, $s = \exp(\tau/\beta)$.

Notice that the value of β can affect the variance in score gives to each share. By keeping the value of β low, the value of early shares decay fast. This implies that if a round has stretched too long, then the value of older shares is almost negligible. Further, if a round finishes quickly, then the payout of early miners will be high as the incentives have to be divided among a smaller set of miners.

Geometric Method

Although the slush method reduces the effects of pool-hopping, it is still not completely shielded against hopping miners. Prior work [216] has shown that any pooled-mining approach that distributes incentives among the participants based on each share they submit cannot be hopping-proof. To make such a system hopping-proof, all the incentives should be given to the miner that generated the share, which solved the challenge. Clearly, such a design is undesirable as it is equivalent to lone mining (single miner gets all the rewards). To resolve the pool-hooping dilemma, some of the Bitcoin mining communities have adopted the *geometric method*.

The geometric method is a hopping-proof mechanism that introduces a set of fixed and variable fees. Fixed fee is a constant value paid to the operator while variable fees is distributed as incentives among the miners. Akin to the score assigned to each share in slush pooling, the variable fees also decays with time. In the geometric method, if I is the block incentive and f is the percentage of fixed fee, then the operator receives fI as fees while the remaining $(1 - f)I$ is distributed as the variable fees. Further, a percentage c of the variable fees is also given to the operator. This c represents the average variable fee and the operator receives a total $c(1 - f)I$ back from the variable fees. Hence, the total payout for the operator is $(c + f - cf)I$. To determine each miner's payout, we have to run through the following steps.

- At the start of a round, choose a counter s and a tracker S_j that helps to track the score of the j-th miner.
- Set $s = 1$ and $S_j = 0$.
- Next, set the decay rate d as $d = 1 - r + r/c$, where $r = 1/D$, and D represents the *difficulty* of reaching PoW target.
- When the j-th miner submits a share, then set $S_j = S_j + sdI$. Next, update $s = sd$.
- Once the target is reached, pay the j-th miner $\frac{(1-f)(d-1)S_j}{sr}$.

Pay-Per-Last-N-Shares

Pay-per-last-N-shares (henceforth referred to as PPLNS) eliminates the notion of rounds from the reward distribution mechanism. It advocates distributing rewards among the miners, which submitted the last N shares in the *period of interest*. This period could also refer to the last N shares submitted before the PoW challenge was resolved. Notice that in PPLNS, miners no longer receive any benefit of mining early.

A simple variant of PPLNS that is not hopping-proof is trivial to design. Assuming that the target difficult D and block incentive I are constant, a simple PPLNS scheme can assign an amount equivalent $\frac{(1-f)I}{N}$ to each of the last N shares. This scheme is not hopping-proof as miners can track the current difficulty and participate when the difficulty is low and leave the pool when the difficulty is high. There are several other variants of PPLNS scheme, some of which are pool-hopping proof [216].

6.2.6   SPECIAL HARDWARE

As mining is the key component to the Bitcoin ecosystem, it is unsurprising to see advances in the underlying mining hardware. A good mining hardware can make the mining process profitable for a miner, if it achieves a high hash-rate while consuming low energy.

Multi-core CPUs. The first generation of Bitcoin mining relied on the multi-core CPUs [227]. Although multi-core CPUs provide some opportunities to parallelize expensive hash computations, they are typically optimized for regular instructions. Hence, considering the high competition in mining the next block, CPU-based mining hardware does not provide any extra boost in finding the valid nonce.

GPUs. Following the successful adoption of GPUs in the parallel programming community, Bitcoin miners switched to using GPUs for increasing their incentives. Furthermore, once the first open-source OpenCL mining source-code was available for use, miners eagerly employed GPUs for mining. Using these OpenCL mining software, miners were able to tune parameters for the GPUs, such as reduce energy, tweak frequency and so on. Moreover, the interest in GPUs propagated as miners were not expected to learn parallelizing their code in order to gain more incentives. However, GPUs have their own limitations: (i) they cannot be used standalone, (ii) waste energy on components non-essential to mining, and (iii) use of multiple GPUs lead to massive costs for cooling and air-flow.

FPGAs. The next evolution of Bitcoin mining led to interests in FPGA-based mining hardware. FPGA miners are considered effective toward bit-operations and rotate-by-constant operations, which are key to fast hashing. Further, advances in FPGA-based mining designs led to elegant unrolling of a single SHA-256 to desired number of times depending on the underlying FPGA hardware. Such a compatible design also led to higher energy consumption than an average FPGA hardware.

ASICs. Application-specific integrated circuit (ASIC) mining hardware are now prevalent in the Bitcoin community. These designs have surpassed their counterparts in both speed and power consumption. Some of the famous ASIC-mining hardware at the time of writing this book were: Antminer S9i [39], DragonMint T1 [129], Whatsminer M20S [200], Avalon6 [53], and so on.

6.2.7 BITCOIN WALLETS

As Bitcoins are accessed through a set of public–private-key pairs, so there is a need to secure the private-keys from a malicious entity. A step in this direction is through the use of Bitcoin *wallets*. Bitcoin wallets can be either described as *hot* or *cold*. Hot wallets are the ones which are connected to the internet or have *online* access. Cold wallets on the other hand are stored offline in a physical medium. Evidently, cold wallets are more secure but less transaction friendly. On the basis of this distinction, a Bitcoin wallet is available in different flavors, such as paper, mobile, web, and desktop. Next, we discuss different types of Bitcoin wallets.

Paper Wallet: A paper wallet facilitates physical storage of a public–private-key pair. Services like BitAddress [33] and Bitcoin Paper Wallet [38] allow Bitcoin users to generate public-private key pairs as QR-codes, which can be then be printed and stored offline. This offline storage makes these addresses immune against hackers and keystroke logging malware.

Physical Bitcoin: Some users have opted for physical storage of Bitcoins in the form of a coin or credit card. In this format, a specified amount of Bitcoins is preloaded in a representational entity. Each physical storage comes with a hidden private-key that can be used to spend the Bitcoins. Note that the private-key is hidden behind a tamper-proof seal, which, if broken, implies that the associated Bitcoins have been spent.

Mobile Wallets: Any Bitcoin user that employs Bitcoins for its day-to-day activities prefers using a mobile wallet. These mobile wallets are essentially Android or iOS applications, which allow users to track and store their Bitcoins. Further, mobile wallets ease the use of Bitcoin as clients can make payments either through the associated application or by scanning the QR-code. Some of the famous mobile wallets include Edge [89], Jaxx [77], and Mycelium [192]. Note that mobile wallets are more vulnerable to hacks and malicious attacks than their cold storage counterparts.

Web Wallets: A web wallet allows a Bitcoin user to access its investment through a web browser. Hence, a web wallet can be accessed from a large array of devices. Akin to the mobile wallets, web wallets too often store private keys on a trusted server. Hence, the security of these wallets is proportional to the reliance on the trusted entity. Some of the examples of web wallets include Coinbase [65], Blockchain [41], and BTC [49].

Desktop Wallets: A desktop wallet facilitates storage of public and private keys on the desktop of a user. Each user downloads and installs a desktop client that stores the required data on the hard drive. Consequently, the security offered by desktop wallets is more than the mobile and web wallets but are still susceptible to malicious attacks as the desktop could have internet access. Some of the examples of desktop wallets are Electrum [95], Bitcoin Armory [34], and Bitcoin Core [35].

Hardware Wallets: Often considered as the most secure form of Bitcoin storage, a hardware wallet stores the private keys of a user in a specific secure hardware. These wallets are more effective than paper wallets as they do not require printing of the keys. In general, only the loss of a hardware wallet can cause a loss of Bitcoins. Some of the examples of these wallets include: Ledger Nano [169], Trezor [219], and KeepKey [220].

6.2.8   ATTACKS ON BITCOIN

Having discussed different aspects of Bitcoin, we know study some of the famous attacks on the Bitcoin ecosystem. These attacks not only affect the integrity of the system but also highlight the key issues in attaining a fully decentralized system.

Double Spending. In Section 6.1, we discussed that each blockchain that employs the PoW protocol can face a 51% attack if the malicious replicas are in control of the 51% computational resources. A key motive for malicious replicas to perform a 51% attack is to double-spend some transactions. Double-spending is a *fraudulent* practice where an owner R of a resource τ attempts to use τ at least twice even when the τ no longer belongs to R after its first usage. Such a practice is often attempted in cryptocurrencies because only digital assets are exchanged between two or more parties and there are no physical assets involved. If a miner owns 51% of the resources, then it has sufficient power to rollback the chain and replace an existing block with a new block.

Selfish mining. This attack is a variation of the 51% attack where malicious miners work in a group and create a private chain [99]. Unlike the 51% attack, a selfish mining attack is possible in Bitcoin if the malicious miners are in control of more than 33% computational resources. The key intuition behind this attack is to waste the resources of honest miners. This can be done by making honest miners work on a *public* fork of the blockchain, while selfish miners operate on their *private* fork.

To perform a selfish mining attack, a small set of malicious miners decide to pool their resources and hide any new block they have created. The attack starts when the malicious miners gain a lead, that is, they find a new block and avoid broadcasting that block to the honest miners. In such a case, the honest miners are unaware, while the selfish miners are mining for the next block, assuming their newly found block as the previous block. Note that the private chain cannot be indefinitely larger than the public chain, as a majority of the miners are honest (control more computational power). So the malicious miners find an appropriate time and release their private chain to all the honest miners. This will force honest miners to switch to the private chain as it has more blocks. Hence, malicious miners end up gaining more benefits, while honest miners lose their computational efforts.

Dusting attack. An adversary can employ a dusting attack to violate the privacy of a miner [181]. In this attack, an adversary sends a tiny amount of Bitcoin to the wallets of good miners in an attempt to track their identities. As dust transactions contain very small amounts, these transactions are often ignored by the miners. However, the adversary can follow the trace and know the identity of its victim. Once the identity of a miner is revealed, then he can be made subject to various targeted attacks such as phishing.

Distributed Denial of Service (DDoS) Attack. A DDoS attack is prevalent on the internet and is employed by attackers to deprive a user of some service. Similarly, an adversary can flood a Bitcoin node with a lot of irrelevant messages to prevent it with communicating with other users [208].

Eclipse Attack. Another way to compromise a Bitcoin miner is through an Eclipse attack [133]. In such an attack, the adversary attempts to modify the view of a good miner by controlling all the connections to and from the victim. Specifically, the miner may waste its resources on mining blocks for a blockchain which does not exist in reality.

Tragedy of Commons. Bitcoin's dependence on the PoW protocol for consensus has made it reliant on miner incentives. These incentives promote miners to act good, which in turn keeps the system healthy (majority of the mining power is in control of the good miners). In Section 6.2.4, we noted that after every 210K blocks, the miner incentives are halved. At such a rate, the miner incentives will soon reach a very small value where to compensate a miner's cost, transaction fees have to be increased significantly.

In such a case, a rational miner would adhere to economic phenomena of *Tragedy of the Commons*, that is, would accept opportunities that maximize its profit [28, 130]. Further, if all the miners indulge in such rational practices, then instead of making any extra profit, every miner would end up at a loss. For example, in Bitcoin, if there is no cap on a transaction's fee, then some users may offer higher fees than others to get their transactions included in the next block. Moreover, if there is no limit on the number of transactions placed in a block, then apart from selecting the high fee transactions, a rational miner would include the lower fee transactions to maximize its gains. This practice would discourage users from paying higher fees in the future. As a consequence, the overall miner gains will reduce with time. Note that the current version of Bitcoin avoids the threat of Tragedy of Commons by fixing the block size to 1 MB. As a result, there is a bound on the number of transactions that a miner can include in a block.

6.3   ENERGY-AWARE PROOF-OF-X PROTOCOLS

In the previous chapter, we studied the consensus based on *Proof-of-Work* protocol. As the PoW protocol requires its miners to spend their computational resources in an attempt to propose the next block, it necessitates use of massive energy. To reduce the dependency of permissionless blockchains on energy-consuming protocols, prior works have introduced the notion of energy-aware consensus protocols such as *Proof-of-Stake* and *Proof-of-Space*. In this section, we analyze the design of these protocols and some of their variants.

6.3.1   PROOF-OF-STAKE

In consensus based on PoW protocol, miners (or replicas) have to deplete their computational resources in order to solve the challenge. Each miner who controls a fraction p of the total computational power, has a probability nearly equal to p to create the next block. Hence, PoW's security principle lies around sacrificing computational resources and power.

Proof-of-Stake (henceforth referred to as PoS) presents a principle that contrasts the resource usage philosophy of PoW. In a blockchain system employing PoS protocol, a replica possessing a higher stake than the other replicas gets a higher chance to create a new block [26]. Specifically, the probability a replica possessing a fraction p of the total stakes in the system creates the next block is p.

The idea around PoS began to appear initially in a discussion between some Bitcoin users [36]. It was suggested as a way to reduce the excessive computational resources consumed due to the PoW protocol. Since then, several works have tried to employ the idea around PoS.

The key security rational behind PoS is that the replicas who have some stake involved in the system are also well-suited to ensure its security.

Definition 6.3   Let S be a system consisting of a prover P and a verifier V. Assume that the total number of coins in the system are c and P holds p of these coins. Let there be an unbiased dice with total c outcomes that announces the next node to create a block. Given S, the probability of P creating the next block is p/c. When P creates a block, it sends the block along with the outcome of unbiased dice and V can easily verify if P holds c coins.

We use Definition 6.3 to illustrate the general working of a PoS protocol. PoS protocol states that the probability any stakeholder proposes the next block is equal to its current stake. Although the blockchain community has a consensus on the general definition of PoS, each new system has brought forth a different variation of PoS [26, 40, 154, 155]. Further, some of these systems call themselves as the *pure* PoS systems while terming others as non-pure extensions. We prevent digressing into such a direction and look at all these designs from an academic standpoint. In the rest of this section, we look at several such variations.

6.3.2   PEERCOIN

PPCoin or Peercoin [155] is often regarded as the first implementation of PoS. The key motivation behind Peercoin's design was to implement a crypto-currency that does not require participating replicas to spend its resources in performing large computations. As the initial versions of Peercoin were unsafe, it has undergone several revisions to yield a stable protocol [26]. From Peercoin's perspective, these version updates were readily possible as Peercoin is maintained by a centralized organization, which periodically transmits signed checkpoints to synchronize replica states. Notice that this is in sharp contrast with the blockchain philosophy, which expects the system to be maintained in a decentralized manner without control of a single authority.
Peercoin's PoS model is based around the concept of *coinage*. Specifically, a stakeholder's ability to create the next block is determined on its value of coinage.

Definition 6.4   Let a stakeholder R in a system S hold p coins for d days. The coinage $\mathfrak{A}$ of this stakeholder R in this system S is $p \times d$.

Definition 6.4 states the trivial mechanism for calculating the coinage for different stakeholders. In Peercoin's PoS protocol, coinage is used to determine the stake held by a stakeholder. Hence, in Peercoin, the probability a stakeholder R gets to propose the next block is dependent on its coinage. This is in contrast to the PoW protocol where each replica increases its chance of proposing the next block by acquiring more computational resources; replicas in Peercoin's PoS continuously attempt to increase their coinage. Notice that the PoS protocol also requires miners to generate a hash that meets the target but the difficulty of target is kept very low (typically one hash is sufficient to reach the target).

Based on the above definition, it is evident that for running the Peercoin's PoS protocol, each stakeholder needs to have access to some stake. In a cryptocurrency like Peercoin, the stake is often represented by the number of coins in possession. To generate a common denomination, Peercoin learns from another cryptocurrency, Bitcoin, and employs the PoW protocol for initial coin generation. Further, akin to the PoW-based blockchain systems, which require every miner to spend its resources in an attempt to propose the next block, each stakeholder in Peercoin's PoS also spends its coinage when it creates the next block.

Example 6.5   Consider a system S with two stakeholders R1 and R2. Assume both R1 and R2 have 10 coins each, and they have held these coins for 10 and 20 days, respectively. This indicates that R1 has acquired a coinage of 100 while R2 has acquired a coinage of 200. As R2 has a higher coinage, so it has a higher probability of creating the next block. Assume this is the case, and R2 is selected to propose the next block. Under such conditions, R2 will spend its coinage while proposing a new block. Following the new block, the coinage of R2 reduces to zero while that of R1 remains at 100.

From Example 6.5, we can observe that each stakeholder needs to lose its coinage in order to propose a new block. Specifically, once a stakeholder R is selected to propose the next block (probabilistically, based on its coinage), R creates the block and its coinage is set to *zero*. Notice that only the coinage of R is reset and its invested stake (total number of coins) remains the same. This gives R ample opportunity to propose another block in the future. Hence, each stakeholder in Peercoin is also termed as a coin *minter*, that is, it transfers the coins back to its account.

To ensure Peercoin's PoS remains decentralized and has active participation, the protocol also includes incentives for its stakeholders. Each stakeholder that successfully creates the next block receives a block reward. Further, all the participating stakeholders annually receive 1% of their stake as rewards.

Fairness Considerations

Initial versions of Peercoin's PoS protocol lacked the fairness criterion. In these versions, any stakeholder with the highest stake has the highest probability to propose the next block in the chain. Although each stakeholder loses its coinage once it creates the next block, any stakeholder with highest coinage can be selected several times is succession to propose subsequent blocks if its stake is much larger in value than the other participants. For example, assume stakeholder R1 has a stake of $10K$ coins while R2 has a stake of 10 coins. In such a setting, R2 may have to wait for at least 100 days before it can match the coinage of R1. Further, if R1 receives some reward for each new block it creates, then there can be a significant increase in the wait time of R2.

To ensure the system is fair to all the stakeholders, Peercoin introduced some changes to its PoS protocol. The modified PoS protocol requires every stakeholder to wait for 30 days after it successfully proposes a new block. This strategy improves the probability for other stakeholders to create a new block. Further, in Peercoin, each stakeholder's stake reaches a maturity after 90 days, that is, they have highest probability of proposing the next block.

Nothing-at-Stake Attack

Although Peercoin's PoS protocol attempts for fairness, initial versions of its design faced a security challenge due to existence of *rational* stakeholders. A rational stakeholder will always aim to maximize its profit, an expected behavior in a democracy in correspondence with the Nash equilibrium [26]. Rational stakeholders can destabilize the system by participating in multiple chains in at attempt to maximize their gains.

A rational stakeholder could get blocks from distinct *forks* of the blockchain. This could be a result of a malicious activity or network lag in the block propagation. To maximize its returns, a rational stakeholder would attempt to propose the next block for each such fork. As stakeholders do not lose any actual resources (like computational energy in PoW), so they are free to propose blocks on different chains. These stakeholders could use their coinage to extend two or more forks of the chain. This could result in an ever-expanding divergent network. One way to mitigate this problem is by restricting the coinage of each stakeholder to a single chain and marking its stake burnt as soon as it creates a block.

Bribe Attacks

PoS protocol does a little in preventing a malicious owner from bribing other replicas. Specifically, an adversary can bribe other high-stake replicas to sign his choice of blocks. This in turn can be used to perform a double-spending attack.

Bribery attacks work till the gains of the adversary surpass the value of the bribe. Any adversary can attempt at creating its own fork of the blockchain by bribing the high-stakeholders with incentives. Further, the adversary can easily take the support of these stakeholders to undo existing blocks and replace them with other blocks. Note that although in theory, this attack can be achieved in PoW, each replica in a PoW-based system would need to accumulate excessive computational resources to undo and add new blocks. Hence, such an attack is unlikely to take place in the PoW protocol. In case of Peercoin's PoS, as stakeholders only loose coinage and not actual stake, such an attack is possible.

6.3.3 PROOF-OF-ACTIVITY

In the previous section, we discussed how Peercoin's PoS protocol significantly reduces the amount of resource consumed by Bitcoin's PoW protocol. However, the proposed PoS protocol also faces a series of unresolved challenges, which make it more vulnerable in comparison to the PoW protocol. This led to the design of *Proof-of-Activity* (henceforth referred to as PoA) protocol [28], which presents a hybrid design that employs both PoW and PoS protocols. The key intuition behind the PoA protocol is that the monetary incentives are not sufficient enough to prevent PoW miners from acting maliciously, and hence, they need assistance from stake-

Miner-role (run at the i-th miner M_i) :

1: Run PoW protocol to generate an empty block header $\mathsf{H}_{B_p} = \langle \text{digest}(\mathsf{B}_{p-1}), t, n, T_D \rangle_{\mathsf{M}_i}$ at index p
2: Broadcast H_{B_p}.
3: Await receipt of $\mathsf{B}_p = \langle U, \mathbb{T}, \langle \delta \rangle_{\mathsf{S}_j} \rangle$
4: Extend the blockchain with p-th block B_p

Stakeholder-role (running at the j-th S_j) :

5: Await receipt of well-formed H_B from some miner.
6: Compute $\delta = \text{digest}(\mathsf{H}_B)$.
7: **for** l in 1 to $|\mathfrak{S}|$ **do**
8:     Compute $\Delta_l = \delta || \text{digest}(\mathsf{B}_{k-1}) || F_l$.
9:     $X = $ Run *follow-the-satoshi* protocol with Δ_l
10:    **if** $X = \mathsf{S}_j$ **then**
11:        **if** S_j among the first $l-1$ stakeholders. **then**
12:            Broadcast $\langle \delta \rangle_{\mathsf{S}_j}$.
13:        **else**
14:            Await receipt of $U = \{\langle \delta \rangle_{\mathsf{S}_k}\}$ from other stakeholders, $\mathsf{S}_k \in \mathfrak{S}, 1 \leq k \leq |\mathfrak{S}| - 1$
15:            Broadcast $\langle U, \mathbb{T}, \langle \delta \rangle_{\mathsf{S}_j} \rangle$
16:        **end if**
17:    **end if**
18: **end for**
19: Await receipt of $\mathsf{B}_p = \langle U, \mathbb{T}, \langle \delta \rangle_{\mathsf{S}_j} \rangle$
20: Extend the blockchain with p-th block B_p

Figure 6.6: The Byzantine commit algorithm of PBFT (client and primary roles).

holders who have their assets involved in the system. Further, PoA attempts at reducing the massive energy costs due to PoW mining.

In PoA, the system consists of both miners and stakeholders. Miners perform the task of computing a complex hash (PoW), while stakeholders validate through their stake (PoS). One of the key challenges with protocols employing PoW mining is that the security of the system relies on miners, which are motivated by incentives. As a result, there can be several attacks on these systems (discussed in previous sections) because miners will attempt to increase their profits to compensate for their computational costs.

PoA divides the tasks between miners and stakeholders. In Figure 6.6, we illustrate the PoA protocol run at the miners and stakeholders. The protocol starts with each miner M attempting to generate an *empty* block header H_{B_p} at index p, $p > 0$. Although this block header H_{B_p} contains no transactions, the miner has to follow the steps in Section 6.1 to find a nonce n that matches the current target T_D. Once a miner finds a valid nonce n, it broadcasts H_{B_p} to all the nodes[4] on the network. This empty block header H_{B_p} helps to identify the $\mathfrak{S} > 0$ stakehold-

---

[4]We use the term nodes to refer to the collection of miners or stakeholders.

ers, which will validate the corresponding block. Specifically, PoA requires each mined block to be validated by $\mathfrak{S}$ distinct stakeholders.

When the j-th stakeholder S_j receives H_{B_p}, it first verifies the accompanying nonce n. If the nonce is valid, then S_j determines if it belongs to the set $\mathfrak{S}$. If this is the case and if S_j is among the first $|\mathfrak{S}| - 1$ stakeholders, then S_j computes hash of H_{B_p}, signs this hash with its private key, and broadcasts this signature.

The $|\mathfrak{S}|$-th stakeholder $\mathsf{S}_{|\mathfrak{S}|}$ awaits receiving signatures from all the other stakeholders. It also verifies the nonce associated with H_{B_p}. Once $\mathsf{S}_{|\mathfrak{S}|}$ receives all the required data, it is ready to add content to the block B_p at the p-th index. It does so by selecting a set of unconfirmed transactions $\mathbb{T}$,[5] collecting the signatures of the $|\mathfrak{S}| - 1$ stakeholders (set U), and including its signed hash to H_{B_p}. Finally, the $\mathsf{S}_{|\mathfrak{S}|}$ broadcasts the block B_p onto the network. Each node that receives this block can verify its validity, and if valid, appends it to its local blockchain.

We use Figure 6.7 to illustrate the steps taken to confirm a block of transactions in PoA protocol. First, miners M_1, M_2, and M_3 compete to propose the next (empty) block using the PoW protocol. Assume miner M_3 wins this challenge and broadcasts the block header H_B on the network. Each stakeholder uses this block header H_B and runs *follow-the-satoshi* protocol to determine whether it is among the $|\mathfrak{S}|$ stakeholders ($|\mathfrak{S}| = 3$), which will participate in the creation of the block corresponding to H_B. In this figure, stakeholders S_1 and S_2 verify the nonce, sign the block and broadcast the signature on the network. Finally, stakeholder S_3 includes these signatures of the two other stakeholders, adds unconfirmed transactions, and broadcasts the block on the network.

Follow-the-Satoshi Algorithm

During the PoA protocol, each stakeholder runs a subroutine *follow-the-satoshi* to determine if it belongs to the set $\mathfrak{S}$ of validating stakeholders. This algorithm requires tracing the path of a *satoshi*[6] until finding a stakeholder. Specifically, this satoshi (s) is a pseudorandom value selected from the set of zero and the total number of satoshis minted until the last block. Next, each block where this satoshi s was transferred to a new address is inspected. This process of inspecting the blocks continues till the final address which holds s is determined.

In PoA protocol, prior to running the *follow-the-satoshi* protocol, each node computes the hash of block header B and concatenates this hash with hash of the previous block and $\mathfrak{S}$ suffix values to generate $\mathfrak{S}$ distinct combinations. Next, each combination is hashed and the resulting hashes act as an input to the *follow-the-satoshi* protocol.

---

[5]Unconfirmed transactions refer to the transactions that are valid and have not been included in any other existing block.

[6]The term Satoshi is used to refer to the smallest unit of exchange in the Bitcoin system, which was kept to honor the anonymous Bitcoin founder with the name Satoshi Nakamoto.

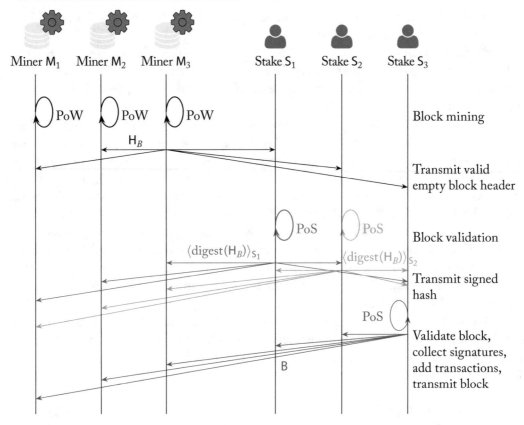

Figure 6.7: An illustration of how PoA protocol achieves consensus that employs both PoW and PoS protocols. Here, we assume the number of stakeholders needed to validate the block are 3. Stakeholders 1, 2, and 3 employ *follow-the-satoshi* protocol to discover themselves as the validating stakeholders, in order.

6.3.4 OTHER PROOF-OF-STAKE VARIANTS

Following the interest in Peercoin and PoA protocols, blockchain researchers have proposed several interesting variations and/or optimizations to the PoS protocol. As it is impossible to cover all such protocols, in this section, we briefly discuss a few of these designs.

Ouroboros

The key aim behind the design of Ouroboros [154] was to present formally a safe and live implementation of the PoS. Hence, Ouroboros builds on top of *Chains-of-Activity* protocol [26]. Like other PoS protocols, Ouroboros also requires some stakeholder to propose the block. To achieve this task, Ouroboros assumes a *synchronous* setting where the total time interval is divided into *slots*.

In each slot, some stakeholder proposes the block.[7] Ouroboros employs randomization to determine the identity of a proposer for each slot. Specifically, the current stake of a node R acts as a parameter to determine R's probability of proposing the next block. This implies that higher the stake, higher is the probability for a node to act as a proposer. Hence, Ouroboros expects a uniform distribution of stake to prevent proposer skewness.

Delegated Proof-of-Stake

Delegated Proof-of-Stake [40] (henceforth referred to as DPoS) promotes an hybrid approach where the system is neither fully decentralized nor centralized. Specifically, DPoS requires the users of its network to elect a set of *delegates*, which are responsible for proposing the next block. Notice that each user can vote for several delegates. Once a set of delegates are elected, they all sign the block and broadcast the block along with the signatures on the network.

The key assumption in this design is that the amount of nodes (delegates) to trust in the system are few. Further, the elected delegates must act good otherwise they risk losing opportunities of future participation and incentives. The major criticism with DPoS's design is its centralized architecture as the right to create a new block is only with a subset of users.

Bonded Proof-of-Stake

Bonded Proof-of-Stake [173] (henceforth referred to as BPoS) requires each participating stakeholder to deposit some of its stake as a security deposit. This deposited stake provides the users of the system a sense of trust as if a stakeholder acts malicious, it risks losing its deposit. Ethereum's Casper [50] is an example of a BPoS protocol.

The major criticism toward the BPoS design is that it blocks an honest stakeholder's deposit for the duration of its participation in the consensus protocol. As PoS protocols advocate the principle of *higher the stake, higher the probability of proposing the next block*, so stakeholders in a BPoS system are required to block large deposits to improve their chances of creating the next block and receiving the resulting incentive.

6.3.5   PROOF-OF-SPACE

Yet another energy efficient variant to the *Proof-of-Work* consensus is the *Proof-of-Space* [15, 88, 203] (henceforth referred to as PoC) consensus protocol. Akin to PoW and PoS protocols, which require miners to either compute an expensive hash function or maintain high stakes, consensuses based on PoC require miners to maintain non-trivial amount of *disk-space*. Similar to the case for PoS protocols, different PoC protocols tend to claim their design as the *true Proof-*

---

[7]Ouroboros permits cases where there are no block proposers for some slot.

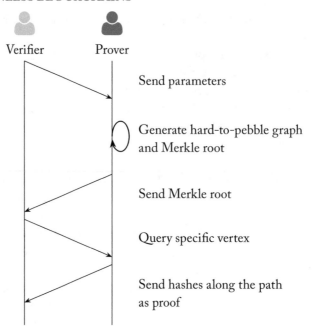

Figure 6.8: An illustration of how a prover and a verifier participate in a single run of the PoC protocol. The protocol starts with the verifier sending values for source vertices and a function H that allows the prover to generate a hard-to-pebble graph.

of-Space implementation [15, 88, 203]. We avoid digressing into this discussion and illustrate the general paradigm.

Definition 6.6   Let $\mathfrak{R}$ be a system consisting of a prover P and a verifier V. Assume that P holds a data $\mathfrak{F}$ of size N while V has an access to some information x about $\mathfrak{F}$. Given x, V sends a query Q to P. If P has access to $\mathfrak{F}$, then P sends a reply y, which V can easily verify.

We use Definition 6.6 and Figure 6.8 to sketch out the basic steps in a PoC protocol. PoC protocol expects each prover P to have access to a non-trivial amount of space of size N. P uses this space to hold a data $\mathfrak{F}$, which could be any large file or graph. Further, V has access to some information x regarding $\mathfrak{F}$, which allows it to distinguish between a byzantine and non-byzantine prover. To perform this check, V sends specific queries to P regarding $\mathfrak{F}$, which P can only answer if it maintains $\mathfrak{F}$.

A correct PoC protocol needs to take into account several malicious attacks and performance tradeoffs. For instance, there needs to be mechanism, which ensures that the prover generates the non-trivial space consuming data $\mathfrak{F}$ and maintains it throughout the duration of the protocol. Notice that PoC cannot require V to generate and transmit the large data $\mathfrak{F}$ to P as that would necessitate massive communication and computation complexity for V. Further,

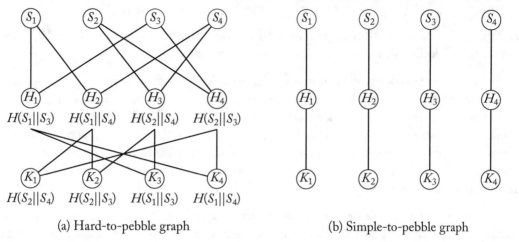

(a) Hard-to-pebble graph   (b) Simple-to-pebble graph

Figure 6.9: Comparison of different graph pebbling schemes. To generate a hard-to-pebble graph, each inner vertex is computed as the hash of the concatenation of two parent vertices.

if P is malicious, then it may attempt to reuse the space by deleting $\mathfrak{F}$ and re-generating it when required. Hence, the process of re-generating $\mathfrak{F}$ should not be trivially cheap. Next, we present a PoC protocol that prevents these issues [88].

Dziembowski et al. [88] present a PoC protocol that employs *hard-to-pebble graphs* to fulfill the requirement for non-trivial data $\mathfrak{F}$. In their scheme, authors employ *hard-to-pebble graphs* to derive a space-consuming function. A graph is termed as *hard-to-pebble* if to uncover information regarding a desired vertex requires access to information on several other verticies. For instance, in Figure 6.9, we present a hard-to-pebble graph that has been constructed through hashing. In this figure, the value associated with each internal vertex is computed by concatenating and hashing two parent vertices. An example of such an interconnected graph that can be used in PoC is PTC graph [206].

In the protocol presented by Dziembowski [88], each pair of a prover and a verifier participates in two phases, namely, *initialization* and *execution*. The PoC protocol starts with the initialization phase where the verifier V sends the prover P a set of parameters. These parameters help to define a hash function H. Next, P uses H to label the vertices of a hard-to-pebble graph G and stores these labels as data $\mathfrak{F}$. Further, P commits to G by computing a Merkle hash root of the labels of G and sends this to V. Now, when V wants some proof from P, it simply queries for label of some vertex in the graph G. V can easily validate the correctness of a response from P through the committed Merkle root.

ATTACKS AND CRITIQUES AGAINST PROOF-OF-WORK

Although PoC protocol tries to present itself as an inexpensive alternative to PoW, it faces challenges of similar nature, which question its widespread adoption.

Hardness of Pebbling. PoC protocol relies on a hard-to-pebble graph to guarantee safety. It is unclear what is the minimal hardness expected from such a hard-to-pebble graph to be of any practical use. Any blockchain that employs PoC protocol will need to first quantify the minimum hardness of the input graph. Further, it is unclear if the chosen value of hardness will remain constant over time as the number of replicas participating in the consensus will increase over time. If such an increase of hardness of the graph occurs periodically, then PoC will face similar reduction in throughput as faced by PoW-based blockchains.

Race to Larger Drives. PoW-based systems such as Bitcoin face huge energy challenges as the difficulty of the PoW target is increased periodically. This is the case because miners continue to invest in efficient hardware that can increase their probability of finding the correct nonce. Similarly, with the adoption of PoC-based consensus protocols, users may try to buy large *hard-drives* in an attempt to increase their available space. This could lead to newer attacks that are characteristically similar to PoW's 51% attack.

6.4   ETHEREUM

The success of Bitcoin led to the design of another blockchain-based cryptocurrency, Ethereum [244]. Akin to Bitcoin, Ethereum also employs *Proof-of-Work* protocol to achieve consensus among its miners. However, Ethereum provides far greater transaction support to its users by allowing them to use and deploy decentralized applications (Dapps) or *smart contracts*. Any application developer can represent its service as a smart contract and deploy it on the Ethereum network, which can then be called by the users to employ required services. To deploy and/or use a smart contract, users of Ethereum's network have to pay in *ethers*—monetary unit of exchange in Ethereum.

A key manner in which Ethereum distinguishes itself from other cryptocurrencies is its support for contract services. Further, Ethereum network visualizes itself as a Web3 network where any user can deploy its application in a decentralized manner, which in turn can be employed by other users to fulfill required tasks.

6.4.1   ACCOUNTS IN ETHEREUM

In Section 6.2, we showed that Bitcoin follows the *unspent transaction model* (UTXO), that is, each user can only transfer unused Bitcoins. To do this, each user needs to specify the addresses to its Bitcoins as inputs, which are transferred to other users. A major shortcoming of this design is a lack of a clean infrastructure that supports transfer of partial Bitcoins. For instance, if a user has 10 bitcoins on an address and it wants to only transfer 5 Bitcoins, then it needs to write two transactions to achieve this task—one transaction to transfer 5 Bitcoins to the intended recipient and another transaction to transfer 5 Bitcoins back to itself.

In contrast, Ethereum employs an *account-based* model. In the Ethereum network, accounts are categorized under two heads: *user accounts* and *contracts*. A *user account* is used to track the ethers owned by account owners. In Ethereum, creation of a user account implies generating a private key, following which the user can generate multiple public-keys associated with that private key. Each of these public-keys can be distributed by the user to exchange ethers with other users.

Each *contract* deployed on the network is also associated with an account. Any user that wants to access a smart contract creates a transaction that interacts with the account associated with the corresponding smart contract. Each contract account also has an address which is represented by 42 hexadecimal characters.

6.4.2 ETHEREUM VIRTUAL MACHINE

To run its decentralized network, Ethereum relies on the Ethereum Virtual Machine (henceforth referred to as EVM) [244]. Each node in the Ethereum network can act as a *full node*, *light node*, or *archive node*. *Full nodes* store all the data and verify each transaction relayed on the network. *Light nodes* only store the block headers and can verify the correctness of data through these headers. Light nodes may need to fetch data from other full nodes for validating and executing each transaction. *Archive nodes* are simply the storage nodes for holding data and querying records. Hence, each node that wants to mine on the Ethereum network can either act as a full node or a light node.

When a client sends a transaction for execution, each miner R captures this transaction and places it in its local pool. Once R is ready to verify and execute this transaction, it runs it through the EVM. Note that in Ethereum, application developers can write smart contracts in only two languages, Solidity and Vyper. The compiled code from these languages is essentially a *bytecode*, which is interpreted by the EVM. This bytecode includes different opcodes that lay down steps for EVM to perform.

For each instruction that is executed by the EVM, there is an associated cost, which is measured in terms of Ethers (ETH). Specifically, it is the duty of the transaction or smart contract creator to reserve and pay this amount prior to the execution. The gas cost is denoted in multiples of GWEI where 1 ETH = 10^{-9} GWEI.

6.4.3 STORAGE AND QUERYING

In Chapter 6.1.2, we discussed the design and use of Merkle trees. Merkle trees help to amortize communication costs by preventing the need to transmit all the transactions in each block. This is achieved by computing the Merkle root of all the transactions in a batch, and only including this Merkle root in the block header. Any node can use this Merkle root to verify the *inclusion* of a transaction in the corresponding block.

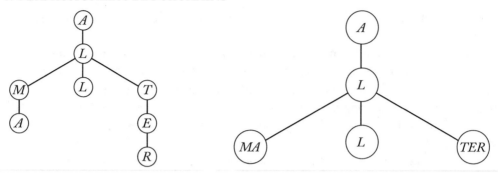

Figure 6.10: Data compaction through Patricia tries. The figure on the *left*, represents a simple trie where each node stores a single character while the figures on the *right* represents a Patricia trie which helps in data compaction.

As Ethereum allows clients to interact with smart contracts, so simple testing the inclusion property is not sufficient. Hence, Ethereum employs a data-structure that learns from two unique data-structures: Merkle trees and Patricia Tries [191]. This data-structure is referred to as a *Merkle Patricia Trie* (MPT) in the Ethereum community. Before diving into the details of an MPT, we first explain the design of a Patricia Trie.

Patricia trie is a variant of radix trees, which has been traditionally adopted for information coding. Specifically, a Patricia trie helps in achieving efficient data compaction and access. If a tree T includes a node N that has only one child C, then on building a Patricia trie T^P from T, there will be a single node N^P that represents both N and C. In cases where a Patricia trie stores strings, common prefixes are also stored in a single node. Other known use cases of Patricia tries include IP routing and lookup algorithms [218, 242]. We use the following example to illustrate a simple Patricia trie.

Example 6.7   Consider an application that wants to stores three arbitrary length keys (*ALL*, *AlMA*, and *ALTER*) into a standard trie. We use Figure 6.10 to illustrate the design of such a trie. Clearly, this representation is not efficient as it requires a total of 8 nodes to represent 3 keys. Notice that some of the nodes in this trie have only one child. This opens up opportunities to employ a Patricia trie to store these keys compactly. On the right-hand side of Figure 6.10, we illustrate the corresponding Patricia Trie. This compacter representation requires only 5 nodes.

Merkle Patricia Trees

Ethereum introduces a data-structure that employs properties of both Patricia trees and Merkle trees to efficiently maintain the state at each participant. Ethereum community uses the term Merkle Patricia Trie (MPT) to denote such a data structure. A key reason Ethereum employs

Merkle Patricia Tries is because they help in yielding answers to many more queries than just checking if a transaction in a block.

Akin to Patricia trees, each node[8] in the tree holds a [key:value] mapping. Before storing a key, each full node computes the cryptographic hash of the key, which helps in achieving Merkle authentication. As Ethereum employs the *hexadecimal* number system to represent values, so each key can start with 16 distinct numbers $(0,1,2,...,f)$. Further, each key can include several such numbers, which may reside at different levels in an MPT. The process of traversing these characters of a key (*path*) to extract the corresponding value is termed as a *lookup*.

To facilitate implementation, Ethereum's MPT includes four distinct type of nodes: root, branch, extension, and leaf. The *root node* stores the Merkle hash of all the children. The *branch node* helps to represent the common key parts. Hence, each branch node can store up to 17 items, *path* to 16 keys (each representing one number), and a value. The *extension node* stores the part of a key which can be compacted, and a *leaf node* stores the actual value corresponding to the key. As leaf and extension nodes help to compact the data in a trie, they contain only two items. However, there needs to be a mechanism to distinguish between the representations for a leaf node and an extension node. Further, it can be difficult to distinguish between *odd* and *even* length paths. We use the following example to explain and resolve these issues.

Example 6.8   Let us assume we want to construct a Merkle Patricia Trie that can store the following four key value pairs: ['in', 'preposition'], ['ink', 'noun'], ['inking', 'verb'], and ['happy', 'adjective'].

First, we need to compute the hash of each key and value. For the sake of explanation, we only employ hexadecimal representation for the keys and use the string format for the values. Assume the following hexadecimal representation for each of the above keys:

['in', 'preposition'] → <68 6d> : 'preposition'
['ink', 'noun'] → <68 6d 6a> : 'noun'
['inking', 'verb'] → <68 6d 6a 68 6d 66> : 'verb'
['happy', 'adjective'] → <67 60 6f 6f 78> : 'adjective'

Using this representation, we can create the following MPT, which helps to efficiently store and track all the four keys.

The MPT presented in Example 6.8 represents each character of the key by a pair of nibbles (1 nibble = 4 bits). Further, we observe the following: (1) the first character of the hashed representation for all the four keys is 6, and (2) the hashed representation of keys 'in', 'ink', and 'inking' share some prefix. These observations suggest that the root of the corresponding MPT is connected to a branch node, which has *two* non null entries to represent the keys with *distinct* prefixes while rest of the entries are set to null.

---

[8]For the sake of clarity, in rest of this section, we use the terms *node* to refer to a vertex in MPT and *full node* to refer to Ethereum nodes.

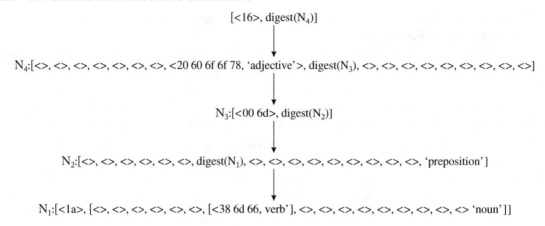

Pad	Node Type	Path Length
00	Extension	Even
1	Extension	Odd
20	Leaf	Even
3	Leaf	Odd

Figure 6.11: Prefixes for Ethereum's Merkle Patricia Trie to distinguish between Leaf nodes and Extension nodes.

As discussed earlier, there is a need to distinguish between odd and even length paths, and leaf and extension nodes. To do so, Ethereum follows the rules in Figure 6.11 and adds a prefix to the remaining path. For example, if the remaining path (characters) in the key are < 64 68 > and this will be part of a extension node, then the stored path will be < 20 64 68 >. With this information in hand, let us try to understand the MPT of Example 6.8.

The root of this MPT is an extension node, which stores the first common character. As this is a single character (odd), so 1 is used as a prefix. The root also stores the merkle root hash of the complete tree, which is simply the hash of branch node N_4. The branch node stores the key 'happy' as a leaf node at the *seventh* location (next character for 'happy' is 7). Further, the branch node also includes a hash of the node N_3. So why is the complete representation of 'happy' stored at the branch node N_4? This is the case because the key 'happy' is not sharing any prefix with any other string. Next, we use another extension node to represent the common prefix 'in'. If we continue following this way, then at node N_1 we complete storing all the keys.

TRIES IN ETHEREUM

Next, we describe how these Merkle Patricia tries are used by Ethereum. Specifically, Ethereum employs *four* distinct tries to manage all the data: State trie, Transaction trie, Transaction receipt trie, and Storage trie [244].

State Trie is also often referred to as World State trie. It is a key-value mapping from user addresses to account state. Ethereum implements the state trie as an MPT and the root of this trie is stored in each block. The account state used in a State Trie is generated by serializing the contents in an account using Recursive Length Prefix (RLP) algorithm. This account state comprises of: (i) a *nonce* that tracks number of transactions from this address, (ii) a *balance* to denote Ethers held by this account, (iii) the *storage root* of this account, and (iv) the *codeHash*, which is the hash of the EVM code that is executed when this account is called. Notice that State trie constantly updates as a new block is added to the chain.

Transaction Trie helps to track all the transactions in a block. This implies that each block has its own transaction trie. The root of a transaction trie is also stored inside the corresponding block. Each transaction in a transaction trie includes several fields: (i) *nonce* denotes the sequence number for a transaction; (ii) *gasPrice* denotes the amount of Wei to be charged per unit of gas for the computational costs due to execution; (iii) *gasLimit* denotes the maximum amount of gas to be charged for executing this transaction; and (iv) *value* denotes the amount to be transferred.

Transaction Receipt Trie helps to log information regarding the execution of a transaction. This information can be used to generate and disseminate a proof of execution. Each transaction receipt includes information regarding *total gas spent* post transaction execution, logs generated during transaction execution, and transaction execution status.

Storage Trie helps to store the data regarding an Ethereum smart contract. We already noted above that the root of a storage trie is part of each account. Notice that this trie is only useful for contract accounts.

6.4.4 ETHASH PROOF-OF-WORK PROTOCOL

In Section 6.2.6, we discussed several advancements in mining hardware technology that allow miners to achieve higher profits with lower costs. Although these hardware advancements make mining profitable, they increase the probability of a centralized blockchain ecosystem. Clearly, a centralized cryptocurrency can act as a sink to 51% attacks. Notice that the introduction of ASIC-mining hardware has only fueled these concerns. Hence, with the aim of preventing control over Ethererum by ASIC miners, Ethereum version 1.0 employs the ETHASH protocol for consensus among its miners.

ETHASH is a PoW-based consensus protocol that employs a variant of Dagger–Hashimoto [97] algorithm. The key aim of this algorithm is to make the consensus *memory-*

hard,[9] which forces a miner to use a hardware that supports large memory storage. To achieve memory-hardness, ETHASH generates a pseudorandom DAG (*directed-acyclic-graph*) and requires miners to regularly query this DAG to find the correct nonce that can solve the current target. As the difficulty increases, the size of this DAG also increases, which increases the amount of available memory. Notice that a large DAG cannot be stored in devices with smaller memories, which makes it hard to use with ASIC devices. The overall protocols works as follows.

- A *seed* is determined from the current set of blocks.

- The seed helps in generating a 16 MB pseudorandom *cache*, which is stored at light nodes.

- The cache helps in generating a pseudorandom DAG that ensures each item in this DAG only depends on a subset of items in cache. This DAG is stored at full nodes and miners.

- The current block header and a random nonce are hashed together to fetch a slice of data from the DAG.

- The resulting slice is hashed and is compared against the current target. If the result is less than the target, then the nonce is accepted.

The size and contents of the DAG are not permanent. After every 30,000 blocks, the DAG is updated. Further, the size of DAG increases when it becomes easier to reach the target. Ethereum ecosystem started with a DAG of 1 GB and as of writing this text, it has reached nearly 4 GB [144].

6.4.5   ATTACKS ON ETHEREUM

Although Ethereum showcases itself as a safer and programmatically richer infrastructure in comparison to Bitcoin, in recent years it has undergone several attacks [16, 58]. In this section, we enlist some of those attacks.

Reentrancy Attack. This attack can occur during execution of a smart-contract. Specifically, a reentrancy attack takes place when a smart contract S calls an external function F, and the function F ends up calling S before the completion of S's execution. This attack allows an adversary to bypass the integrity checks until the caller contract runs out of gas. A reentrancy attack was first observed as a DAO attack where a hacker stole up to $60 million [58].

Frozen Ether. This is a vulnerability which was a result of Ethereum contract accounts disallowing spending Ethers. Specifically, Ethereum permits users to transfer money to their

---

[9]Notice the similarity between the ETHASH protocol and *Proof-of-Space* protocol where the latter aims to achieve consensus by making each block proposer store a hard-to-pebble graph (refer to Section 6.3.5.)

contract accounts but once this money was available in the contract account, it can no longer be spent [58]. This attack was first observed on a Parity wallet [201].

Empty Account. Earlier versions of Ethereum allowed empty accounts to be part of state trie. Notice that empty accounts have zero nonce, zero balance and no code. Although an empty account performs no functionality, allowing it to be a part of state trie requires performing all the bookkeeping tasks. This allows an attacker to create a massive number of empty accounts and cause a Denial-of-Service attack [60].

Uncle Blocks. In the Bitcoin protocol, the miners compete among themselves to propose the next block for the chain. This competition can lead to forks in the blockchain. To resolve such a situation, one of the chains is given priority over other, which leads to discarding one of more blocks (or forks). Clearly, this practice causes a tremendous loss to the losing miner and discourages all miners from acting honestly.

To resolve this scenario, Ethereum came up with the notion of Uncle or Ommers blocks [244]. An uncle block is a valid block, which could not be part of the main blockchain. To prevent miner losses, Ethereum allows each miner to include identity of any known uncle block in the next block. On a closer look, the idea of having uncle block is risky as it allows miners to act as selfish and continuously propose uncle blocks to increase their profits [58].

6.5 CONCLUDING REMARKS

The intuition behind the design of any permissionless blockchain is to allow any node to participate in the consensus, i.e., an *open membership* setting that offers a greater degree of decentralization. Specifically, these systems aim for a system that preserves the anonymity of the participants or at least guarantees them a pseudo-anonymity. To satisfy such a requirement, permissionless blockchains have to rely on protocols such as PoW or PoS to achieve consensus (i.e., voting) among all the participants [126]. In essence, they simulate the notion of identity—a necessary barrier for casting a legitimate vote—by (1) introducing a computational proof making it prohibitively expensive to cast an illegal vote (cf. PoW) at the cost of damaging our environment and planet or (2) by forcing to invest a sufficient stake in order to economically align the interest of participants and the success of the chain (cf. PoS).

First, the capability of hiding identities of the participants may not be desirable or even possible in every context. For example, there may exist an organization that may prefer to offer their customers a democratic voice in maintaining the ledger on the condition of knowing the identities of every participant as *a priori*. *Second*, recent analysis of the cryptocurrencies that have adopted the permissionless model have revealed a series of attacks such as selfish mining due to the monetization as the means to instill a well-behaving democratic participation [16, 99, 133, 208]. Many such attacks are motivated by the incentive-based sustainability model of permissionless applications. *Third*, as permissionless chains are more prone to the divergence of world views due to forks, which not only results in an unprecedented delay to assume transaction as confirmed, but they may cause a social divide in the community maintaining the ledger collectively.

These challenges with the design of permissionless blockchains have forced large-scale enterprises to shy away, at least for the time being, from their adoption and lean towards the design of *permissioned* technology [126, 187]. We envision a wider adoption of the permissionless setting that is arguably more resilient by construction. We further observe a unique opportunity at the crossroad of permissioned and permissionless, a unified model that offers both superior efficiency and resiliency while ingraining the decentralization and democratization virtues of our society.

6.6   BIBLIOGRAPHIC NOTES

Following the success of Bitcoin and PoW-based consensus in permissionless blockchains, several works have proposed new designs and protocols that either target higher throughputs or propose safer agreements [22, 98, 111, 158].

Bitcoin-NG [98] suggests a protocol that works in two stages. In the first stage, a leader is elected using the PoW protocol. Next, this leader continuously proposes new blocks until it is replaced. This design helps Bitcoin-NG to achieve higher throughputs that Bitcoin.

Byzcoin [158] introduces the notion of consensus groups, which hold the right to propose the next block. Each miner becomes part of a consensus group by finding the correct PoW nonce. Next, one of the miners in the consensus group acts as a leader and runs the PBFT protocol to propose the next block. To avoid PBFT's quadratic communication complexity, Byzcoin employs threshold signatures. *PeerCensus* [78] introduces a strongly consistent variant of Bitcoin. Specifically, all the miners in PeerCensus compete to propose a new block. Once a miner finds a block, it puts it front of a committee of nodes, which participate in a standard BFT consensus such as PBFT or Zyzzyva, to decide on the next block to be appended to the chain. *Hybrid Consensus* [204] builds on top of PeerCensus and proposes a model where miners follow the PoW protocol to propose a new block, which is approved by a committee of members. A key difference between HybridConsensus and protocols like PeerCensus and Byzcoin is that the former provides the same byzantine resilience guarantee as traditional BFT protocols, that is, HybridConsensus can handle up to 1/3 byzantine replicas, while the latter can only handle corruption of 1/4 replicas. *Solida* [4] is yet another protocol that combines traditional BFT consensus and PoW protocol to yield an efficient variant to Bitcoin's consensus. Solida employs the PoW protocol to elect the members of a committee and runs the PBFT protocol among the members of the selected committee to order client transactions.

A key concern with all the PoW-based consensus protocols is that they require expensive cryptographic computations. In Section 6.3.1, we recognized that one solution in this direction was to employ PoS-based consensus. With the introduction of Peercoin's PoS protocol, several other cryptocurrencies, such as NXT [232], Netcoin [103], and BlackCoin [236], have shown interest in PoS-based consensus. Apart from the variants of PoS protocol that we discussed in Section 6.3.4, Bentov et al. [29] present a theoretical framework that encapsulates different properties expected by a PoS protocol. They do this by theoretically laying down their PoS protocol (Snow White) that builds on top of their earlier work, Sleepy Consensus [205].

Following the design of energy efficient alternatives to PoW such as PoS and PoC, several other *Proof-of-X* consensus protocols have been proposed [21, 32, 148, 221]. Ball et al. [21] employ standard algorithmic problems such as Orthogonal Vectors, 3SUM, and All-Pairs Shortest Path to yield a PoW protocol that have known theoretical complexity. The key intuition behind this design is that PoW consensus employed by existing cryptocurrencies is based on SHA256 hashing, which does not have a provable guarantee. A lack of such provable guarantees leads to a heuristic design, which cannot be extended to other applications. *Proof-of-Exercise* [221] requires PoW miners to perform useful expensive computations such as matrix computations. Specifically, this approach promotes a service where a miner's energy not only helps in running consensus but also provides solutions for another application. *Proof-of-Retrievability* [148] is similar to the PoC protocol as it requires a prover to store a large file $\mathfrak{F}$ and provide access to $\mathfrak{F}$ to any verifier. Equihash [32] presents a PoW variant, which is based on the generalized birthday problem. Equihash makes PoW protocol memory intensive to prevent use of ASICs while ensuring the verification of result is cheap. *Proof-of-Authority* [202] designates a set of nodes as the authorities or leaders. These authorities are entrusted with the task of creating new blocks and validating the transactions. *Proof-of-Authority* marks a block as part of the blockchain if it is signed by majority of the authorized nodes.

The most well known application for these *Proof-of-X* protocols are cryptocurrencies such as Bitcoin, Ethereum, and Peercoin. Since the inception of these cryptocurrencies, several new permissionless applications have been proposed. Next, we list some of these applications and their designs.

Algorand [107] is a PoS-based cryptocurrencies that employs verifiable random functions to elect nodes that will propose new blocks and committee members that will select the next block to append to the chain. Higher the stake a node holds, greater is its probability of getting elected. Further, Algorand does not require PoW protocol during any phase of its consensus.

Ripple [57] can be visualized as both a payment framework and cryptocurrency. It facilitates transfer of commodities between two or more users through a set of trusted nodes. These trusted nodes run a consensus protocol to select and order incoming user transactions. *Stellar* [175] also aims to be a commodity exchange platform. However, Stellar aims to be a exchange platform for common users while Ripple aims large scale banks. To order its user transactions, Stellar employs federated voting. *Avalanche* [228] supports development of decentralized blockchain applications and commodity exchange platforms. It also provides support for a cryptocurrency that helps order transactions, and achieves consensus through the Avalanche consensus protocol. *Celo* [104] provides its users access to a cryptocurrency and tools for designing permissionless applications. Celo selects a set of validators based on the value of their stake to order client transactions. Hence, it employs a variant of the PoS protocol.

In comparison to Bitcoin, a key reason that the users prefer Ethereum to develop a variety of decentralized applications is its ability to execute complex smart contracts. This led to introduction of RSK [170], which facilitates writing smart contracts on top of Bitcoin blockchain. Blockstack [7] also provides a support for building scalable decentralized applications on top of Bitcoin blockchain. To commit any transaction in its chain, Blockstack requires its miners to participate in its *Proof-of-Transfer* consensus protocol. Truffle Blockchain Group [234] builds on top of Ethereum to provide access to a suite of tools that facilitate creating smart contracts on several different blockchain platforms, while Consensys [67] provides access to APIs that facilitate designing large-scale applications on top of Ethereum framework.

Bibliography

[1] M. Abd-El-Malek, G. R. Ganger, G. R. Goodson, M. K. Reiter, and J. J. Wylie. Fault-scalable byzantine fault-tolerant services. *SIGOPS Oper. Syst. Rev.*, 39(5):59–74, 2005. DOI: 10.1145/1095809.1095817 114

[2] I. Abraham, G. Gueta, D. Malkhi, L. Alvisi, R. Kotla, and J.-P. Martin. Revisiting fast practical byzantine fault tolerance, 2017. https://arxiv.org/abs/1712.01367 xix, 17, 20, 87, 88, 110, 111

[3] I. Abraham, G. Gueta, D. Malkhi, and J.-P. Martin. Revisiting fast practical byzantine fault tolerance: Thelma, velma, and zelma, 2018. https://arxiv.org/abs/1801.10022 xix, 17, 20, 87, 88, 110, 111

[4] I. Abraham, D. Malkhi, K. Nayak, L. Ren, and A. Spiegelman. Solidus: An incentive-compatible cryptocurrency based on permissionless byzantine consensus, 2017. https://arxiv.org/abs/1612.02916 222

[5] I. Abraham, D. Malkhi, K. Nayak, L. Ren, and M. Yin. Sync HotStuff: Simple and practical synchronous state machine replication. In *IEEE Symposium on Security and Privacy (SP)*, pages 106–118, 2020. DOI: 10.1109/SP40000.2020.00044 112

[6] M. Al-Bassam, A. Sonnino, S. Bano, D. Hrycyszyn, and G. Danezis. Chainspace: A sharded smart contracts platform, 2017. http://arxiv.org/abs/1708.03778 167

[7] M. Ali, A. Blankstein, M. J. Freedman, L. Galabru, D. Gupta, J. Nelson, J. Soslow, and P. Stanley. PoX: Proof of transfer mining with Bitcoin, 2020. https://blockstack.org/pox.pdf 224

[8] N. Alon, H. Kaplan, M. Krivelevich, D. Malkhi, and J. Stern. Scalable secure storage when half the system is faulty. *Inf. Comput.*, 174(2):203–213, 2002. DOI: 10.1006/inco.2002.3148 117, 167

[9] N. Alon, H. Kaplan, M. Krivelevich, D. Malkhi, and J. Stern. Addendum to scalable secure storage when half the system is faulty. *Inf. Comput.*, 205(7):1114–1116, 2007. DOI: 10.1016/j.ic.2006.02.007 117, 167

[10] Y. Amir, C. Danilov, D. Dolev, J. Kirsch, J. Lane, C. Nita-Rotaru, J. Olsen, and D. Zage. Steward: Scaling byzantine fault-tolerant replication to wide area networks. *IEEE Trans. Dependable Secur. Comput.*, 7(1):80–93, 2010. DOI: 10.1109/TDSC.2008.53 111, 167

[11] Y. Amir, C. Danilov, J. Kirsch, J. Lane, D. Dolev, C. Nita-Rotaru, J. Olsen, and D. Zage. Scaling byzantine fault-tolerant replication to wide area networks. In *International Conference on Dependable Systems and Networks (DSN'06)*, pages 105–114, 2006. DOI: 10.1109/DSN.2006.63 83, 96, 111, 146, 151, 167

[12] M. J. Amiri, D. Agrawal, and A. E. Abbadi. CAPER: A cross-application permissioned blockchain. *Proc. VLDB Endow.*, 12(11):1385–1398, 2019. DOI: 10.14778/3342263.3342275 167, 173, 174

[13] M. J. Amiri, D. Agrawal, and A. El Abbadi. SharPer: Sharding permissioned blockchains over network clusters, 2019. https://arxiv.org/abs/1910.00765v1 167

[14] E. Androulaki, A. Barger, V. Bortnikov, C. Cachin, K. Christidis, A. De Caro, D. Enyeart, C. Ferris, G. Laventman, Y. Manevich, S. Muralidharan, C. Murthy, B. Nguyen, M. Sethi, G. Singh, K. Smith, A. Sorniotti, C. Stathakopoulou, M. Vukolić, S. W. Cocco, and J. Yellick. Hyperledger fabric: A distributed operating system for permissioned blockchains. In *Proc. of the 13th EuroSys Conference*, page 30:1–30:15, ACM, 2018. DOI: 10.1145/3190508.3190538 xix, 18, 169, 173, 174, 183

[15] G. Ateniese, I. Bonacina, A. Faonio, and N. Galesi. Proofs of space: When space is of the essence. In *Security and Cryptography for Networks*, pages 538–557, Springer, 2014. DOI: 10.1007/978-3-319-10879-7_31 211, 212

[16] N. Atzei, M. Bartoletti, and T. Cimoli. A survey of attacks on ethereum smart contracts (SoK). In *Principles of Security and Trust*, pages 164–186, Springer, 2017. DOI: 10.1007/978-3-662-54455-6_8 220, 221

[17] P.-L. Aublin. Vers des protocoles de tolérance aux fautes Byzantines efficaces et robustes. Ph.D. thesis, Université de Grenoble, 2014. https://tel.archives-ouvertes.fr/tel-01549111 106, 111

[18] P.-L. Aublin, R. Guerraoui, N. Knežević, V. Quéma, and M. Vukolić. The next 700 BFT protocols. *ACM Transactions on Comput. Syst.*, 32(4), 2015. DOI: 10.1145/2658994 111

[19] P.-L. Aublin, S. B. Mokhtar, and V. Quéma. RBFT: Redundant byzantine fault tolerance. In *Proc. of the IEEE 33rd International Conference on Distributed Computing Systems*, pages 297–306, 2013. DOI: 10.1109/ICDCS.2013.53 106, 111

[20] Y. Baek, Joonsang Zheng. Simple and efficient threshold cryptosystem from the gap Diffie-Hellman group. In *GLOBECOM'03. IEEE Global Telecommunications Conference*, 3:1491–1495, 2003. DOI: 10.1109/GLOCOM.2003.1258486 82, 111

[21] M. Ball, A. Rosen, M. Sabin, and P. N. Vasudevan. Proofs of work from worst-case assumptions. In *Advances in Cryptology—CRYPTO 2018*, pages 789–819, Springer, 2018. DOI: 10.1007/978-3-319-96884-1_26 223

[22] S. Bano, A. Sonnino, M. Al-Bassam, S. Azouvi, P. McCorry, S. Meiklejohn, and G. Danezis. SoK: Consensus in the age of blockchains. In *Proc. of the 1st ACM Conference on Advances in Financial Technologies*, pages 183–198, 2019. DOI: 10.1145/3318041.3355458 222

[23] R. A. Bazzi. Synchronous byzantine quorum systems. *Distrib. Comput.*, 13(1):45–52, 2000. DOI: 10.1007/s004460050004 114

[24] M. Belotti, S. Kirati, and S. Secci. Bitcoin pool-hopping detection. In *Proc. of 4th IEEE International Forum on Research and Technology for Society and Industry*, pages 1–6, 2018. DOI: 10.1109/RTSI.2018.8548376 199

[25] M. Ben-Or. Another advantage of free choice (extended abstract): Completely asynchronous agreement protocols. In *Proc. of the 2nd Annual ACM Symposium on Principles of Distributed Computing*, pages 27–30, 1983. DOI: 10.1145/800221.806707 19

[26] I. Bentov, A. Gabizon, and A. Mizrahi. Cryptocurrencies without proof of work. In *Financial Cryptography and Data Security*, pages 142–157, Springer, 2016. DOI: 10.1007/978-3-662-53357-4_10 xx, 18, 204, 205, 207, 210

[27] I. Bentov, P. Hubáček, T. Moran, and A. Nadler. Tortoise and hares consensus: The meshcash framework for incentive-compatible, scalable cryptocurrencies, 2017. https://eprint.iacr.org/2017/300 168

[28] I. Bentov, C. Lee, A. Mizrahi, and M. Rosenfeld. Proof of activity: Extending Bitcoin's proof of work via proof of stake (extended abstract). *SIGMETRICS Perform. Eval. Rev.*, 42(3):34–37, 2014. DOI: 10.1145/2695533.2695545 204, 207

[29] I. Bentov, R. Pass, and E. Shi. Snow white: Robustly reconfigurable consensus and applications to provably secure proof of stake, 2016. https://eprint.iacr.org/2016/919 223

[30] C. Berger and H. P. Reiser. Scaling byzantine consensus: A broad analysis. In *Proc. of the 2nd Workshop on Scalable and Resilient Infrastructures for Distributed Ledgers*, pages 13–18, ACM, 2018. DOI: 10.1145/3284764.3284767 18

[31] A. Bessani, J. Sousa, and E. E. Alchieri. State machine replication for the masses with BFT-SMART. In *44th Annual IEEE/IFIP International Conference on Dependable Systems and Networks*, pages 355–362, 2014. DOI: 10.1109/DSN.2014.43 172

[32] A. Biryukov and D. Khovratovich. Equihash: Asymmetric proof-of-work based on the generalized birthday problem. *Ledger*, 2:1–30, 2017. DOI: 10.5195/ledger.2017.48 223

[33] bitaddress.org. bitaddress.org—open source javascript client-side Bitcoin wallet generator, 2020. https://www.bitaddress.org/ 201

[34] Bitcoin Armory. Bitcoin armory—Python-based fully-featured Bitcoin wallet software, 2020. https://btcarmory.com/ 202

[35] Bitcoin Core. Bitcoin Core: Bitcoin, 2020. https://bitcoincore.org/ 202

[36] Bitcoin Forum. Proof of stake instead of proof of work, 2011. https://bitcointalk.org/index.php?topic=27787.0 204

[37] Bitcoin Wiki. Comparison of mining pools, 2020. https://en.bitcoin.it/wiki/Comparison_of_mining_pools 198

[38] bitcoinpaperwallet.com. Bitcoin paper wallet generator: Print offline tamper-resistant addresses, 2014. https://bitcoinpaperwallet.com/ 201

[39] Bitmain. Antminer S91, 2020. https://www.bitmain.com/ 201

[40] BitShares-Core Contributors. Bitshares documentation, 2020. https://how.bitshares.works/_/downloads/en/master/pdf/ 205, 211

[41] Blockchain.com. Blockchain.com—the most trusted crypto company, 2020. https://www.blockchain.com/ 202

[42] R. Boichat, P. Dutta, S. Frølund, and R. Guerraoui. Deconstructing Paxos. *SIGACT News*, 34(1):47–67, 2003. DOI: 10.1145/637437.637447 112

[43] J. Bonneau, A. Miller, J. Clark, A. Narayanan, J. A. Kroll, and E. W. Felten. SoK: Research perspectives and challenges for Bitcoin and cryptocurrencies. In *IEEE Symposium on Security and Privacy*, pages 104–121, 2015. DOI: 10.1109/SP.2015.14 192

[44] G. Bracha and S. Toueg. Asynchronous consensus and broadcast protocols. *J. ACM*, 32(4):824–840, 1985. DOI: 10.1145/4221.214134 16, 19

[45] Braiins. World's first Bitcoin mining pool—Slush Pool, 2020. https://slushpool.com/home/ 199

[46] E. Brewer. CAP twelve years later: How the rules have changed. *Computer*, 45(2):23–29, 2012. DOI: 10.1109/MC.2012.37 5, 6, 19

[47] E. A. Brewer. Towards robust distributed systems (abstract). In *Proc. of the 19th Annual ACM Symposium on Principles of Distributed Computing*, page 7, 2000. DOI: 10.1145/343477.343502 5, 6, 19

[48] BTCC. Bitcoin Ethereum futures trading with leverage, 2020. https://www.btcc.com/ 190

[49] BTC.COM. BTC.com—wallet for Bitcoin and Bitcoin Cash, 2020. https://wallet.btc.com/ 202

[50] V. Buterin and V. Griffith. Casper the friendly finality gadget, 2017. http://arxiv.org/abs/1710.09437 211

[51] C. Cachin and M. Vukolic. Blockchain consensus protocols in the wild (keynote talk). In *31st International Symposium on Distributed Computing*, 91:1:1–1:16, Schloss Dagstuhl, 2017. DOI: 10.4230/LIPIcs.DISC.2017.1 18

[52] J.-Y. Cai, R. J. Lipton, R. Sedgewick, and A. C.-C. Yao. Towards uncheatable benchmarks. In *Proc. of the 8th Annual Structure in Complexity Theory Conference*, pages 2–11, IEEE, 1993. DOI: 10.1109/SCT.1993.336546 186

[53] Canaan. Avalon6, 2016. https://www.canaan.io/ 201

[54] M. Castro. Practical byzantine fault tolerance. Ph.D. thesis, Massachusetts Institute of Technology, 2001. http://hdl.handle.net/1721.1/86581 xix, 11, 17, 19, 24, 71, 111

[55] M. Castro and B. Liskov. Practical byzantine fault tolerance. In *Proc. of the 3rd Symposium on Operating Systems Design and Implementation*, pages 173–186, USENIX, 1999. xix, 11, 17, 19, 24, 69, 71, 111, 170, 178

[56] M. Castro and B. Liskov. Practical byzantine fault tolerance and proactive recovery. *ACM Trans. Comput. Syst.*, 20(4):398–461, 2002. DOI: 10.1145/571637.571640 xix, 11, 17, 19, 24, 71, 111

[57] B. Chase and E. MacBrough. Analysis of the XRP ledger consensus protocol, 2018. https://arxiv.org/abs/1802.07242 185, 223

[58] H. Chen, M. Pendleton, L. Njilla, and S. Xu. A survey on Ethereum systems security: Vulnerabilities, attacks, and defenses. *ACM Comput. Surv.*, 53(3), 2020. DOI: 10.1145/3391195 220, 221

[59] J. Chen and S. Micali. Algorand, 2016. https://arxiv.org/abs/1607.01341 111

[60] T. Chen, X. Li, Y. Wang, J. Chen, Z. Li, X. Luo, M. H. Au, and X. Zhang. An adaptive gas cost mechanism for ethereum to defend against under-priced DoS attacks. In *Information Security Practice and Experience*, pages 3–24, Springer, 2017. DOI: 10.1007/978-3-319-72359-4_1 221

[61] B. Chor and L. Moscovici. Solvability in asynchronous environments. In *30th Annual Symposium on Foundations of Computer Science*, pages 422–427, IEEE, 1989. DOI: 10.1109/SFCS.1989.63513 19

[62] B. Chor and L.-B. Nelson. Solvability in asynchronous environments II: Finite interactive tasks. *SIAM J. Comput.*, 29(2):351–377, 1999. DOI: 10.1137/S0097539795294979 19

[63] B.-G. Chun, P. Maniatis, S. Shenker, and J. Kubiatowicz. Attested append-only memory: Making adversaries stick to their word. *SIGOPS Oper. Syst. Rev.*, 41(6):189–204, 2007. DOI: 10.1145/1323293.1294280 90, 111

[64] Coin Sciences Ltd. Multichain—open source blockchain platform, 2020. https://www.multichain.com/ 170, 183

[65] Coinbase. Coinbase—buy and sell Bitcoin, Ethereum, and more with trust, 2020. https://www.coinbase.com/ 202

[66] B. T. H. Company. AntPool, 2020. https://antpool.com/ 190

[67] ConsenSys. Blockchain technology solutions—ethereum solutions, 2020. https://consensys.net/ 224

[68] ConsenSys. ConsenSys Quorum, 2020. https://consensys.net/quorum/ 170, 183

[69] B. F. Cooper, A. Silberstein, E. Tam, R. Ramakrishnan, and R. Sears. Benchmarking cloud serving systems with YCSB. In *Proc. of the 1st ACM Symposium on Cloud Computing*, pages 143–154, 2010. DOI: 10.1145/1807128.1807152 179

[70] Corda. Corda—open source blockchain platform for business, 2020. https://www.corda.net/ 183

[71] M. Correia, G. S. Veronese, and L. C. Lung. Asynchronous byzantine consensus with $2f + 1$ processes. In *Proc. of the ACM Symposium on Applied Computing*, pages 475–480, 2010. DOI: 10.1145/1774088.1774187 90, 111

[72] M. Correia, G. S. Veronese, N. F. Neves, and P. Verissimo. Byzantine consensus in asynchronous message-passing systems: A survey. *Int. J. Crit. Comput.-Based Syst.*, 2(2):141–161, 2011. 18

[73] J. Cowling, D. Myers, B. Liskov, R. Rodrigues, and L. Shrira. Hq replication: A hybrid quorum protocol for byzantine fault tolerance. In *Proc. of the 7th Symposium on Operating Systems Design and Implementation*, pages 177–190, USENIX, 2006. 114

[74] CryptoFish, LLC. Multipool—a Bitcoin, Litecoin, and Altcoin mining pool, 2016. https://www.multipool.us/ 190

[75] H. Dang, T. T. A. Dinh, D. Loghin, E.-C. Chang, Q. Lin, and B. C. Ooi. Towards scaling blockchain systems via sharding. In *Proc. of the International Conference on Management of Data*, pages 123–140, ACM, 2019. DOI: 10.1145/3299869.3319889 167, 173, 174

[76] A. de Vries. Bitcoin's growing energy problem. *Joule*, 2(5):801–805, 2018. DOI: 10.1016/j.joule.2018.04.016 18, 185, 188

[77] Decentral Inc. Jaxx liberty: Secure blockchain wallet, exchange and portfolio, 2020. https://jaxx.io/ 202

[78] C. Decker, J. Seidel, and R. Wattenhofer. Bitcoin meets strong consistency. In *Proc. of the 17th International Conference on Distributed Computing and Networking*, ACM, 2016. DOI: 10.1145/2833312.2833321 222

[79] P. Diamantopoulos, S. Maneas, C. Patsonakis, N. Chondros, and M. Roussopoulos. Interactive consistency in practical, mostly-asynchronous systems. In *IEEE 21st International Conference on Parallel and Distributed Systems (ICPADS)*, pages 752–759, 2015. DOI: 10.1109/ICPADS.2015.99 19

[80] Diem Association. Welcome to diem–diem documentation, 2020. https://developers.libra.org/docs/welcome-to-libra 169, 184

[81] T. T. A. Dinh, J. Wang, G. Chen, R. Liu, B. C. Ooi, and K.-L. Tan. BLOCKBENCH: A framework for analyzing private blockchains. In *Proc. of the ACM International Conference on Management of Data*, pages 1085–1100, 2017. DOI: 10.1145/3035918.3064033 179

[82] D. Dolev. Unanimity in an unknown and unreliable environment. In *Proc. of the 22nd Annual Symposium on Foundations of Computer Science*, pages 159–168, IEEE, 1981. DOI: 10.1109/SFCS.1981.53 15, 17, 19

[83] D. Dolev. The byzantine generals strike again. *J. Algorithm*, 3(1):14–30, 1982. DOI: 10.1016/0196-6774(82)90004-9 15, 17, 19

[84] D. Dolev and R. Reischuk. Bounds on information exchange for byzantine agreement. *J. ACM*, 32(1):191–204, 1985. DOI: 10.1145/2455.214112 17, 19

[85] D. Dolev and H. R. Strong. Authenticated algorithms for byzantine agreement. *SIAM J. Comput.*, 12(4):656–666, 1983. DOI: 10.1137/0212045 15, 16, 19

[86] S. Duan, M. K. Reiter, and H. Zhang. BEAT: Asynchronous BFT made practical. In *Proc. of the ACM SIGSAC Conference on Computer and Communications Security*, pages 2028–2041, 2018. DOI: 10.1145/3243734.3243812 19, 113

[87] C. Dwork and M. Naor. Pricing via processing or combating junk mail. In *Advances in Cryptology—CRYPTO'92*, pages 139–147, Springer, 1992. DOI: 10.1007/3-540-48071-4_10 186

[88] S. Dziembowski, S. Faust, V. Kolmogorov, and K. Pietrzak. Proofs of space. In *Advances in Cryptology—CRYPTO*, pages 585–605, Springer, 2015. DOI: 10.1007/978-3-662-48000-7_29 xx, 18, 211, 212, 213

[89] Edge. Edge—blockchain wallet and security platform, 2020. https://edge.app/ 202

[90] M. Eischer and T. Distler. Scalable byzantine fault tolerance on heterogeneous servers. In *13th European Dependable Computing Conference (EDCC)*, pages 34–41, IEEE, 2017. DOI: 10.1109/EDCC.2017.15 98, 111

[91] M. Eischer and T. Distler. Scalable byzantine fault-tolerant state-machine replication on heterogeneous servers. *Computing*, 101(2):97–118, 2019. DOI: 10.1007/s00607-018-0652-3 98, 111

[92] A. El Abbadi, D. Skeen, and F. Cristian. An Efficient, Fault-Tolerant Protocol for Replicated Data Management. In *Proceedings of the Fourth ACM SIGACT-SIGMOD Symposium on Principles of Database Systems*, pages 215–229. ACM, 1985. DOI: 10.1145/325405.325443. 18

[93] A. El Abbadi and S. Toueg. Availability in Partitioned Replicated Databases. In *Proceedings of the Fifth ACM SIGACT-SIGMOD Symposium on Principles of Database Systems*, pages 240–251. ACM, 1985. DOI: 10.1145/6012.15418. 18

[94] M. El-Hindi, C. Binnig, A. Arasu, D. Kossmann, and R. Ramamurthy. BlockchainDB: A shared database on blockchains. *Proc. VLDB Endow.*, 12(11):1597–1609, 2019. DOI: 10.14778/3342263.3342636 168, 169

[95] Electrum Technologies. Electrum Bitcoin wallet, 2020. https://electrum.org/ 202

[96] Ethereum Foundation. BTC Relay: A bridge between the Bitcoin blockchain and Ethereum smart contracts, 2017. http://btcrelay.org 168

[97] Ethereum Foundation. dagger-hashimoto—ethereum wiki, 2020. https://eth.wiki/concepts/dagger-hashimoto 219

[98] I. Eyal, A. E. Gencer, E. G. Sirer, and R. Van Renesse. Bitcoin-NG: A scalable blockchain protocol. In *Proc. of the 13th USENIX Conference on Networked Systems Design and Implementation*, pages 45–59, 2016. 187, 222

[99] I. Eyal and E. G. Sirer. Majority is not enough: Bitcoin mining is vulnerable. *Commun. ACM*, 61(7):95–102, 2018. DOI: 10.1145/3212998 187, 188, 198, 203, 221

[100] F2Pool. F2Pool: Leading Bitcoin, Ethereum and Litecoin mining pool, 2020. https://www.f2pool.com/ 190

[101] M. J. Fischer and N. A. Lynch. A lower bound for the time to assure interactive consistency. *Inform. Process. Lett.*, 14(4):183–186, 1982. DOI: 10.1016/0020-0190(82)90033-3 16, 19

[102] M. J. Fischer, N. A. Lynch, and M. S. Paterson. Impossibility of distributed consensus with one faulty process. *J. ACM*, 32(2):374–382, 1985. DOI: 10.1145/3149.214121 8, 13, 14, 19

[103] N. Foundation. NETCOIN—currency designed for you and the net, 2019. http://netcoin.io/ 222

[104] T. C. Foundation. Celo protocol—celo docs, 2020. https://docs.celo.org/v/master/celo-codebase/protocol 223

[105] E. Gabber, M. Jakobsson, Y. Matias, and A. J. Mayer. Curbing junk e-mail via secure classification. In *Proc. of the 2ond International Conference on Financial Cryptography*, pages 198–213, Springer, 1998. DOI: 10.1007/BFb0055484 186

[106] J. Gehrke, L. Allen, P. Antonopoulos, A. Arasu, J. Hammer, J. Hunter, R. Kaushik, D. Kossmann, R. Ramamurthy, S. T. V. Setty, J. Szymaszek, A. van Renen, J. Lee, and R. Venkatesan. Veritas: Shared verifiable databases and tables in the cloud. In *Proc. of the 9th Biennial Conference on Innovative Data Systems Research*, CIDRDB.org, 2019. 169

[107] Y. Gilad, R. Hemo, S. Micali, G. Vlachos, and N. Zeldovich. Algorand: Scaling byzantine agreements for cryptocurrencies. In *Proc. of the 26th Symposium on Operating Systems Principles*, pages 51–68, ACM, 2017. DOI: 10.1145/3132747.3132757 96, 111, 223

[108] S. Gilbert and N. Lynch. Brewer's conjecture and the feasibility of consistent, available, partition-tolerant web services. *SIGACT News*, 33(2):51–59, 2002. DOI: 10.1145/564585.564601 6, 19

[109] G. Golan Gueta, I. Abraham, S. Grossman, D. Malkhi, B. Pinkas, M. Reiter, D.-A. Seredinschi, O. Tamir, and A. Tomescu. SBFT: A scalable and decentralized trust infrastructure. In *49th Annual IEEE/IFIP International Conference on Dependable Systems and Networks (DSN)*, pages 568–580, 2019. DOI: 10.1109/DSN.2019.00063 xix, 17, 20, 83, 110, 111

[110] W. J. Gordon and C. Catalini. Blockchain technology for healthcare: Facilitating the transition to patient-driven interoperability. *Comput. Struct. Biotechnol. J.*, 16:224–230, 2018. DOI: 10.1016/j.csbj.2018.06.003 18

[111] V. Gramoli. From blockchain consensus back to byzantine consensus. *Future Gener. Comput. Syst.*, 107:760–769, 2020. DOI: 10.1016/j.future.2017.09.023 222

[112] GroupFabric Inc. Bitcoin miner—the free easy-to-use Bitcoin miner, 2020. https://www.groupfabric.com/bitcoin-miner/ 189

[113] R. Guerraoui, N. Knežević, V. Quéma, and M. Vukolić. The next 700 BFT protocols. In *Proc. of the 5th European Conference on Computer Systems*, pages 363–376, ACM, 2010. DOI: 10.1145/1755913.1755950 111

[114] R. Guerraoui, P. Kuznetsov, M. Monti, M. Pavlovic, and D.-A. Seredinschi. Scalable byzantine reliable broadcast. In *33rd International Symposium on Distributed Computing (DISC)*, 146:22:1–22:16, Schloss Dagstuhl, 2019. DOI: 10.4230/LIPIcs.DISC.2019.22 111

[115] B. Guo, Z. Lu, Q. Tang, J. Xu, and Z. Zhang. Dumbo: Faster asynchronous BFT protocols. In *Proc. of the ACM SIGSAC Conference on Computer and Communications Security*, pages 803–818, 2020. DOI: 10.1145/3372297.3417262 19, 113

[116] S. Gupta. Resilient and Scalable Architecture for Permissioned Blockchain Fabrics. In *Proceedings of the VLDB 2020 PhD Workshop co-located with the 46th International Conference on Very Large Databases*, volume 2652 of *CEUR Workshop Proceedings*. CEUR-WS.org, 2020. 18, 169

[117] S. Gupta, J. Hellings, S. Rahnama, and M. Sadoghi. An in-depth look of BFT consensus in blockchain: Challenges and opportunities. In *Proc. of the 20th International Middleware Conference Tutorials, Middleware*, pages 6–10, ACM, 2019. DOI: 10.1145/3366625.3369437 18, 169, 183

[118] S. Gupta, J. Hellings, S. Rahnama, and M. Sadoghi. Blockchain consensus unraveled: Virtues and limitations. In *Proc. of the 14th ACM International Conference on Distributed and Event-based Systems*, pages 218–221, 2020. DOI: 10.1145/3401025.3404099 18, 169, 183

[119] S. Gupta, J. Hellings, S. Rahnama, and M. Sadoghi. Building high throughput permissioned blockchain fabrics: Challenges and opportunities. *Proc. VLDB Endow.*, 13(12):3441–3444, 2020. DOI: 10.14778/3415478.3415565 18, 169, 183

[120] S. Gupta, J. Hellings, S. Rahnama, and M. Sadoghi. Proof-of-Execution: Reaching Consensus through Fault-Tolerant Speculation. In *Proceedings of the 24th International Conference on Extending Database Technology*, 2021. xix, 17, 18, 20, 83, 85, 110, 111, 172, 183

[121] S. Gupta, J. Hellings, and M. Sadoghi. Brief announcement: Revisiting consensus protocols through wait-free parallelization. In *33rd International Symposium on Distributed Computing (DISC)*, 146:44:1–44:3, Schloss Dagstuhl, 2019. DOI: 10.4230/LIPIcs.DISC.2019.44 xix, 17, 18, 20, 98, 106, 108, 109, 111, 150, 165, 172, 183

[122] S. Gupta, J. Hellings, and M. Sadoghi. RCC: Resilient Concurrent Consensus for High-Throughput Secure Transaction Processing. In *37th IEEE International Conference on Data Engineering*. IEEE, 2021. to appear. xix, 17, 18, 20, 98, 106, 108, 109, 111, 150, 165, 172, 183

[123] S. Gupta, S. Rahnama, J. Hellings, and M. Sadoghi. ResilientDB: Global scale resilient blockchain fabric. *Proc. VLDB Endow.*, 13(6):868–883, 2020. DOI: 10.14778/3380750.3380757 xix, 18, 20, 83, 96, 98, 110, 111, 115, 146, 165, 166, 167, 169, 172, 183

[124] S. Gupta, S. Rahnama, and M. Sadoghi. Permissioned blockchain through the looking glass: Architectural and implementation lessons learned. In *Proc. of the 40th IEEE International Conference on Distributed Computing Systems*, 2020. xix, 18, 109, 169, 172, 179, 183

[125] S. Gupta and M. Sadoghi. EasyCommit: A Non-blocking Two-phase Commit Protocol. In *Proceedings of the 21st International Conference on Extending Database Technology, EDBT 2018, Vienna, Austria, March 26-29, 2018*, pages 157–168. OpenProceedings.org, 2018. DOI: 10.5441/002/edbt.2018.15. 128

[126] S. Gupta and M. Sadoghi. Blockchain transaction processing. In *Encyclopedia of Big Data Technologies*, pages 1–11, Springer, 2019. DOI: 10.1007/978-3-319-63962-8_333-1 185, 188, 221, 222

[127] S. Gupta and M. Sadoghi. Efficient and non-blocking agreement protocols. *Distributed Parallel Databases*, 38(2):287–333, 2020. DOI: 10.1007/s10619-019-07267-w. 128

[128] V. Hadzilacos and J. Y. Halpern. Message-optimal protocols for byzantine agreement. *Math. Systems Theory*, 26(1):41–102, 1993. DOI: 10.1007/BF01187074 17, 19

[129] Halong Mining. DragonMint T1 Miner, 2018. https://halongmining.com/ 201

[130] G. Hardin. The tragedy of the commons. *Science*, 162(3859):1243–1248, 1968. DOI: 10.1126/science.162.3859.1243 204

[131] T. Haynes and D. Noveck. RFC 7530: Network file system (NFS) version 4 protocol, 2015. https://tools.ietf.org/html/rfc7530 19, 71

[132] Hedera Hashgraph, LLC. Hedera Hashgraph, 2020. https://hedera.com/ 184

[133] E. Heilman, A. Kendler, A. Zohar, and S. Goldberg. Eclipse attacks on bitcoin's peer-to-peer network. In *Proc. of the 24th USENIX Conference on Security Symposium*, pages 129–144, 2015. 203, 221

[134] J. Hellings, D. P. Hughes, J. Primero, and M. Sadoghi. Cerberus: Minimalistic multi-shard byzantine-resilient transaction processing, 2020. https://arxiv.org/abs/2008.04450 xix, 18, 20, 162, 167, 183

[135] J. Hellings and M. Sadoghi. Brief announcement: The fault-tolerant cluster-sending problem. In *33rd International Symposium on Distributed Computing (DISC)*, page 45:1–45:3, Schloss Dagstuhl, 2019. DOI: 10.4230/LIPIcs.DISC.2019.45 xix, 18, 115, 129, 150, 165, 166, 167, 183

[136] J. Hellings and M. Sadoghi. The fault-tolerant cluster-sending problem, 2019. https://arxiv.org/abs/1908.01455 xix, 18, 115, 129, 150, 165, 166, 167, 183

[137] J. Hellings and M. Sadoghi. Coordination-free byzantine replication with minimal communication costs. In *23rd International Conference on Database Theory (ICDT)*, 155:17:1–17:20, Schloss Dagstuhl, 2020. DOI: 10.4230/LIPIcs.ICDT.2020.17 xix, 18, 115, 116, 165, 166, 167, 183

[138] J. Hellings and M. Sadoghi. ByShard: Sharding in a byzantine environment, 2021. to appear. xix, 18, 20, 167, 172, 183

[139] J. Hellings and M. Sadoghi. Byzantine cluster-sending in expected constant communication, 2021. to appear. 115, 129, 167

[140] J. L. Hennessy and D. A. Patterson. *Computer Architecture: A Quantitative Approach*, 5th ed., Morgan Kaufmann, 2011. 174

[141] M. Herlihy. Atomic cross-chain swaps. In *Proc. of the ACM Symposium on Principles of Distributed Computing*, pages 245–254, 2018. DOI: 10.1145/3212734.3212736 19, 168

[142] M. Herlihy. Blockchains from a distributed computing perspective. *Commun. ACM*, 62(2):78–85, 2019. DOI: 10.1145/3209623 18

[143] M. P. Herlihy and J. M. Wing. Linearizability: A correctness condition for concurrent objects. *ACM Trans. Program. Lang. Syst*, 12(3):463–492, 1990. DOI: 10.1145/78969.78972 173

[144] Investoon. DAG size calculator, 2020. https://investoon.com/tools/dag_size 220

[145] Z. István, A. Sorniotti, and M. Vukolić. StreamChain: Do blockchains need blocks? In *Proc. of the 2nd Workshop on Scalable and Resilient Infrastructures for Distributed Ledgers*, pages 1–6, ACM, 2018. DOI: 10.1145/3284764.3284765 173

[146] M. Jakobsson and A. Juels. Proofs of work and bread pudding protocols. In *Secure Information Networks: Communications and Multimedia Security IFIP TC6/TC11 Joint Working Conference on Communications and Multimedia Security (CMS'99)*, pages 258–272, Springer, 1999. DOI: 10.1007/978-0-387-35568-9_18 186

[147] A. Juels and J. G. Brainard. Client puzzles: A cryptographic countermeasure against connectiondepletion attacks. In *Network and Distributed Systems Security (NDSS) Symposium 1999*, The Internet Society, 1999. 186

[148] A. Juels and B. S. Kaliski. Pors: Proofs of retrievability for large files. In *Proc. of the 14th ACM Conference on Computer and Communications Security*, pages 584–597, 2007. DOI: 10.1145/1315245.1315317 223

[149] M. N. Kamel Boulos, J. T. Wilson, and K. A. Clauson. Geospatial blockchain: Promises, challenges, and scenarios in health and healthcare. *Int. J. Health. Geogr.*, 17(1):1211–1220, 2018. DOI: 10.1186/s12942-018-0144-x 18

[150] A. Kamilaris, A. Fonts, and F. X. Prenafeta-Boldú. The rise of blockchain technology in agriculture and food supply chains. *Trends Food Sci. Technol.*, 91:640–652, 2019. DOI: https://doi.org/10.1016/j.tifs.2019.07.034 169

[151] R. Kapitza, J. Behl, C. Cachin, T. Distler, S. Kuhnle, S. V. Mohammadi, W. Schröder-Preikschat, and K. Stengel. CheapBFT: Resource-efficient byzantine fault tolerance. In *Proc. of the 7th ACM European Conference on Computer Systems*, pages 295–308, 2012. DOI: 10.1145/2168836.2168866 90, 110, 111

[152] M. Kapritsos, Y. Wang, V. Quema, A. Clement, L. Alvisi, and M. Dahlin. All about eve: Execute-verify replication for multi-core servers. In *Proc. of the 10th USENIX Conference on Operating Systems Design and Implementation*, pages 237–250, 2012. 113

[153] J. Katz and Y. Lindell. *Introduction to Modern Cryptography*, 2nd ed., Chapman and Hall/CRC, 2014. 179, 187

[154] A. Kiayias, A. Russell, B. David, and R. Oliynykov. Ouroboros: A provably secure Proof-of-Stake blockchain protocol. In *Advances in Cryptology—CRYPTO*, pages 357–388, Springer, 2017. DOI: 10.1007/978-3-319-63688-7_12 205, 210

[155] S. King and S. Nadal. PPCoin: Peer-to-peer crypto-currency with Proof-of-Stake, 2012. https://www.peercoin.net/whitepapers/peercoin-paper.pdf xx, 18, 205

[156] V. King and J. Saia. Breaking the $o(n^2)$ bit barrier: Scalable byzantine agreement with an adaptive adversary. *J. ACM*, 58(4), 2011. DOI: 10.1145/1989727.1989732 112

[157] Kiv. GUIMiner, 2012. https://sourceforge.net/projects/guiminerscryptn/ 190

[158] E. Kokoris-Kogias, P. Jovanovic, N. Gailly, I. Khoffi, L. Gasser, and B. Ford. Enhancing Bitcoin security and performance with strong consistency via collective signing. In *Proc. of the 25th USENIX Conference on Security Symposium*, pages 279–296, 2016. 222

[159] E. Kokoris-Kogias, P. Jovanovic, L. Gasser, N. Gailly, E. Syta, and B. Ford. OmniLedger: A secure, scale-out, decentralized ledger via sharding. In *IEEE Symposium on Security and Privacy (SP)*, pages 583–598, 2018. DOI: 10.1109/SP.2018.000-5 168

[160] C. Kolivas. Cgminer: ASIC and FPGA miner in c for Bitcoin, 2018. https://github.com/ckolivas/cgminer 189

[161] R. Kotla, L. Alvisi, M. Dahlin, A. Clement, and E. Wong. Zyzzyva: Speculative byzantine fault tolerance. *SIGOPS Oper. Syst. Rev.*, 41(6):45–58, 2007. DOI: 10.1145/1323293.1294267 xix, 17, 20, 87, 110, 111, 178

[162] R. Kotla, L. Alvisi, M. Dahlin, A. Clement, and E. Wong. Zyzzyva: Speculative byzantine fault tolerance. *ACM Trans. Comput. Syst.*, 27(4), 2010. DOI: 10.1145/1658357.1658358 xix, 17, 20, 87, 110, 111

[163] R. Kotla, A. Clement, E. Wong, L. Alvisi, and M. Dahlin. Zyzzyva: Speculative byzantine fault tolerance. *Commun. ACM*, 51(11):86–95, 2008. DOI: 10.1145/1400214.1400236 xix, 17, 20, 87, 110, 111

[164] J. Kwon and E. Buchman. Cosmos whitepaper: A network of distributed ledgers, 2019. https://cosmos.network/cosmos-whitepaper.pdf 19, 168

[165] L. Lamport. The part-time parliament. *ACM Trans. Comput. Syst.*, 16(2):133–169, 1998. DOI: 10.1145/279227.279229 112, 133, 152

[166] L. Lamport. Paxos made simple. *SIGACT News*, 32(4):51–58, 2001. DOI: 10.1145/568425.568433 112, 133, 152

[167] L. Lamport, R. Shostak, and M. Pease. The byzantine generals problem. *ACM Trans. Program. Lang. Syst.*, 4(3):382–401, 1982. DOI: 10.1145/357172.357176 10, 15, 19

[168] L. Lao, Z. Li, S. Hou, B. Xiao, S. Guo, and Y. Yang. A survey of IoT applications in blockchain systems: Architecture, consensus, and traffic modeling. *ACM Comput. Surv.*, 53(1), 2020. DOI: 10.1145/3372136 18

[169] Ledger SAS. Hardware wallet—state-of-the-art security for crypto assets, 2020. https://www.ledger.com/ 202

[170] S. D. Lerner. RSK Bitcoin powered smart contracts, 2019. https://www.rsk.co/Whitepapers/RSK-White-Paper-Updated.pdf 224

[171] B. Li, W. Xu, M. Z. Abid, T. Distler, and R. Kapitza. Sarek: Optimistic parallel ordering in byzantine fault tolerance. In *12th European Dependable Computing Conference (EDCC)*, pages 77–88, IEEE, 2016. DOI: 10.1109/EDCC.2016.36 98, 111

[172] C. Li, P. Li, D. Zhou, W. Xu, F. Long, and A. Yao. Scaling nakamoto consensus to thousands of transactions per second, 2018. https://arxiv.org/abs/1805.03870 168

[173] W. Li, S. Andreina, J.-M. Bohli, and G. Karame. Securing Proof-of-Stake blockchain protocols. In *Data Privacy Management, Cryptocurrencies and Blockchain Technology*, pages 297–315, Springer, 2017. 211

[174] J. Liu, W. Li, G. O. Karame, and N. Asokan. Scalable byzantine consensus via hardware-assisted secret sharing. *IEEE Trans. Comput.*, 68(1):139–151, 2019. DOI: 10.1109/TC.2018.2860009 xix, 17, 20, 90, 96, 111

[175] M. Lokhava, G. Losa, D. Mazières, G. Hoare, N. Barry, E. Gafni, J. Jove, R. Malinowsky, and J. McCaleb. Fast and secure global payments with stellar. In *Proc. of the 27th ACM Symposium on Operating Systems Principles*, pages 80–96, 2019. DOI: 10.1145/3341301.3359636 223

[176] L. Luu, V. Narayanan, C. Zheng, K. Baweja, S. Gilbert, and P. Saxena. A secure sharding protocol for open blockchains. In *Proc. of the ACM SIGSAC Conference on Computer and Communications Security*, pages 17–30, 2016. DOI: 10.1145/2976749.2978389 168

[177] D. Malkhi, K. Nayak, and L. Ren. Flexible byzantine fault tolerance. In *Proc. of the ACM SIGSAC Conference on Computer and Communications Security*, pages 1041–1053, 2019. DOI: 10.1145/3319535.3354225 112

[178] D. Malkhi and M. Reiter. Byzantine quorum systems. *Distrib. Comput.*, 11(4):203–213, 1998. DOI: 10.1007/s004460050050 114

[179] D. Malkhi and M. Reiter. Secure and scalable replication in Phalanx. In *Proc. 17th IEEE Symposium on Reliable Distributed Systems*, pages 51–58, 1998. DOI: 10.1109/RELDIS.1998.740474 114

[180] Y. Mao, F. P. Junqueira, and K. Marzullo. Mencius: Building efficient replicated state machines for wans. In *Proc. of the 8th USENIX Conference on Operating Systems Design and Implementation*, pages 369–384, 2008. 112

[181] J. Mapperson. Understanding Litecoin's dusting attack: What happened and why, 2019. https://cointelegraph.com/news/understanding-litecoins-dusting-attack-what-happened-and-why 203

[182] J.-P. Martin. Fast byzantine consensus. In *Proc. of the International Conference on Dependable Systems and Networks*, pages 402–411, IEEE, 2005. DOI: 10.1109/DSN.2005.48 88, 110, 111

[183] J.-P. Martin and L. Alvisi. Fast byzantine consensus. *IEEE Trans. Depend. Secur. Comput.*, 3(3):202–215, 2006. DOI: 10.1109/TDSC.2006.35 88, 110, 111

[184] J.-P. Martin, L. Alvisi, and M. Dahlin. Small byzantine quorum systems. In *Proc. International Conference on Dependable Systems and Networks*, pages 374–383, IEEE, 2002. DOI: 10.1109/DSN.2002.1028922 114

[185] R. C. Merkle. A digital signature based on a conventional encryption function. In *Advances in Cryptology—CRYPTO'87*, pages 369–378, Springer, 1988. DOI: 10.1007/3-540-48184-2_32 120, 188

[186] A. Miller, Y. Xia, K. Croman, E. Shi, and D. Song. The honey badger of BFT protocols. In *Proc. of the ACM SIGSAC Conference on Computer and Communications Security*, pages 31–42, 2016. DOI: 10.1145/2976749.2978399 19, 113

[187] C. Mohan, B. C. Ooi, and G. Vossen. Distributed computing with permissioned blockchains and databases. *Dagstuhl Rep.*, 9(6):69–94, 2019. DOI: 10.4230/DagRep.9.6.69. 222

[188] G. E. Moore. Cramming more components onto integrated circuits. *IEEE Solid-State Circuits Soc. Newsl.*, 11(3):33–35, 2006. DOI: 10.1109/N-SSC.2006.4785860 173

[189] S. Moran and Y. Wolfstahl. Extended impossibility results for asynchronous complete networks. *Inf. Process. Lett.*, 26(3):145–151, 1987. DOI: 10.1016/0020-0190(87)90052-4 13, 19

[190] I. Moraru, D. G. Andersen, and M. Kaminsky. There is more consensus in egalitarian parliaments. In *Proc. of the 24th ACM Symposium on Operating Systems Principles*, pages 358–372, 2013. DOI: 10.1145/2517349.2517350 112

[191] D. R. Morrison. PATRICIA—practical algorithm to retrieve information coded in alphanumeric. *J. ACM*, 15(4):514–534, 1968. DOI: 10.1145/321479.321481 216

[192] Mycelium. Mycelium wallet, 2020. https://wallet.mycelium.com/ 202

[193] S. Nakamoto. Bitcoin: A peer-to-peer electronic cash system, 2009. https://bitcoin.org/bitcoin.pdf xx, 2, 18, 169, 173, 185, 189

[194] A. Narayanan and J. Clark. Bitcoin's academic pedigree. *Commun. ACM*, 60(12):36–45, 2017. DOI: 10.1145/3132259 18

[195] S. Nathan, C. Govindarajan, A. Saraf, M. Sethi, and P. Jayachandran. Blockchain meets database: Design and implementation of a blockchain relational database. *PVLDB*, 12(11):1539–1552, 2019. DOI: 10.14778/3342263.3342632 169

[196] K. J. O'Dwyer and D. Malone. Bitcoin mining and its energy footprint. In *25th IET Irish Signals and Systems Conference and China-Ireland International Conference on Information and Communications Technologies (ISSC/CIICT)*, pages 280–285, 2014. DOI: 10.1049/cp.2014.0699 185, 188

[197] K. Okupski. Bitcoin developer reference, 2016. https://github.com/minium/Bitcoin-Spec 191, 197

[198] OpenCores.org. BTCMiner—open source Bitcoin miner, 2018. https://opencores.org/projects/btcminer 189

[199] M. T. Özsu and P. Valduriez. *Principles of Distributed Database Systems.* Springer, 2020. DOI: 10.1007/978-3-030-26253-2 18, 167

[200] (PangolinMiner). Whatsminer M20S with PSU, 2020. https://pangolinminer.com/ 201

[201] Parity Technologies. Security alert, 2017. https://www.parity.io/security-alert-2/ 221

[202] Parity Technologies. Blockchain infrastructure for the decentralised web, 2020. https://www.parity.io/ 223

[203] S. Park, A. Kwon, G. Fuchsbauer, P. Gaži, J. Alwen, and K. Pietrzak. SpaceMint: A cryptocurrency based on proofs of space. In *Financial Cryptography and Data Security,* pages 480–499, Springer, 2018. DOI: 10.1007/978-3-662-58387-6_26 211, 212

[204] R. Pass and E. Shi. Hybrid consensus: Efficient consensus in the permissionless model. In *31st International Symposium on Distributed Computing (DISC),* 91:39:1–39:16, Schloss Dagstuhl, 2017. DOI: 10.4230/LIPIcs.DISC.2017.39 222

[205] R. Pass and E. Shi. The sleepy model of consensus. In *Advances in Cryptology—ASIACRYPT,* pages 380–409, Springer, 2017. DOI: 10.1007/978-3-319-70697-9_14 223

[206] W. J. Paul, R. E. Tarjan, and J. R. Celoni. Space bounds for a game on graphs. In *Proc. of the 8th Annual ACM Symposium on Theory of Computing,* pages 149–160, 1976. DOI: 10.1145/800113.803643 213

[207] M. Pease, R. Shostak, and L. Lamport. Reaching agreement in the presence of faults. *J. ACM,* 27(2):228–234, 1980. DOI: 10.1145/322186.322188 9, 15, 19

[208] A. Pillai, V. Saraswat, and Arunkumar V. R. Smart wallets on blockchain—attacks and their costs. In *Smart City and Informatization,* pages 649–660, Springer, 2019. DOI: 10.1007/978-981-15-1301-5_51 203, 221

[209] Poolin. Poolin mining pool—a great Bitcoin and multi-cryptocurrency mining pool, 2020. https://www.poolin.com/ 190

[210] B. Project. Bitcoin Core version 0.11.2 released, 2015. https://bitcoin.org/en/release/v0.11.2 191

[211] T. Qadah, S. Gupta, and M. Sadoghi. Q-Store: Distributed, multi-partition transactions via queue-oriented execution and communication. In *Proc. of the 23rd International Conference on Extending Database Technology*, pages 73–84, OpenProceedings.org, 2020. DOI: 10.5441/002/edbt.2020.08 173

[212] T. M. Qadah and M. Sadoghi. QueCC: A Queue-oriented, control-free concurrency architecture. In *Proc. of the 19th International Middleware Conference*, pages 13–25, ACM, 2018. DOI: 10.1145/3274808.3274810 173

[213] M. O. Rabin. Efficient dispersal of information for security, load balancing, and fault tolerance. *J. ACM*, 36(2):335–348, 1989. DOI: 10.1145/62044.62050 117, 167

[214] S. Rahnama, S. Gupta, T. Qadah, J. Hellings, and M. Sadoghi. Scalable, resilient and configurable permissioned blockchain fabric. *Proc. VLDB Endow.*, 13(12):2893–2896, 2020. DOI: doi.org/10.14778/3415478.3415502 xix, 18, 169, 172, 183

[215] A. Rejeb, J. G. Keogh, S. Zailani, H. Treiblmaier, and K. Rejeb. Blockchain technology in the food industry: A review of potentials, challenges and future research directions. *Logistics*, 4(4), 2020. DOI: 10.3390/logistics4040027 18, 169

[216] M. Rosenfeld. Analysis of Bitcoin pooled mining reward systems, 2011. https://arxiv.org/abs/1112.4980 198, 199, 200

[217] M. Sadoghi and S. Blanas. Transaction Processing on Modern Hardware. Synthesis Lectures on Data Management. Morgan & Claypool Publishers, 2019. DOI:10.2200/S00896ED1V01Y201901DTM058. 128

[218] R. Sangireddy, N. Futamura, S. Aluru, and A. K. Somani. Scalable, memory efficient, high-speed IP lookup algorithms. *IEEE/ACM Trans. Netw.*, 13(4):802–812, 2005. DOI: 10.1109/TNET.2005.852878 216

[219] SatoshiLabs. Trezor hardware wallet (official)—the original and most secure hardware wallet. 202

[220] ShapeShift. KeepKey—hardware wallet, 2020. https://shapeshift.io/keepkey/ 202

[221] A. Shoker. Sustainable blockchain through proof of exercise. In *IEEE 16th International Symposium on Network Computing and Applications (NCA)*, pages 1–9, 2017. DOI: 10.1109/NCA.2017.8171383 223

[222] V. Shoup. Practical threshold signatures. In *Advances in Cryptology—EUROCRYPT*, pages 207–220, Springer, 2000. DOI: 10.1007/3-540-45539-6_15 82, 111

[223] A. Skidanov and I. Polosukhin. Nightshade: Near protocol sharding design, 2019. https://near.org/downloads/Nightshade.pdf 168

[224] Y. Sompolinsky, Y. Lewenberg, and A. Zohar. SPECTRE: A fast and scalable cryptocurrency protocol, 2016. https://eprint.iacr.org/2016/1159 168

[225] C. Stathakopoulou, T. David, and M. Vukolić. Mir-BFT: High-throughput BFT for blockchains, 2019. https://arxiv.org/abs/1906.05552 98, 109, 111, 165

[226] G. Taubenfeld and S. Moran. Possibility and impossibility results in a shared memory environment. *Acta Inf.*, 33(1):1–20, 1996. DOI: 10.1007/s002360050034 19

[227] M. B. Taylor. Bitcoin and the age of bespoke silicon. In *Proc. of the International Conference on Compilers, Architectures and Synthesis for Embedded Systems*, pages 1–10, IEEE, 2013. DOI: 10.1109/CASES.2013.6662520 200

[228] Team Rocket, M. Yin, K. Sekniqi, R. van Renesse, and E. G. Sirer. Scalable and probabilistic leaderless BFT consensus through metastability, 2020. https://arxiv.org/abs/1906.08936 223

[229] G. Tel. *Introduction to Distributed Algorithms*, 2nd ed., Cambridge University Press, 2001. 18, 167

[230] Tendermint. Tendermint—building the most powerful tools for distributed networks, 2020. https://tendermint.com/ 170, 183, 184

[231] The Linux Foundation. Hyperledger—open source blockchain technologies, 2020. https://www.hyperledger.org/ xix, 18, 169, 183

[232] The Nxt community. Nxt whitepaper, 2016. https://nxtdocs.jelurida.com/Nxt_Whitepaper 222

[233] H. Treiblmaier and R. Beck, Eds. *Business Transformation Through Blockchain*. Springer, 2019. DOI: 10.1007/978-3-319-98911-2 18

[234] Truffle Blockchain Group. Sweet tools for smart contracts—truffle suite, 2020. https://www.trufflesuite.com/ 224

[235] M. van Steen and A. S. Tanenbaum. *Distributed Systems*, 3rd ed., Maarten van Steen, 2017. https://www.distributed-systems.net/ 18, 167

[236] P. Vasin. BlackCoin's Proof-of-Stake protocol v2, 2014. https://blackcoin.org/blackcoin-pos-protocol-v2-whitepaper.pdf 222

[237] G. S. Veronese, M. Correia, A. N. Bessani, and L. C. Lung. Spin one's wheels? byzantine fault tolerance with a spinning primary. In *Proc. of the 28th IEEE International Symposium on Reliable Distributed Systems*, pages 135–144, 2009. DOI: 10.1109/SRDS.2009.36 107, 111

[238] G. S. Veronese, M. Correia, A. N. Bessani, and L. C. Lung. EBAWA: Efficient byzantine agreement for wide-area networks. In *Proc. of the IEEE 12th International Symposium on High-Assurance Systems Engineering*, pages 10–19, 2010. DOI: 10.1109/HASE.2010.19 98, 111

[239] G. S. Veronese, M. Correia, A. N. Bessani, L. C. Lung, and P. Verissimo. Efficient byzantine fault-tolerance. *IEEE Trans. Comput.*, 62(1):16–30, 2013. DOI: 10.1109/TC.2011.221 xix, 17, 20, 90, 91, 110, 111

[240] F. Voight. P2Pool—the official homepage of the P2Pool software, 2017. http://p2pool. in/ 190

[241] H. Vranken. Sustainability of Bitcoin and blockchains. *Curr. Opin. Environ. Sustain.*, 28:1–9, 2017. DOI: 10.1016/j.cosust.2017.04.011 18, 185, 188

[242] M. Waldvogel, G. Varghese, J. Turner, and B. Plattner. Scalable high speed IP routing lookups. In *Proc. of the ACM SIGCOMM'97 Conference on Applications, Technologies, Architectures, and Protocols for Computer Communication*, pages 25–36, 1997. DOI: 10.1145/263105.263136 216

[243] J. Wang and H. Wang. Monoxide: Scale out blockchains with asynchronous consensus zones. In *16th USENIX Symposium on Networked Systems Design and Implementation (NSDI)*, pages 95–112, 2019. 168

[244] G. Wood. Ethereum: A secure decentralised generalised transaction ledger, 2016. EIP-150 revision. https://gavwood.com/paper.pdf xx, 18, 19, 169, 170, 185, 214, 215, 219, 221

[245] G. Wood. Polkadot: Vision for a heterogeneous multi-chain framework, 2016. https://polkadot.network/PolkaDotPaper.pdf 19, 168

[246] M. Wu, K. Wang, X. Cai, S. Guo, M. Guo, and C. Rong. A comprehensive survey of blockchain: From theory to IoT applications and beyond. *IEEE Internet Things J.*, 6(5):8114–8154, 2019. DOI: 10.1109/JIOT.2019.2922538 18

[247] Y. Xiao, N. Zhang, W. Lou, and Y. T. Hou. A survey of distributed consensus protocols for blockchain networks. *IEEE Commun. Surv. Tutor*, 22(2):1432–1465, 2020. DOI: 10.1109/COMST.2020.2969706 18

[248] Y. Yang. LinBFT: Linear-communication byzantine fault tolerance for public blockchains, 2018. https://arxiv.org/abs/1807.01829 83, 111

[249] M. Yin, D. Malkhi, M. K. Reiter, G. G. Gueta, and I. Abraham. HotStuff: BFT consensus with linearity and responsiveness. In *Proc. of the ACM Symposium on Principles of*

Distributed Computing, pages 347–356, 2019. DOI: 10.1145/3293611.3331591 xix, 17, 20, 80, 83, 107, 109, 110, 111, 184

[250] M. Zamani, M. Movahedi, and M. Raykova. RapidChain: Scaling blockchain via full sharding. In *Proc. of the ACM SIGSAC Conference on Computer and Communications Security*, pages 931–948, 2018. DOI: 10.1145/3243734.3243853 168, 173, 174

[251] K. Zhang and H.-A. Jacobsen. Towards dependable, scalable, and pervasive distributed ledgers with blockchains. In *IEEE 38th International Conference on Distributed Computing Systems (ICDCS)*, pages 1337–1346, 2018. DOI: 10.1109/ICDCS.2018.00134 185

[252] W. Zhao. Fast Paxos made easy: Theory and implementation. *Int. J. Distrib. Syst. Technol.*, 6(1):15–33, 2015. DOI: 10.4018/ijdst.2015010102 112

Authors' Biographies

SUYASH GUPTA

Suyash Gupta is pursuing doctoral research at the Computer Science Department at University of California, Davis. At UC Davis, he is a senior member of Exploratory Systems Lab and works under the supervision of Prof. Sadoghi. He also works as the Lead Architect at the blockchain company Moka Blox. Prior to joining UC Davis, he started his doctoral research at the Department of Computer Science at Purdue University. He earned a Master of Science degree from Purdue University in 2017 and transferred to UC Davis to complete his research. He also received a Master of Science (Research) degree from Indian Institute of Technology Madras in 2015. His current research focuses on attaining safe and efficient, fault-tolerant consensus in distributed and blockchain applications. He also has published works that present efficient optimizations and design for parallel and distributed algorithms. In his free time, Suyash likes to code and has won awards at several hackathons.

JELLE HELLINGS

Jelle Hellings is currently a Postdoc Fellow in the Exploratory Systems Lab led by Prof. Sadoghi at UC Davis. Since 2018, his work focusses on exploring the theoretical limitations of future high-performance resilient data processing systems, this with the aim of exploring new directions for data processing in malicious environments.

Jelle Hellings studied Computer Science and Engineering at the Eindhoven University of Technology, Netherlands. At the TU/e, he finished his graduate studies with a research project focused on external memory algorithms for indexing data that can be represented by trees or directed acyclic graphs. The results of which were presented at SIGMOD 2012. Following, he moved to Hasselt University, Belgium, to pursue his doctorate at the Databases and Theoretical Computer Science research group. There, his main focus was on the study of the expressive power of graph query languages. Furthermore, he also studied constraints for semi-structured data, graph querying via walks and via context-free languages, counting-only queryes, and temporal join algorithms.

MOHAMMAD SADOGHI

Mohammad Sadoghi is an Assistant Professor in the Computer Science Department at the University of California, Davis. Formerly, he was an Assistant Professor at Purdue University and Research Staff Member at IBM T.J. Watson Research Center. He received his Ph.D. from the University of Toronto in 2013. He leads the ExpoLab research group with the mission to pioneer a resilient data platform at scale, a distributed ledger centered around a democratic and decentralized computational model (ResilientDB Fabric) that further aims to unify secure transactional and real-time analytical processing (L-Store). He envisioned ResilientDB to serve as a platform to foster "creativity." He has co-founded a blockchain company called Moka Blox LLC, the ResilientDB spinoff. He has over 90 publications in leading database conferences/journals and 34 filed U.S. patents. His ACM Middleware'18 paper entitled "QueCC: A Queue-oriented, Control-free Concurrency Architecture" won the Best Paper Award. He served as the Area Editor for *Transaction Processing in Encyclopedia of Big Data Technologies* by Springer. He has co-authored the book *Transaction Processing on Modern Hardware*, Morgan & Claypool Synthesis Lectures on Data Management. He regularly serves on the program committee of SIGMOD, VLDB, Middleware, ICDE, EDBT, Middleware, ICDCS, and ICSOC and has been an invited reviewer for *TKDE, TPDS, JPDC,* and *VLDBJ.*